Copyright Consciousness

Dave Fossum

COPYRIGHT CONSCIOUSNESS

Musical Creativity and Intellectual Property in Turkey

Wesleyan University Press   Middletown, Connecticut

Wesleyan University Press
Middletown, CT 06459
www.wesleyan.edu/wespress
© 2025 David Christian Fossum
All rights reserved
Manufactured in the United States of America
Designed by Mindy Basinger Hill / Typeset in Minion Pro

Portions of chapter 2 were published concurrently in *Law and Social Inquiry* as "Legal Consciousness and Cultural Intimacy in Turkey's Intellectual Property Reform."

The publisher gratefully acknowledges the support of the AMS 75 PAYS Fund and the General Fund of the American Musicological Society, supported in part by the National Endowment for the Humanities and the Andrew W. Mellon Foundation.

Library of Congress Cataloging-in-Publication Data

Names: Fossum, David Christian, 1979– author.

Title: Copyright consciousness: musical creativity and intellectual property in Turkey / David Christian Fossum.

Description: [First.] | Middletown, Connecticut: Wesleyan University Press, 2025. | Series: Music/culture | Includes bibliographical references and index. | Summary: "An ethnography of copyright law in Turkish music, integrating this information into broader narratives about Turkish society, the nature and value of musical creativity, and the histories of national genres"— Provided by publisher.

Identifiers: LCCN 2024058186 (print) | LCCN 2024058187 (ebook) | ISBN 9780819501752 (cloth) | ISBN 9780819501769 (paperback) | ISBN 9780819501776 (ebook)

Subjects: LCSH: Copyright—Music—Turkey. | Music trade—Turkey. | Music—Social aspects—Turkey.

Classification: LCC ML3790 .F685 2025 (print) | LCC ML3790 (ebook) | DDC 346.04/8209561—dc23/eng/20241202

LC record available at https://lccn.loc.gov/2024058186

LC ebook record available at https://lccn.loc.gov/2024058187

5   4   3   2   1

To the creators of Turkey's music,
anonymous and known

Kim var idi, biz bu elde yoğ iken

Who was here when we were not yet in this country?

KARACAOĞLAN

CONTENTS

Acknowledgments xi

Note on Orthography xv

Introduction 1

ONE Copyright Reform and Cultural Modernization 28

TWO Constituting Legality in the Music Sector 52

THREE Essentializing Creativity: Authorship and Anonymity 83

FOUR Copyright and Traditionalism in State Broadcasting 108

FIVE When Copyright Meets Folk Music 132

SIX Collectors, Copyright, "Kiziroğlu": Formal Law
and Everyday Legality 165

Conclusion 195

Appendix 203

Glossary 209

Notes 213

Works Cited 235

Index 263

ACKNOWLEDGMENTS

Like any work of authorship, this book is in many ways a collective creation. I could not have undertaken the research or completed the writing of the book without the contributions of many other individuals. It is overwhelming to reflect now upon how many shared their knowledge and supported my project. They are too many to name, especially among the generous and hospitable communities who hosted me in Turkey. I am grateful to all of them. Here I wish to acknowledge a few to whom I am particularly indebted. Any errors are my own.

First and foremost, I must acknowledge the teachers to whom I owe my knowledge of Turkey's rich music traditions: Hüsnü Aydoğdu, Ruhi Ayangil, Necati Çelik, Şendoğan Karadeli, Nevzat Karakış, Mehmet Ali Sanlıkol, and Ümit Şimşek. All of them furthermore offered assistance, care, and mentoring in ways that transcend the category of "teacher." A few individuals in Turkey became absolutely crucial to my research, offering repeated consultation, wisdom, access, and/or further connections to other sources invaluable for my project: Bünyamin Aksungur, Halil Atılgan, Erdal Erzincan, Martin Greve, Songül Karahasanoğlu, Gül Okutan Nilsson, Erdem Özdemir, Ulaş Özdemir, Yücel Paşmakçı, Hasan Saltık and Kalan Records, Süleyman Şenel, and Metin Uzelli. I am grateful for the support of Yelda Özgen Öztürk and the late Şehvar Beşiroğlu at Istanbul Technical University's Center for Advanced Studies in Music (MIAM). I was also welcomed by faculty, students, and director Adnan Koç down the hill at ITU's Turkish Music State Conservatory. Staff and leadership at MESAM, MSG, and MÜ-YAP were helpful and generous to me, especially Recep Ergül, Zeynep Özkan, Ahmet Türkoğlu, and Gülcan Tutkun. Several courts also offered crucial access and knowledge, especially the Istanbul 1st, 2nd, and 4th and the Ankara 2nd Civil Law Courts for Intellectual and Industrial Rights. Others stand out for their knowledge-sharing, encouragement, assistance, and generous hosting.

These included İsmail Altunsaray, Aytekin Ataş, Mustafa Avcı, Tümer Avcı, Sinan Ayyıldız, Gürsoy Babaoğlu, Ahmet Ozan Baysal, Haydar Gögercin, Cenk Güray, Cem Erdost İleri, Onur Kocamaz, Hüseyin Korkankorkmaz, Kutay Derin Kugay, Erdem Şimşek, the late Nedret Ural, Burcu Yıldız, the community of TUMAÇ, and members of the Asitane-i İsmail Rumi Foundation. Many other individuals generously granted interviews or shared their perspectives in conversations; some of these I cite in the book, and others have been anonymized or have not made it into the manuscript, but I am grateful to all of them. Living and researching in Turkey would not have been possible without the friends who helped make my work less stressful and my life more enjoyable and meaningful, and in some cases even offered occasional research assists: Joe Alpar, Turgay Bayındır, Robbie Beahrs, Osama Bedawe, Salih Demirtaş, Ayşe Erarslan, Alex Kreger, Peter Klempner, Franco Mazzi, Sylvia Önder, Robert Reigle, Will Sumits, and others in the communities that welcomed me in Istanbul.

Many colleagues also offered professional guidance and feedback on drafts of the manuscript. Most significantly, Marc Perlman exceeded my greatest expectations for what a dissertation advisor might offer, and he continued shaping my ideas as I wrote the book. I am also grateful for the many contributions of the rest of my Brown University dissertation committee: Kiri Miller, Sonia Tamar Seeman, and Joshua Tucker. Esther Viola Kurtz read every word of my drafts and offered solidarity through grad school and the writing process. My mentors from my MA degree at Wesleyan University provided a solid foundation in ethnomusicology, especially Mark Slobin, Su Zheng, and Eric Charry. At Arizona State University, I am fortunate to have had wonderful colleagues who have offered feedback and support: Sabine Feisst, Matt Fiorentino, Heather Landes, Kay Norton, Catherine Saucier, Peter Schmelz, Ted Solis, Sandy Stauffer, Christi Jay Wells, colleagues from the Melikian Center for Eurasian and East European Studies, and participants in a Research Cluster and a Fellowship, both funded by the Humanities Institute. Trevor Reed has been an inspiring colleague, collaborator, and reader of my drafts. I am also grateful to colleagues and mentors at the University of Pittsburgh, where I began writing this book as a Dietrich School of Arts and Sciences Humanities Center Post-Doctoral Fellow: Jonathan Arac, Shalini Ayyagari, Olivia Bloechl, Randall Halle, Adriana Helbig, Farbod Honarpisheh, Mike Madison, David Marshall, Marcy Pierson, Deane Root, Andrew Weintraub, and others active at the Humanities Center and in the Music Department. I also wish to thank Stephen Blum and Denise Gill for their support and inspiration. Other professional colleagues offered thoughtful input or readings of portions of the manuscript: Olufunmilayo Arewa, Veit Erlmann, Aman Gebru, Erol Köymen, George Murer, Federica Nardella, Jacob Olley, Anali Perry, Zvi Rosen, Guy Rub, David Samuels, Jessica Silbey, Semin Tunalı, Aleysia Whitmore, Melikian Center colleagues, and two anonymous manuscript peer reviewers. I also wish to thank Ron Herron for his friendship and encouragement throughout the years I wrote the book.

This book builds on dissertation research that was funded in part by the US Department of State, Educational and Cultural Affairs, under an American Research Institute in Turkey dissertation research fellowship (2013–2014). It was also made possible in part by financial assistance from the Ruth Landes Memorial Research Fund, a program of the Reed Foundation (2015). Other phases of research were funded by ASU's Humanities Institute and the Melikian Center, as well as the University of Pittsburgh's Center for Russian and East European Studies.

NOTE ON ORTHOGRAPHY

In this text I include Turkish words and names as spelled in the original Turkish alphabet without transliterating them to the English alphabet. The modern Turkish alphabet contains a few letters not used in English or which are pronounced differently than in English, as follows:

C/c	as "j" in jug
Ç/ç	as "ch" in "choice"
Ş/ş	as "sh" in "show"
Ğ/ğ	silent, lengthens preceding vowel
İ/i	as "ee" in "feet"
I/ı	no English equivalent; a schwa sound deep in the throat (approximately like "uh")
Ö/ö	as in German "schön"; closest English equivalent is the "ir" in "bird"
Ü/ü	as in German "über"; like "ue" in "clue" with the tongue lifted toward the palate

Diacritics marking circumflex vowels (â, û, î) are sometimes used in loanwords from Persian and Arabic to indicate the lengthening of a vowel or palatalization of a preceding consonant. All translations from Turkish interviews and sources are by the author unless otherwise noted.

Copyright Consciousness

Introduction

Early in my research for this book, I interviewed a former board member from one of Turkey's two competing copyright collecting societies for musical authors. These are agencies that copyright holders authorize to license certain uses of their works so that they can accrue royalties. The board member was eager to give an interview but did not want me to audio record it, since she felt that if I took only written notes she would speak more freely about the many problems she had witnessed during her time on the board. In my hastily scribbled notes from the conversation, I've captured one of her more colorful statements: "In Turkey, authors' rights have become discarded rights,"[1] a phrase that puns on the similar sounding *telif* (authorship) and *telef* (wasted or discarded).

———

In 2022, I had a rushed initial meeting with Recep Ergül, the recently elected president of MESAM, the larger and older of the two collecting societies. Ergül took the opportunity to rehearse a series of political talking points about the challenges facing the organization as he carved out fifteen minutes for me between other meetings. Describing the still relatively low licensing income and resulting royalties that the society was able to collect and distribute after decades of trying to develop the copyright infrastructure, he told me: "Regarding the point at which we've arrived in the process we've been in, we're maybe in thirty-fifth place in the world, and among the lowest ranked [countries] in Europe. This is because the copyright consciousness [*telif bilinci*] hasn't developed enough. It hasn't been explained well enough that copyright is a fundamental right, one that needs to be understood as a matter of liberty. And there's another cause [of the low collections] as well, and that's the late date at which Turkey's system was formed" (Recep Ergül, interview with the author, June 14, 2022).

———

A musician and music scholar who responded enthusiastically to my request for an interview turned out to have a wealth of ideas about the problem of applying copyright in Turkey. As if shooting from the hip, he peppered me with a rapid-fire, stream-of-consciousness series of critiques, thanking me at the end of the interview for prompting him to assemble his thoughts about copyright. One of his main points was that the European-derived body of law was a poor cultural fit for Turkey. Contrasting aspects of Turkish culture with the emphasis on individuality in Western culture, he told me, "In the Orient, there's a mystical culture and way of life. It's more about belonging to a society. There's the concept of a community [*cemaat*]; I'm an individual belonging to a community. We need to discuss who the 'I' is when distributing property. And in folk music, it belongs to a community. The musician is expressing the feelings of a community."

———

As these opening vignettes suggest, for many actors in Turkey's music sector, it seemed that the country's copyright regime was a work in progress at best, dysfunctional at worst. As suggested by the notion of authors' rights (*telif hakları*) being "discarded" (*telef*) or by the industry rankings that MESAM president Ergül cites, by most accounts Turkey's music sector has so far failed to reach its potential in terms of copyright-related income. For the better part of four decades, the state has invested in a series of reforms to shore up its once little-enforced intellectual property (IP) laws, including copyright alongside areas such as patent, trademark, and industrial design. Yet the project seemed to be ongoing. One of the most common assessments of the situation was that "the system hasn't settled" (*sistem oturmadı*).[2]

Most indicative of the state of progress in Turkey's copyright reform is the overall low royalty income that the collecting societies bring in. During one interview, a record producer pulled up a spreadsheet filled with International Federation of the Phonographic Industry (IFPI) global sales data, showing how Turkey lags far behind countries that are comparable in terms of per capita income and level of economic development, particularly in annual revenue

2 *Copyright Consciousness*

from performing rights and digital platforms. While some referenced such industry reports, others framed the issue in terms of their own pocketbooks. One prominent arranger and MESAM member—someone who held a share of rights to quite popular songs—pulled out his cell phone to show me a message from MESAM that notified him of his meager quarterly royalty distribution of 24.20 TL (about 10 USD at the time). In addition to quantifiable metrics like annual licensing income, musicians and industry executives described to me a variety of other frustrations they experienced: the glacial pace at which lawsuits progressed through the courts, the hassle of obtaining licenses to record previously published works, and the disordered and incomplete state of the databases that collecting societies used for distributing royalties.

Copyright stakeholders—such as the collecting society board member to whom it seemed authors' rights had become "wasted" rights—are thus often acutely aware of a tension between what the law seems to promise and the lived reality of copyright. They may also feel a need to make sense of or resolve this tension in various ways. Perhaps, as the musician and music scholar proposed, we should account for it in terms of a cultural difference between the western European contexts that first gave rise to copyright and the social context of Turkey, where some people viewed IP as a modernizing or westernizing import. For some, as I describe at length in this book, this cultural difference means that copyright does not suit certain local genres, especially folk music. Perhaps, however, this imagined cultural difference was not an insurmountably essential one, but merely a matter of making up for the lost time when copyright had been little applied in the country and of inculcating a respect for IP rights among the general population, as Ergül seems to suggest.

My aim in this book is not to provide a normative account suggesting how to resolve the issues that my interlocutors identified. Rather, at its core, the book is concerned with how actors make sense of and respond to the music copyright system's purported failures and perceived injustices, often by integrating their experiences into larger narratives about Turkish society, the nature and value of musical creativity, or the histories of national genres. My focus is not on copyright statutes drawn up in opaque legalese by parliamentary committees and applied in austere courthouses through the ritual power wielded by a judge in a robe. Social scientists who write about the role of law in everyday life often refer to "legality": law not as it exists "on the books" (Pound 1910) but rather as an emergent phenomenon that mediates social action not only in formal institutional but also in everyday settings (S. Silbey 2005, 347). Especially in this sense, law is

Introduction **3**

not made only by legislative assemblies and carried out in the courts, but constituted anywhere it informs social practices, including musical ones. Thus, a broad range of actors—judges, lawyers, and copyright bureaucrats, but also musical performers and composers, record producers, and music publishers—play an active role in shaping copyright legality. Another vignette may clarify the point.

———

In one conversation that I've recorded in my field notes, a musician and conservatory instructor cited the widely circulating idea that an "eight-measure rule" determined the line between a permissible borrowing of a chunk of melody and an illegal infringement. Songwriters or composers were often said to rely on this guideline when appropriating a preexisting tune into their own work: if eight full measures of the tune were the same, they might be successfully sued, but if they altered one note in this stretch, or if they borrowed less than eight bars, they were in the clear. The musician thought the guideline silly, and he had formulated a sophisticated musicological critique of it. He pointed out that if you had eight measures of melody you wanted to steal from someone else, you could simply change the meter of the melody to fit the eight measures into six or four bars. He proceeded to sing a melody, counting the measures by conducting with his hand, and then to sing the same melody while conducting in a different meter. He leveraged this clever point to critique the copyright system.

While the discourse about the eight-measure rule extended even into such elaborate critiques, upon investigation it turned out to be a myth. Staff at a collecting society's member relations department—which I had been told relied upon the rule to resolve disputes among members—rolled their eyes knowingly when I asked about it, calling it an "urban legend" (*şehir efsanesi*).[3] In fact, there didn't seem to be any such rules for drawing a bright line between infringement and a case of two similar but distinct melodies.[4] Yet even a former board member from the society told me she thought the society used the rule.

———

When many citizens think of the law, they may imagine it to exist in a kind of transcendent realm removed from everyday life. But the law also shapes all sorts of everyday activities. Think of composers wishing to incorporate a preexisting tune and unsure how much they can borrow without infringing upon the rights in

4 *Copyright Consciousness*

the borrowed melody (it's easy to see why a clear guideline like an eight-measure rule might appeal). Here, how composers imagine the law will shape their creative choices. This emergent legality may motivate people's actions: a composer may go ahead and borrow seven bars of a tune, for example. Conversely, the sense that a bright-line rule for permissible borrowing is silly (however apocryphal) may stimulate critical reflection on the role of law in regulating creative life, inflecting the very normative discourse that legitimates copyright itself. People may think of copyright law as embodying unquestionable normative values, as when Ergül framed it as "a fundamental right" and "a matter of liberty." They may also sense a disparity between the promise of IP norms and the realities of how the law plays out in their lives, reading this as a sign of some larger fact about Turkey or the world. Such critical reflection may also inform the law "on the books" in turn. For example, a sense that copyright is incompatible with a country's folk traditions may motivate efforts to create special legal provisions to protect them.

Sociolegal scholars use the term *legal consciousness* to refer to how citizens enact and interpret legality both through their actions and through how they conceptualize and talk about the law. I build upon this body of scholarship through my account of legality in Turkey's music industry, tracking diverse actors' *copyright consciousness*. In my opening vignette, Ergül uses the term "copyright consciousness" (*telif bilinci*) to refer to the internalization of copyright norms (which purportedly remains insufficiently realized in Turkey). I often encountered the phrase used in similar ways in official discourse promoting copyright enforcement. By titling my book *Copyright Consciousness*, I invoke both the sociolegal concept of legal consciousness and this distinct but overlapping sense in which those most invested in developing Turkey's copyright regime deployed it. I analyze such normative discourse while also documenting how diversely positioned actors mobilize, take up, critique, or resist copyright in their engagements with music.

WHY COPYRIGHT?

When I first began my dissertation fieldwork in Turkey in 2013, I knew I wanted to research folk music. I was interested in the creative processes that had produced it and how nationalist and folkloristic ideologies had shaped it. But it had not occurred to me to research copyright issues. Few ethnomusicologists had given the topic sustained attention (though my dissertation advisor, Marc Perlman, was one of the few). There were good reasons for this: studying copyright meant

Introduction 5

potentially wading into a world of ugly conflicts, attempting to trace a complicated tangle of money flows (data about which were not easily accessible), and familiarizing oneself with the esoteric legal doctrines and byzantine technicalities that shaped stakeholders' experiences (e.g., Krueger 2019). As I began studying folk music and conducting interviews, however, I gradually came to see it as an arena where three compelling research questions converged.

The first is the most obvious. Copyright represents a policy regime for valuing and regulating creativity, as framed by legal doctrines and concepts such as originality, authorship, expression, and rights.[5] Such concepts of authorship and ownership contrast with the often collective or collaborative ethos of compositional practices in many traditional genres and with the Romantic notion of folkloric "anonymity" often invoked to account for the origins of Turkey's folk music. How then, I wondered, might copyright shape musical creativity in Turkey? How might copyright fail to accommodate locally specific concepts of authorship and ownership, especially those common in folk music? Conversely, how might an effort to accommodate any such localized concepts shape copyright legality in Turkey?

My second research question had to do with identity and cultural policy. A major theme in the scholarly literature on the music of Turkey has been how official institutions and ideologies have mediated musical production and reception as part of the state's nation-building project since the founding of the Turkish Republic in 1923 (Balkılıç 2009, 2018; Bates 2016; A. Erol 2012; Gill 2017; Greve 2017; Köymen 2022; Markoff 1986; O'Connell 2016; Öztürkmen 1993; Seeman 2019; Stokes 1992; Tekelioğlu 1996, 2001; Woodard 1999; among many others). This rich vein of scholarship reveals how state institutions constructed and promoted particular genres such as folk music—often modernizing them in the process—as symbols with which citizens could affiliate, thus learning to think of themselves as a part of the modern nation to which such culture belonged. Of course, this modernist reformism (Turino 2008, 16) has been a fraught project contested by those seeking a more inclusive vision of belonging to Turkey. Framing a genre as national culture often involved curating it to exclude, marginalize, censor, reframe, or revise songs, tunes, and practices that complicated the official narratives—for example those of Kurdish, Armenian, Greek, Laz, Roman, Arab, or other minorities. Since the 1990s the Turkish state had mostly defanged its top-down cultural reformism, opening a limited space for multiculturalist discourse and largely leaving it up to the market to sway and respond to the public's taste, though ethnonationalist approaches persist, and the

6 *Copyright Consciousness*

prospect of nationalist backlash remains (Yıldız 2018). In this environment, copyright emerged as an important cultural policy regime, one wielding a particular set of powers that some of my fieldwork interlocutors seemed highly attuned to: It promised to financially reward musical production (at least potentially). The cost of copyright licensing could sometimes obstruct artists' musical projects. And there was always the prospect of ugly lawsuits over contested authorship claims or licensing negotiations. Meanwhile, as some of my opening vignettes suggest, developing the copyright regime represented an urgent project with collective stakes. Yet it wasn't clear what relation this project bore to the older nationalist cultural reformism (if any). It didn't seem that minority musics were blocked from copyright protection, for example, and if copyright somehow helped either reinforce or reshape identity discourses, it wasn't clear to me what the mechanism was. Some scholarship has revealed how citizens have carried official ideologies into the private sphere, through consumption that displayed political commitments, in the neoliberal context of post-1980s Turkey (Özyürek 2006; Gill 2017, 52–57). Critical legal scholarship has meanwhile considered how IP laws—despite their ostensible color-blindness—might reproduce patterns of racial injustice (Vats 2020), while national anxieties may be projected into discourse about piracy (Dent 2020; Johns 2009, 454–60; Stobart 2010, 38–47). How, I wondered, might copyright mediate sociality or senses of self and belonging?

My third question overlaps with the first two in some ways. As the narratives about Turkey's purportedly late arrival to the copyright game suggest, developing the domestic system meant harmonizing and integrating it with an international network of IP laws and administrative bodies. Both scholarly and lay narratives often analyze such processes in terms of globalization or cultural imperialism. They argue that IP disproportionately benefits international corporations based in the global North, or that it regulates creative production according to Eurocentric norms of authorship and ownership.[6] The story that emerged as my fieldwork progressed, however, seemed more complicated than this. While some of my interlocutors expressed versions of the cultural imperialism thesis (see also Karlıdağ 2010), most musicians and other actors seemed to take it for granted that an improved copyright regime was necessary for and beneficial to the country's music industry. Some even viewed it as a potential tool for *combatting* cultural imperialism and *promoting* Turkish culture. Furthermore, I often encountered distinctive aspects of Turkey's copyright laws, doctrines, and policies. For example, worldwide—and especially within Europe—it is unusual (though not unheard of) to have multiple competing collecting societies for

Introduction **7**

musical authors, as Turkey does. IP represents what anthropologists Aihwa Ong and Stephen J. Collier called "a global form," which has "a distinctive capacity for decontextualization and recontextualization, abstractability and movement, across diverse social and cultural situations and spheres of life" (2005, 11). Where such global forms appear in a specific context, they interact with other elements (preexisting "values, procedures, and substantive forms") in a heterogeneous and unstable conglomeration of interacting elements that they call a "global assemblage" (9–11). Attuned to such dynamics, I found myself interested in the distinctive aspects of Turkey's copyright regime, which might illustrate domestic actors' agency in reshaping the global form. Such contingencies complicate an otherwise straightforward import of a purportedly "Eurocentric" legal regime. In what ways had copyright been adapted to the local historical and political context? What accounted for the particular form that Turkey's copyright regime took?

Putting legality at the center of the analysis helps to cast some of the answers to these questions into relief. At its core, the book argues that as an emergent aspect of social life, copyright legality is mutually constitutive with concepts of personhood and senses of self and identity. Constituting legality is a contingent endeavor, one that involves everyone from lay listeners to high court judges, all of whom come with their own values, interests, and prior experiences. That said, neither is the process totally random. As theories of legal consciousness have suggested, constituting legality is a social, intersubjective process, one patterned by recurring frames and narratives. Because the process recruits actors whose perspectives have been informed by the prior history of, say, the promotion of official folk music and its attendant narratives about creativity and identity, such social imaginaries also mediate copyright legality. The contingency of this process through which actors negotiate legality means that the national IP system also takes on a distinctive form. Meanwhile, since copyright regimes are national in jurisdiction but also tied to international legal frameworks and political-economic relationships, the project of establishing an effective one in Turkey resonates with and inflects larger discourses about the nation's place in the world. With this book I thus aim to clarify the dynamics of how copyright legality emerges, though even the richest ethnographic or historical account will necessarily be partial.

8 *Copyright Consciousness*

WHY TURKEY?

It was some combination of serendipity and the vagaries of musical taste that drew me to Turkey for my dissertation fieldwork, and as I have mentioned, my interest in the law developed after I had already chosen the country as a place to work. That said, the country turned out to present a compelling subject for a monograph on music copyright, particularly since one of the rationales for copyright law is that it is supposed to promote creative production. Turkey boasts one of the world's most vibrant music industries, where listeners enjoy a diverse array of genres and tend to consume far more locally produced music than international. There are the genres that had long been promoted through the cultural reformism that held sway in state broadcasting and other official institutions: Western art music (including that made by Turkish composers), folk music (*halk müziği*, itself a congeries of diverse localized or regional forms), and the urban practices long cultivated at the Ottoman court or Sufi lodges and recontextualized as Turkish classical music in the republican era. Even within these officially promoted forms, musicians and commentators contest the genre boundaries, stylistic norms, and meanings attached. Countless popular genres have thrived, meanwhile, outside the official channels, often promoted and sold on the lightly regulated private record market and, since the 1990s, in private broadcasting. Turkish citizens have always been well attuned to cultural currents circulating abroad, and they both consume and contribute to international genres like jazz, tango, rock, and hip-hop and produce localized variants or extensions of them, often in versions that self-consciously incorporate elements of native genres.

Copyright—or its relative absence—appears to have profoundly shaped this rich music scene, though perhaps not in the ways one might expect. As I describe in greater detail in chapter 1, local music companies proliferated in a lax copyright environment that had made the national market unprofitable for major multinational companies after the arrival, beginning in the 1950s, of sound recording formats that could be cheaply and easily produced or pirated, like the 45 RPM record and the cassette tape. Then, in the 1980s to 1990s, European Union accession negotiations, market liberalization, and trade agreements drove a dramatic overhaul of the country's IP system that transformed musical ownership and creativity. The state squelched piracy, invested in developing domestic IP expertise, liberalized mass media, revised legal statutes, and created the conditions for multinational music companies to take up shop. In this book, I will refer to these processes as "IP reform" or "copyright reform." As I describe

Introduction 9

in greater detail in chapter 1, the state long enjoyed a monopoly in broadcasting, which it leveraged for cultural nation-building. Concurrently with IP reform, media were privatized in the early 1990s, though the state broadcasting agency, Turkish Radio and Television (TRT), continues to exist alongside private outlets, patronizing a variety of musical forms. The recording industry operated privately even through the era of the state's broadcasting monopoly, but since the mid-1980s, the Cultural Ministry has regulated the agreements between publishing rightsholders and labels, who are required to register recorded works in a database at the Ministry and to purchase anti-piracy seals that they affix to physical recordings sold in the marketplace.

The project of copyright reform enlists a broad range of state, private, and civil society actors. The Cultural Ministry's copyright office oversees statutory revisions (which must also ultimately pass through Parliament), draws up regulations on collective management, establishes anti-piracy measures, and sometimes mediates licensing negotiations among rightsholders and commercial users of copyrighted repertoire. The judicial system, a civil law system that resembles those of several continental European countries, has featured specialized intellectual and industrial property rights courts since an intensive period of legal reform in the early 2000s, though the most conclusive and precedent-setting decisions come from the court of last instance, the Court of Cassation (Yargıtay). Collecting societies, while regulated by the Cultural Ministry, are privately founded and run by leaders elected from among the membership. Members authorize the societies to administer their rights so that they can receive royalties when their music is performed or sold. Two main collecting societies, MESAM and MSG, manage the rights of composers, lyricists, arrangers, and publishers; this includes both performing rights (when works are played live, broadcast, streamed, or heard over speakers in a public space) and mechanical rights (when physical copies of recordings of works are sold). MÜ-YAP is the domestic record industry association, and it also functions as a collecting society, administering labels' rights in sound recordings—at least when they are played in public commercial spaces (since 2012 the labels have individually negotiated deals with digital service providers). Turkey's copyright statute also stipulates that recording artists have a right to their performances captured in a sound recording; these rights are managed by the collecting society MÜYORBİR.[7] That Turkey's IP reform recruits such a range of actors to the project of shoring up legal enforcement and developing the system for rights management, often via active membership in collecting societies built on democratic models, invites comparisons with broader contexts

10 *Copyright Consciousness*

where scholars have emphasized the participatory processes that constitute citizens as political subjects (Lazar 2013; Holston 2013, 95). Music scholars have only begun to examine how engagement with bureaucratic structures, including NGOs, have made musicians into political subjects negotiating the substance of citizenship in the era of (neo)liberal political transitions since the 1970s (Stokes 2023, 57–76). While the changes wrought by Turkey's IP reform have arguably been radical, the copyright regime continues—to the chagrin of stakeholders—to underperform by many measures, and the copyright collecting societies, industry executives, Cultural Ministry bureaucrats, courts, and legal professionals involved all seemed to view themselves as active participants in a reform that is ongoing.

The tensions among these factors—the diversity and incredible creativity to be found on the domestic music scene, the dramatic IP reform that occurred over the past several decades, and the disappointments that persisted through the reform—seemed indicative of Turkey's geopolitical position on the fringe of Europe and made the country a rich copyright case study. I suspect that scholars tracking copyright in similarly positioned countries—those lying outside or on the margins of the global North—will find aspects of Turkey's music copyright story familiar or instructive (see Dent 2020; Darian-Smith 2002; Wang 2019; among others).

WHY LEGAL CONSCIOUSNESS?

When I began my fieldwork, few models existed for writing an ethnographic monograph on copyright, especially in contexts beyond North America or western Europe. Several excellent books have addressed this lacuna more recently, including Jessica Silbey's *The Eureka Myth* (2014) and *Against Progress* (2022), Alex Dent's *Digital Pirates* (2020), Veit Erlmann's *Lion's Share* (2022), and Larisa Kingston Mann's *Rude Citizenship* (2022), all works that have influenced my own thinking.[8] Edited volumes such as *Copyright Africa* (Röschenthaler and Diawara 2019) and *Putting Intellectual Property in Its Place* (Murray, Piper, and Robertson 2014) have also expanded the ethnographic literature on the topic. Yet particularly considering the growing importance of IP rights for the music industries (Williamson and Cloonan 2013, 23) and that musical production in many countries has been reshaped by copyright reform efforts akin to Turkey's since the 1990s, the topic remains under-researched. A number of music scholars have addressed copyright-related topics in shorter writings—an article or a section of a book—but these have often taken a relatively narrow focus: examining

Introduction **11**

the controversy over authorship in a specific song (Lindahl 2004; Manuel 2006), describing cultures of piracy (Stobart 2010), or critiquing the effects of copyright doctrines and case law on musical creativity (Brooks 2005; Demers 2006; McLeod and DiCola 2011; Scales 2005). In other studies, copyright has been implicated for its role in a larger phenomenon that was the true focus of the research: the political economy of the music industries, for example (Marshall 2013; Taylor 2016; Wallis and Malm 1984), or how technologies of distribution alter musical forms or patterns of marketing and consumption (Drott 2018; Hassan and Kopf 2018; Hesmondhalgh and Meier 2018; Meier and Manzerolle 2019; Negus 2019; Prey 2016; Wallis et al. 1999). The research questions that drove my fieldwork led me to strive for a more holistic picture of the copyright ecosystem, and the concept of legal consciousness provides a framework for sketching such a picture.

Legal consciousness has been glossed as "the ways people understand and use law" (Merry 1990, 5) and "participation—through words and deeds—in the construction of legal meanings, actions, practices, and institutions" (Ewick and Silbey 1998, 247; see also Cowan 2004; Halliday and Morgan 2013). The concept is often closely associated with the study of law "in everyday life" (Sarat and Kearns 1993; Ewick 2015). We may think of the everyday as the world situated outside formal legal institutions, that which the law seeks to regulate, though scholars have also critiqued the assumption that law can be separated out from society in any real way that transcends analytic purposes (Blumenthal 2012; R. Gordon 1984, 60, 102–9). Scholarship in this area has furthermore described the law and everyday as mutually constitutive (e.g., Halliday and Morgan 2013, 3). As sociolegal scholars David Engel and Frank Munger put it, "Law is one of the elements that constitute the categories and routines of everyday life; and, in turn, these very categories and routines—and the individuals who participate in them—give form and meaning to the law . . . The term 'legal consciousness' is now widely used to characterize the two-way process and the behavior and cognition of the social actors who participate in it" (2003, 11).

The traditional emphasis of legal consciousness research on the "everyday" may also suggest that it most closely relates to research on laypersons' understandings of legality, and indeed, much scholarship in this arena has been primarily concerned with the perspectives of lower-income and marginalized people, often with the aim of highlighting the inequalities that the legal system (re)produces (see Cornut St-Pierre 2019, 327, for a useful survey). In music, an analogous topic might be how musicians or media users take up, resist, subvert, or conceptualize copyright and its associated norms (Kjus 2019; Edwards et al. 2015;

12 *Copyright Consciousness*

Mann 2022; Street and Philips 2017). However, legal consciousness researchers have also studied elite actors such as judges (Yngvesson 1988; Somanawat 2018), bureaucrats (Richards 2015), and corporate lawyers (Tungnirun 2018). Pointing out that "there is no reason to think that the collective construction of legal meanings and legal structures should happen exclusively in the daily routine of ordinary people and that their experience alone should be the key to law's true nature," legal scholar Pascale Cornut St-Pierre suggests focusing not on "the study of law in everyday life but rather the study of law as a cultural practice" (2019, 328–29; see also Ewick and Silbey 1998, 23).

These definitions suggest several ways in which legal consciousness suits an ethnomusicological approach to the law. First, focusing on legal consciousness affords a broad view of copyright and the numerous types of actors it implicates, from shop owners playing copyrighted music over their speakers, to musicians, to collecting society officials and IP courts. For many readers, the word "copyright" may suggest first and foremost spectacular lawsuits over alleged plagiarism in hit songs, but few copyright disputes reach a court verdict, and most are settled out of court. Studies that primarily analyze case law necessarily focus on the outcomes of a few, exceptional cases (although appellate court decisions do set important precedents and shape industry approaches to copyright management). For most rightsholders, the importance of copyright law lies less in its availability as a resource for settling disputes than in how it sets the terms for an administrative system that pays music creators. In my own research, I found that stakeholders were most often concerned with the workings of such everyday copyright management, though press announcements about the outcomes of legal disputes among songwriters did periodically cause a stir on the music scene. Answering my research questions about the relationship between the larger project of IP reform and the longer history of cultural reformism in Turkey meant understanding something of actors' lived experience of the transactional, rights-management aspect of copyright that largely played out in collecting societies and the offices of publishers, labels, distributors, and digital service providers, where the interests of creators existed in tension with those of the corporate agents who helped get their music to listeners. And while a relatively small percentage of musicians earn a substantial living from copyright-related income (DiCola 2013), many more aspired to breach that small percentage. Others were implicated in the copyright system because of the cost and hassle of licensing. It also seemed to me that a huge range of individuals with few copyright stakes of their own nonetheless contested or reaffirmed the norms of creativity and control

Introduction **13**

that helped constitute an emergent copyright legality in and out of the courts and collecting societies. I was interested in how a particular legality emerged from this larger copyright ecosystem, since "the observation of difference can reveal the contingency of various taken-for-granted aspects of a particular legal culture" (Halliday 2019, 866).

My first, most obvious ethnographic observation was that a variety of actors involved in the music industry and the larger project of IP reform understood it in terms of a progress narrative. According to this narrative, the country lagged behind in the game of building a copyright system that might compare favorably with that in other places, where, many of these individuals seemed to assume, a well-functioning system was in place (see chapters 1 and 2). There was a dissonance between what copyright seemed to promise and the lived reality of how it played out in Turkey, whether quantifiable in terms of meager royalty income or suggested by other purported dysfunctions of the system. This dissonance could be viewed as a version of what law and society scholarship long called "the gap between the law on the books and the law in action." During the 1960s–1970s heyday of this "gap studies" paradigm, progressive scholars sought to show how the law as implemented in life failed to achieve its purported aims. By pointing out such failures, scholars suggested ways to address or close this gap. This approach was later critiqued on several grounds. One critique was that objectively identifying unified ideals or aims of laws might be impossible (Feeley 1976, 498–500). Later scholars have allowed for a vision of the law as more complex, indeterminate, and unpredictable, or as something that might be wielded for different aims by different actors.[9] Scholars furthermore grew disappointed in the power of gap-studies research to effect social and legal change (Gould and Barclay 2012, 326; see also Sarat 1985).

One way to view legal consciousness research is that it addresses such critiques by asking not how to resolve such "gaps" the researcher identifies, but rather by ethnographically documenting how actors themselves perceive and seek to resolve or account for such gaps (Gould and Barclay 2012). In attending to actors' reported experiences of an underdeveloped or dysfunctional copyright system, this book thus aligns with approaches to legal consciousness that take the tensions between ideal and reality of the law as a necessary feature of legality, one whose manifestations should be probed ethnographically. While I do hope that my account highlights the contingency of copyright legality as currently constituted, perhaps opening a space to imagine alternative possibilities for Turkish IP, I suggest no policy proposals and make no normative recommendations.

14 *Copyright Consciousness*

In asserting that constituting legality is a contingent endeavor (à la R. Gordon 1984, cf. Tomlins 2012), I do not mean to suggest that it is completely random or that nothing constrains the possibilities (S. Silbey 2005, 330). What I mean to stress is the wide variety of agents who may contest and shape it—even if significant differences exist in their power and resources to do so. Scholars have often emphasized that it is marginalized people who most often resist dominant understandings of legality (Brisbin 2010). Nor is it, as the most cynical realist account might have it, a straightforward matter of the law reflecting the interests of the powerful. The most often-cited theorization of legal consciousness—and the most influential upon my own take on the subject—is that advanced by sociologists Patricia Ewick and Susan Silbey in their classic study *The Common Place of Law* (1998). Ewick and Silbey describe legal consciousness as multidimensional, made up of a set of seemingly contradictory stories about the law that are in fact mutually reinforcing in a way that sustains the law's hegemony. In chapter 2 I similarly examine legal consciousness as a multidimensional phenomenon as I strive to clarify the dynamics of how copyright legality is constituted in Turkey. Among my observations is the presence of a culturally intimate dimension in which citizens are able to reconcile the tension between the ideals and practice of the law—the gap between what copyright seems to promise and the reality of how it plays out—because it makes sense in terms of familiar, often self-orientalizing narratives about Turkey's place in the world (cf. Herzfeld 2005). This culturally intimate dynamic was another of my earliest and most frequent observations in my interactions and conversations about copyright. While it seemed important and unavoidable to write about it, I was also bothered by a sense that making it too central to my account might be reductive, since my interlocutors were savvy, cosmopolitan individuals who often had their own reflexive, critical perspective on these nonetheless persistent self-stereotypes. Approaching legal consciousness as multidimensional appealed to me in part because it allowed me to contextualize this cultural intimacy as one aspect of a more complex picture of copyright legality in Turkey's music sector.

Integrating my observations about cultural intimacy meanwhile allows me to show how legality plays a key role in identity or subject formation, a traditional interest of ethnomusicologists that remains little examined in the literature on legal consciousness. A few strains of existing sociolegal scholarship resonate with this concern. Sociolegal scholars Lynette Chua and David Engel name an "identity school" of legal consciousness research that highlights how "the place of law in people's lives is intimately connected to their sense of who they are"

Introduction **15**

(2019, 338). However, this literature tends to focus on how legal categories such as disability forge identity-based political constituencies, rather than examining the relationship between legality and larger social imaginaries such as ethno-nationalisms. Elsewhere, Engel has also identified a "communities of meaning" approach to legal consciousness, according to which citizens' sense of legality is bound up with images of community (Engel 1998, citing Greenhouse 1988 and Yngvesson 1988). A few more recent studies similarly highlight how citizens reproduce national and racial imaginaries while constituting legality (Aliverti 2019; Hertogh and Kurkchiyan 2016). Where Engel views this as an approach distinct from the "power and resistance" school of Ewick and Silbey, however, I integrate these apparently disparate concerns, showing how widely circulating social imaginaries mediate the processes that produce the law's hegemony. In taking up the concept of legal consciousness, then, I inflect sociolegal models of legality while relating copyright to a core concern of ethnomusicology.

WHY FOLK MUSIC?

While I intend my ethnographic account of legal consciousness to suggest numerous applications for the music scholar interested in IP, modeling an approach that might apply to any genre of music, chapters 3 to 6 of the book form an extended examination of a genre that presents particular complications for copyright: folk music. Although IP remains a little-researched area in ethnomusicology, if there is one issue that has drawn these scholars to the topic, it is how the concepts of individualized authorship and ownership that underpin copyright laws contrast or clash with the collective creative practices often thought to produce "folk," Indigenous, and other noncanonical musical forms around the world. In Turkey, folk literature and folk music specialists have long celebrated the idea that folklore is "anonymous" (*anonim*), where the idea of anonymity entails not only an epistemological status (that its creators are unknown) but also an ontological one: that it is produced through creative processes that render it the expression of a collective rather than of individuals. My aim is not to document a "Turkish" way of understanding creativity and ownership, but rather to show how actors negotiate the tension between copyright and the idea of musical folklore as anonymous and collective heritage. In the process, I intervene in a long-running conversation within (ethno)musicological and legal scholarship on folk and traditional music.

Legal scholars have argued that copyright law is predicated upon a particular understanding of authorship often dubbed "the Romantic author": the idea that individual geniuses bring forth works ex nihilo, a feat that justifies their control over the works as property (Boyle 1996; Jaszi 1991; Woodmansee 1984; Woodmansee and Jaszi 1994; cf. Barron 2006; Cummings 2010). Copyright therefore requires that cultural products conform to particular notions about authorship: that artistic works have identifiable individual authors and that they be fixed products rather than fluid processes, for example. Much music made in traditional contexts around the world fails to meet these requirements. Items are subject to constant flux and variation, are understood to arise from communal creative processes, and/or are thought to be so old as to have passed their potential terms of protection in any case. They therefore fall outside of the purview of copyright law. Legal scholar Rosemary Coombe has analyzed the situation in terms of what historian James Clifford called the "the art-culture system": copyright law affords protection, according to a logic of possessive individualism, to "great artists" who produce works "understood to embody the unique personality of their individual authors," while "tribal" or Indigenous artifacts are authenticated by a sense that they are ahistorical, inhabiting an unchanging mythic time, affording them protection only under laws of cultural property (1998, 216–19; cf. Clifford 1988).

The first wave of ethnomusicological attention to copyright fretted over where this left the folk, traditional, or Indigenous musics that were often the focus of the discipline. In an early consideration of these issues, for example, Anthony Seeger tracked the authorship and ownership concepts of the Indigenous Amazonian Suya people, who believe songs belong to the first person or group who sings them and not to whoever composed them (1991; 1992, 347; the composers, meanwhile, may be fish, animals, or plants). Among Seeger's worries was that the songs he recorded and published on behalf of the Suya might be popularized and copyrighted by some more powerfully positioned recording artist (1991, 38). Such fears played out perhaps most dramatically and famously in the case of Deep Forest, a French duo who produced popular worldbeat electronica albums that incorporated ethnographic field recordings in a way that scandalized ethnomusicologists (Feld 1994, 2000; Mills 1996; Zemp 1996).[10] In response to such concerns, the World Intellectual Property Organization (WIPO) has long sponsored efforts to formulate protection schemes for uncopyrightable practices and expressions claimed by cultural groups, though such (usually *sui generis*) schemes confront a series of conceptual challenges, and they have not often been

Introduction 17

implemented (Boateng 2011; Brown 2003; Dutfield 2003; Erlmann 2022, 109–73; Noyes 2011; Perlman 2011; Robinson, Abdel-Latif, and Roffe 2017).

A prize-winning paper by ethnomusicologist Anthony McCann framed the clash between copyright and traditionality as a matter even more fundamental than the unethical exploitation of individual songs and recordings. He sounded the alarm that the forays of the copyright collecting society IMRO into the realm of Irish traditional music threatened to commodify a genre that, he argued, had long been based on a gift economy (2001). His likening of copyright to an enclosure of a commons of traditional musical resources partook in the environmentalist metaphors that legal scholars like James Boyle were leveraging at the time to advocate for preserving, in the face of the rapidly expanding scope and reach of IP laws, a public domain of culture upon which creators should be free to draw (1996, 2008; Kapczynski 2008; Lessig 2016; Litman 1990). Media scholars echoed the idea, excoriating copyright law for squelching appropriative forms of musical creativity (Mcleod 2005; Vaidhyanathan 2003).

There is an underexamined tension between the twin progressive impulses underlying the critique of the public domain's "enclosure" and the movement for *sui generis* protections for traditional culture or Indigenous knowledge (W. Gordon 2003, 627). The tension is particularly striking where the same individuals support both movements, as at the seminal Bellagio Convention of 1993, which culminated in a declaration that leveled a critique of copyright's grounding in Romantic author ideology as it called both for new protections for traditional culture and for preserving access to the public domain (Karaganis 2012). Highlighting the contradiction between these two political aims, legal scholars Anupam Chander and Madhavi Sunder leverage examples of private interests controlling IP derived from traditional culture to point out that "the public domain steps in just where the romantic author ceases to deliver property rights to the powerful. The romantic author cannot justify corporate control over these important, global information resources, but the romantic public domain can" (2004, 1346; see also Rosenblatt 2019).

More recently, some scholars have been prone to question the assumption, underlying this entire discussion, that copyright laws are in fact Eurocentric and/ or incompatible with traditional or Indigenous musics. In an early critique of the assumption, Martin Scherzinger drew parallels between European Romanticism's author myths and Shona beliefs about musical creativity (1999; see also 2014, 178; Bigenho 2002). Adding to the observations of other scholars who had tracked African musicians' savvy engagements with copyright, Caspar Melville has pointed out that while the Malian *jeliw* he writes about "work in an ancient tradition," they are also "able to adapt and navigate the rough waters of international copyright with the help of European publishers, so as to ensure income for themselves and the continuation of their musical tradition" (2017, 13).[11] The idea that copyright is Eurocentric "can tend to reproduce the notion of the African musician as a passive victim" (13; cf. Collins 2006; Perullo and Eisenberg 2015; Skinner 2012). It is also worth recalling that when the definition of folk music was debated in the early 1950s at the International Folk Music Council, delegates who hailed from or had researched in countries of the global South, such as U Khin Zaw of Burma, pushed back on the idea that folk compositions could not be newly produced by individuals (IFMC 1953, 14; Cowdery 2005, 809–10); in such scholars' views folk songs could be individually created, presumably making them copyrightable. To be sure, traditional or Indigenous creators often have good reasons to view ownership of works as collective even where they have a strong subjective awareness of having individually produced them (Bigenho 2002, 199–225; Boateng 2011, 11–12; McDonagh 2018). But acknowledging individual authorship of the collectively owned is distinct from constructing traditional creativity and canonical authorship as radically different. Adding to her previous critiques of Boyle's cultural environmentalism, Sunder has more recently argued that "reifying the public domain may have the unintended effect of congealing traditional knowledge as 'the opposite of property,' presenting poor people's knowledge as the raw material of innovation—ancient, static, and natural—rather than as intellectual property—modern, dynamic, scientific, and culturally inventive" (2012, 129–30).

In focusing on folk music through much of this book, I build extensively upon this last strain of critique that complicates the notion that copyright or its underlying author concepts are essentially Eurocentric. As I examine in chapters 3 to 6, folkloric anonymity, while framed as an outcome of natural processes, was in fact constructed during the twentieth-century project of collecting and promoting folk music. Turkey's IP reform then altered the stakes of folk music's purported anonymity. A renewed copyright regime incentivized new claims to authorship and stoked fierce debates about how the law should be applied in the genre. My choice of folk music as a genre study, then, occasions a contribution to a long-standing debate within ethnomusicology while promising a rich set of answers to my research questions about how copyright affects authorship and ownership concepts and how the prior history of nationalist cultural reformism—and responses to it—might shape copyright legality in Turkey today.

Introduction **19**

WHY AND HOW I LEARNED WHAT I LEARNED

Creativity has been a focus of mine since I first decided to study ethnomusicology after learning to play and admire a two-stringed lute called a *dutar* while living in Turkmenistan in 2004–2006. My earliest research projects sought to clarify the nature of creative agency—and master performers' understandings of it—in instrumental performance on the dutar. In complicating the idea of folkloric anonymity, I am taking a cue from the musicians I had learned from in Turkmenistan before my fieldwork in Turkey. While playing compositions that had been passed down and reshaped over generations and were thus collective and anonymous "folk" products of a sort, these gifted performers also remembered and celebrated how performer-creators of previous generations, whose names were well-known, authored specific contributions to such traditional works, crafting them into distinctive variants (Fossum 2015, 2017). In the spirit of this understanding of creativity, I place individual creative agency at the center of my research. That said, I have sometimes wondered whether this persistent research interest also reflects a hangover of my conservative upbringing, in which I was taught to cherish the "great works" of the mostly European men contributing to the Western canon. I also have a past life as a performer of rock, a genre with its own romanticisms around the guitar hero. It seems possible that I am also in some way perpetuating this focus on celebrating the individual achievements and contributions of "Romantic authors" even as I have decentered the Western canon in my own work. If this is the case, however, I can also credit a resonance between indigenous Turkmen and Western Romantic values for driving me to the insights at which I have arrived in my research.

Whatever the reasons, my interest was piqued when, on the heels of my experience in Turkmenistan, I first encountered Turkish folk music in its state-sponsored form, packaged as it was with a folkloristic narrative about the "anonymity" of the songs and tunes that had emerged as a collective expression of the Anatolian people. My first teacher of Turkey's folk music was Hüsnü Aydoğdu, a retired staff musician from TRT, the state broadcasting institution that had curated and promoted something of an official canon of folk music: the TRT Folk Music Repertoire. Hüsnü hoca, as I called him (*hoca*, pronounced "HO-ja," meaning "teacher"), was forging a new life for himself and his family in my native Washington, DC, metropolitan area, and he had assembled a motley ensemble of amateur enthusiasts of the music. At the time (2007–2008), it was the closest thing I could find to my recent experience of studying Turkmen dutar. The group

20 *Copyright Consciousness*

convened weekly to perform some of the simpler songs and tunes from the TRT Repertoire in a style that I would later understand was modeled on one of the agency's famous broadcast ensembles, "Voices from the Homeland" (*Yurttan Sesler*). Hüsnü hoca remains a dear friend, and he helped me immensely during my later fieldwork in Turkey. He is a thoughtful individual with his own critical perspective on official folklore, but it was in his ensemble that I first encountered some of the folkloristic narratives that I examine at length in this book and that seemed to charge the genre with a Romantic aura of authenticity.

The data presented in this book were collected over several periods of research in Turkey, beginning with my dissertation fieldwork (August 2013–May 2014, January–November 2015, and June–July 2016) and continuing with post-doctoral follow-up fieldwork during the summers of 2018, 2019, 2022, and 2023. During this research I was based in Istanbul, though I made many trips to other cities and towns around Turkey—especially Ankara but also İzmir, Antalya, Diyarbakır, Bursa, and villages from the shores of the eastern Black Sea and the Aegean to the Toros mountains—to conduct interviews and attend concerts or festivals.

My fieldwork involved not only participant observation but also what legal anthropologist Hugh Gusterson calls "polymorphous engagement" in his discussion of projects that involve "studying up": that is, research on the relatively powerful in the corporate or bureaucratic world, including the legal professionals and copyright officials whose perspectives interested me. Such an approach entails "interacting with informants across a number of dispersed sites, not just in local communities, and sometimes in virtual form" and "collecting data eclectically from a disparate array of sources in many different ways" (1997, 116; see also Donovan 2007; Nader 1974). While my fieldwork methods were polymorphous in this sense—and different methods often overlapped in messy ways—I place my methods into three rough categories for purposes of offering the reader a sketch of how I learned what I learned.

First, I engaged in the classic ethnographic method of participant observation in musicking by taking music lessons and playing with musicians, especially folk music. My instrument of choice was the *bağlama*—a long-necked lute with three courses of strings that is the most popular instrument for performing folk music in Turkey and to which some of my prior knowledge and motor memory of guitar- and dutar-playing transferred. After the aforementioned Hüsnü hoca, my first teacher in Turkey was Ümit Şimşek, an outstanding player and even more gifted pedagogue who was based, before his tragic passing in 2020, at the private music school of his brother-in-law, the prominent bağlama virtuoso

Introduction 21

Erdal Erzincan. Ümit hoca and Erzincan were members of the Alevi religious minority whose music constitutes a key subgenre of folk music, though official institutions like TRT long censored Alevi songs that expressed beliefs diverging from Sunni orthodoxy. Erzincan was an important figure in a cultural revival that has brought greater visibility to Alevi belief and cultural practices since the 1980s (see Dressler 2008; A. Erol 2009; Kreger 2023; U. Özdemir 2015; Pinkert 2016). Bağlama virtuosos like Erzincan were great innovators of technique for the instrument, having built considerably upon the classic, mainstream approach best exemplified by the famous "Voices from the Homeland" ensemble (see chapters 3 to 5).

As my research progressed, however, I came to see a value in improving my knowledge of this older, broadcast ensemble approach to folk music long promoted by institutions such as TRT and the Folklore Foundation (Folklor Kurumu), which I had first encountered in Hüsnü hoca's group. Thus, in spring 2014 I seized an opportunity to rehearse and perform with an ad hoc folk music orchestra led by Yücel Paşmakçı, a respected folk music performer, teacher, and former director of TRT's Folk Music Division. The rehearsals and concert were held at Istanbul Technical University (ITU), whose Turkish Music State Conservatory, founded in 1976, was the oldest conservatory teaching musical forms native to Turkey, where conservatories had previously focused only Western classical music. ITU has hosted a number of foreign ethnomusicologists working in the country, including me. As I worked to learn the repertoire for the Paşmakçı orchestra, a long-time ITU bağlama teacher named Şendoğan Karadeli pulled me under his wing, and in our lessons, he guided me to a deeper understanding of the standardized set of techniques for performing folk music from around Turkey, as developed in state broadcasting ensembles. He has remained a great friend and teacher for me.

For yet another perspective on the music, I sought out a highly respected folk music artist named Nevzat Karakış, who defied institutionalized approaches to learning. He refused payment for lessons, preferring to meet in a café in Istanbul's left-leaning Kadıköy neighborhood, where a community of folk music enthusiasts, many of whom were members of ethnic minorities, joined in our conversations (my reciprocation for the knowledge he shared often involved buying drinks and food for the group). In a soft, slow-to-speak manner that indexed a learned thoughtfulness, Nevzat hoca drew on an encyclopedic knowledge of folk songs and tunes and his impressive personal library of publications on the subject to critique the official narratives that had helped construct the folk music genre. He was a well-connected, keen observer of the folk music scene, and our lessons focused less on performance technique than on understanding song texts and the historical contexts in which they had emerged. His critical take on state folklore and the market for folk music offered a counterpoint to the official folkloristic narratives and the IP-normative perspectives I often encountered in my conversations about copyright with those engaged in IP reform.

In addition to my work with Ümit hoca, Şendoğan hoca, and Nevzat hoca, I furthermore made time to study Turkey's indigenous urban art music traditions with *ud* (fretless lute) master Necati Çelik and *kanun* (plucked zither) master Ruhi Ayangil (I had received some initial grounding in the United States from the multitalented Mehmet Ali Sanlıkol). While I conceptualized this learning as separate from my copyright research, these teachers occasionally offered relevant perspectives on copyright or connected me with helpful individuals in the industry.

The second category of fieldwork approaches involved interviews and conversations, of varying degrees of formality, with musicians, IP lawyers and experts, music company executives, and individuals involved in copyright collecting societies or government institutions (the Cultural Ministry, TRT, or courts). My music teachers, local academics, and my growing network of contacts in the music scene often provided connections to these individuals, but many were also approachable in other ways. While quickly changing during my fieldwork, the recording industry was still partly concentrated in Unkapanı, an industrial manufacturing hub with rows of storefronts where record producers often welcomed visitors for conversation over a tea. The offices were often frequented by former and current recording artists as well, many of whom were interested in my project. Even some IP court judges were approachable, I found, if one popped into the office of their clerks (*kalem*) to make an appointment (to my astonishment, on some occasions they invited me straight in to hear about my research and offer their thoughts). Legal professionals were usually quite busy, however, and while some were surprisingly generous with their time, I often had only a few minutes with them. On one occasion, a prominent entertainment lawyer let me interview him while we sat in traffic in his car as he drove between meetings. In contrast to such copyright-related interviews, which sometimes felt high-pressure and rushed, researching topics such as the history of TRT could feel luxurious, as the timing of my project meant that many of the individuals knowledgeable about the 1960s–1980s era that most interested me were retired and eager to talk about their lives.

Introduction **23**

It is common for researchers to cite the number of interviews they conducted, and in keeping with this, I catalogued my formal interviews in a spreadsheet. By the end, I tallied ninety-five interviews with eighty-six different individuals (there were some whom I interviewed more than once, and some cases in which I interviewed two or three individuals at a time). I find such a count dissatisfying, however, since I also had countless informal conversations in which I often encountered perspectives and comments I preserved in fieldnotes and, where appropriate, cite anonymously. Such conversations often occurred around music lessons, academic symposia, record label offices, or hangouts at bars and cafés.

The third category of research I undertook involved archival and library searches. I spent many long afternoons at the law library of Bilgi University, where numerous tomes of Turkish IP scholarship and proceedings of legal symposia could be found. To my surprise, I also found that transcripts for relevant meetings—advisory meetings for TRT, for example, or the negotiations between copyright collecting societies and industry associations for music copyright licensees—had been published and could be tracked down, even if few copies had been produced. Through a formal petition process, some IP courts also granted me limited access to lawsuit case files relevant to my project, though drawing upon these has its challenges, since Turkish privacy law stipulates harsh penalties for publicizing personally identifiable information from lawsuits. In the end—in keeping with the book's focus not on "the law on the books" but on a more expansive view of legality—I have not found it necessary to cite more than a few details from copyright cases, though my general understanding of Turkish law benefitted from reading them.

My own positionality as a white, cis-male US citizen also likely shaped both my access to data and how my interlocutors presented it to me. I sometimes wondered, for example, to what extent my status as a foreign doctoral researcher from an elite American university granted me access others may not have had. And where my interviewees described the purportedly backward or underdeveloped state of Turkish copyright, to what extent were such assessments provoked by their interaction with someone who hailed from a country where, they might imagine, the copyright system functioned in a way to which they aspired for their own system (cf. Dent 2020, 23)?[12] This dynamic is one reason that I have incorporated archival and published sources produced independently of my own research to corroborate what I encountered in interviews and conversations. I invite the reader to consider such complexities as they read and assess my account.

What I hope emerges from this multifaceted methodological approach is a holistic (if partial) picture of legality as constituted by a range of actors: musicians (both performers and creators of copyrighted content); industry executives, including record producers, distributors, and music publishers; copyright collecting society officials; lawyers and judges; bureaucrats from the Cultural Ministry or TRT; music journalists; listeners; and licensees for commercial uses of music. These categories also frequently overlapped. For example, the leaders of the musical authors' copyright collecting societies (MESAM and MSG) are elected from among the societies' membership, meaning that they are also composers or songwriters (and not infrequently, recordings artists, publishers, or even record producers as well).

THE PLAN OF THE BOOK

Having introduced the concepts and research contexts that shape this book, let me now offer a road map for how I progress through my account. Chapters 1 and 2 provide an overview of copyright and legal consciousness in Turkey's music sector generally, while chapters 3–6 focus on the folk music genre. Chapter 1 offers a diachronic account of copyright's development in the country's music industry. In its early years, the passage of a new copyright statute was caught up in the projects of shoring up the Turkish Republic's sovereignty and the state's effort to modernize society. Once passed, the law was only loosely enforced in the music sector for decades despite the determined activism of a few composers. I highlight a series of narratives about the situation that emerge from this history. The chapter thus orients the reader to the book's historical context while augmenting existing scholarly accounts of modernity and nationalism in Turkey and of the global dynamics of copyright. Chapter 2 offers an ethnographic account of the legal consciousness of judges, lawyers, collecting society officials, publishers, musicians, record producers, and licensees involved in these processes. I document multiple dimensions of these actors' copyright consciousness, showing how the history sketched in chapter 1 provides the narratives that pattern how they constitute legality today. This chapter offers my most direct and sustained engagement with theories of legal consciousness.

Chapters 3 and 4 track how the folk music genre was constructed in terms of a legal consciousness that frames the music as incompatible with copyright. Chapter 3 reviews how official institutions of folklore established and curated the genre of folk music in Turkey from the 1920s to 1970s. I survey historical data about rural creative practices to problematize the widespread theory that

Introduction **25**

folk songs emerge from a collective process that renders them anonymous. I also trace the appropriation of European concepts of authorship in Turkey's urban art music since the nineteenth century. I argue that while creativity in both folk and post-Ottoman art music (also called Turkish classical or art music) involves similar collective processes, proponents of the anonymity theory filtered out such similarities as they constructed the boundaries between the two genres. Chapter 4 documents how the idea of anonymity informed 1970s–1980s policy at TRT, the state agency that held a broadcasting monopoly and curated a canon of folk music as national culture. I draw on archival data and oral history to examine policies established by traditionalists at the agency. These policies were meant to guard the authenticity of the genre in the face of a series of social and technological developments that seemed to threaten the viability of anonymous, collective creativity, a situation that resonated with larger scholarly debates about orality and literacy at the time. I argue that such policies were in part a reaction to early copyright activism among folk music performers who claimed to have composed folk songs. In response to the traditionalist policies that sought to exclude or marginalize such music, some folk music artists then presented their own work as anonymous to access the airwaves. Such practices muddied the metadata on authorship, complicating these artists' efforts to claim rights when copyright became better enforced after the 1980s.

Chapters 5 and 6 ethnographically document how the narrative construction of folk music heritage outlined in chapters 3 and 4 mediates the legal consciousness of the actors who implement copyright in the genre today. Chapter 5 outlines how these actors respond to a series of issues they encounter, including contested authorship claims, the problematic documentary record of authorship, and the fear that the copyright system offers no protection against supposedly corruptive uses of folk music heritage. I also account for a policy idiosyncratic to Turkey, whereby arrangers of anonymous folk music were long offered only a limited (10 percent) royalty. I show how the policy was shaped by folkloristic ideologies that led copyright officials to minimize the value of folk music arrangements. The policy illustrates how localized discourses of creativity and national belonging shape copyright legality, though music sector politics, legal doctrine, and bureaucratic convenience are also key factors. Chapter 6 examines how formal law may stand in tension with extralegal norms or established customs, a situation actors negotiate as they constitute legality. I document a debate among musicians, legal scholars, and copyright administrators about the possibility of creating a copyright for collectors of anonymous folk songs. They debate the issue through the lens of a paradigmatic case I analyze at length: a famous rural musician is labeled the "collector" of a traditional song he reinvents and popularizes. He attempts to gain legal recognition for his contributions, which judges and bureaucrats struggle to fit into the categories of copyright law. Recognizing a right in folk song collection would represent an unusual adaptation of copyright, one motivated by a localized history of valorizing the figure of the folk music collector. Yet an imperative for consistency with legal doctrine and international practice constrains the possibilities for interpreting and adapting formal law.

A brief conclusion ties these ethnographic data to my larger argument that constituting copyright legality is a contingent process in which a broad range of actors participate as they take up legal concepts, assert their interests, and reproduce or contest ideologies of creativity and belonging. I also point to the significance of these findings and to directions for future research. An appendix, intended primarily as a reference for legal scholars, provides an overview of the key features of Turkish copyright law.

Introduction **27**

ONE

Copyright Reform and Cultural Modernization

At the end of June 2015, the streaming platform Apple Music was launched in 110 countries. Apple listed the countries on its website. To the disappointment of many Turkish consumers, Turkey was not on the list. In a column titled "Why Don't We Have Apple Music?" published several days later, pop culture journalist Mehmet Tez commented, "When I was a kid, albums came late, films came late, books came late, technology came late, fashions, trends came late. Now it's 2015. You think everything has changed. No. It's the same story. This is our fate. It's our country in a nutshell" (Tez 2015).[1]

The holdup, as identified by Tez as well as by a few industry insiders in their social media posts and in my conversations with them, seemed to be Apple's inability to come to terms with Turkey's copyright collecting societies for musical authors, MESAM and MSG, which issue licenses for commercial uses of copyrighted repertoire, redistributing this income as royalties to composers, lyricists, and publishers. With such negotiations occurring behind closed doors, it was hard to know what the sticking points were, though recording artists around the world have complained about the low royalties paid by streaming services, and some balked at Apple's plan not to pay royalties during its initial free, three-month trial period for the platform.[2] Some executives used the press to portray Apple Music as acting on bad faith and disregarding the rights of Turkish rightsholders by attempting to open without negotiating a licensing agreement. Another journalist, Cengiz Semercioğlu, drew on an interview with these executives to spin an anti-imperialist narrative, objecting to how "one of the world's giant companies" was "treating Turkey like a third world country" and "looking down with scorn" (2016). In my own conversations with industry executives at the time, however, some suggested the collecting societies were demanding an up-front lump payment that was outside of the usual payment structures for streaming deals. The most cynical reading was that Turkish industry executives with an interest in domestic digital service providers of music services (TTNet and Turkcell) held positions on the boards of the collecting societies, and that they were negotiating for high, guaranteed minimums in their deals to create an entry barrier for international platforms such as Apple Music, Spotify, and YouTube seeking to access the Turkish market. In an interview I conducted during the delay, a board member from one of the societies was understandably vague about the details of the negotiation but offered: "Since we have to make agreements together with other collecting societies, it was to the disadvantage of some."[3]

One industry executive who was eager to see Apple Music launch posted a series of since-deleted tweets bemoaning the situation. In June 2015 he suggested that the societies "wanted more than was their right." In September, he tweeted, "While our copyright societies continue to consider, @AppleMusic is opening even in China." Tez's column meanwhile echoed commonly circulating complaints about the artist-run authors' copyright societies: "I'm saying this openly: let MESAM and MSG quit this work and hand it over to professionals" (Tez 2015). The collecting society board member I had interviewed, however, was confident that there would be an agreement in the end.

Indeed, by February 2016, the parties had come to a licensing agreement, and the service opened. Yet the journalist Tez had found the brief delay indicative of a larger fact about Turkish society. The industry executive's dig that Apple Music was opening "even in China" drove home the point. Tez's article implied a narrative that Turkey's copyright system fell short of standards embodied in international practice, and that this was typical for the country. Semercioğlu's take, meanwhile, seemed to locate the Apple Music delay in a larger history of the country's semi-colonial marginalization at the hands of western imperialism.

———

Turkey's copyright regime is a work in progress. All jurisdictions must accommodate the disruptive nature of new technologies for distributing music, through ever-evolving administrative structures, legal revisions, and contractual arrangements, but in Turkey there is a sense that the system remains un-

Copyright Reform and Cultural Modernization **29**

derdeveloped even aside from this larger dynamic. Those whom copyright touches—everyone from industry executives to consumers—often interpret their experiences of this emergent copyright regime in terms of a series of recurring narratives. In the theoretical terms I propose in the introduction of this book, these narratives mediate their copyright consciousness, their enactments of copyright legality through discourse and social action. The public discourse around Apple Music's opening in Turkey illustrates this dynamic well. For example, while Tez chalked up Apple Music's belated opening to a specific issue (the insufficiently professionalized nature of the collecting societies), it also seemed to typify for him something more fundamental about Turkey. His rhetoric implicitly takes international practice as a normative standard for how copyright should operate in Turkey, and it characterizes the delay relative to the 110 countries in which Apple Music had already launched as an example of the country's larger tendency to lag behind in the game of progress. In short, a common understanding of the country's history and geopolitical positioning shaped his copyright consciousness.

In this chapter, I draw on interviews as well as archival and secondary sources to sketch a history of copyright's development in Turkey, showing how a series of recurring narratives emerge from this history and shape how actors with stakes in copyright frame the process. Addressing a lacuna in existing scholarship, I argue that IP reform represents a cultural modernization project akin to others that musicologists of Turkey have described. This project has also been contested in ways that resonate with larger tensions in international copyright. One such tension involves how to balance the rights of authors against the public's interest in having access to works, especially where these contribute to cultural modernization. Another tension lies in how the Turkish state has sought to sustain its sovereignty even as it seeks to integrate its IP laws and infrastructure internationally. This analysis sets up the next chapter, where I offer an ethnographic account of how such tensions and narrative framings mediate the copyright consciousness of actors in the music sector today.

After an initial discussion that locates copyright reform within the larger context of cultural (especially musical) reformism in Turkey, I break up my history of Turkish copyright into several rough periods. In the early republican period (1923–1950), the drafting of a copyright statute was caught up in the politics of the Turkish state's larger effort to shore up its sovereignty. In what I call the "dark age of copyright" (1950–1980), the country had a little-enforced statute on the books and a few determined activists sought to assert their rights. In the era of reform (1980–2010), the state became invested in building an administrative infrastructure for enforcing copyright in music and other industries. The rise of digital distribution platforms marks the most recent period (2010–present), which aligns with my own period of fieldwork in the country and which I describe in greater detail in the next chapter.

CULTURAL REFORMISM IN TURKEY

I argue that the ongoing effort to reform Turkey's IP laws and administrative structures to harmonize and integrate them with international IP laws and structures must be understood within the context of a longer history of cultural reformism dating back to the late Ottoman Empire. The empire had been waning in power relative to its European counterparts since the end of the seventeenth century, when it began to suffer a series of military defeats and to cede some of its vast territory (İnalcık and Quataert 1994; Quataert 2000). In the wake of the Ottoman Empire's final collapse after World War I, Mustafa Kemal (Atatürk) emerged as the leader of a successor nation-state, the Republic of Turkey, founded in 1923.

While Turkey is thus a postimperial state, it also shares much with postcolonial states. One of the founding Kemalist ideologies of the Turkish Republic was a linear idea of modern progress, in which modernity was located in "the West." According to this idea, Ottoman society remained "feudal" and "semi-colonial" in comparison to "contemporary" western Europe, where capitalism had developed (Ahmad 1993, 78). It had been relegated, in other words, to what historian Dipesh Chakrabarty called the "waiting room" of European historicism (2009, 8; see also Ahıska 2010). While Ottoman leadership had sought to reform some of its institutions on Western models as early as the first half of the nineteenth century, the eventual collapse of the empire seemed to prove that these reforms had not been radical enough (Ahmad 1993; Berkes 1998; İnalcık and Quataert 1994, 759–943; Lewis 1961; Landau 1984; Mardin 2006; Özman 2010). It was therefore necessary to revolutionize society within the new Republic of Turkey, a feat that the Kemalist leadership attempted to accomplish through a series of top-down cultural reforms. They switched from the Islamic calendar to the Western (Gregorian) calendar, replaced the Arabic script with a Latin one, banned head gear that distinguished men according to traditional social and religious categories, and repressed the Sufi orders (Ahmad 1993, 79–83).

Copyright Reform and Cultural Modernization **31**

Cultural Modernization in Music

As many scholars have described, Ottoman and early republican cultural reforms extended to the realm of music, where institutions of patronage were radically altered, and the state attempted to promote specific musical forms as exemplary of a desired national culture (Balkılıç 2009; O'Connell 2016; Gill 2017; Paçacı 1999; Stokes 1992; Tekelioğlu 2001). Political elites and musicians alike sought to westernize music in the Ottoman empire beginning at least by the early nineteenth century. In the Ottoman context, musical practices were characterizable in terms of *alaturka* (in the style of the Turk) and *alafranga* (in the Frankish style, an ethnic identifier that came to be applied to stylistic practices associated with the West; O'Connell 2000, 2005, 2016). These labels also took on a particular valence in the context of the rising political power and prestige of European empires, as *alafranga* became a marker of progressiveness among the Ottoman elite. One landmark moment arrived in 1826, when Sultan Mahmud II disbanded the elite Janissary corps as part of the westernization of military institutions. Accordingly, the traditional *mehter* military band, which had consisted of Janissary corps members, was replaced with a Western-style military band (Popescu-Judetz 1996, 63).[4] In 1831 a new music academy, the Muzıka-i Hümayun, was formed, and musicians were brought from Italy to teach Western musical practices (O'Connell 2005, 185). During the *Tanzımat* reform era (1839–1876), Western musical forms such as opera were increasingly performed in Istanbul, not only because of such state-sponsored cultural reforms but also because of the growing population of Levantines—non-Muslims of European descent—in the city (Aracı 2010). Meanwhile, elements of Western musical knowledge and style were appropriated into alaturka practices: musicians adopted forms of written notation (first in a cipher system known as *hamparsum* and later using modified staff notation); they harmonized local, formerly monophonically or heterophonically performed melodies; and they worked Western frameworks into their music-theoretical treatises (O'Connell 2005, 186; see also Ayangil 2008).

In the context of the founding of the Republic of Turkey in 1923, alaturka became associated with a backward Ottoman past that must be shed altogether in favor of a modernity associated with Western forms. Key to this shift were the ideas of nationalist sociologist Ziya Gökalp (1876–1924), who set up a tripartite scheme distinguishing Western music, Eastern music, and national music.[5] By "Eastern" music he meant those alaturka urban practices that would later be salvaged as traditional Turkish art or classical music. He asserted that these were in fact derived from Byzantine practices transmitted to the Arabs, Persians, and Ottomans via Islamic philosopher and music theorist al-Farabi (ca. 870–950). This music, he alleged, was un-Turkish, unnatural, and less developed than Western music. By national music, Gökalp meant music that could be found among the rural, Turkish-speaking Anatolian folk, whose practices he claimed they had carried with them when they had migrated from Central Asia. Gökalp advocated synthesizing this music with Western classical forms in order to create a modern national music (Gökalp 1959, 299–300).

Gökalp's theories stimulated a renegotiation of the categories that framed musical practice. Alaturka music was proscribed from being taught in schools, while instruction in Western music was promoted. From 1930, a number of Western music specialists, including Paul Hindemith, were invited to the country to help develop knowledge of the music. The institutional support for the repertoire now known as Turkish art music was drastically reduced in favor of Western music (O'Connell 2000, 133–34). Between 1934 and 1938, alaturka music was banned from the radio (B. Aksoy 2008, 190–91). Meanwhile, efforts to collect folk music began in earnest in the late 1920s, with expeditions by members of Istanbul Conservatory, and continued more extensively in the 1930s to 1950s, under the leadership of Muzaffer Sarısözen, a music teacher and later radio ensemble director who maintained an archive at Ankara State Conservatory.

The proponents of traditional urban alaturka practices salvaged their music in part by adopting some of Gökalp's terms, by further westernizing its theory and performance practice, and by erasing signifiers of the Ottoman past (Gill 2017, 47–48). Musicologist Hüseyin Sadettin Arel, for example, argued that such urban musical practices could be traced to the same Central Asian Turkic origins to which Anatolian folk music could, and that they therefore also represented a music appropriate to Turkish nationalism (1969). Rauf Yekta, one of the few remaining proponents of urban alaturka traditions at Istanbul Conservatory after the founding of the republic, led efforts to appropriate the tools of Western musicology to classicize traditional urban musical practices (O'Connell 2005, 189; see also Jäger 2015). True to the ambivalence associated with modernization, today's Turkish classical musicians often advance a loss narrative that frames westernizing interventions as a discursive rupture that signaled the end of their tradition, even as they continue to play the repertoire (Gill 2017).

As I discuss further in chapters 3–6, from the late 1930s the state leveraged a monopoly in broadcasting to promote officially sanctioned versions of both rural folk music and alaturka, restyled in nationalist terms as Turkish folk music and

Copyright Reform and Cultural Modernization **33**

Turkish art music, respectively. While Turkish composers trained in Western art music did undertake the kind of synthesis Gökalp envisioned, under Sarısözen's leadership folk music repertoire was more effectively popularized, in formats that modernized it by transcribing and fixing it in staff notation and arranging it for tuxedo-clad radio ensembles who played a standardized form of the folk lute bağlama and sang in unison. This approach to modernizing and promoting folk music was less literally informed by Western classical performance practice than were the Gökalp-inspired syntheses that worked folk tunes into symphonies or piano suites. Western art music and some carefully censored forms of popular music also found their place on state radio and (from the mid 1960s) television. A greater variety of popular music, however, could be found on the lightly regulated private market for recordings. A number of scholars, including those I have cited above, have examined these approaches of the Turkish state toward music in depth. Here, my purpose is to augment existing accounts by locating and clarifying the role of copyright law—long peripheralized in such accounts—within the state's larger cultural reform program.

COPYRIGHT AND MODERNISM IN THE EARLY REPUBLIC

My argument here is that the history of the larger republican project of cultural reformism shapes how the actors involved in contemporary copyright reform understand and participate in the process. To grasp this relationship, it helps to know something of the early history of legal reform in the Republic of Turkey. The early republic's Kemalist leadership imagined that in modern Western societies, laws codified and expressed customs and traditions that organically emerged from the bottom up. By contrast, in Turkey they sought to impose legal forms based on Western models to alter traditions and customs in a top-down fashion and so to modernize them (Göle 1996, 76; Üskül Engin 2014, 33). For example, they adapted the Swiss Civil Code to replace the role of traditional Islamic Sharia law in regulating family life and inheritance (Ahmad 1993, 80; Caporal 1982; Göle 1996; Miller 2000; Özsu 2010; Versan 1984). A similar set of assumptions about the power of copyright law to modernize creative production in Turkish society attended legal reforms in the arena of IP. For example, one narrative often invoked in discourse about copyright is that the Ottomans had been late to adopt the printing press (in 1727–1729) relative to countries in western Europe. As Atatürk put it one speech, "Three centuries of observation and hesitation were needed, of effort and energy expended for and against, before the old laws and their exponents would permit the entry of printing into our country. . . . It is our purpose to create completely new laws and thus to tear up the very foundations of the old legal system" (Lewis 1961, 268–69).[6] Policymakers and activists calling for copyright reform have often referenced the purportedly meager nature of Ottoman print culture that this historical resistance to the printing press created. At the First Turkish Congress on Publishing (1939), for example, participants lamented both the small number of books that had been printed in the Otto-man era and how authors and publishers were currently suffering injustices as their rights were being neglected (*Birinci Türk Neşriyat Kongresi* 1939, 10–25).[7] A committee appointed from among the congress' participants found Turkey's copyright statute, a holdover from the late Ottoman era (1910), to be deficient when compared to the statutes of other countries on a number of counts (67–78).[8] According to their findings, legal reform was necessary to help raise the country's print culture to modern standards (Hirsch 1985, 430).

The early republic's leadership also sought to develop a robust national econ-omy to ensure national sovereignty. In their view, the Ottoman Empire had been effectively reduced to the status of a European colony (Ahmad 1993, 93). They saw Turkey as a mainly agrarian economy lacking domestic capital. Late Ottoman policy had turned the country into "a colony of foreigners" (93), a peripheral supplier of raw materials to nations of the industrialized metropole, from whom they imported finished products, developing a crippling balance of trade deficit in the process.[9] The hardships wrought by the global depression that began in 1929 particularly roused anti-imperialist resentment toward Western powers, whom many Turks came to view as exploiting the colonial periphery and impinging on Turkish sovereignty (Lewis 1961, 275–78). To consolidate Turkish sovereignty by developing the national economy, the Kemalists developed the policy of *etatism*. Under etatism, the state intervened in the capitalist economy through protection-ist trade policies and established and operated certain enterprises alongside the support of private industry (Barlas 1998, 76–107). Because the Kemalist leadership furthermore viewed industry as synonymous with civilization (Ahmad 1993, 93), they also viewed economic development and national sovereignty through the frame of progress toward modernity.

The Kemalists' international policy went hand in hand with cultural nation-building and with developing a strong national economy, and it aimed to put the country on equal footing with western European powers. This meant nei-ther pursuing isolationism nor continuing an asymmetrical internationalism that reinforced the colonial dynamic. Rather, they undertook "a balancing act

Copyright Reform and Cultural Modernization **35**

aimed at the symmetric internationalization of the nation-state in the making" (Liebisch-Gümüş 2019, 28).[10] While this balancing act involved avoiding certain international entanglements, copyright may have appeared to be an arena in which Turkey could integrate internationally without too great a threat to its sovereignty. Furthermore, as part of the economic addendum to the 1923 Lausanne Agreement, the treaty in which the Allied powers recognized the sovereignty of the Republic of Turkey, the country was required to join the Berne Convention, the international agreement that sets minimum standards of copyright protection (Öztrak 1970; Hirsch 1985, 304).

When policymakers discussed acceding to Berne and revising the copyright statute, they debated how to balance the republic's developmental priorities with its symmetric internationalist approach. On the one hand, for those who framed copyright in terms of authors' moral rights or in terms of the need to meet the latest and highest standards of IP protection recognized in the West, it seemed necessary to pay foreign authors their due for translations of their works.[11] On the other hand, because of the priority Kemalists placed upon cultural westernization, many pointed out the need to make the "great works" of Western civilization accessible to the Turkish reading public. Denying foreign authors a right in translations of their works would ensure that translations could be published easily and cheaply in Turkey. Such an approach would also bolster the fledgling national publishing sector; it thus aligned with other protectionist policies aimed at developing domestic industry (see for example *Birinci Türk Neşriyat Kongresi* 1939, 12, 73–78).[12] The latter position initially won out, and other signatories of the Lausanne Agreement objected to Turkey's refusal to recognize the rights of foreign authors in translated works. They thus rejected Turkey's first bid to join the Berne Union in 1931 (Ricketson and Ginsburg 2022, vol. 3, §11.17).

Turkey remained out of the Berne Convention until a new copyright statute addressing these objections was passed in 1951. The new statute was drawn up by Ankara law professor Ernst Hirsch who—like many of the foreign music specialists invited to help reform musical education in the country—was a German Jewish émigré fleeing the political situation at home. Hirsch modeled the Turkish law on the German statute. He connected the passage of the new statute to the victory of the Democratic Party, whose agenda included trade liberalization, in the country's first multi-party elections in 1950 (1985, 432).[13] Turkey had also emerged from World War II in an economically and socially uncertain state and geopolitically positioned between the two diverging ideological poles of the budding Cold War. After World War II, the Soviet Union sought to claim territory in northeast Turkey and to ensure its own access to the Bosphorus and Dardanelles straits. These developments impelled Turkey to shore up its relations with Western powers by joining the Organization for European Economic Cooperation (1948), the Council of Europe (1949), and NATO (1952) around this time (see Bilgin and Bilgiç 2012, 3; Gönlübol 1975; Karpat 1975). Acceding to Berne may have helped consolidate such ties, and the new copyright statute made this possible.[14]

LIFE IN THE DARK AGE OF COPYRIGHT

Despite the passage of the 1951 copyright statute and Turkey's accession to the Berne Union, little seems to have initially changed within the country's music sector as a result. In my interviews with music industry actors and in many published sources that describe this period, a series of narratives emphasize how copyright remained loosely enforced in the country over the next three decades. The 1910 law had given composers the right to authorize reproductions of their works in published scores, and it also afforded them mechanical rights—the rights to authorize and profit from recordings of their works in physical media like records.[15] However, while the most successful composers might be paid a percentage based on sales of a record, they complained that this percentage was low, that sales figures were impossible for composers to verify, and that many worked in exchange for only a one-time, fixed fee (*fiks*; Ünlü 2004, 387–91; see also MESAM 2007, 30). The 1951 statute went further by recognizing performing rights—the rights of composers to compensation when their works are performed live or broadcast—but no system for tracking performances and distributing royalties was initially created.

When drafting the 1951 statute, Hirsch had argued that, in keeping with the principles of etatism, the state should be responsible for forming copyright collecting societies—the organizations that license and track the uses of copyrighted works and distribute royalties to rightsholders. Some within the Education Ministry felt, however, that under etatism the state acted patronizingly toward citizens, and that artists should form the societies. Recalling the debate in his memoir, Hirsch anticipated later critiques of the artist-run collecting societies, MESAM and MSG, that were eventually formed in Turkey. "Having lived in Turkey for 18 years and being somewhat acquainted with the mentality of those whose interests were in question," he wrote, "I explained that I didn't have much hope that these people would show the necessary energy to found this type of society and protect their interests." The artists in question were "caught up in a completely individualistic attitude" and would not accomplish something that could only be attained by "cooperative behavior" (Hirsch 1985, 432). As a result of the debate, the statute included a compromise provision in which artists had a six-month window from the signing of the statute to form societies, after which point the state would do so. Subsequently no artist-formed society emerged, but the state also failed to follow through on forming a society.[16]

Musicians also described having little awareness of copyright in the decades following the passage of the statute. In my conversations with veteran Anatolian Rock singer and one-time MESAM president Ali Rıza Binboğa, for example, he recalled that when his song "Yarınlar Bizim" (The tomorrows are ours) was selected as Turkey's entry for the Eurovision contest in 1975, he was advised to register the work with the French collecting society SACEM so that he could collect royalties when it was played abroad. Prior to this he had had no idea that he could collect royalties for such uses. Binboğa emphasized to me that if he—an educated urbanite with a university degree in engineering—had been unaware of his rights, how much less so the rural musicians like iconic bard Âşık Veysel who were attaining national fame in the 1960s and 1970s? Other veteran musicians also recalled how, if a songwriter had written a song, and the song became a top single, whether the songwriter themselves or another artist performed it, record producers might have a large number of their artists perform the song, especially in the early days of the height of its popularity. Initially, the label might pay the songwriter for the rights to use that song, but as more and more people performed it, the songwriter received no new payments for the rights in the subsequent recordings. Exacerbating the issue was the power asymmetry between musicians and record producers, who often understood copyright law to a much greater extent and had unwitting musicians sign contracts that involved not only licensing the specific use of a work but also stipulating extreme terms that Binboğa caricatured as, "Whatever happens on this planet or another planet all the rights over these things in any form are mine."[17] Nevzat Sümer (1927–2018), a Turkish art music composer and *kanun* player credited as the founder of MESAM, further described to me how artists shied away from turning to the courts to assert their rights and demand money from record producers because they regarded it as "degrading" (*zül*).

While the dominant narratives I encountered emphasized this lack of awareness of copyright on the part of musicians and the lack of a system for proper copyright enforcement, some of my interlocutors complicated this narrative.

38 *Copyright Consciousness*

Metin Uzelli, the second-generation owner of the independent Turkish label Uzelli Records, told me how his father had gotten into the business in Germany during the early 1970s. Because he was distributing in Germany, he had to make his contracts with Turkish recording artists conform to German copyright law. He specifically recalled how his father had registered Âşık Veysel as a member at the German copyright collecting society GEMA, for example, and he would send checks for royalties to GEMA, who would in turn mail payments to Veysel in Turkey. Uzelli kept careful records on such transactions, and I was able to see a few examples. But Uzelli's careful and conscientious practices may have been exceptional.

In the realm of performing rights—the rights of copyright holders when their works are broadcast or performed live—there were both similarities and differences to the situation with mechanical rights—the rights of composers when their works are captured and sold as physical recordings. Until the privatization of broadcast media in the 1990s, if performing royalties for local consumption were to be collected from broadcasting, they would have to come first and foremost from Turkish Radio and Television (TRT), the state agency that long held a monopoly on broadcasting. The fees TRT paid to Turkish artists appearing on the outlet were often perceived as minimal.[18] Artists were usually happy to perform nonetheless, if only for the publicity. Some composers also recalled TRT paying royalties on *foreign* works, because foreign rightsholders demanded it, but they complained that *Turkish* authors were not receiving royalties for performances of their works in broadcasts (MÜZKO 1978, 16–17).

Despite the narrative emphasis on musicians' lack of awareness of copyright, there was a history of copyright activism among a few musicians dating back to the 1960s. Sümer, for example, had been active as a labor organizer among musicians since the late 1950s. In addition to running a promotion group for musicians and founding musicians' unions at the Ankara and Istanbul Radio stations in the 1960s (see TRT 1972a), he also collaborated with law professor Halit Kemal Elbir to run publishing outfits that sought to collect royalties for Turkish art music composers from record labels and TRT. They accomplished this via registrations with SACEM, the French collecting society, though they had limited success (MESAM 2007, 25). Sümer saw the founding of MESAM, Turkey's first collecting society for musical composers and lyricists, as the culmination of this activism (interview, September 12, 2015). Atilla Özdemiroğlu (1943–2016), a prominent composer, arranger, and film scorer who also held a law degree, had likewise run publishing operations that collected some royalties for compos-

Copyright Reform and Cultural Modernization **39**

ers in the 1970s, and he sought to organize musicians on the issue of copyright (MESAM 2007, 32–33).

Another copyright activist was a musician and lawyer named Cemil Demirsipahi (1933–2013), who plays a key role in my account of the policies of TRT's folk music division.[19] Demirsipahi, who had studied law under copyright statute author Hirsch, initiated a lawsuit over his gold record "Aman güzel yavaş yürü (Cano)" (Kaplan n.d., 4, 6).[20] This was one of the first lawsuits over music copyright in Turkey; the 1962 decision established several legal precedents and was frequently cited in legal scholarship in subsequent years.[21] By the late 1970s, Demirsipahi was collaborating with a group of industry activists who formed an organization called MÜZKO.[22] The group held a series of conferences at hotels to try to organize and to raise awareness among musicians about their legal rights. As the culmination of a series of meetings, Demirsipahi drew up the organization's founding statutes, together with a foreword outlining the need for a national collecting society (MÜZKO 1978).

Demirsipahi looked with suspicion at the foreign collecting societies, SACEM and GEMA, who he thought were neglecting or even exploiting Turkish composers' rights. He claimed that Turkish composers who signed their rights over to these organizations did not receive their due in return; rather, the societies were taking disproportionate cuts from these earnings and using them to support "their own cultural musics." They allegedly did this by adding extra middlemen into the distribution process, perhaps consuming the royalties entirely. This contrasted with what he imagined were substantial royalties that *were* being paid to SACEM's French members (MÜZKO 1978, 20; see also "Cemil Demirsipahi ile söyleyiş" 2005, 292). "It would be a mistake to give the management of our cultural music to other countries," he wrote (MÜZKO 1978, 14). He suspected the foreign societies of attempting, via their contractual agreements in Turkey, to "become masters [*hakim*] over our musical market" and "arbiters of the proportions [of foreign and Turkish music] in radio and television broadcasts" (14).

In another kind of narrative about this period of copyright history in Turkey, the lack of legal enforcement constituted an environment that stimulated local production at the expense of rightsholders, especially those located abroad. As chronicled in Cem Kaya's 2014 documentary *Remake, Remix, Rip-off*, a prolific local film industry flourished in the 1960s and 1970s as filmmakers capitalized on the lack of copyright enforcement to repeatedly recycle plots, interpolate unlicensed clips from Hollywood films, and freely insert recorded music into their soundtracks.[23] Within music, similar dynamics were at play. The early his-

40 *Copyright Consciousness*

tory of the recorded music industry in Turkey was dominated by foreign companies who operated through local representatives—often members of religious minorities. From about 1930, these companies had merged under the umbrella of EMI, which owned a record plant in the Yeşilköy neighborhood of Istanbul. The bulk of records were produced on three major labels—Odeon, His Master's Voice, and Columbia—for several decades, until smaller, local companies gradually began to form in the 1950s, with increasing forays into the market by new local players through the 1960s (see Ünlü 2004; Çakmur 2001, 155–65, 185–90; Karlıdağ 2010, 180–90).

The 45 RPM record, a new technology that arrived in Turkey in the late 1950s, was cheaper and easier to produce than the older 78 RPM format, altering market conditions in a way that disrupted the dominance of the major foreign firms in the Turkish recording industry. In 1964, an Istanbul entrepreneur named İzzet Şefizade opened a record plant where he manufactured records not only for his own label, *Diskofon*, but also for other small record companies, some of whom began pressing pirated versions of records released by the multinational major firms (Çakmur 2001, 187–88). Barış Çakmur, a political scientist who wrote his dissertation about Turkey's music industry, argues that this development lowered the cost of records and ate into the profits of the major firms. An increasing number of local firms were able to enter the market because of the low overhead that resulted from the relatively cheap production costs of 45 RPM records and the lack of royalty payments paid to composers because of loose copyright enforcement. The state's monopoly over broadcasting, which it leveraged to forward its cultural reform program rather than to promote commercially produced records, further contributed to the labels' low overhead by limiting the possibilities for promotion. However, it also heightened uncertainty about the demand for new releases. All of these conditions, together with the lack of anti-piracy enforcement, led to EMI's departure from the Turkish market, to the bankruptcy of the larger domestic firms, and to the proliferation of small local firms who could survive on lower profit margins. The arrival of cassette technology reinforced these conditions by making unauthorized copying even easier and cheaper (Çakmur 2001, 186–90; cf. Manuel 1993, 30–31; Johns 2009, 442).[24]

In the early 1970s, the proliferating local record labels had become concentrated in a single, recently built, brutalist-style block of offices in Istanbul's Unkapanı neighborhood. Record producers and musicians I spoke with recalled how this concentration of the music industry in a single area fostered neighborly relations and informal business practices among local music companies,

Copyright Reform and Cultural Modernization 41

including reciprocal favors, verbal agreements, or irregular, informally drawn up contracts for some kinds of transactions. The situation militated against the kind of careful record-keeping that might have facilitated royalty payments tied to sales. Some summaries of record producers' practices of the time suggest that while relatively conscientious firms existed, they were not the norm (MÜZKO 1978, 15). One anonymous record producer even flatly stated that their label paid *no* royalties in the 1970s and 1980s, which helped keep overhead low (Çakmur 2001, 189).

One way to read this history, then, is that the lack of copyright enforcement in the music sector aligned with the priorities of etatism by fostering industry in the hands of private Turkish capital.[25] At the same time, for copyright stakeholders, the experience of this "dark age" of copyright exemplified the country's ongoing backwardness vis-à-vis international standards of IP protection. The account of composer and performer Sadettin Kaynak provides an early example of this sort of copyright consciousness (Ünlü 2004, 389–90). Kaynak had attempted to sue nightclub owners over the use of his works in live performances at their venues, but the courts ultimately found in favor of the nightclubs, apparently because the 1910 law that was in effect at the time of his suit made no provision for performing rights. Kaynak had become inspired to open copyright lawsuits after traveling to Berlin in 1928 and seeing how performing rights were administered there. "Not only the [performing] artist, but the nightclub owner makes money on the composer's work [in Turkey]. But when it comes to copyright, they evade it," he said in an interview with a newspaper. "We have to secure law and order; in fact, it's essential that we do so. Every country gives authors' rights to composers. But with us [*bizde*], the composer is always rowing against the current" (389–90). Similarly, the singer Esin Avşar described how she had failed to earn any money from her hit record "Yok Yok" (No, no), citing how record pirates had "held a gun to the head of" her record producer. She punctuated the anecdote with an expression commonly deployed to characterize such an outcome as typical: "Burası Türkiye!" (This is Turkey! [i.e., such conditions are to be expected]; 2008, 78).

The perspectives of 1970s copyright activists offer another example of copyright consciousness. Demirsipahi and other early copyright activists saw copyright as a modern ideal ratified by Turkey's statute, which Demirsipahi described as "an extremely civilized [*son derece medeni*] law" ("Cemil Demirsipahi ile söyleyiş" 2005, 292). They sought to organize Turkish copyright stakeholders to develop a national copyright system like those that existed elsewhere. However, the gap

42 *Copyright Consciousness*

between this ideal of the law and the reality of the system in Turkey spoke to long-held anxieties about the country's semi-colonial position relative to Europe. Thus, Demirsipahi and Özdemiroğlu viewed organizations like SACEM and GEMA as quasi-imperialist entities who pushed Turkish composers to copyright's colonial periphery. This perception may have been reinforced through a colonialist kind of condescension they experienced in their interactions with international organizations.[26] Özdemiroğlu recalls a meeting with representatives from SACEM and the International Federation of the Phonographic Industry (IFPI) in Paris, at which he and the Turkish representatives declared that they wanted to organize their own collecting society and for SACEM and GEMA to withdraw their direct involvement in Turkey.[27] The SACEM officials reportedly replied condescendingly, telling him that running a collecting society was very complicated work, that countries in North Africa and the Middle East had delegated the task to them for this reason, and that Özdemiroğlu and his Turkish colleagues wouldn't be able to do it themselves (MESAM 2007, 32).

THE ERA OF REFORM

By all accounts, the 1980s initiated a period of significant change in the relevance of copyright law to Turkey's music sector. Musicians I spoke with tended to talk about the era starting in the 1980s in terms of what happened "when copyright entered the matter" (*telif hakları işe girince*), "when copyright arose" (*telif hakları ortaya çıkınca*), or even (inaccurately) "when the copyright law appeared" (*telif hakları kanunu ortaya çıkınca*). Record producers, lawyers, and judges, too, recalled the dramatic shifts that occurred during the 1980s and 1990s, even if they were familiar with the longer legal history and often had more nuanced ways of characterizing the developments of the time.

Driving this "rise of copyright" was a series of larger political developments. Under the leadership of Prime Minister and, later, President Turgut Özal, the government implemented a series of economic policy reforms that were in tune with the larger international wave of neoliberalism at the time and with Özal's desire to integrate Turkey's economy with Europe's. Despite a period of liberalization in the 1950s, the state's prevailing approach to the economy prior to 1980 had been a mixed one featuring planned industrialization through import substitution and public enterprises that complemented private ones (Hale 1981; Sunar 1996). Özal's government, by contrast, emphasized a free market approach to trade.

Heightened IP enforcement went hand in hand with this policy of trade liber-

Copyright Reform and Cultural Modernization **43**

alization. A 1983 revision to the copyright statute re-introduced the possibility of forming copyright collecting societies, and some of the music sector's copyright activists, led by Sümer, capitalized on this moment to found MESAM. A 1981 court decision mandated that TRT begin paying copyright royalties to Turkish composers whose works were broadcast on the network (see Beşiroğlu 1999, 313–29; Avcı 2021, 70). The 1986 Law on Cinematic, Video, and Musical Works furthermore required that new sound recordings be registered with the Cultural Ministry, who maintained a database of the compositions captured in these recordings so that mechanical licensing could be better tracked. The ministry required that official seals called banderoles (*bandrol*) be affixed to sound recordings and books to track their sales and thus reign in the market for informally produced or pirated products.

The 1990s saw further, even more dramatic reforms. The state liberalized broadcasting in the early 1990s, ending TRT's monopoly and allowing a series of private television and radio stations to enter the market. This in turn altered music companies' business models, as it again became possible to promote records through music broadcasting on the new stations that emerged (Çakmur 2001, 194). Turkey's participation in a Customs Union with Europe in 1995, together with the multilateral Trade Related Aspects of Intellectual Property (TRIPS) agreement, drove a series of further changes for copyright implementation (Keyder 1996). The state created specialized IP courts and a Patent Institute to develop local IP expertise and enforcement, and in subsequent years an EU project sent a number of Turkish legal experts and judges to be trained in Europe. A 1995 revision to the statute furthermore recognized the rights of record producers in the sound recordings they produced, the rights of performers in the performances captured in these recordings, and broadcasters' rights over their broadcasts (Karlıdağ 2010, 168).[28] The record producers and recording artists eventually formed collecting societies (MÜ-YAP and MÜYORBİR, respectively) to capitalize on these rights.[29] With improved prospects for promoting popular music recordings and stronger copyright enforcement promising to make the national music sector more profitable, international music companies meanwhile reentered the Turkish market.

The copyright statute was revised repeatedly, in 2001, 2004, and 2008, as the Turkish state sought to harmonize its laws with EU regulations, further empower and improve the functioning of collecting societies, and ramp up anti-piracy efforts. The revisions arose out of negotiations among the Cultural Ministry, legal experts, trade associations representing commercial users of copyrighted media, and representatives for copyright owners; these parties met periodically to propose and debate draft revisions or additions to the statute. External pressures, such as EU accession negotiations and Turkey's appearances on the US Trade Representative's priority watch list for IP protection and market access practices, often drove such efforts. IP infringements became subject to criminal prosecution tied to harsher and harsher penalties, while a series of police actions sought to sweep city streets of the informal sector merchants hawking unauthorized reproductions of software or music (Karlıdağ 2010, 172, 210, 219–22). However, the corruptibility of the banderole system (Çakmur 2001, 267–69; 2002, 53–55) and judicial reluctance to execute the new, harsh penalties for infringement initially limited the effectiveness of anti-piracy efforts (Karlıdağ 2010, 219). Meanwhile, the spread of broadband internet in Turkey in 2004–2005 brought the unauthorized copying of music online. Sales of physical recordings peaked in 2004 (218).

MUSIC COPYRIGHT IN TURKEY AT THE TIME OF MY RESEARCH

With the benefit of a few years' hindsight, I would argue that the start of my own ethnographic fieldwork in 2013 aligned with a few important shifts in the story of Turkey's copyright reform. First, on-demand streaming platforms including Spotify, Apple Music, and YouTube were replacing downloading as the primary way in which listeners consumed recorded music. These platforms provided cheap and easy access to a huge catalogue that eliminated much of the appeal of illegal downloading. Second, the political context was evolving. Kemalist political ideologies have been decentered to some extent by the conservative perspective of the Justice and Development Party (AKP) that has dominated Turkey's politics for more than twenty years. The AKP has challenged the Kemalists' secularism in defining the Turkish nation and has, in many ways, sought to reorient the country away from Europe and toward a distinct regional Islamic or Middle Eastern modernity (A. Aslan 2013). Political events such as the government's response to the 2013 Gezi protests jeopardized Turkey's EU accession negotiations, one of the drivers of IP reform. On the other hand, Turkey continues to undergo an "identity crisis" in which a strong desire to be recognized as belonging to Europe combines with the experience of rejection and failure in the EU accession process (Babül 2017, 14). This dynamic reinforces the narratives according to which Europeans and other foreigners were meddling in Turkey's affairs in

Copyright Reform and Cultural Modernization **45**

a quasi-colonial manner (Babül 2017, 97, 129, 151; see also Ahıska 2010, 54–63; Ahmad 1993; Oran 2007, 55).

Given this context, it makes sense that in some conversations I still encountered the anti-imperialist nationalism that motivated certain initial reactions to the international integration of Turkey's copyright system and its music sector, and yet I also had the sense that it had come to seem outdated to many in the industry. International music companies were providing work for many of the people I interacted with, and distribution channels such as the aforementioned streaming platforms had become nearly global in their reach. Turkish media such as television programs (the soundtracks for which provided lucrative opportunities for some musicians and publishers) were themselves finding a significant international market. All of this created a widespread sense that the international integration of Turkey's music industry was a fait accompli. That is not to say that no one perceived any dissonances between Turkey's copyright system and imagined international standards, but rather that the international standards seemed to hold an even more unquestionable status. Most of those participating in the process of IP reform remained motivated to continue harmonizing Turkey's laws with those of Europe and developing the copyright bureaucracy, but a revision to the copyright statute in the works for several years had sunk on the government's agenda by the time I began my research, and—due to the inability of parties with opposing interests to agree on the revisions—had been abandoned by my follow-up research in 2022.

Despite all of these developments, however, based on most of my conversations with those in music sector it seemed that the more things changed, the more they stayed the same. Most fundamentally, Turkey continued to lag behind comparable countries in overall copyright licensing income. CISAC, the international federation of national collecting societies for musical authors, publishes annual reports that rank countries by overall music copyright income collected that year. In the 2022 report, the United States led the list with over two billion euros collected, while France, Japan, the United Kingdom, and Germany followed with 800–950 million euros collected each (CISAC 2022a). After this, there was a drop off to Italy at about 300 million euros, followed by a series of countries in the 100–300-million-euro range. Turkey checked in at number thirty-three with 21.7 million euros collected, behind several countries roughly comparable in terms of geopolitical positioning and degree of industrialization: Poland, the Czech Republic, Hungary, and Romania. Turkey outstrips these countries in population size, however; it thus fell to forty-sixth in music copyright income as a percentage of GDP, and below the top fifty on the rankings by collections per capita. Many industry actors saw the relatively low licensing income that Turkish collecting societies were able to bring in as indicative of the poor, still underdeveloped state of the copyright system.

My interlocutors pointed to a series of ongoing issues that the collecting societies and other actors in the IP bureaucracy were trying to resolve. Musicians and industry executives alike connected the low licensing income to disorganization or unprofessionalism within the collecting societies, especially MESAM and MSG. Indeed, the very presence of two competing societies presented a host of problems. Most countries feature a single collecting society per rights area, since operating as a monopoly both maximizes rightsholders' bargaining power and creates a convenient, one-stop-shop for users who wish to purchase licenses (Gervais 2010; Handke and Towse 2007). MSG, Turkey's second society for musical composers, lyricists, arrangers, and publishers, had formed in the late 1990s after a revision to the copyright statute allowed for competing societies in the same rights area. By most accounts, MSG was founded when Dağhan Baydur, a musician and music publisher who had been leading an effort to expand performing rights licensing while serving on MESAM's board, became frustrated with what he saw as the society's lack of professionalization and its resistance to his licensing operation, and he decided to split off and form his own society (see Fossum 2024). Industry executives and lawyers recalled that major international publishing firms had also played a role in MSG's founding, which they saw as an opportunity to better control the path of royalty streams. The presence of two societies confused the commercial users of copyrighted repertoire to whom the societies sought to sell licenses. These licensees had been known to express frustration about the need to purchase a license from a second society after they had purchased one from the first, or—according to a more cynical reading—they used the situation as an excuse to stall or resist licensing (Kural 2005, 247; *İşyerleri için* 2004, 31–33). Some collecting society officials and lawyers also recalled that since both societies claimed to represent some of the same foreign repertoire in Turkey, double payments were sent overseas, negatively impacting the overall royalty pool available to domestic rightsholders. The two societies' databases that catalogued copyrighted works and their rightsholders furthermore often conflicted with each other, and critics in the industry frequently complained that the databases were generally disorganized and incomplete. As a solution to some of these problems, in 2008 the four societies (MESAM and MSG, along with the record producers' society MÜ-YAP and the recording artists' society MÜYORBİR)

Copyright Reform and Cultural Modernization **47**

organized a common licensing protocol, selling a combined license for the rights managed by all four of the societies and attempting to coordinate their databases. These collaborative efforts later collapsed, however. At a low point, MESAM and MSG were expelled from CISAC in June 2021, "follow[ing] longstanding conflicts and breaches of the Confederation's professional rules that caused operational inefficiencies and low royalties for creators" (CISAC 2022b). At the time of my final phase of research in 2022–2023, MESAM and MSG were again coordinating their efforts, and MESAM's new leadership boasted about new collective management software they had developed and that both societies would use moving forward. Other actors in the music sector remained cynical about the prospects for improving the situation.

Another of the issues that collecting society officials, industry executives, and IP experts were most concerned about was licensing the many public spaces (*umumi mahaller*) where copyrighted music was often put to commercial use. Such spaces included shops, cafés, hotels, restaurants, bars, and concert venues— all businesses who benefited commercially from the power of music, whether played over loudspeakers or live on a stage, to attract patrons and customers. These public uses of music require an additional license that one does not automatically acquire simply by purchasing a CD or a subscription to a streaming service. Licensing these uses is perhaps the primary function of collecting societies, who send teams of officials and lawyers to these venues to pressure their owners to purchase licenses, often by threatening legal action. In Turkey, many industry insiders felt that this licensing income was especially important because they suspected that, compared to music streamed over the internet or played on television, a relatively higher percentage of music played in bars, cafés, and teahouses around the country was of domestic origin, meaning that a high percentage of this licensing income could potentially be kept within Turkey rather than sent to rightsholders overseas.[30] Yet most of these smaller users remained unlicensed as the collecting societies faced a series of logistical and legal obstacles. One issue rightsholders cited was a series of court decisions that interpreted the copyright statute's regulations regarding penalties for unlicensed uses in such a way that the resulting fines were often minimal, reducing users' incentive to purchase licenses. On the other hand, in my own conversations with courts, some framed the legally required penalty for such infringement (three times damages plus interest) as unnecessarily harsh, harsher than the fines imposed in other countries. Industry executives meanwhile complained that these lawsuits moved painfully slowly, often dragging on for many years. The slow pace of adjudication also affected lawsuits determining copyright ownership and infringement among songwriters, which presented a set of issues I discuss in greater detail in chapter 5.

All of these factors contributed to a widespread sense that Turkey's copyright regime, and especially its collecting societies, continued to compare unfavorably with the systems established in other countries. In March 2021, I presented a version of the material in this chapter to a group of Turkish musicians and music scholars. After my talk, several audience members remarked on Hirsch's comments that composers in Turkey were "caught up in a completely individualistic attitude" and would not exhibit the kind of "cooperative behavior" necessary for collective management of copyright (Hirsch 1985, 432). One commented that there wasn't "seriousness" (*ciddiyet*) among those running MESAM and MSG, while others cited the ongoing presence of rival camps among society members, and one recalled the uncivil atmosphere of a recent general membership meeting of one of the societies, in which opposing sides had dramatically hurled accusations at each other. All of this appeared indicative of the still developing or dysfunctional nature of the country's copyright regime.

CONCLUSION

In this chapter, I have sketched a history of copyright reform in Turkey, but along the way, I have highlighted a narrative of modernization that motivated many of the actors involved and informed how they interpreted the project. As an extensive scholarly literature on the music of Turkey has shown, the republican idea of modernization through westernization drove a cultural agenda that transformed the country's musical traditions in many ways. In part, I intend this chapter to augment those existing accounts by foregrounding the previously overlooked role of copyright reform among the other cultural—and especially musical—reforms such scholars have described.

Several aspects of the story I have told here furthermore speak to larger themes in the legal and sociolegal studies literature. Policymakers and courts everywhere negotiate a tension between the rights of authors and the interests of the broader public. Stakeholders and lawmakers in early republican Turkey strived to strike a balance between these two imperatives in a country where the state sought to modernize culture and develop the domestic economy. In doing so, they anticipated a debate that played out several decades later in a variety of post-colonial contexts and especially during the 1967 conference regarding the

Copyright Reform and Cultural Modernization **49**

Stockholm Revision to the Berne Convention. Here, there emerged a widespread movement in which developing countries pushed back on Berne terms that privileged rightsholders in developed countries at the expense of the needs of their own publics (Olian 1974; Ricketson and Ginsburg 2022, vol. 3, §15.03–15.33). The example highlights how the wider-spread tension between authors' rights and public interest inflects the politics of the transnational relations baked into copyright. My account of the "dark age" of copyright and of the ongoing—by most accounts insufficient—IP reform process in Turkey furthermore presents a rich case study of the gap between the ideals and practice of the law. I approach this gap as an aspect of actors' copyright consciousness: how they constitute copyright legality through both discourse and social action. In the next chapter, I theorize this copyright consciousness as multidimensional, constituted through a set of perspectives that the actors involved take up at different moments in their construction of copyright legality. Since part of my argument is that Turkey's specific history informs this process, let me draw, by way of conclusion, a few connections between the history I have sketched and the dimensions of copyright consciousness that I theorize in the next chapter.

First, the historical progress narrative provided a normative grounding for the project of copyright reform: Turkey needed to modernize its laws by bringing them in line with international standards to reform society and so make it modern. Thus bureaucrats, legal scholars, and musician-activists alike advocated the adoption of legal doctrines, standards of protection, and systems for administering copyright that were modeled on international practices. At the same time, many actors approached the project pragmatically, balancing the pursuit of lofty IP ideals with more localized concerns. The early republic's leaders sought forms of economic and legal integration that they might leverage to shore up the new country's sovereignty without compromising an equal footing with European powers on the world stage. They balanced copyright harmonization with promoting domestic economic development in part by initially limiting the rights of foreign authors in translations of their works. Nor was such a pragmatic approach to copyright limited to high-level political actors. Within the "dark age" of copyright, record producers capitalized on the lack of copyright enforcement to run profitable music companies by, at least in some cases, avoiding paying royalties to musical authors. Later, copyright activists within the music sector mobilized to demand legal reform and the development of effective bureaucratic structures for administering copyright, asserting an agency in realizing international IP norms at home.

50 *Copyright Consciousness*

There were also critical perspectives that framed the reality of the Turkish system as discordant with the ideals of the law. According to an anti-imperialist narrative, Turkish actors resent the semi-imperialist relationship they perceive to lurk within international—especially Turkish-European—relations. This anti-imperialist schema shaped the early republican leadership's cautious approach to Berne standards that might hinder the development of domestic publishing. Through a similar frame, Demirsipahi critiqued the presence of the French and German collecting societies (SACEM and GEMA) in Turkey, viewing them as extracting royalty income at the expense of Turkish composers and imposing a cultural agenda that was at odds with the promotion of Turkish national culture. More fundamentally, the contrasting normative and critical narratives often mapped onto an imagined difference between the domestic copyright system and other systems abroad. The longstanding narrative that Turkish society could be modernized in a top-down fashion through legal reform suggests that such a reflexive awareness of a contrast between domestic and international legal systems characterizes legal consciousness in Turkey, where actors often located the ideal legal order internationally, but questioned the legitimacy and effectiveness of the domestic copyright regime. That copyright had been loosely observed for so many years furthermore reinforced a widespread sense that Turkey had to "catch up" with the best developed copyright systems operating elsewhere, and the situation often seemed to resonate with larger anxieties about Turkey's standing in the world. Such anxieties reflect another aspect of copyright consciousness, a culturally intimate one in which those with stakes in copyright understand the system's shortcomings as typical of Turkey (cf. Herzfeld 2005). Recall from the opening anecdote of this chapter, for example, how the pop culture journalist Mehmet Tez saw the delayed launch of Apple Music as an instance of a cultural time lag that felt all too familiar.

In the next chapter, I offer an ethnographic account of the legal consciousness of contemporary actors in the copyright system and the music sector, showing how these normative, pragmatic, critical, and culturally intimate perspectives work together to pattern the constitution of copyright legality today.

Copyright Reform and Cultural Modernization **51**

TWO

Constituting Legality in the Music Sector

> As you know there's a thesis that people always talk about, how correct
> it is I don't know; why is it that all Muslim countries have stayed backward?
> I can't say if this idea is correct or not but it's an observation. And there's
> another observation. But this one is definitely correct. What is it? The
> countries that place the most importance on intellectual property
> and protect it are the most developed countries.
>
> (*İşyerleri için 2004*, 41)

This is how the judge of one of Istanbul's specialized intellectual property courts framed the stakes of copyright licensing when she spoke at a summit, sponsored by the city's Chamber of Commerce, that brought together the leadership of professional organizations for Turkey's touristic businesses (hotels, retailers, and transit operators) with the leadership of copyright collecting societies. The latter included MESAM and MSG, which administer the rights to musical compositions and lyrics, and MÜ-YAP, which manages record labels' rights in sound recordings. Legally, the touristic businesses are required to purchase licenses from the collecting societies for their uses of copyrighted music (such as when they play it over the speakers in a hotel lobby, store, or bus for their clientele). The users often resist paying for music or haggle for lower rates. A lawyer from MÜ-YAP had depicted such resistance in stark terms in his own address to the summit:

> When you look at the international structure since the eighteenth century,
> international efforts drive internal laws, so on the one hand internationally
> there is a universality to the order. They say, "Brother, you're going to protect

property. You're going to put importance on human rights, pay the cost of intellectual rights." On the other hand you have the local order, a few national realities, and taking these few national realities into consideration, you're saying, "Brother, the conditions in my country are different. To get the guilty to confess, it might be necessary to beat them. Maybe even torture them." Or maybe I don't have to pay for rights related to intellectual property, or when I get a refrigerator, I can take it without paying and say, "Someday later we'll talk about the money." . . . In the end, it is the people of a country that create that kind of order. But that is your internal order, and if you continue to operate according to these rules, you cannot be a member of international society. . . . We have to accept international norms. (İşyerleri *için* 2004, 24–25)

Both the judge and the MÜ-YAP lawyer are heavily invested in what I am calling copyright reform in this book: the efforts to shore up anti-piracy enforcement, develop domestic IP expertise, and establish a bureaucratic apparatus that effectively collects licensing income and efficiently distributes it as royalties to rightsholders. That individuals with such professional stakes in copyright would advocate so strongly for it is hardly surprising; their remarks seem aimed at pressuring the professional organizations by depicting them as an element keeping Turkey from joining the modern, international order. More striking is how their rhetoric suggests an acute awareness of group status, that there are collective stakes for everyone involved. Copyright norms are framed as unquestionable because they are universal; if Turkey fails to respect them, the rhetoric suggests, it will be a second-rate, backward country.

The users seemed to take some aspects of this framing for granted. A representative for the hospitality industry commented, "In earlier meetings or in the molding of public opinion it was said that the tourism [sector] doesn't want to pay copyright . . . but within Turkey the touris[tic business operators] are a relatively civilized society; no one is opposed to paying copyright; actually copyright is going to be paid and has to be paid. This is very natural, and there's nothing to say against this" (*İşyerleri için* 2004, 29). Having affirmed the normative grounding offered by the MÜ-YAP lawyer and the judge—that paying for copyright is "natural" and those who do so are "civilized"—the representative pivots, however, toward a pragmatic consideration of the disparity between such lofty IP ideals and more concrete economic considerations: "Sir, we can't forget the realities of the country in my opinion; I mean we compare everything with [how things are] abroad, and that's beautiful and good; why don't we compare

Constituting Legality in the Music Sector **53**

the base pay [here] with the base pay abroad, or the price of a hotel where you stay overseas with the price of a hotel here? In other words, the expenses have to be presented in parallel with the income" (29).

In his pivot, the hospitality industry representative thus shifts between two perspectives on copyright legality: one an affirmation of IP's normative basis and the other a pragmatic engagement with the question of how the idealized vision of copyright should be realized in the immediate context.[1] In this chapter, I track such shifting perspectives on copyright to sketch an ethnographic account of legal consciousness as I encountered it in Turkey's music sector, defined broadly to include not only musicians and music company executives but also lawyers and government officials concerned with copyright, courts, and licensees of copyrighted music. Within this account, I describe the normative and pragmatic perspectives between which the hospitality industry representative pivots as two dimensions of legal consciousness, how citizens participate in constituting legality through their discourse and action.

I highlight two further aspects of legal consciousness as well. Within what I call a critical dimension, actors observe purported shortcomings, dysfunctions, or injustices of the copyright system, often attributing them to self-interested actors wielding their power unfairly. For example, in an interview, Anatolian Rock icon Ali Rıza Binboğa—who was president of MESAM and present at the summit with the industry organizations—described to me how MESAM was "taking our copyright, in other words our rights, from the hands of dominant powers [*egemen güçler*]." These "dominant powers" included the tourism industry and broadcasters who used their economic and political importance to lobby the government for favorable terms of copyright licensing. Such a critical awareness also seems implicit in the MÜ-YAP lawyer's and the judge's comments on the licensees' resistance, or, conversely, in those of the hospitality industry representative who suggests that the licensing fees demanded are unfair. A fourth and final dimension of legal consciousness that I identify is a culturally intimate one. Here, the apparent failures of the copyright system make sense in terms of widely circulating essentialisms about what it means to be a citizen of Turkey (cf. Herzfeld 2005). This aspect of legal consciousness is in clear evidence at the summit, where all three individuals I have cited seem to express an anxiety that a failure to license copyright might confirm a stereotype about the country's backwardness.

In identifying these multiple dimensions to legal consciousness, I draw loose inspiration from the many sociolegal studies that depict legality as multifaceted,

54 *Copyright Consciousness*

constituted through the seemingly contradictory ways that people approach the law. For example, the sociologists Patricia Ewick and Susan Silbey (1998) described how in the context of 1990s New Jersey, where they conducted extensive ethnographic research, citizens imagined the law as a transcendent realm removed from the particulars of the everyday, its legitimacy grounded in its impartiality. To remain relevant to citizens' lives, however, the law must also be available to them as a strategic resource to leverage in the world; when narrating this aspect of legality, they described or treated the law as if it were a game to be played. While these two stories of the law seemed contradictory, they mutually worked to reinforce the law's power: "Challenges to legality for being only a game, or a gimmick, can be repulsed by invoking legality's transcendent reified character" while "dismissals of law for being irrelevant to daily life can be answered by invoking its gamelike purposes" (230). A third thread consisted of resistive tactics (à la de Certeau 1984) and critical discourse that while it depends upon recognizing the contradictions between ideal and practice—in fact reinforces the law's authority by affording the disempowered a space of agency without disrupting its hegemony (233). Other studies have built upon such an approach to legal consciousness. Criminologist Prashan Ranasinghe (2010) describes how members of business improvement associations confronting public disorder express a profound ambivalence toward the law, articulating a reverence for it while also finding themselves disenchanted with its outcomes. Similarly, legal scholar Pascale Cornut St-Pierre describes how corporate tax lawyers affirm a classical story of the law as a set of coherent rules that states establish and by which lawyers play; their deployments of legal technique, however, reveal that they in fact "use the rules to produce something new and unexpected" (2019, 344).

While many studies have thus shown legal consciousness to consist of multiple, seemingly contradictory but in fact mutually reinforcing aspects, two factors give a particular character to legal consciousness of copyright—what I call copyright consciousness—in Turkey. The first is the nature of copyright law itself. Copyright regimes are national in jurisdiction, and so they implicate everyone in the domestic music industries together. It makes allies of music-makers who operate in different genres and who identify with divergent political positions, but who are often united as members of collecting societies looking to increase the overall royalty pool. It also sets up a series of sometimes opposing interests: between record labels and publishers or songwriters, who compete for slices of the royalty pie, for example, or between rightsholders and the owners of public spaces such as shops and bars. National copyright regimes are, however, shaped

Constituting Legality in the Music Sector **55**

by the terms that international treaties such as the Berne and Rome Conventions establish, and countries often work to harmonize their statutes with those of other countries they view as key trade partners (for Turkey, these are usually EU states). Copyright collecting societies meanwhile maintain sometimes fraught cooperative relationships with societies in other countries where their members' music might also be performed and thus accrue royalties. All of this means that copyright sets up a set of sometimes cooperative, sometimes combative relationships among both domestic and international actors. A second factor shaping copyright consciousness in Turkey is the country's geopolitical positioning on the margins of Europe, where copyright can become caught up in larger political-economic struggles for national sovereignty, favorable trade relations, and the cultural modernization that the republic's founding ideologies framed as necessary for equal membership in an international order led by Western powers (see chapter 1).

These factors produce a reflexivity to legal consciousness, a group status awareness not often present in legal consciousness studies set in North America or western Europe, though it is likely a common feature of legal consciousness in developing countries or those positioned on the margins of the global North. For example, sociolegal scholars Marc Hertogh and Marina Kurkchiyan (2016) compare legal consciousness in the United Kingdom, Poland, and Bulgaria. In their account, UK citizens favorably compared the legitimacy and effectiveness of their own legal system to those in other countries, while Polish and Bulgarian citizens were often cynical about their own countries' legal systems, a view that contrasted with their positive perceptions of EU law. As I will show, this reflexive aspect of legal consciousness runs through all four of the dimensions that I identify: the normative, the pragmatic, the critical, and the intimate. It also presents an answer to one of my main research questions in this book: how it is that an ostensibly identity-blind cultural policy regime like copyright mediates identity construction and subjectivity. The project of establishing a well-functioning copyright system in the country is a collective one that matters for rightsholders' livelihoods and the vitality of the music sector as a whole. But those involved in the project must make sense of the perceived gap between the law's ideals and practice: how the copyright system seems dysfunctional at worst, underdeveloped at best. Actors tend to interpret the situation not only in terms of copyright law itself but also in terms of larger narratives about the country's historical, cultural, and political positioning.

In what follows, I examine each of the four dimensions of copyright consciousness in turn. Just as Ewick and Silbey identify the cultural schema of the law as

56 *Copyright Consciousness*

a game, I trace a series of cultural schemas that pattern how actors constitute these dimensions of legality. I call them cultural schemas to emphasize that while they often involve a narrative, the schemas can be as evident in how they shape actors' behavior as they are in explicit discourse (compare Halliday 2019, 863). In order to illustrate the dynamic interrelation among the dimensions, I then provide a case study of how a variety of actors experience and respond to one issue with the copyright regime: the challenge of authorizing new recordings of copyrighted works. In a brief conclusion, I consolidate these observations, summarizing the picture of copyright consciousness I have sketched and connecting it to the themes of the coming chapters.

THE NORMATIVE DIMENSION: COPYRIGHT AS IDEAL

Actors in Turkey's music sector invoked two cultural schemas that depicted the law in idealized terms and affirmed its normative basis. In the first, they located the ideal copyright system in an imagined international realm; in the second, they invoked the unquestionable rights of authors over their work.

Locating the Ideal Abroad

As described in chapter 1, Turkey's copyright statute was initially modeled on Germany's, and many of its revisions have been driven by larger efforts to harmonize the country's IP laws and regulatory system with those in Europe, in order to facilitate greater international economic integration. Furthermore, the republic's founding ideologies identified western Europe as the vanguard of modern civilization and a model for reforming the country's own social and political institutions. Copyright has furthermore long been coordinated by international treaties such as the Berne and Rome Conventions. It should hardly be surprising, then, that a broad range of actors working in the country's IP bureaucracy and the music sector tended to ground copyright's normative basis in an imagined international realm or, more specifically, in western European standards and models. In my numerous interviews and conversations with copyright administrators, executives, and musicians, they often referenced "how things are overseas" (*yurt dışında olduğu gibi*) or "in the West" (*batıda*) when suggesting models for how Turkey's copyright system should be organized or run. It was not always clear whether these formulations were meant to reference a set of specific countries. Often they seemed to conjure a vague international imaginary, perhaps akin to what ethnomusicologist Louis Meintjes called "overseas" in her discussion of South African musicians who had toured abroad. Meintjes describes how, "viewed, imagined, and desired from the postcolonial, postapartheid, and professional backwaters, overseas becomes idealized as everything the local is not" (2003, 242; cf. Yurchak 2005, 158–206).

In some cases, actors explicitly tied this international grounding of copyright norms to republican ideologies of modernization, for example by praising Turkey's statute as modern and "extremely civilized" ("Cemil Demirsipahi ile söyleyiş" 2005, 292; see chapter 1).[2] In addition to the resonance with republican ideologies that entailed modernizing Turkish society in the image of an idealized "West," this tendency to locate a normative model for copyright internationally makes sense because the process of IP reform has been driven by efforts to harmonize Turkey's laws with those of European countries, and it has often involved training judges in Europe and bringing in consultants from abroad to advise on legal revisions and policy. Leadership of the musical authors' collecting societies, MESAM and MSG, also attend meetings sponsored by the international collecting societies' federation, CISAC, where they tune into the latest developments in other countries. Rightsholders may receive royalties when their music is performed abroad and may assign foreign collecting societies such as SACEM the right to manage their overseas royalties, giving them a point of comparison for the workings of the domestic societies. Industry executives, meanwhile, often have relationships with multinational music companies, from whom they gain an awareness of copyright management structures abroad.

Authors' Rights as Human Rights

An additional normative grounding for copyright lay in the idea of authors' rights as moral or human rights. Here, it is worth noting that there are different philosophical justifications for copyright law. Anglo-American laws rationalize copyright according to a utilitarian logic that frames it as a monopoly granted over the right to make copies of a work in order to allow its author to profit from it. In theory, this incentivizes creators to contribute to the production of knowledge and culture for the good of the greater public.[3] To ensure long-term public access to works and to limit copyright owners' control (monopolies being otherwise anathema to liberal economic theory), copyright laws set term limits on protection and allow for certain unlicensed uses. In Turkey as in continental Europe, by contrast, copyright laws are rationalized in terms of a version of Hegelian

58 *Copyright Consciousness*

personality theory: a work is the protectable property of an author to the extent that it reflects or constitutes some aspect of the author's personality. The Turkish statute requires that, to be protectable, works must exhibit *hususiyet*, originality that necessarily bears traces of the author's personality (Yavuz, Merdivan, and Türkay 2013, 64). According to this logic, authors (and even their families) have a moral investment in their works that justifies not only a set of economic rights but also certain moral rights: the right to be acknowledged as the author when one's work is copied, displayed, or performed; the right to prevent alterations to a work; and so on. Differences in terminology between Anglo-American and continental laws reflect this philosophical distinction ("copyright" vs. various cognates of the term "authors' rights": the German *Urheberrecht*, the French *droit d'auteur*, and the Turkish *telif hakları*). On the other hand, copyright laws on both sides of the Atlantic are informed in some ways by both of these distinct justifications; even in continental systems, there are limits to terms of copyright protection, for example (for a fuller discussion, see Gervais 2010, 13–14; Ginsburg 1990; Hughes 1988; Boyle 2008).

While this ideal of copyright as a matter of the moral rights of authors derives from continental legal doctrine, it also informs actors' legal consciousness. It frames copyright as a fundamental right whose neglect must be all the more objectionable for its moral valence. In my research, I found that composers and songwriters—especially those who had the most at stake in copyright or who had been active in collecting societies—often spoke of authors' rights in terms of human rights. Sezen Aksu, one of the best-selling songwriters and recording artists in Turkey, for example, appeared on television to speak out about copyright during a period of intensive IP reform in the late 1990s. In one clip posted to her official YouTube channel, she tells a television audience:

> The problem of copyright is that we have this image of a few personalities, a few characters, going around and just saying to our people, to the public, that we aren't getting our money for our compositions, our works, our lyrics. Now in the West it's the complete opposite, where they say creators' rights are given to the individual, in other words the creator of the work. These belong to the creator. So it is a matter of both economic and of moral rights. . . . So, acknowledging moral rights, from the position of the people going around door to door looking for their rights—this is the pursuit of a democratic right no different from women's rights, animal rights, human rights, children's rights. ("Sezen Aksu" 2015)

Note how Aksu both characterizes authors' rights as a human right (downplaying their economic transactional aspect) and figures the West as the place where such rights are properly recognized and respected. Thus, the habit of locating transcendent IP ideals elsewhere introduces a reflexive element to this perspective on the law, a critical subtext according to which someone like Aksu affirms the ideals of copyright while also highlighting how the ideals have not been realized in Turkey.

The framing of authors' rights as an unquestionable kind of human right also informs policy. For example, when I interviewed an official from the Cultural Ministry (which oversees copyright collecting societies), she told me that "in Turkey, the author [*eser sahibi*] has a certain sacred status [*kutsallık*]."[4] She offered this statement as an explanation of the policy that music publishers were not full, voting members of the copyright collecting societies. Because publishers were not authors, but rather companies whom composers and songwriters had only authorized to manage their rights, they were classified as "benefitting members" (*yararlanan üye*), able to receive royalty checks from the societies but not to vote in elections for a society's governing board.[5]

THE PRAGMATIC DIMENSION: COPYRIGHT AS PRACTICE

If one aspect of copyright consciousness legitimized the law by telling a story about its grounding in internationally derived legal concepts and a European philosophical tradition that framed authors' rights as transcendent and self-evident, another set of cultural schemas domesticated copyright, affirming its everyday relevance to actors in Turkey's music sector.

Playing the Copyright Game

In Ewick and Silbey's classic account, citizens often described legality in terms of a game, as "a terrain for tactical encounters through which people marshal a variety of social resources to achieve strategic goals" (1998, 28). In my own research, I found many examples of actors in the music sector strategically and pragmatically engaging the law in a similar way. A good example comes from the opening of this chapter: the hospitality industry representative did not challenge the normative story about copyright as an unquestionable universal ideal; while he agreed that touristic businesses should and will pay for copyright, he sought to negotiate the exact cost of such a license, in this case by strategically suggesting that the price demanded did not sufficiently account for differences in income in Turkey vis-à-vis elsewhere. Yet such practical engagement involved not only negotiating the copyright regime's concrete terms, but also pursuing strategies for profiting from it as it currently existed. One recording artist whose career I followed closely during my research pieced together his income through a combination of concert performances, running a music school, and selling recordings. He savvily incorporated copyright-based revenue streams into this income. Around the time that digital streaming took off in Turkey, he left his long-time record label to start his own, presumably so that he could retain his master rights, which are much more lucrative in the streaming environment than are composition rights. For a period, he held an elected (and salaried) position within one of the collecting societies; a variety of musicians and industry executives suspected that those holding such positions were most interested in the stable income they provided. This strategy of combining copyright-related revenue with other means of deriving an income from music is a widespread one (e.g., Hesmondhalgh et al. 2021, 18).

Building the Copyright System

While I encountered such examples of a game-like engagement with the law, I also found that a different cultural schema more often shaped this pragmatic aspect of copyright consciousness: my interlocutors frequently invoked the image of copyright as a "system" in whose construction they participated. While copyright stakeholders had international copyright norms on their side, realizing them in Turkey required shoring up public consensus around respecting IP and developing the bureaucratic apparatus for licensing music copyright and distributing royalties. These two projects were also interconnected, since the well-functioning copyright system these actors sought to build depended upon users of copyrighted music becoming accustomed to paying licensing fees that the system would effectively distribute. For actors taking up this pragmatic perspective on legality, the task was a tall one, but not impossible.

Take, for example, this excerpt from a 2018 interview I conducted with a rights-holding musician and producer who had previously served on the board of one of the collecting societies:

> DF: What is your basic sense of, like, the state of copyright now in Turkey? Can you say generally what you think?

MUSICIAN/PRODUCER: I think it's an opportunity. I mean, we are the last stop to the general, let's say, state of copyright. I mean, after [the] Turkish border there is no copyright for a few thousand, what, ten thousand kilometers. So we are the end of the culture or the end of the business. And copyright is a very [sensitive] topic. It needs educated composers and educated right[s] holders, and they have to understand what a civil organization is, what an association is. . . .

DF: You mean collecting societies?

MUSICIAN/PRODUCER: Yes. And because you need this consciousness, you need copyright consciousness. And we are working on it in Turkey, I mean it's not easy. It takes—maybe it will take another hundred years! You never know—maybe it's not our generation that will solve it, because if you look at central Europe, it was a few generations [that] had to work on copyrights until it was established today. In Turkey copyright is young. It started maybe in the '70s really. And it was organized maybe in the '90s, and reorganized now. And it may take some time. So I think it's growing. It's developing. The copyright consciousness is growing, and we are trying to educate people and make them understand why copyright is important.[6]

This musician—whose ability to speak with me in German-accented English indexed his cosmopolitan perspective and connections with western Europe—depicts Turkey as "the last stop" for copyright, suggesting an image of the copyright system as a rail line extending from a metropole out into the still-developing provinces. Here, Turkey is positioned as the most remote location in the rail network. Within this image, Turkey's system lags behind the more established national copyright systems (which, as the rail image suggests, probably lie in western Europe). However, it is still connected, and establishing a fully developed copyright system is achievable, even if it requires the hard work of educating people. This individual put this work on the shoulders of rightsholders themselves: "It's not the officials," he told me. "The officials, we cannot expect anything from the officials. We have to demand from them something. We have to go there and say 'we want this, this, this, this, because this, this, this, this.' And only then can it happen." Such rhetoric emphasizes the participatory nature of constituting legality, framing it as a function of direct democracy that cannot rely on action delegated to bureaucratic elites (cf. Holston 2022). Within this vision, the rightsholders can, with work, get what they need from the copyright system. His vague phrase "because this, this, this, this" seems to suggest how they should

62 *Copyright Consciousness*

legitimate their demands in terms of international IP norms. When I asked him what rightsholders should demand, he listed "a proper law that protects them" and, referencing the issue of performing rights licensing, "cooperation with [the] ministry of internal affairs, cultural affairs, and municipalities for the collection of performing rights from *all* commercial spaces."

While other industry actors I spoke with voiced more cynical perspectives on the copyright system (as I discuss below), those who took up the hard work of educating rightsholders and the public, lobbying for legal revisions, or improving collecting societies' licensing efforts were acting on a sense that they had some power to improve things. The transcendent ideals on which the law was based might—someday—be realized in the form of a well-functioning copyright system.

The account of one entertainment lawyer I interviewed who had worked for MESAM paints a picture of how committed some of these activists were: "When I started at MESAM in 1997 we had three lawyers. The lawyers had no computer. That's how poor MESAM was. My colleague who worked in [the member relations department] would give us their computer when their work ended at 5 p.m., and we wrote petitions at night. The next day we would open lawsuits. That's how bad it was. MESAM couldn't collect any royalties. . . . The salaries and whatnot were also low. People who had truly devoted themselves to [the cause of] copyright were working there." She also recalled how, especially in these early days before the state established dedicated IP courts and sent judges overseas to receive specialized training in IP law, she found it necessary in her role as a representative of music rightsholders to educate the courts about how rights management worked:

I am a graduate of Istanbul Law. Even though I graduated in [19]90, I finished school without learning a word about copyright. Of course, the judges, the courts, aren't going to know either. In our country, when you say "professional union" [*meslek birliği*, the Turkish word for collecting society], a lawyer's union of bars, an association of architects or accountants or something comes to mind. When we opened the first lawsuits in 1997, the civil courts would respond [by saying], "Who are you? How are you collecting money like this? Are you collecting extortion? Where did you come from?" The judge of the 8th civil court, very hard-working, was a judge who wanted to learn about the topic more deeply. I used to speak with them, explain it to them. When I was preparing the first cases, underneath [the files we submitted] we would first put [the

Constituting Legality in the Music Sector **63**

copyright statute], then the regulations on collecting societies [*meslek birliği tüzüğü, tip statüsü*], and MESAM's founding documents. In other words, are we really rightsholders [*eser sahipleri*] or not, what are we collecting—we would explain this. The law came out in 1952, but what is copyright [*telif*], no one knew.

A variety of actors articulated this pragmatic approach to copyright consciousness through such explicit reflections (often cast in heroic terms about the effort required for raising awareness and building the copyright system). However, there were many other times when their *actions* implied or constituted a pragmatic approach to the law. For example, one record producer frustrated with how courts interpreted the terms of authorization agreements in lawsuits over sound recordings decided to become a court-registered expert witness so that he might voice his perspective in legal briefs.

THE CRITICAL DIMENSION

The law appears, then, as both transcendent ideal and worldly endeavor. In the context of Turkish copyright, one story of legality locates the ideal of the law in unquestionable norms better realized elsewhere (perhaps western Europe), while within another, pragmatic construction of the law, actors domesticate legality by figuring these ideals as realizable in Turkey. But they often do so in an aspirational way. In my many conversations with actors in the music industry and the IP legal infrastructure, they were quick to point out the many dissonances they perceived between the ideals of international copyright and the ways the still-developing domestic system functioned in practice. Stakeholders were often acutely aware of such perceived shortcomings of the judicial system and copyright infrastructure, whether they quantified the issue in terms of unrealized licensing income or rather recalled more qualitatively the frustrations they had encountered in their interactions with the legal bureaucracy. They might therefore feel a need to reconcile the apparent contradiction between the law as ideal and practice, finding ways to make sense of or make do with the situation.

A recurring theme in the literature on legal consciousness is how "the contingency and indeterminate authority of legality afford the opportunity for conflict about the meaning and application of the hegemonic power of legality and define a space or a field for thought and action that challenges its constitutive or instrumental power" (Brisbin 2010, 26). Identifying the tensions between the ideals and practice of the law—the contingency and indeterminacy of legality—opened just such a space in the ethnographic context I encountered. One industry executive, for example, decried the apparent irrationality and unpredictability of legal outcomes in Turkey, describing how going to court was "like a coin flip." Consider also the musician, cited in the introduction of this book, who critiqued the idea that one could legally borrow up to eight measures of a melody. While the idea turned out to be a copyright urban legend with no basis in actual case law, it pointed to a larger observation: that copyright doctrines produce indeterminacy and result in arbitrary outcomes. In my conversations with them, some IP courts meanwhile critiqued how judicial precedents had vested expert witness testimony from musicologists with too much authority, making it impossible to rule in a way that challenged this testimony.[7] In one case, expert witnesses had suggested that there should be no finding of infringement in a lawsuit over an advertising jingle because the jingle was short. The court, which disagreed with the report's understanding of the (quite low) threshold of originality required for a melody to be copyrightable, had ordered new reports, because the appeals court would likely overturn their ruling if they decided in a way that contradicted the musicological experts. Courts I spoke with unfavorably compared such situations to procedure in Europe.

Sometimes such critiques simply seemed aimed at identifying an issue with the copyright system as it currently existed, perhaps with a pragmatic approach to the matter in mind. Perhaps, for example, those offering such critiques were hoping that if their observations made it into my published account, it might help draw attention to an issue that could be addressed through policy improvements. Most of the time, however, purported shortcomings of the Turkish copyright system seemed to appear as a sign of something else, as a part of a larger pattern. Despite the contingent and contested nature of legality, I observed recurring cultural schemas that seemed to shape how actors critically reflected upon or responded to such tensions. Here I identify two such cultural schemas that seemed to pattern what I call the critical dimension of copyright consciousness.

Copyright as a Field of Self-Interested Action That Produces Injustice

Early in my research for this book, I sat having tea with a musician and student attending one of Turkey's best conservatories. When I mentioned that I wanted to write about copyright in the country's music industry, he cringed as if I had dragged my fingernails across a chalkboard. "Copyright . . ." he repeated. "Are you

Constituting Legality in the Music Sector **65**

aware of the fights that have occurred over copyright?" He advised me to ask soft, indirect questions in my interviews and warned me of some of the interpersonal conflicts I needed to be aware of, that I should not mention [musician X] in the presence of [musician Y]. The conversation has stuck in my memory as one of the first instances in which I encountered the common idea that the state's efforts to shore up copyright enforcement had stoked interpersonal conflict in the music sector, including litigious behavior among rightsholders. In many interviews and conversations, musicians would question the validity of lawsuits over melodic similarities by pointing out that the combinatory possibilities for constructing a melody were finite: "Anyway, there are only eight notes," one musician put it (others, acknowledging chromaticism, might expand the count to twelve notes). In some such comments, musicians seemed to echo more widely circulating critiques of copyright law itself: how it can allegedly squelch creativity by reframing transformative appropriations or accidental similarities as infringements (e.g., Demers 2006; Vaidhyanathan 2003). Such discourse suggests that many cases of alleged infringement that hit the headlines in fact reflected the inevitability of melodic similarity that greedy and litigious composers refused to acknowledge (see also Avcı 2021, 60). While these critiques often thus seemed directed at copyright law itself, they also implied a cultural schema in which copyright had established a set of power relations among stakeholders, and many dissatisfactory outcomes of the copyright system might be chalked up to the tendency of actors to wield their power in self-interested and unjust ways (such as through unwarranted litigiousness).

In some cases, this cultural schema was voiced through explicit discourse, but in other cases it was more evident through action. The world of Turkish copyright lent itself to certain resistive tactics analogous to those that, for example, the socially marginalized actors of Ewick and Silbey's account employed (such as avoiding interactions with the law or "taking the law into their own hands"; 1998, 180–220). Collecting society officials and industry lawyers often seemed to feel relatively empowered to respond to their dissatisfaction with the system by working to reform it. Working musicians less involved in the copyright infrastructure tended more often to turn to resistive tactics when the law's application seemed unjust. One night, for example, I attended a performance of works by a renowned composer at a relatively small cultural center, joining the musicians for dinner afterward. Knowing that I was researching copyright, one of the musicians mentioned to me that the composer's heirs were known to tightly control live performance of their testator's works, and so they had simply not reported the repertoire performed to the composer's collecting society.[8] In another case, a recording artist complained to me about the membership criteria of the recording artists' collecting society, MÜYORBİR, which at the time stipulated a minimum number of times that one's tracks had been downloaded before one qualified. Aspiring MÜYORBİR members sometimes viewed such criteria as designed to favor more popular recording artists who wielded greater power in the society, redirecting non-member performers' royalties to themselves. As we sat having tea at a café, the recording artist, who pointed out that the download criterion presents a significant obstacle in an era when listeners are far more likely to stream than to download tracks, was downloading his album repeatedly on his own phone in an effort to reach the threshold. While actors engaging the normative dimension of legality construct the law as impartial, acts of resistance were responses to a recognition that certain individuals—the wealthiest and most popular recording artists or the heirs to the rights to the songs of a famous composer—leveraged their disproportionate power over copyright licensing or royalty distribution for personal gain.

Composers, recording artists, and their representatives frequently complained that record producers leveraged their disproportionate understanding of copyright and their power as gatekeepers to pressure them into signing exploitative contracts. One musician described the situation of a recording artist he knew who had made an album, paid for the entire production costs herself, and went to a label to have it produced and put on the market. The producer agreed but made the recording artist pay the banderole fees and also sign over control of all the master rights. When the artist later wanted to authorize a television program to use a track from the album, the producer wouldn't agree to it. Worse, some record producers, often by virtue of the fact that they also had a few composition credits to their names, had taken up leadership positions on the collecting society boards, creating what some saw as a conflict of interest.

Record producers, publishers, and a variety of musicians all frequently blamed the internal power dynamics of MESAM and MSG for the overall low licensing income in the sector. The societies are run by boards elected from the membership. This arrangement is supposed to align the interests of the society's leadership with those of its members. Many people I spoke with in the music sector complained, however, that this approach put musicians, rather than better-trained legal experts or professional administrators, in charge of the societies.[9] The societies' internal electoral politics could get heated in ways that many saw as counterproductive. During my fieldwork, this was perhaps most visible in the high-profile conflict between Alevi bağlama virtuoso Arif Sağ and arabesk icon Orhan Gencebay, former friends who began to hurl vitriol at each other via news media as they competed for the presidency of MESAM (e.g., Sözcü 2014). The implication of many such complaints that I heard from a variety of industry actors was that those fighting for elected positions were interested in them for the salaries attached to them, and that this incentivized them to stage ineffectual political performances aimed at shoring up their electoral bases within the societies rather than undertaking the work necessary to improve the functioning of the societies and the licensing income they brought in. The situation could also be tied back, however, to larger international power dynamics. One independent record label executive characterized the societies' electorally based leadership model as carbon copied from international institutional structures promoted by the international federation of musical authors' societies, CISAC. He thought the international majors—influential within CISAC via their publishing arms—wanted collecting societies to work this way because it inhibited their effectiveness, allowing the majors to better control money flows.

One former MESAM official commented to me that at a general membership meeting at which Arif Sağ had been elected president, it seemed to her that most of the members in attendance had been Alevi. As she pointed out, Alevis—a marginalized and sometimes violently oppressed religious minority in the country—were disproportionately represented within the music industry.[10] She chalked Sağ's victory up to "denominationalism" (*mezhepçilik*), which she perceived to be on the rise in Turkey. She didn't think it had been a factor in previous elections. Collecting society members were also thought to vote in organized blocks in order to put colleagues from their own political communities or musical genres into posts on the Board of Directors. For musicians working in genres that make up a relatively small market segment (Turkish art music as opposed to pop music, for example), these elections can be particularly fraught. There is more at stake than identity politics or even choosing the most competent person for the job. The Board of Directors has the power to rejigger such internal policies as membership criteria and royalty distribution formulas. Turkish art music composers, for example, have long been able to attain full membership in MESAM if they have a minimum number of compositions represented in the state broadcasting agency's official Turkish Art Music Repertoire, regardless of how much airplay these compositions receive. Under different membership criteria, they might be excluded from voting. There was a widespread perception that partisanship or genre-based factionalism drove the electoral politics rather

68 *Copyright Consciousness*

than considerations of competence for the job of increasing licensing income or improving distribution databases.

The idea that factionalism held back progress was salient enough that the MESAM leadership elected in 2021, which had run as a ticket calling themselves the "Unity and Innovation Group," featured musicians from a variety of genres and political orientations and had made depoliticization a point of its platform. Folk music artist Recep Ergül, the newly elected president, was an outspoken critic of the former leadership's purported ineffectiveness, fiscal irresponsibility, and unresponsiveness to members. Yet privately, many industry actors were skeptical that the new leadership would be any different. When I mentioned the lawsuit this new MESAM leadership had opened against German collecting society GEMA—apparently over its performing rights distribution scheme that allegedly reduced royalties for Turkish rightsholders—an industry executive I spoke with characterized the suit as a political performance that would not effect meaningful change (see Gazete Duvar 2022).

Other critical observations targeted the relations among collecting societies and other corporate actors in the copyright ecosystem. Copyright stakeholders often perceived broadcasters and other commercial users of copyrighted music to hold a position of disproportionate power that they wielded in licensing negotiations or that they leveraged to influence legal revisions and policy. Referencing the ongoing problems that the presence of two competing collecting societies for musical authors (MESAM and MSG) created, one entertainment lawyer commented to me that "our country—especially because users don't want to pay for copyright—isn't structured in such a way as to resolve [the presence of] more than one society." The comment seemed to imply that representatives for these users were lobbying to maintain a situation that they were able to exploit for their own benefit, since the rivalry between the two societies weakened them both: in periods when the societies failed to coordinate their licensing efforts, the users often resisted purchasing a license from the second society after purchasing one from the first.

Copyright as Cultural Imperialism

According to another cultural schema, some actors accounted for the copyright system's ongoing problems—the injustices it afforded, or the fact that progress on its construction seemed too slow—by framing copyright reform as cultural imperialism. They pointed either to how copyright law privileged more powerfully positioned international actors or to how it represented a Eurocentric, foreign imposition on Turkish culture. As described in chapter 1, in the early Turkish Republic the legacy of the late Ottoman past, in which European powers leveraged debt obligations to ensure favorable access to Ottoman markets, made a variety of people in Turkey highly cognizant of their own semi-colonial marginalization. This concern seemed reflected in the ideas of Cemil Demirsipahi, for example, who in the 1970s suspected the French and Germans, via SACEM and GEMA, of trying to "become masters over our musical market" (MÜZKO 1978, 14). The conditions have changed since the time of Demirsipahi's remarks, as the Turkish state has committed itself more fully to economic integration with Europe since the 1980s, and many actors in the music sector seemed to view the subsequent return of international music companies to the national market as a business opportunity. Yet some of my interlocutors occasionally disclosed such an anti-imperialist perspective. In one 2022 conversation with an executive of an independent record company, for example, she asked if I'd noticed how lifeless the atmosphere had become in Unkapanı, the cluster of brutalist structures where the Turkish record industry had been largely concentrated for the past fifty years. I answered that yes, I had noticed this, but I wasn't sure if this was because the sector was dying or because music companies were simply leaving Unkapanı for other locations around Istanbul. The latter was happening, she confirmed, but the sector was losing life, a situation she attributed to a colonialist dynamic within the international recording industry. The small labels, she told me, had become sub-labels for the international majors. She also complained that the royalty rates from digital streaming were much lower in Turkey than they were in the United States. She described the international majors as "giant corporations" (*dev şirketleri*), declared that digital distribution had become a monopoly (*dijital tekelleşti*), and that "we're being exploited" (*sömürülüyoruz*).

A former Cultural Ministry official who had worked on copyright statutory revisions in the late 1990s and early 2000s expressed frustration with international IP experts who came to Turkey to advise on the process (throughout our conversation, she sometimes described these experts as representing "the West," sometimes specifically the United States or the European Union). She complained that they didn't take the time to learn Turkish or understand Turkey, and that they dictated revisions without appreciating the sensitivities of the relations among some of the actors involved. Furthermore, the experts had been condescending and critical of the state of copyright in Turkey without considering either the context of how much it had improved in recent years or the fact that, she asserted, the Ottoman empire had possessed a highly developed copyright law when that of the United States—which long pursued lax copyright enforcement as a development strategy (Dutfield 2008, 41–42)—was in a worse state. This official critiqued the West right back, describing how, after World War I, European powers had, on the one hand, capitalized on the moment to seize Ottoman territory, while on the other hand they had demanded that Turkey be developed. She also favorably compared the Ottoman policy in North Africa and the Arab world to later Western colonial policies there.

While this official cited the relatively long history of copyright in the country (dating back to the Ottoman empire), this seemed to represent a minority perspective, and others stressed how historical and cultural differences made copyright an unnatural or imperfect fit for Turkey. As I analyze in greater detail in chapter 3, folk music is often understood to have emerged from forms of sociality predicated on a collectiveness that contrasts with the sort of possessive individualism driving IP (Leach 2007). This purported "collectiveness" is often taken to typify traditional Turkish society in some larger sense, constituting one of the elements of historical and cultural difference from the West. Some of my interlocutors viewed copyright as a foreign imposition that not only fits folk music poorly, but might also have a corruptive, commercializing influence. A recording artist and former collecting society official I interviewed complained that because of copyright, everything had taken on "the quality of commodities [meta halı]," that everyone was pursuing commercialism, and that "this is taking us away from our culture." In our conversations, my teacher Nevzat Karakış often critiqued how copyright had motivated folk music artists to make questionable authorship claims in order to profit from copyright, sometimes veering from their radical political commitments in the process (a particularly salient issue for Karakış, who had been inspired by the iconic recording artist Ruhi Su's leftist take on folk music). I will have much more to say about the intersection of copyright consciousness and folk music in subsequent chapters.

THE CULTURALLY INTIMATE DIMENSION

Recall how in the opening example of this chapter, the judge addressing the meeting between the collecting societies and the tourism industry associations asked, "Why is it that all Muslim countries have stayed backward?" Likewise, the MÜ-YAP lawyer suggested that the tourism sector's resistance to music copyright licensing undermined Turkey's claim to a spot in "international society." Notice

Constituting Legality in the Music Sector 71

the implication that the entire nation's international status is somehow bound up with the hotel and shop owners' payment of licensing fees. Such statements come from actors obviously invested in expanding the effectiveness of the national copyright system and seem aimed at pressuring the professional organizations by depicting them as an element keeping Turkey from joining the modern, international order. The judge furthermore seems to hold strongly secularist views that are not likely shared by everyone involved. But the rhetoric nonetheless belies an expectation that invoking such national anxieties about progress toward modernity might prove effective. Similarly, in one of my interviews with him about such licensing negotiations, former MESAM president Ali Rıza Binboğa characterized the professional organizations' stubborn resistance to paying for public performance licenses as an obstinance typical for Turkish citizens: "With us it's all or nothing; there's nothing in between, no such thing as moderation. With us there's no such thing as 'let's think about it [from this other perspective] for a moment.' If a man believes it's one way, you have to work very hard to convince him otherwise. That's the kind of country we are. We're at the extremes."

A wide variety of actors in the music sector and the copyright bureaucracy related the purportedly dysfunctional or underdeveloped state of the country's IP regime to such larger essentialisms about Turkish society, taking perceived copyright dysfunction as somehow typical of Turkey. Such discourse resonates with anthropologist Michael Herzfeld's theorization of cultural intimacy. Herzfeld describes cultural intimacy as "a rueful self-recognition" of "those aspects of a cultural identity that are considered a source of external embarrassment but that nevertheless provide insiders with their assurance of common sociality" (2005, 3). As Herzfeld points out, "cultural intimacy is, above all, familiarity with perceived social flaws that offer culturally persuasive explanations of apparent deviations from the public interest" (9). Cultural intimacy may work to cohere sociality, since, as Herzfeld puts it, "national embarrassment can become the ironic basis of intimacy and affection, a fellowship of the flawed, within the private spaces of national culture" (29). Cultural intimacy is also a phenomenon that other scholars have documented and discussed in the broader context of Turkey. In her ethnography of EU human rights trainings, Elif Babül has shown that a shared knowledge of how Turkish institutions fail to meet transnational standards forges an intimate sociality among the Turkish bureaucrats who guard such secrets as they perform their institutional role and status for foreign experts (2017, 151–73). Similarly, sociologist Meltem Ahıska suggests that Turkish citizens perform their modernity for a projected Western gaze—how they imagine the West sees them.

This entails outwardly confirming the official narrative of progress while guarding shared, insider knowledge of the failures of such progress, which produces an intimacy among those involved in modernizing processes. Ahıska describes how "narratives of memory about destroyed or missing archives circulate and establish a different register of truth, an intimate truth of loss," since the fragmented memories contained in such archives complicate "the official truth of progress on display for the West" (2010, 39).[11] Other sociolegal scholars of Turkey have similarly highlighted the dissonance that commonly arises when disturbing facts such as histories of political violence are disavowed in courts and official discourse and silenced in the archival record even as many citizens are aware of them (see Ayata and Hakyemez 2013; Ertür 2022, 143–55). It is in such dissonance that cultural intimacy is forged.

Like the critical dimension of copyright consciousness, what I call the culturally intimate dimension involves reconciling the tensions between the ideals and practice of the law. Rather than accounting for such dissonances by pointing to power relations, however, in culturally intimate discourse actors make sense of the situation as a familiar and typical—even if objectionable—part of the experience of being a citizen of Turkey. Such cultural intimacy is furthermore facilitated by the larger social intimacy that the national copyright system constitutes, through "the mechanisms that entangle authors and users, along with a range of material objects, with one another" in what ethnomusicologist Veit Erlmann calls "collective worlding" in his ethnographic account of the South African collecting society SAMRO (2022, 241). Within this intimate space, perceived failures of Turkish copyright can invite explanations that frame the experiences as indicative of some larger fact about Turkish society (cf. Dent 2020, 23).

In several of my interviews, entertainment lawyers or industry executives accustomed to describing legal doctrine or copyright policy in quite nuanced terms suddenly lapsed into familiar essentialisms about a collective self of the sort Herzfeld describes. In one case, a music publishing executive had spent over an hour describing the details of his work to me, and as we spoke about the relative profitability of different forms of rights licensing, the detail arose that he had never heard of income arising from sheet music sales. When I asked why he thought this was so nonexistent in Turkey, he quipped, "Maybe it's because we're a nation that doesn't like to read."

Such expressions of cultural intimacy often took the form of an explicitly self-orientalizing discourse. One of the complexities of cultural intimacy that Herzfeld describes is its ambiguous relationship with official discourse; whereas

Constituting Legality in the Music Sector **73**

official national narratives of Greece emphasize its status as the cradle of European culture whose civilized nature they contrast with Turkish "barbarism," in moments of cultural intimacy Greeks may "dwell on what they perceive as national failings and weaknesses . . . as evidence of their erstwhile condition as the serfs of *varvari*, barbarians" (2005, 82–83). Such self-reflections admit the mutability and historicity of supposedly national traits, like civilization, that state discourse frames as essential and eternal (82–83). Similarly, the forms of cultural intimacy that I encountered in Turkey often belied an anxiety that the official state project of modernizing Turkish society might have been incomplete or insufficient, leaving Turkish citizens lagging in the game of progress.

As a particularly colorful example, a former MESAM board member described a policy for which he had advocated and that the society had failed to put into practice despite the board's approving it. He accounted for the perceived failure as follows: "I think this about it: we are a nomadic society. . . . A settled society has a literate culture. They write, they draw, they pass on information. . . . It's a different way of understanding things. . . . But in [nomadic societies] there's culture, there's culture of course. But they live in one spot, then pick up, go to another place. . . . This will only change with centuries. It's a different system: the West is an information society, a system society. In the Orient, we do things more from the heart."

Where my interlocutors sometimes chalked up the perceived incompetence or dysfunction in the collecting societies to their internal politics, some also saw the situation as typical for Turkey. Dağhan Baydur, owner of the music publishing firm Muzikotek and founder of MSG, described his initial decision to leave MESAM in the late 1990s and form the second society as largely driven by his frustration at the lack of professionalism and competence he encountered on the MESAM board. Having begun his publishing career while living in the United Kingdom in the 1980s, he tended to compare the Turkish copyright system unfavorably to what he had encountered there. "I'll tell you, everything is down to Magna Carta," he told me, referencing the English document mythologized for establishing a set of personal liberties.

> Lack of Magna Carta. Not only copyright, all the problems that we have, is the lack of Magna Carta. I went to the exhibition in London, they found the four parchments signed by King John, the real ones, they're next to Euston station, British Library. They're great, I advise you to go and see those things. . . . [The year] 1215, eight hundred years ago, you know that's the problem. Turkey is

spending what, maybe the third biggest money in European football. You know we didn't go to the football World Cup for some years after spending all that money? In a private company you would be fired in three months. And those people are still the head of the federation. It's something similar to [the situation in] music.

This view resonates with a wider-spread tendency among Turkish citizens with cosmopolitan orientations to unfavorably compare the professionalism of Turkish firms to that of multinationals, and to do so in orientalist terms (Erkmen 2018). Here the discourse is leveraged to account for the many problems—especially low licensing income—that music industry actors face.[12]

CASE STUDY: AUTHORIZING NEW RECORDINGS OF COPYRIGHTED WORKS

Having offered a picture of copyright consciousness in Turkey, identifying a set of recurring stories and frames through which actors in the copyright ecosystem constitute legality, I would now like to offer a case study of one issue in order to show how these dimensions of legality interrelate. My case study focuses on a challenge described by a variety of music industry actors about copyright in Turkey: the process for authorizing recordings of copyrighted works. Worldwide, it is common for copyright owners to reserve the right to grant or deny permission to adapt or synchronize a work—to create a musical arrangement that warrants protection as a derivative work, for example, or to incorporate it into a film score. In exchange for authorizing the adaptation or synchronization, they may also demand a fee (thus soundtrack licensing fees can sometimes constitute a hefty part of a film maker's budget). However, in some jurisdictions, the authorization to record works *without* substantially adapting or synchronizing them is more or less automatic, governed by regulatory systems that require rightsholders to authorize the use and that regulate the fee associated with this authorization. The United States, for example, has set up a system of "compulsory licensing," under which a performing artist who wishes to record a cover version of a song need only write to the copyright owner's publisher to declare the use and send royalties at a rate fixed by a panel of judges called the Copyright Royalty Board.[13] Such compulsory licensing for mechanical rights has been controversial since it first arose in the early twentieth century, with some countries adopting this approach and others rejecting it (see Elton 2011; Ficsor 2010; Ricketson and

Constituting Legality in the Music Sector 75

Ginsburg 2022, vol. 3, §13.59).[14] At issue is the balance between the rights of authors and the vitality of the recording industry, for whom compulsory licensing ensures cheap and easy access to published works.

In Turkey, when seeking authorization for a mechanical license to record a version of another's work, performing artists (or their record labels) must directly negotiate the authorization of the use with the rightsholder, whether the performance constitutes an adaptation or only a performance that does not substantially adapt the work. The upshot of this approach is that when musicians wish to record someone else's song on their albums, the rightsholder(s) must sign an agreement allowing the use, and they can refuse to do so. In return for granting permission, they can also demand a fee, and there is no law or court regulating this fee. In some cases, when a musician is friends with a rightsholder, for example, there may be no fee at all, while a quite established or famous songwriter might demand a substantial price. Musicians might also find themselves on both sides of this tension: as rightsholders, they may appreciate this opportunity to profit from the works they control, but as performing artists, they might also find themselves on the other side of this negotiation, and they often complained about the difficulty and sometimes prohibitively high cost of obtaining permission to record previously published songs on their albums.

Given that rightsholders authorize collecting societies to exercise the rights to their works, one might expect that someone wishing to record a work would seek authorization from the society, and that it might be granted more or less automatically (e.g., Ficsor 2010, 55–58). But the Turkish societies have created a mechanism to ensure that rightsholders retain an ability to refuse to authorize someone to make a sound recording of their works. The Turkish law, like other copyright laws, enumerates a bundle of economic rights accorded a copyright owner: the right to make an adaptation such as a translation or arrangement of the work (*işleme hakkı*), the right to make a commercial reproduction of the work (*çoğaltma hakkı*), the right to commercially distribute reproductions of the work (*yayma hakkı*), the right to publicly perform the work (*temsil hakkı*), and the right to broadcast the work through television or radio or to make it available via a digital platform (*umuma iletim hakkı*). Members of MESAM and MSG do not sign over control of the right of adaptation to the society; this is in keeping with standard practice in many countries, where synchronizing or arranging a work in a substantial way requires authorization from the rightsholder(s). The other four rights represent what collecting societies normally manage on behalf of musical authors, and based on my conversations with those who were

76 *Copyright Consciousness*

active with MESAM in its early days, members formerly signed over control of all these rights to MESAM.[15] However, in 1999 (according to one lawyer who was working for MESAM at the time), MESAM decided to relinquish control of the right of distribution (*yayma hakkı*), handing it back to its members (MSG appears to have subsequently followed this precedent). This meant that someone who wished to record a MESAM member's work could get an authorization for commercial reproduction from the society, but they would have to go directly to the copyright owner for an authorization to distribute copies.[16]

There were several possible explanations for this situation, based on my oral history interviews and a few other sources. According to one explanation, members had been complaining that the royalty income they were receiving at the time was low. The society's income from performing rights licensing was just beginning to develop in the late 1990s. The easier-to-collect mechanical royalties were also low, and by many accounts poorly distributed. Labels may also have been underreporting sales figures, which were, at the time, considered a trade secret that the composition rightsholders could not audit (Çakmur 2001, 246–47). Nor were the Cultural Ministry's figures, based on the sale of banderoles—the anti-piracy seals affixed to CDs and cassettes—accurate, since the banderole system could easily be cheated (see Çakmur 2002). Given these factors, the ability to demand an authorization fee to record one's work represented a potentially valuable income. Second, songwriters were accustomed to long-standing industry contractual practices according to which they received up-front, lump sums in exchange for the songs they wrote for labels (see Çakmur 2001, 243–47). They may have sought to perpetuate this system through MESAM. Finally, some lawyers I spoke with recalled that in MESAM's early days, there were sometimes cases in which a composer objected to a use of their work but were unable to stop it because they had authorized MESAM to administer the rights. In this account, the policy of leaving the distribution right with rightsholders was also envisioned as a way to allow them to prevent such unwanted uses, since MESAM didn't want to be in the business of policing specific uses.[17] They reportedly saw this as the role of a publisher rather than that of a collecting society.

Whatever motivated this approach to authorizing the use of works, the policy was a point of frequent complaint. Particularly among the owners of related rights in sound recordings (performers and record producers), there are many who wish to see it reversed. The matter could become especially frustrating when the control of the rights passed from the author of the work to successors after the author's death. One musician complained to me that he found that

Constituting Legality in the Music Sector 77

the fact that such heirs were usually not themselves musicians made it difficult to negotiate with them. When a composer's heirs control the rights to a work, it may be difficult to communicate the artistic vision and musical style with which one intends to use it. Heirs may also be perceived to view the matter as a primarily commercial transaction, and the song as an asset to be exploited for profit, whereas the original composer might have been more interested in having others perform the work and have primarily artistic rather than commercial concerns. One conservatory instructor related an anecdote about a student who had come up with an arrangement of a song by a famous *âşık* (traditional minstrel; pl. *âşıklar*) and wanted to put it on his album. The âşık's heirs set the price for signing a permission at 4,000 Turkish lira (about 1,500 USD at the exchange rate of the time, a hefty sum for a Turkish student). The student had had to give up on their idea. "When you have to pay 4,000 lira it kills your inspiration," the conservatory instructor remarked.

Throughout my fieldwork, I sometimes heard musicians comment that because of such challenges in acquiring permissions for the use of published songs, recording artists were increasingly composing their own songs, even in the realm of folk music, where original composition has traditionally been a point of controversy. Musicians working in the genre were also known to circulate spreadsheets listing public domain works that they could record without having to worry about unexpected copyright lawsuits. On one occasion, my teacher Nevzat Karakış presented me as an expert on music copyright at the rehearsal of an amateur folk music choir that he directs. During a Q&A, one of the choir members asked me pointedly why copyright laws granted control of the rights in a song to the heirs of composers, heirs who had done nothing to deserve this right. Coming from an amateur folk singer, the question—and the trenchant tone in which it was posed—was a vivid reminder of how the control over works that copyright grants to some individuals seemed particularly objectionable to performers of folk music, which is often perceived as a collective heritage rightly belonging to everyone. I explore this dynamic in greater detail in subsequent chapters.

The problem of obtaining authorizations from copyright holders played out in another arena as well: re-releases of old recordings. According to the system established by the 1986 Law on Cinematic, Video, and Musical Works, record labels releasing new albums have to register the recordings with the Cultural Ministry's Copyright Directorate, presenting full documentation (*muvafakat-name*, "consent form," or *eser işletme belgesi*, "certificate for use of the work") that they had permission to use all the works on the recording and claiming their own right in the recording itself.[18] While this system has undoubtedly helped standardize and regulate rights administration, it created a new set of headaches for the labels. Beginning in 1986, agreements with rightsholders became more standardized than they had been, because the ministry's bureaucracy was making it clear exactly what had to be covered by the agreements to make them satisfactory for registration of the recording and the acquisition of banderoles. But prior to the development of this registration system, the state had refrained from regulating such agreements, meaning that they were drawn up primarily with a bilateral relationship between label and rightsholder in mind. This meant that the agreements prior to 1986 were unstandardized.[19] The altered standards in agreements in turn created problems particularly for labels that wanted to re-release old recordings.[20]

In many cases, reacquiring permissions proves impossible or prohibitively difficult and expensive. Hasan Saltık, the late owner of Kalan Records, told me that problems in this area had caused the label to put an end to its series of re-released "archival" recordings (*arşiv serisi*), a personal favorite of mine. When producing the series, he would track down the artists and composers with a stake in the historical recording he wished to re-release. In many cases the original artists or composers had died, and there would be a set of children or grandchildren who had inherited the rights as part of an estate. The label would pay a fee and sign an agreement with each of them to authorize the re-release. The problem was that they would sign agreements with, say, five heirs, thinking they had acquired the necessary permissions. But after they had begun production, a sixth heir would emerge, complaining that the label had not also come to terms with them, and since the project was already underway or already released, the label would be forced to pay an exorbitant fee to the sixth heir.[21] In other such cases they were simply sued. At some point, the Cultural Ministry tightened its registration policy as well, demanding that the label needed permissions from every heir before they would grant banderoles for the album. But in Kalan's experience, it was impossible to find every heir. In many cases they were not members of a collecting society, making it difficult to locate them or pay them. Thus, Kalan finally dropped its archival series (interview, March 4, 2015; see also Eyüboğlu 2009). Saltık was not the only record label executive to complain to me of this issue.

MÜ-YAP has proposed an amendment to the copyright statute that would establish a system for mandatory licensing for recordings released prior to 1986. This proposal, however, was part of a revised version of the copyright statute

Constituting Legality in the Music Sector **79**

that was under discussion during my research but which ultimately failed to pass when stakeholders with opposing interests could not come to agreement on the details. Meanwhile, many of the country's historic recordings remain rarities that may never be re-released in a new format, and music fans are left to scour the increasingly pricy vintage records in flea markets and used record shops if they wish to hear them.

Returning to my theoretical discussion, my ethnographic data on the issue of authorizing new recordings of works illustrate all the dimensions of legal consciousness that I have identified. For many composers, the power to deny someone the right to record their works was an expression of the law's ideals, its normative grounding in the sacred nature of authors' rights. Turkish art music composer and former MESAM general secretary Dursun Karaca, for example, viewed composers' ability to authorize the use of their works as "a matter of honor included in the moral rights" of artists. He contrasted this with "the completely commercial matter" of the rights of publishers and record producers, which the Turkish law framed as "neighboring rights" (2005, 30).

We have also seen how MESAM's choice to leave the control of the right of distribution with its members reflected a game-like, pragmatic approach to addressing the domestic realities of Turkey's fledgling copyright administrative system in the 1990s. It allowed MESAM members to profit from uses of their works amidst otherwise low licensing income, and it seems to have afforded the continuation of an older economic model for producing albums. MÜ-YAP's proposed statutory provision for mandatory licensing of pre-1986 recordings likewise represented a pragmatic approach to adapting the system for the challenges presented by the domestic context.

Yet some actors perceived a tension between the normative ideals that grounded the power of authorization and the pragmatic considerations at issue. Revised regulations on the authorization to record and reproduce a work failed to sufficiently account for the legacy of older approaches to documenting consent. Some thus saw composers' heirs as wielding the rights they had inherited in unreasonable ways. This tension provoked critical readings of the situation, such as performers of folk music or record producers who were re-releasing historic recordings complaining that their creative visions were being obstructed by how these rightsholders leveraged the law. Industry actors with knowledge of international practice could also unfavorably compare the situation with the compulsory licensing systems established in other countries or with an imagined, better-functioning one. These tensions could provoke intimate readings according to which the seeming unreasonableness of the Cultural Ministry's approach to pre-1986 authorization agreements or the lack of a compulsory licensing system typified the country's dysfunction. One of the lawyers who described to me the history of MESAM's leaving control of the right of distribution with its members was critical of the move. He recalled how he had protested the policy to Cultural Ministry officials who had allowed it. In his account, MESAM had said it didn't want to "take over" (*devralmak*) these rights and thus police uses of works, a role it viewed as rightly that of a publisher. "Usually when I give an example, I choose irritating examples of very absurd people, so that they will understand well," he explained. "And as I said about the collecting societies, they are the representatives of the rightsholders [*eser sahipleri*], aren't they? 'As a lawyer, if I look into a mortgage case, am I taking over the person's house? If I look into a divorce case, am I taking over their wife?' I said to them. There's no need to take over. You're the representative. The collecting society, you're a publisher. Why [does this constitute] taking over [the rights]?" He punctuated his recollection with a culturally intimate statement that framed the policy as typical of something more fundamental about Turkey: "This country is a curious country."

CONCLUSION

In this chapter, I have shown how actors with a variety of stakes in Turkey's copyright regime construct legality in terms of a set of cultural schemas, some of whose origins I have traced in chapter 1. Legal consciousness is not simply a matter of how citizens think about the law; it also shapes legality—the law as it informs social action in everyday life. As Austin Sarat and Thomas Kearns put it, "Law plays a constitutive role in the world of the everyday, yet it is also available as a tool to people as they seek to maintain or alter their daily lives," and "the constitutive power of law, with the characteristic habits, skills, and cultures it enables, always provides room for challenge even as it imposes constraints" (1993, 61). I have explored this dynamic through my discussion of normative and pragmatic dimensions to copyright consciousness in Turkey, where actors also strive to reconcile the tensions between these two dimensions of legality through resistance, critique, and culturally intimate discourse.

The nature of copyright law, which is national in jurisdiction but embedded in a larger international regulatory framework and a set of transnational relationships, makes it distinct from some other areas of the law that legal consciousness scholars have researched. The ethnographic context of Turkey, where

Constituting Legality in the Music Sector **81**

international practice provides a normative grounding less salient in the US context, accounts for further differences. This produces a reflexive awareness of group status that shapes all four dimensions of copyright consciousness in Turkey. It leads actors to imagine that copyright's normative ideals are best realized abroad. Actors taking a pragmatic approach to the law frame the project of developing the country's copyright system as a matter of harmonizing and integrating it with more developed national systems located elsewhere. Critical perspectives on copyright may chalk up the tensions between the ideals and practice of the law to a form of cultural imperialism exploiting differences of culture and power between Turkey and those countries where copyright has had longer to develop. And most dramatically, actors may make sense of their frustrations with Turkey's system by integrating them into culturally intimate narratives about what it means to belong to Turkey. This dynamic likely has parallels beyond Turkey, wherever IP reform is framed as crucial to a country's status as a developed nation.

Whereas scholars such as Ewick and Silbey have pursued a critical agenda in which they attempted to account for how the law's hegemony is sustained despite the persistence of unjust outcomes, the reflexive dynamic that I describe may offer an additional explanation: actors make sense of the tensions between the ideal and practice of the law in terms of familiar, culturally intimate self-stereotypes or in terms of historical and cultural differences that they perceive between Turkey and the Western contexts that gave rise to copyright. However, I also intend such observations to augment a long-standing musicological conversation about cultural reformism and the Turkish nation-state. Musicologists of Turkey have returned again and again to the state's role in forging common cultural, especially musical, symbols as a part of its nation-building project. Yet critical and culturally intimate engagements with a less explicitly nationalist reform project—that of IP law—represent a crucial, often overlooked way that state policy mediates sociality in the music sector and beyond.

In the subsequent chapters, I further draw out the links between copyright legality and nationalist cultural reformism in an extended examination of folk music, a genre defined more than any other in terms of the culturally intimate essentialisms that I have identified here, since many of my interlocutors imagined it to epitomize a mode of collective creation that they contrasted with the Western individualism underlying liberal property regimes.

THREE

Essentializing Creativity
Authorship and Anonymity

This chapter begins with a question:

> In Anatolian folk music, which represents the creativity of the rural segment
> [of the population], foremost among the topics handled are snippets of rural
> life and descriptions of nature. One of the main themes is love. There are no
> complaints about the difficulties of life, but there are revolts against injustice.
> Folk songs [*türküler*], which have anonymous character, do not reflect the
> individual, but the society within which they live, and aside from folk music
> that is based on Sufism, the remaining topics are completely outside of religion.
>
> This text describes which of the following concerning Anatolian folk music?
>
> A) What makes up its contents
> B) That it provides the possibility for folk poets' development
> C) That it does not carry the aim of provoking feelings
> D) That it particularly reflects individual feelings
> E) That its products don't express a love for life (ösym 2010, 3)

I was confronted with this question one evening while hanging out with one of
my teachers, Nevzat Karakış, at the little café where we regularly met, one evening in March 2015. We were in the midst of one of our many discussions about
folk music, singing folk songs and talking about the ideologically motivated

ways that the state had intervened in song texts during the long history of the collection and promotion of folk music through official institutions. A friend of ours, Ahmet, was sitting across the café, his face buried in a practice test for the Finance Ministry Internal Auditor Candidate Exam. Aware of the topic of our conversation, he gave a little shout as he encountered this question in his exam book, reading it aloud to us. The customers in the café chuckled, shouting, "A!"

We might explain the strange presence of such a question about musical folklore in a Finance Ministry exam as simply an ordinary example of a textual excerpt useful for testing reading comprehension skills. After all, answering the question would not require the exam taker to subscribe to the claims made in the textual excerpt itself or even to know much at all about musical folklore.

But in Turkey, folk songs (*türkü*; pl. *türküler*) are everywhere. Musicians of numerous genres have adapted them into their own idioms, and they have often been rewarded for doing so with significant commercial success. Walking past storefronts on the street, flipping through television channels, hitching a ride in one of the noisy, ubiquitous, semiformal minibuses or jitneys (*dolmuş*) that make up a key aspect of the public transit system, attending a demonstration or political rally, or walking into a bar, one is almost bound to encounter a türkü in some form. They are also potent symbols that could serve as expressions of resistance and pluralism for actors on the political left even as they register as national heritage for actors across a range of the political spectrum, from far right to center left. And where türküler can be heard, so, too, can often be found attendant ideologies about their content and origins. I couldn't help reading Ahmet's test prep question as one example of how these ideologies permeate public discourse in subtle ways, mediating the reception of folk music for the millions who encounter it every day.

For example, the text suggests that "there are no complaints about the difficulties of life, but there are revolts against injustice," implying that the rural Turkish folk who have expressed themselves in türküler embody moral qualities valued by nationalism: fortitude, a tireless work ethic, intolerance of injustice. The topics of songs are said to be "completely outside of religion," a useful attribute for the secularist Kemalism that had inspired the bulk of early folkloric collection in the country. And most piquing my own interest, türküler are said to "have anonymous character" and "do not reflect the individual, but the society within which they live." These last points are commonly expressed tenets of a well-known theory about the nature and origins of folk music in Turkey. In fact, one of the striking features about discourse on folk music in the country is the prevalence

84 *Copyright Consciousness*

of the idea of anonymity. The documentary record of how folk music is created is sparse at best, and folk music experts and enthusiasts have exploited this lack of data to elaborate a theory that posits türküler emerging from a collective creative process that renders them anonymous.

So far in this book, I have offered an account of legal consciousness in Turkey's music sector and especially among those actors most involved in intellectual property (IP) reform. Yet I have had little to say about creativity, whose regulation is the primary concern of copyright as a legal regime. In this chapter, I approach the idea of folkloric anonymity as a kind of creative imaginary that defines the genre and shapes how musicians make and how listeners hear folk music. Because of folk music's supposed anonymity, many people, from casual listeners to folk music artists, tend to think of copyright law as rightly having little to do with folk music, since most of it should be in the public domain. The subsequent chapters of this book, which take folk music as an extended case study of how copyright legality emerges in relation to a genre, will complicate such assumptions in a number of ways. Here I examine the imagined oppositionality between copyright and folk music, arguing that in fact this opposition represents a kind of legal consciousness that was central to how the genre was defined. I show how institutionally based folk music experts constructed the idea of anonymity by imagining creativity in folk music as essentially different from creative processes in traditional post-Ottoman urban art music. This account will lay the groundwork for subsequent chapters. In chapter 4, I show how the anonymity idea informed the curation of a kind of canon of folk music at the state broadcasting agency TRT, where, as I argue, policy toward folk music programming was (at least in part) a response to copyright activism among musicians working in the genre. This legacy in turn complicated the application of copyright in folk music in the post-1980s era of IP reform, as I show in chapter 5.

FOLK MUSIC AND COPYRIGHT CONSCIOUSNESS

In arguing that a certain legal consciousness defines the genre of folk music in Turkey, I refer not only to the way musical folklore experts and artists describe the genre in their publications and performances, but also to how it is understood by wider, nonexpert audiences to whom such folkloristic ideas have spread, often via broadcast programs and popularly circulating writings that celebrate Turkey's folk music (and even, apparently, by exam prep books). These nonexpert folk music audiences include the IP legal professionals working to build Turkey's

Essentializing Creativity 85

copyright system. For example, in 2005, the Istanbul Bar Association convened a national symposium on "Intellectual and Industrial Property Rights and Culture." The symposium represented one of many aspects of the ongoing process of IP reform that I outlined in chapter 1. The opening talk of the symposium, given by Mehmet Aydın, the chair of the bar's commission on IP rights, and subsequently published in the symposium's proceedings, asks in all-caps: "WHY HAS AN INTELLECTUAL PROPERTY CULTURE STILL NOT DEVELOPED IN OUR COUNTRY?" (Aydın 2005, 18). The talk cites a number of purported problems with the country's IP regime at the time: an insufficient number of specialized IP courts and judges, the poor quality of expert witnesses, and so on (21). Invoking the oft-mentioned belatedness of the Ottoman Empire's adoption of the printing press and other aspects of industrialization, it furthermore frames these problems as a sign of underdevelopment or backwardness (22; see also chapter 1). Most importantly, the talk chalks up this purported underdevelopment to a lack of consciousness, an insufficient "intellectual property culture" among Turkish citizens: "Within our country's subcultures that aspect of feudal culture that rejects intellectual and industrial property persists." In bold, the transcript declares: "Feudal Culture excludes intellectual rights" (21).

But there's a twist. It turns out—according to the account sketched in the talk—this lingering cloud of "feudalism" and IP backwardness has a silver lining:

> As a positive example, in our country's territory, our country's people have produced tens of thousands of türkü, *deyiş* [poems by traditional singer-poets, often of the Alevi religious minority; pl. *deyişler*], *ağıt* [songs of mourning; pl. *ağıtlar*], and their melodies. All of these are our quite wonderful riches. But the intellectual rights to these türküler do not belong to the first folk minstrel who sang them. Quite naturally, türküler have become public property, because the environment of türküler is not favorable to registration [*tescil*] [of works]. This is because as a result of feudal culture's character, it excludes intellectual property—all of it, even its beneficial aspects. (21)

By this account, a "feudal" environment has produced the country's rich heritage of anonymous türküler, but it has accomplished this at the expense of recognizing individual authors' rights. The talk ties this situation to rurality, asserting that "with urbanization intellectual rights begin to crystallize." Even in an earlier Ottoman period, in a context of "trade guilds and partially urbanized life," it was possible to speak of authors who owned their works: a song by Ottoman art music composer Dede Efendi (1778–1846), a poem by the dervish Yunus Emre (d. 1320?), a play by Ottoman playwright Şinasi (1826–1871), and so on (21).

This account of IP law posits an essential cultural difference between Turkey and the West, in this case defined in terms of the development of an "IP culture," and it projects this difference onto a temporal axis of progress. While "East" and "West" are not explicitly invoked, they are the subtext of the reference to the printing press, since the Ottoman adoption of the printing press was "belated" only in comparison to those countries where its use spread more quickly (i.e., European ones; see chapter 1). In conversation with Edward Said's account of Orientalism (1979), sociologist Meltem Ahıska has theorized Turkey's relationship with narratives that locate modernity in the West as "Occidentalism" (2003, 2010). In Said's famous formulation, Westerners defined themselves as such in relation to their own representations of an oriental Other discursively constructed during the European colonial encounter. For Ahıska, Occidentalism involves neither a simple Westernism nor a spiteful rejection of the West (2010, 41). Rather, in Occidentalism, non-Western subjectivity emerges in relation to non-Westerners' own projections of the Western gaze—how they imagine the West sees the non-West (2003, 365–69). Ahıska documents how this Occidentalist subjectivity continues to inform political discourse and social action, including cultural reform projects, and we might add copyright reform to the list of projects she describes.

Note, for example, how the alignment of individual authorship with modernity and collective, folkloric creativity with traditionality reproduces a European-derived, internationally circulating discourse that constructs authorship and IP law as an aspect of civilizational development. Copyright historian Eva Hemmungs Wirtén traces how French author Victor Hugo, in an 1878 speech advocating for international copyright legislation, explicitly linked the recognition of authors' rights to notions of universal human rights and to civilizational progress toward modernity (2004, 14–37). Similarly, historian Monika Dommann describes how nineteenth-century efforts to internationalize copyright commonly invoked a civilizational progress narrative, one that praised authors' rights "as the achievement of the 'European cultural group of civilized states,'" (2019, 23). The French philosopher Michel Foucault, in his famous essay "What is an Author?," likewise locates "a privileged moment of individualization" in the seventeenth or eighteenth century, when named, individual authorship began to be expected as an authenticator of literary discourses in Western civilization, whereas previously "their anonymity [had] caused no difficulties since their

Essentializing Creativity **87**

ancientness, whether real or imagined, was regarded as a sufficient guarantee of their status" (2003, 377, 383). Dommann further asserts that "[a] cultural code that equated progressiveness with the rejection of tradition and that favored written notes over oral transmission is constitutive of music law in the nineteenth century" (2019, 23). She points out that in the first legal commentary on musical authors' rights, the Austrian lawyer and musician Johann Vesque von Püttlingen contrasted collective folkloric and individual artistic modes of creation when he wrote that "a collective creation would go against the innermost essence of artistic production; in music, creative conception is typically tied to the inner life of the individual" (24).

The sort of legal consciousness that frames individual authorship as modern and European and denies the coeval-ness of the collective, anonymous creativity supposedly typical of rural Turkey seems to figure into the Occidentalist dynamic that Ahıska points out. At least, this is true to the extent that a tendency to claim and identify with the genre, contrasting its creative processes to modern authorship, represents a response to a projected Western gaze. Nor is Turkey unique as a place where creative imaginaries figure into Orientalist discourse, where modern authorship may be mapped onto "the West" and other creative modalities mapped onto "the East." Ethnomusicologist Laudan Nooshin has suggested, for example, that a discursive contrast figuring Iranian classical music as "improvised" and Western classical music as "composed" has been central to an Orientalist process of alterity-construction (2003; 2015, 10). Indeed, debates in international fora about how and whether to protect folklore (often under updated rubrics such as *traditional culture* or *indigenous knowledge*) through *sui generis* IP schemes tend to take it for granted that such cultural expressions are created through modalities distinct enough from canonical forms of authorship that individuals cannot claim a copyright in them under existing mechanisms (e.g., Blakeney 1999; Dutfield 2003; Karaganis 2012; cf. Aragon 2014, 14). One of my contributions in this chapter will be to show that, at least in Turkey, this imagined incompatibility between folklore and copyright had to be constructed.

Returning to the talk at the Istanbul Bar Association symposium, note how it posits a difference not only between Turkey and an imagined West, but also within Turkey, between an urban center already primed for intellectual property law and a rural periphery too backward for it. The reference to (Hammamizade İsmail) Dede Efendi is telling. The Istanbul-based composer is often hailed as the greatest exemplar of the urban musical traditions currently labeled Turkish or Ottoman classical (or art) music. As I argue in this chapter, the mostly rural-derived genre of folk music (the "türkü, deyiş, ağıt, and their melodies") was constructed, at least in part, in contradistinction to such post-Ottoman art music. Here, the IP symposium's opening talk reproduces a common contrast that folk music experts have often drawn between Turkey's individually authored art music and collectively and anonymously generated folk music. For example, the folk music artist Nida Tüfekçi, a powerful figure within official institutions of musical folklore in the 1970s to 1980s (see chapter 4), said the following:

> Music is currently being studied in two forms. . . . In terms of musical production, one is music made by a person [kişi], for example a song [şarkı] by Cevdet Çağla, this carries a personal mark, or let's say one of Dede Efendi's works, this is Dede Efendi's work. To take the problem on from this point, there are two factors in the production of music. One is the component of individual art, to put it another way works made through personal creation; the other is the common property of the people, music whose owner is unknown, products of folklore, we can talk about all the arts that fall within the bounds of folklore at once. Folk Music takes the place of the second category I talked about. Thus there is one Turkish Music, one branch of this is individual [ferdi] art, one branch is collective [toplumsal] art. (TRT 1974, 162–63)[1]

As I argue in the rest of this chapter, imagining such an essential difference between the creative modalities of Turkish folk and art musics erases many complexities of actual creative practice, since both genres involve both individual and collective forms of creative agency. Yet as the comments I have cited from both folk music experts (Tüfekçi) and nonexperts (the Bar Association's IP commission chair, Aydın) suggest, imagining such a contrast in creative modality is central to how the genre of folk music is understood and defined in Turkey. Furthermore, since the moral rights of named, individual authors ground copyright rights, and folk music is usually understood to be anonymous and collectively composed, I argue that the genre is also defined in terms of a certain legal consciousness: folk music is that which is not protectable by copyright and rightly belongs to the public. We can also view this idea as a corollary of several aspects of the legal consciousness I discuss in chapter 2. The framing of authors' rights as modern and civilized grounded what I call the normative dimension of copyright consciousness. The contrast between the Euro-American legal doctrines regarding authorship and the creative modalities assumed to produce Turkey's folk music, meanwhile, was central to a critical narrative of copyright as cultural imperialism.

While the centrality of such a legal consciousness to the genre's definition

Essentializing Creativity **89**

makes folk music a particularly apt case study for the present book, there is furthermore a way in which many of my interlocutors also took its imagined collective modality of creativity to typify Turkey in a larger sense.[2] For example, a lawyer and former IP court judge whom I interviewed invoked an Orientalist contrast between Western individualism and a general collectiveness in Turkish culture. She told me, "We are not close to individuality" (*bireyselliğe yakın değiliz*), and "We did everything collectively" (*kollektiv yapmışız her şey*). She described how people in Turkey, especially in village contexts, often listen to the radio or watch television together at a café rather than alone at home, that this is how people are accustomed to consuming such media, thinking of it as "ours" and not "yours and mine." Implying that such collective listening habits blurred the line between private consumption and public commercial use, she cited this tendency as a reason for resistance to the licensing of broadcast music in public spaces (though such resistance is not unique to Turkey; see Litman 2006, 33). She told me, "Copyright seems wrong to us" (*ters geliyor bize*). In another case, a musician and music scholar (cited at the opening of this book) described how people in the Orient hadn't "lived with the concept of earning money. There was no capitalism. So copyright, capitalism, this legal system, when it comes, there are problems, because the culture doesn't fit the law." Linking this essentialism about Turkish society with folk music specifically, he told me that "in the Orient, there's a mystical culture and way of life. It's more about belonging to a society. There's the concept of a community [*cemaat*]; I'm an individual belonging to a community. We need to discuss who the 'I' is when distributing property. And in Turkish folk music, it belongs to a community. The musician is expressing the feelings of a community."

This self-orientalizing take on Turkish society has not gone uncontested, and neither has the idea of anonymous, collective, folkloric creativity (see chapter 4). Yet such ideas do circulate widely, and they frequently attend folk music production and reception. They also inform a widespread, rough-and-ready sense that copyright doesn't or shouldn't really apply in folk music, which represents a heritage rightly belonging in the public domain. Legal and musical folklore experts have also explicitly argued that türküler are not protectable works in the sense defined by copyright law (Etili 2005; see also Stokes 1992, 55–58). Urban art music and other popular or classical genres, so the rough generalization goes, are more properly the subject of copyright protection since the compositional process in these genres more closely adheres to modern conventions of authorship.

As I show in the next several chapters, the application of copyright law to the genre has proven more complicated than this scheme suggests. Part of the reason, as I argue in this chapter, is that the distinctions are drawn too sharply, accentuating differences and erasing similarities in a process we might call "essentializing creativity."[3] The compositions of urban art music may *seem* ready-made for the assignation of individual rights, and the heritage of rural music for the public domain. However, this is because this status was achieved by the prior deployment of two Romanticisms: Romantic authorship (the idea of a genius creating autonomous works ex nihilo) and folklore, which were mapped onto these two genres, respectively, in a process that differentiated them. The accentuation and the erasures involved in this deployment helped constitute the genres in question. But—as we shall see in subsequent chapters—it also complicated matters when copyright began to be enforced more stringently in the 1980s and there were new stakes in how generic differences were imagined.

CREATIVITY IN POST-OTTOMAN ART MUSIC

The genre called (post-)Ottoman or Turkish art or classical music consists of an aggregate of repertoires developed in diverse contexts, though these repertoires are structured around a common melodic-modal system (*makam*) and a common metrical system (*usûl*), and in some cases the same musicians and the same melodies straddled multiple contexts.[4] The repertoire includes instrumental and vocal music patronized at the Ottoman court, ritual music of Mevlevi and other urban Sufi lodges, and light classical song genres performed in entertainment venues in the nineteenth and twentieth centuries. Despite the nationalist framing of the genre as "Turkish," Armenians, Greeks, Jews, Romani, and other people have contributed significantly to its repertoire and performance practice. For this reason, I prefer the term "post-Ottoman art music" when not specifically referencing the nationalist framing of the genre.

Romantic author-like understandings of creativity in post-Ottoman art music, like that implied by Tüfekçi's depiction of the art/folk contrast, sit in an uneasy relationship with other views that emphasize the genre's history as a primarily oral tradition. In discussing this tension, my aim is not to locate a specific moment in which Romantic notions of authorship may have emerged within (post-)Ottoman art music; rather, I wish to highlight how the complex historical record can afford contrasting readings of the situation, allowing scholars and ideologues to pursue divergent historicist agendas. On the one hand, it is possible to emphasize continuities and similarities between Ottoman and European

Essentializing Creativity 91

notions of authorship, arguing that Romantic notions of the author can be traced to longer-standing Ottoman practices (as implied by Tüfekçi's contrast with folk music). On the other hand, it is possible to emphasize the distinctness of Ottoman creative traditions vis-à-vis European ones, framing Romantic authorship notions as a relatively recent, foreign import, an argument that may appeal to critics of modernist reformism or to those who wish to contest the boundaries drawn between folk and art musics.

Ottoman musicians long transmitted their music without the aid of written notation, and while this approach did not preclude authorship attributions, it made fidelity to a composer's score impossible.[5] Instead, performers were expected to be faithful to the authoritative versions learned from masters in the context of an orally-based transmission system known as *meşk* (Behar 1998). Even after written notation became widespread, teachers have continued to orally transmit crucial knowledge about style, technique, the workings of the *makam* system, and attendant social values. Many musicians have seen musical variability and change as inevitable and even desirable in this context, though such contingencies are tempered by norms around rendering compositions correctly.

The historian of Ottoman music Cem Behar has assembled examples that highlight how this tension—between an assumed mutability and variability to compositions and a Romantic *werktreue*-like notion of fidelity to a composer's original version—has persisted in *makam*-based performance practices for centuries (2013; see also 1998, 80–97). The mid-seventeenth-century manuscript of Polish-born Ottoman musician Ali Ufki records two variants of the same tune without passing judgment on either (Behar 2013, 5); writing a half century later, however, another foreign-born Ottoman musician, Demetrius Cantemir, seems motivated to identify and preserve supposedly original versions as intended by the composer (6). Similarly, an eighteenth-century Ottoman biographical dictionary praises certain musicians' purported ability to perform "the works of old masters as they were composed originally" (6). In the twentieth century, Hafız Ahmet Efendi, son of the famous nineteenth-century composer Zekai Dede, resigned from his post at the newly founded Istanbul Conservatory over a dispute about how to correctly render in published notation a single note in a piece he had learned from his father (8). Yet composers like Cevdet Çağla and Refik Fersan (1893–1965), both of whom employed written notation, authorized multiple versions of their own works as "correct" or "original" (9).

The relationship between the composer and the performer also differs in post-Ottoman art music vis-à-vis the canonical relationship envisioned in (post-)

Romantic era Western art music. In the *meşk* context, there has never been a strict specialization into roles of composer, performer, and teacher, as a master musician must play a bit of each, a situation resembling that of pre-Romantic European music (Behar 2006, 403; Goehr 2007). One mark of instrumental competence, for example, is the ability to properly perform the improvisational genre *taksim*; this entails internalizing and enacting many of the same principles that govern composition. Furthermore, since notations are usually skeletal and meant to be elaborated, it is the performer's job to flesh out this skeleton in idiomatically appropriate ways. My lessons with *ud* master Necati Çelik involved learning his own, highly elaborated versions of classic works. These versions were somewhat variable, and yet consistent enough that they were recognizably his own. Developing such a performance version thus also involved a sort of (re) composition on the part of the performer.

(Post-)Ottoman art music compositions changed over time as generations of musicians reshaped them according to shifting stylistic trends, personal preferences, and the vagaries of memory, particularly prior to the widespread adoption of written notation. Where old repertoire items were periodically written down at various times in Ottoman music history, manuscripts evince the workings of oral transmission on these compositions, which appear in variants and versions that sometimes differ from each other significantly, often becoming more elaborate over time (Wright 1988). Given such complications, musicologist Ralf Martin Jäger partially credits "the transmitting community" for shaping these polymorphous compositional entities he dubs "*opus*-clusters" in contrast to the notionally singular "works" of European composers (2015, 39–42).

An occasional looseness or flexibility around authorial attributions has further compounded these complexities. Consider for example the tradition of *nazire*, in which musicians compose a new work based upon or inspired by another's. Over time *nazire* compositions were sometimes confused with the originals, which could become credited to the composer of the *nazire* (Feldman 1990, 85). Sometimes composers' names have been simply forgotten or were never recorded, and a minority of repertoire items are from manuscripts that note no author; these are sometimes marked as anonymous (*laedri* or *meçhul*).[6] At various historical junctures, musicians have also resorted to pseudographia, crediting mythical or historical forebears with compositions that were in some cases novel inventions (Feldman 2015, 115–30; see also Feldman 1990, 91–95; Wright 1992).

If the compositional process in post-Ottoman classical music differs so much from that envisioned by Romantic author formulations, why was there histori-

Essentializing Creativity 93

cally such a strong tendency for Ottoman musicians to attribute compositions to individual composers—a practice that may date back to the sixteenth century (Feldman 1990, 87)? One possibility has been proposed by musicologist Walter Feldman, who argues that Ottoman musicians saw themselves as contributing to a cosmopolitan tradition of music stretching geographically into Iran and Central Asia and historically back to the Greeks, rather than creating a wholly new, "national" Ottoman one. Later Ottoman musicians maintained a repertoire of classic works attributed (pseudographically or otherwise) to mythical and historical musical ancestors within this cosmopolitan tradition; this established the continuity of an imagined musical lineage in which they could ground their authority. They then distinguished the place of their community within this larger tradition by authoring new repertoire items that contributed to it (Feldman 1990, 87). Analyzing the periodic rise and fall of practices of authorial attribution in the broader Islamic world, music historian Eckhard Neubauer argues that in times of political-economic decline, the individualized author concept disappears, and that it reappears in periods of revival (1997, 363).

These authorship concepts may not correspond exactly to the modern myth of the self-expressive "Romantic author" producing works ex nihilo. Yet there are some signs that European Romanticism may have motivated such autonomous author-like perspectives in Ottoman and republican Turkish musical contexts by at least the time of the *Tanzimat* reforms (1839–1876), some of which aimed to remold Ottoman institutions, often modeling them on western European ones. Scholars of Ottoman poetry have explicitly examined shifting notions of originality and authorship in this period. The classical Ottoman lyric tradition depended upon reformulating a series of canonical metaphors into new variants that could be prized as original (and attributed to a specific author) without being so novel as to be illegible as part of the tradition. These recurring metaphors—the rose as the beloved's face and the garden as the body, for example—were central to a metaphysical allegory in which the lover's desire for the beloved stood in turn for the subject's devotion to the sultan and his love for God (Öztürk 2016, 139–42). Contrasting this sort of originality with later ideas of authorship, Walter Andrews compares the tradition to "improvised jazz, rock, or hip-hop, where masters of the art render common themes in unique and original ways and the less accomplished only mix and match familiar riffs" (2006, 7–8).[7]

The primacy of this lyric tradition was challenged in the second half of the nineteenth century by a literary movement called "the new literature." Literary scholar Veysel Öztürk has shown how the writer Namık Kemal, one of the

94 *Copyright Consciousness*

leaders of this movement, critiqued Ottoman verse traditions by characterizing as "fantasy" the allegorical way they envisioned the outer world. Exponents of the new literature movement, in contrast, sought to create realist depictions of their own impressions of the outer world through a distinct authorial voice, an approach appropriated from European literature. Öztürk argues that while these writers did not explicitly formulate their critique of older poetic traditions in terms of originality, their realism was predicated upon a new kind of autonomous, imaginative subjectivity for which the classical Ottoman lyric tradition allegedly left no space because of its restrictions on personal creativity (2016). For Kemal, advocating this new literary subjectivity was part of a larger political project in which he explicitly promoted envisioning Ottoman citizenship in terms of post-Enlightenment Western notions of the liberal subject, attempting to reconcile such a vision with the traditional Islamic concept of community (*umma*). While this last aspect of his project was critiqued by secularist republican reformers, his thought has significantly informed Turkey's political and literary discourse (Mardin 1962, 283–336).

I am not aware of a study that systematically traces a similar internalization of Romantic authorship notions in (post-)Ottoman art music, and it is beyond the scope of this book to provide one. A few historical details suggest, however, that such a process may have predated the republican-era tendency to dichotomize folk and art musics. Beginning around the middle of the nineteenth century, for example, composers turned from the once-dominant, large-scale, compound compositional suite form *fasıl* toward a new style of the shorter song form *şarkı*. Such shifts toward shorter and livelier musical forms might have several explanations, and ethnomusicologist Federica Nardella sees it as a continuation of existing trends in lyrical practice in the classical Ottoman lyric tradition (2023, 130). Nonetheless, calling this trend "Romantic," music historian Bülent Aksoy argues that within this new şarkı, composers wrote melodic themes that were identifiably individual and personal in style. Rather than older, classical Ottoman or Persian poetry, they set contemporary poetic texts of the "new literature" movement (including those of Namık Kemal), whose feelingful Romanticism seems to be reflected in the musical style as well (1981, 1231; cf. Nardella 2023, 109–55). Jäger likewise notes the appearance of a notion of composers' identifiable individual styles after 1850 (2015, 41).[8] In the early republican era, the singer Münir Nurettin Selçuk sought to modernize post-Ottoman art music by refashioning it into a concert idiom modeled upon European art music. This approach seems to have entailed a stricter distinction between composer and performer roles. When he

Essentializing Creativity **95**

was critiqued for altering the texts of the poems set to the songs he performed, for example, he responded by invoking something like Romantic *werktreue* and its appeal to the composer's authority as embodied in the score. He insisted that those lyrical changes had been inserted by the composer; as the performer, his role was limited to "expressing nuances . . . according to the strength of his own feelings even if a musical work is fixed" (O'Connell 2016, 156–57).

A more extensive study of this issue is beyond the scope of this book. My main point here is to emphasize that versions of Romantic author ideology circulate among post-Ottoman art musicians and their public, but they exist in tension with other practices and values surrounding musical creativity that seem to emphasize collectivism. The contemporary tendency to view post-Ottoman classical pieces as autonomous works brought forth by an individual author may reflect what Lydia Goehr has called the "conceptual imperialism" of the work concept: later post-Ottoman classical works may have been composed with a Romantic "work" concept in mind, while surviving repertoire of the past that was not so composed has nonetheless been understood as such retroactively under a "derivative" application of the concept (see Goehr 2007, 245–57). Such an emphasis on individualism in post-Ottoman art music may also be contextual. In certain contexts, its collectiveness and traditionality may be foregrounded, especially where its practitioners and scholars wish to emphasize its distinctiveness from Western art music and in particular to celebrate the traditional *meşk* transmission system. But individualistic aspects are foregrounded particularly in discourse that differentiates the genre from folk music.

CREATIVITY IN RURAL TRADITIONS

In contrast to the general tendency to credit individual composers in post-Ottoman classical music, the category of folk music is often understood to consist of "collective" or "folkloric" works, in Tüfekçi's terms above, or—to use the most common relevant keyword in Turkey—"anonymous" (*anonim*) works. The term "anonymous" can be used in a few different senses, and I often heard musicians applying it quite loosely in copyright contexts to describe not only works of unknown authorship but also works that had entered the public domain because they had reached the limits of their terms of copyright protection, even where there was an acknowledged author—be it a historical Anatolian bard like the seventeenth-century figure Karacaoğlan or a Western composer like Beethoven.[9] Coming from folk music artists and experts, however, it most often referenced

96 *Copyright Consciousness*

a specific folkloristic theory according to which folk songs and tunes emerge from a creative process that renders it not the work of an individual but of a collective. Indeed, even where a Karacaoğlan might be acknowledged, it was often assumed that the extant version of the türkü had become so reshaped in the oral transmission process that it could be considered anonymous.

According to the anonymity theory, a türkü begins its life as the utterance of an individual—be it the bearer of a regional musical tradition or a complete musical amateur—who has been compelled by some powerful happenstance (called an *olay*) to express their feelings in song. Folkloristic accounts often figure these individuals not as composers but as "burners," drawing on an indigenous term for türkü creation (*yakmak*) used as early as the sixteenth century (Şenel 2015, 198). In doing so, however, burners take up musical and poetic idioms distinct to the region where they live, and musical folklorists often assert that türküler capture not only such individuals' feelings but also those shared by a rural community, a regional folk. Members of the community then learn and pass the türkü on to future generations, and in the process of oral transmission—often called "the anonymity sieve" (*anonimlik süzgeci*)—the melody and the poem may be reshaped and refined, eventually filtering away all traces of the individual who had uttered its initial version. The process—so the theory goes—reworks the türkü into an expression rightly belonging to the people.[10]

Motivated in part by the nationalist ideas of sociologist Ziya Gökalp (see chapter 1), musicians and folklorists in the early republic began traveling around the country to collect folk songs and tunes that Gökalp envisioned as the true musical culture of the Turkish nation, publishing collections of folk songs in various forms and also academic writings about them (see Altınay 2000; Şenel 1999; Öztürkmen 1993; Tan 2008).[11] But many of the figures key to these early efforts also seemed inspired by international currents in folklore. Mahmut Ragıp Gazimihal (1900–1961), a classical violinist and instructor at Istanbul Municipal Conservatory who was one of the most prominent of these early republican figures to take up the project of national musical folklore, had studied in both Berlin and Paris and was later involved in the International Folk Music Council (Gazimihal 2006, v). He included in his early book on türkü extensive bibliographies of works by foreigners on Turkish and other folklore (72–134). Another founding Turkish folklorist, Hamit Zübeyir Koşay (1897–1984), seems to have read extensively in Hungarian, German, Russian, and French (see Koşay 1974). He attended carefully to developments in folklore abroad, in particular to Hungary, the pan-Turanian project of identifying traces of ancient Ural-Altaic culture,

Essentializing Creativity **97**

and scholarship on shamanism in Central Asia. His *Guide to Ethnography and Folklore* (*Etnografya ve Folklor Kılavuzu*, 1939) was subtitled "Prepared on the Basis of Hungarian Language Publications" and included a chapter on music penned at his request by Ahmet Adnan Saygun, who had worked closely with Hungarian composer Bela Bartok on the latter's musical folklore expedition in Turkey the previous year. Saygun, who received much of his musical training in Paris as one of the famous "Turkish Five" composers of the early republican era, later became an active member of the International Folk Music Council (IFMC). Halil Bedi Yönetken, who had studied in Prague, Berlin, and Paris (Yönetken 2006, 174), and Ahmet Kutsi Tecer, who had studied philosophy at the Sorbonne (Gökdemir 1987), were key collaborators with the Sivas music teacher and later radio ensemble director Muzaffer Sarısözen in the Ankara State Conservatory folk music collection expeditions that documented, between the mid-1930s and the early 1950s, the several thousand songs and tunes that make up the core of today's folk music repertoire.

Given these connections to international folklore, it should hardly be surprising that the anonymity theory so widespread in Turkey resembles the ideas of a few foreign folklorists. In his book on English folk song, Cecil Sharp cited the German mystic Jakob Böhme's idea about folkloric creativity, that "first of all one man sings a song, and then others sing it after him, *changing what they do not like*"; Sharp added, "Whether or not the individual in question can be called the author is another matter altogether. Probably not, because the continual habit of 'changing what they do not like' must, in the course of time, ultimately amount to the transference of the authorship from the individual to the community" (1965, 12–13; emphasis added by Sharp). A version of Sharp's theories became the official position of the IFMC in the 1940s and '50s under the leadership of his protégé Maud Karpeles (see Cowdery 2005; IFMC 1953, 1955; Karpeles 1951; Williams 1953; Wiora 1949). The French anthropologist Arnold van Gennep's guidebook *Le Folklore* (1924), which advances similar ideas about folkloric creativity, served as the basis for the *Guide for Collectors of Folklore* (*Halk Bilgisi Toplayacılarına Rehber*), published in Turkey by the Folklore Association (*Halk Bilgisi Derneği* 1928), and was later translated by the Turkish folklorist Pertev Naili Boratav.

The anonymity theory so widespread in Turkey appears to be an elaboration on these more broadly circulating ideas. However, after this first generation of early republican folklorists, the genre was cultivated and promoted by individuals less in tune with international currents in folklore. As described in chapter 1, figures such as Gazimihal and Saygun were inspired to carry out Gökalp's vision of creating a national music by synthesizing the music of the rural Turkish folk with Western concert idioms.[12] While versions of this approach still exist today, the genre of folk music was promoted more successfully by popular musicians on the record market (Ünlü 2004) and through radio and television programs that featured ensembles accompanying themselves on indigenous folk instruments, as I describe in greater detail in chapter 4. State broadcasting outlets (consolidated in the 1960s as TRT) served as a kind of school of folk music where many folk music artists were trained, and they proved particularly influential from the 1950s to the 1980s. The figure most often held up as a founding father figure for this school of folk music performance was Sarısözen, who served as a key folk song collector, archivist, pedagogue, and champion of the music. Sarısözen notably lacked the international credentials and connections of other republican folklorists, as did subsequent generations of folk music promoters, including Tüfekçi, who passed on and elaborated the anonymity theory apparently in part by grafting native terms and concepts such as "burning" and the importance of the instigating event (*olay*) onto internationally circulating folkloristic theories of creativity.

As I describe in the next chapter, Turkish folkloristics' anonymity theory is controversial and sometimes contested. My concern here is to show how—as in the case of post-Ottoman art music—a closer look reveals the realities of rural creativity to be more complex than the anonymity theory suggests. However, there are two major challenges to providing a satisfying account of creative processes in the genre of Turkish or Anatolian folk music. First, this genre label is an umbrella term stretched over a vast diversity of localized musical practices that it pulls awkwardly together into a single category. These include songs of funeral lamentation often sung by professional mourners; melodies strung together one after another by players of *davul* (a double-headed drum) and *zurna* (a loud double reed instrument) for dancing at outdoor weddings; the songs associated with the culture of irregular militia called *zeybek*; the sacred songs of the Alevi religious minority; songs excerpted from local versions of the Eurasian Turkic epic-singing traditions; and much more. It seems clear that the many people who contributed to these traditions did not envision themselves as contributing to a unified genre of national folk music with a consistent set of creative norms attached to it, at least until recently.

Second, the creative processes from which folk songs and tunes have emerged are poorly documented, a fact that valorizers of the genre have exploited to celebrate its "anonymity." However, the period of the 1920s to the early 1950s, in which the bulk of the national canon of folk music was documented, followed

Essentializing Creativity **99**

the violent displacement of non-Muslims and Kurds in the World War I era and coincided with a period of state violence and forced internal resettlement of much of the population (for overviews see Kirişci 2008; Üngör 2011). While anonymity is often naturalized through discourse that romanticizes it as the outcome of a collective creative process, to what extent might it also represent an epistemic rupture achieved through violent means? Accounts of efforts to document orally transmitted music at this time suggest how source musicians may sometimes have been reticent to provide information about the sources of their music. Sarısözen recalled the following from one of his 1944 expeditions, for example: "We went to the Elazığ People's House. The windows of the People's House were low. As we were taking a break from our collection efforts in one of the first-floor rooms, drinking coffee and smoking cigarettes, the source musician felt so distressed that he took advantage of the sprawling conversation to escape by jumping out of the window. It was the season for intense work, not weddings or celebrations, and furthermore, that source musician had been brought [to us] from his village by the military police. Of course he's going to escape!" (Elçi 1997, 28).

The biography of Sarısözen in which this anecdote appears is typical of Turkish folkloristics in leveraging the example to play up the hardships overcome by the folklorist. Not mentioned is that Elazığ had been transformed into a base of military operations for asserting control over the area just seven years prior to Sarısözen's visit. The operation involved the killing and forced displacement of much of the population of the neighboring, heavily Kurdish-Alevi Dersim region, and several Kurdish leaders were taken to the Elazığ People's House before being executed (Sipahi 2021, 69–70). According to one source, the window-jumping musician was Sılemano Qız (aka Süleyman Doğan or Sılo Qıc, ca. 1915–2019), a Kurdish Alevi singer-poet who accompanied himself on violin (M. Aslan 2010, 208). Qız had been an eyewitness of the Dersim operation, reportedly surviving only because he was able to play music for the soldiers.[13] Other accounts of folkloric expeditions describe collectors' overhearing their sources' expressions of fear and suspicion that they might be spies, and in some cases source musicians were known to withhold or change information or songs when speaking with a collector (Balkılıç 2009, 182–85). Furthermore, some of the genres in question are primarily women's practices. It seems possible that traditional Islamic values according to which women should be concealed could have militated against recognition of authorship in some cases (184–85).[14] Anonymization may have been overdetermined, since Sarısözen and other folk music collectors did not ask their informants to name the authors of the songs and tunes they performed in

100 *Copyright Consciousness*

any case.[15] Yet while existing scholarship has often critiqued the identity politics of musical folklore in Turkey, it has insufficiently examined the potential for a mutually reinforcing dynamic between the construction of folkloric anonymity specifically and political power, including the early republican politics of memory and nationalist history-writing.

Despite the shortcomings of the documentary record, ethnographic data and the literature on folk music's constituent traditions do make it possible to provide a few case studies that suggest the variety and complexity of creative processes that shaped the songs and tunes that make up the bulk of the genre's repertoire today.

Women's Songs of Mourning

The genre of ağıt—sung poetry of mourning—illustrates some of these complexities. The practice of spinning and singing ağıtlar varies greatly from region to region and community to community within Turkey, but here I synthesize some general observations described by other scholars to survey the range of forms of creativity involved (Kemal 2014; Başgöz 2008, 76–82; Güven 2013). Many ağıtlar begin as verses improvised to simple melodies during funeral rites in village contexts.[16] A woman among the mourners begins by improvising a verse, sometimes borrowing from a stock of well-known ağıt poetic lines or images, and usually conforming to traditional poetic forms. The poetry helps incite crying, and the other women repeat the newly uttered poetic verses. The same woman may continue, inventing a new verse describing the virtues of the deceased or articulating the pain of the bereaved, or another woman may take a turn. The process continues in the days and weeks following a funeral. While according to Islamic law, bodies are buried promptly, there can be some delay before more distantly located friends and relatives are able to come pay their respects. When these arrive, the women of the village take up the ağıt-spinning again, building on reconstructions of the initial ağıtlar that emerged on the day of the burial. Over time, a repertoire of verses composed to mourn a particular person develops as women of the village repeat and rework them.

Folklorists' accounts make it easy to see how ağıt-composing can be a collaborative endeavor far removed from the kind of creativity envisioned in Romantic author accounts. Yaşar Kemal, a famous leftist author who as a young man in the 1940s published a folkloristic book on ağıtlar in his native village in southern Turkey, described attempting to reconstruct which woman had composed which

Essentializing Creativity **101**

verse in an ağıt for İbiş, the son of a village dervish. İbiş's ağıt "was composed by all the women of his village. I didn't collect İbiş's ağıt from one woman; I took a part of it from more or less every woman in the village. I tried to get the name of the woman who had composed each part of it, but everything had gotten so mixed up together that I couldn't sort it out, and I began simply writing down the verses" (2014, 28). During the process of uttering ağıtlar, verses sung to remember other, past loved ones might also emerge as grief recalls grief in a manner akin to what ethnomusicologist David Samuels called "iconicity of feeling" (2004; cf. de la Bretèque 2016, 34). Thus, ağıtlar can incorporate verses not only composed by different women, but also inspired by different people.

On the other hand, certain individuals can play key roles in composing or shaping ağıtlar. Kemal mentions two sisters—Hasibe and Telli Hatun—renowned both for their role as repositories of a repertoire of ağıtlar and also as inventors of ağıtlar. Such women were often hired by families of the deceased to come to the funeral and mourn; in such cases one of them might carry more or less the entire process of composing ağıt verses (2014, 27). Kemal mentions transcribing from Hasibe and Telli Hatun "both their own and others' ağıtlar," implying that the sisters had maintained some sense of authorship or ownership over their own ağıtlar, distinguishing them from others (10). Ağıtlar might also be composed some time after a death by someone close to the deceased, by an ağıt specialist like one of the Hatun sisters, or by an âşık (see below). Kemal even describes ağıtlar that dying individuals composed for themselves when they knew that death was imminent (46). While individuals might draw on stock images—another collective aspect of ağıt creativity—Kemal's account celebrates how these often appear in strikingly novel variations; he also cites examples of an individual inventing a new image that gets taken up by others and becomes a stock image (41).

Furthermore, the ağıtlar that achieve wider circulation beyond the village go through an entexualization process, that is, a "process of rendering discourse extractable, of making a stretch of linguistic production into a unit—a text—that can be lifted out of its interactional setting" (Bauman and Briggs 1990, 73; see also Silverstein and Urban 1996; Wilf 2014, 405). This process involves further individual interventions. As folklorist İlhan Başgöz observed, it would be disrespectful to write down ağıtlar in the context of ritual mourning where they are first produced. Rather, someone has to subsequently recall or reconstruct the ağıt for it to be written down and published. This may be the same person who initially composed it, but in this later process of assembly, she has more time to consolidate and refine the ağıt. She may rework the ağıt to fit it into standard poetic forms, cull verses or add them, or combine verses from different rituals into one. Echoing the language of the personality theory underlying continental copyright laws (see chapter 2), Başgöz asserts that a widely circulating, more-or-less fixed ağıt will "bear the stamp" of this figure, who "bears the tradition" (2008, 79–80). Such figures may also be central to the process known as *türküleşme* ("türkü-fication"), by which the best known ağıt verses, those that circulate as regional or national folk music, become set to a unique, fixed tune (Güven 2013). Actors in mass media such as popular performers or record producers can also play a key role in such entextualization processes by creating fixed versions of normally open and variable türküler (Stokes 1992, 67–69; Güven 2013, 126; Bates 2016, 39–43).

Anatolian Singer-Poets

My second, contrasting case study focuses on the figure of the *âşık*, a traditional singer-poet who usually accompanies himself (or more rarely, herself) on the bağlama or *saz*, the long-necked lute that is the most widespread instrument within the folk music genre (see Erdener 1995; E. Özdemir 2013; Reinhard and di Olivera Pinto 1989; Şenel 2007). Âşıklar usually learn this craft through master-disciple relationships, and in the course of this education, are either given or choose a pen name, a *mahlas*, which they incorporate into the final verse of each poem as a kind of signature. In addition to singing original poems (called *deyişler*),[17] the âşık also sings the poems of previous âşıklar. These are referred to as *usta malı*, the property of masters.

As the practices of *mahlas* and performing attributed *usta malı* suggest, âşıklar clearly value individual authorship and ownership, at least when it comes to the verbal aspect of the art form as opposed to the musical. Individual authorship of âşık poems is also relatively well-documented, since âşıklar have long written down theirs and others' poems in notebooks (*cönk*). There also seem to be long-standing norms against plagiarism. Because of such emphases on remembered individual authorship, early republican folk literature specialists debated whether âşık poetry in fact belonged to the category of folklore, of which they usually took anonymity to be a defining criterion (e.g., Güney 1953, 10; Boratav 1942, 26).[18]

There are also collective and intertextual aspects of âşık creativity. Âşıklar from the northeast of Turkey partake in improvised duels that require the competitive or collaborative construction of poetic dialogue on the spur of the moment, for example. In these and more individualized compositional contexts, âşık poetry further draws on stock rhymes and images and conventional verse forms and

Essentializing Creativity 103

meters. As in post-Ottoman classical music and Ottoman *divan* poetry, there is also a tradition of *nazire*, writing poems inspired by a prior poem. However, at least among some contemporary âşıklar with whom I spoke, the line between nazire and plagiarism was not always clear. Further complicating notions of originality and authorship, there also appear to be traditions of pseudographia in âşık music. The âşık Ali İzzet Özkan claimed, for example, that he had composed poems and attributed them to the sixteenth-century revolutionary Pir Sultan Abdal, locating this practice in a long tradition of such attributions to this figure (Özkan and Başgöz 1979, 43).

The extent to which melodic creativity similarly involves individual authorship among âşıklar—and the historical depth of any such individual melodic authorship practices—is open to debate. Unlike âşık poems, melodies were not written down until very recently. Even for contemporary âşıklar I spoke with, the lyric seemed to be the defining element of the songs they proudly claimed. According to one common saying among âşıklar, "hava müşterektir, söz sahibinindir." The saying translates to something like, "The air is common, the lyric belongs to its writer," but exploits the double meaning of *hava* (air) in Turkish: like the English word *air*, the word *hava* can refer both to a musical melody and to the air around us (see Fossum 2023b, 40). Indeed, there are many examples of âşıklar singing different poems to the same tune. Tüfekçi argued that this phenomenon lent âşık songs as a genre an essentially "anonymous character" in keeping with his view that anonymity was the defining characteristic of folk music (1992). On the other hand, as in the case of ağıtlar, through the process of "türkü-fication" (*türküleşme*) some of the most widely circulating âşık poems become associated with a fixed, unique melody to which others avoid singing alternate lyrics (E. Özdemir 2013, 58).

It also seems clear that in the modern era, in which âşık music circulates through mass-mediated sound recordings, tunes may be composed for a specific lyric, and are sometimes claimed by the âşık who authored the lyric. Do such notions of melodic authorship extend back to an era that predates technologies for recording the tunes, or before copyright in music might have incentivized authorship claims?[19] In the case of older türküler, the tunes may also be significantly reshaped during oral transmission, as suggested by türküler documented in different variants. Some âşıklar take the presence of a unique tune attached to a given âşık poem as evidence that the author of the poem had also composed the tune. One âşık I spoke with imagined the seventeenth-century âşık Köroğlu to have composed the tune for the widely circulating song "Kiziroğlu," which

Köroğlu sings about an adversary in the course of the epic tale sung about him in northeastern Turkey (see chapter 6). But experts are often skeptical even of more recent claims to melodic authorship in folk music. Furthermore, even when âşıklar's melodic authorship is acknowledged, musicians and folklore experts often purport the similarity of many such melodies to each other to minimize the originality involved.[20]

The melodies to many âşık songs have also been composed not by âşıklar but by musicians who specialize in performing türküler and who may encounter an âşık poem in written form and choose to sing it. There are well-documented examples of this practice among contemporary urban musicians, but there have long been such türkü specialists operating in village contexts around Anatolia. Neşet Ertaş (1938–2012), the famous folk musician from Kırşehir, attributed a number of well-known tunes to his father Muharrem Ertaş (1913?–1984; see for example Akman 2006, 36). In the *Abdal* tradition to which the two belonged, such performers use the term *havalandırmak* (to "tunify" or "breathe air into") for the act of setting a poem to a melody, potentially putting the poem into greater circulation in the process (Parlak 2013, 1:244–45, 333).[21] While bağlama virtuoso and music professor Erol Parlak's enormous two-volume biography of Neşet Ertaş repeatedly emphasizes Abdals' lack of concern for wealth or monetary rights to songs (e.g., 240–49), it also reports an anecdote that suggests a sense of ownership over their repertoire. According to the anecdote, a still young but already renowned Muharrem Ertaş appeared at a wedding at which a group of performers from the nearby town of Hacıbektaş were performing instead of him, "disrespecting" him in the process (Parlak is not explicit as to what disrespectful act they committed). When one of the musicians invited requests from the audience, Ertaş replied to them: "Sing whatever you want, but sing nothing from Muharrem Ertaş, my son Neşet Ertaş, my in-law Hacı Taşan, or my nephew Çekiç Ali!" These latter three were his best-known students—masters in their own right—in addition to being his relatives, and together they constituted the current pantheon of the region's top musicians. The host of the wedding replied—with good reason—"But what is left that they can sing, Muharrem!?" (288–89, citing A. Yılmaz 2008, 183–84).

———

From these two case studies, it should be clear that creative processes in folk music's constituent traditions are varied, complex, and in most cases poorly

Essentializing Creativity 105

documented. The generalized theory of anonymous folkloric creation defines anonymity as an essential characteristic of folk music in the face of details that complicate the story. Were Hasibe and Telli Hatun, the famous ağıt-spinners featured by Kemal, authors of their ağıtlar? Or were they mere compilers, cogs in a more collaborative or collective machine that had churned out the songs? Mere nodes in a larger network? The question presumes that works taken to be more canonical of Romantic authorship, such as works in the Western art music genre, aren't also entextualizations of the collaborative, collective, or unfixed.[22] The traditions now framed as Turkish or Ottoman classical music and Turkish or Anatolian folk music involve both individual and collective forms of creative agency. Yet the genres are often defined in terms of generalizations that essentialize the creative processes that generate their constituent songs and tunes, foregrounding individualized creativity in art music and collective creativity in folk music.

CONCLUSION

In this chapter, I have argued that the genre of folk music, an umbrella term that lumps together a huge variety of localized musical practices, is defined in terms of a certain legal consciousness, one that figures the genre as that which rightly lies outside the scope of copyright. This legal consciousness relies in turn upon an essentializing account of the creative practices from which türküler and folk tunes have emerged. In particular, this construction of the genre has been achieved through a discursive contrast with urban art music traditions. I have analyzed this situation at length partly as a contribution to the international debates about creating legal mechanisms to protect folklore or traditional culture, such as those occurring at WIPO's Intergovernmental Committee on Intellectual Property and Genetic Resources, Traditional Knowledge and Folklore (Robinson, Abdel-Latif, and Roffe 2017). Where much of this literature assumes that such culture is produced through creative modalities that make them a poor fit for direct copyright protection, the case of Turkey's folk music shows how this imagined incompatibility with copyright had to be constructed.

By way of conclusion, let me suggest two further takeaways from my account, upon which I will build in the coming chapters. First, the legal consciousness that attends folk music shaped the documentary record of authorship and complicated the implementation of copyright in the genre, as we shall see in subsequent chapters. Second, I wish to highlight the contingency of how copyright legality has been constructed in the folk music arena. Given the complex histories of creativity in the genre's constituent traditions, there are other ways that the genre could have been defined in relation to copyright. As I describe in the next chapter, some individuals with stakes in folk music copyright have in fact leveraged such alternative accounts as they contest the anonymity theory and make claims on the rights in folk music.

FOUR

Copyright and Traditionalism in State Broadcasting

In the mid-1970s, at the peak of a heated interpersonal conflict, folk music doyen Nida Tüfekçi was reportedly sentenced to a week in jail. At the time, Tüfekçi held a powerful position as interim director of the Music Division at Turkey's official state broadcasting organization, Turkish Radio and Television (TRT). A journalist from the youth culture magazine *Hey* recalls catching the moment of his sentencing in a photo that accompanied a story reveling in the scandal. Tüfekçi paid a fine rather than standing behind bars, but the journalist, Taner Dedeoğlu, vividly remembers capturing his image as he stood with one arm raised and an incredulous look on his face as he stood before the judge. Dedeoğlu was a beat reporter covering TRT, and he had received a tip about Tüfekçi's hearing from Cemil Demirsipahi, a lawyer, musician, and sometimes TRT performer who had accused Tüfekçi of defamation, precipitating the jail sentence. Demirsipahi apparently hoped to further embarrass Tüfekçi by drawing press attention to his conviction (Taner Dedeoğlu, interview, June 27, 2018).[1]

The defamation charge was the culmination of an escalating battle between Tüfekçi and Demirsipahi, a battle fueled no doubt by a personality clash and professional rivalry, but whose lines were drawn in ideological terms. Tüfekçi's peers considered him a staunch traditionalist with strong opinions about what counted as folk music and how best to preserve it and present it to the public. Demirsipahi was known as a progressive, open to experimentation, change, and creative interventions into folk music.[2] The defamation charge had arisen when Demirsipahi performed the backing music for a television program, improvising melodies on his bağlama to accompany footage of Anatolian village scenery. Dedeoğlu, who claims to remember the program well, characterized the music as "independent music" (*özgün müzik*), a label often used to describe music that diverges from the conventions of well-established genres in Turkey. Tüfekçi, who objected fiercely to the non-traditional performance when he saw it, wrote a formal note to the head of the TRT television office, in which he declared Demirsipahi to be "not an artist."[3] It was this statement that had warranted the jail sentence (Taner Dedeoğlu, interview, June 27, 2018).

The conflict between Tüfekçi and Demirsipahi had long been simmering, the defamation charge only a boiling point. At the core of the conflict lay an ideological disagreement over a question about creativity in folk music: is it possible to compose a folk song? Tüfekçi held an uncompromising view that folk music had to be an anonymous, collectively produced expression of the folk, and any individual attempt to write an original folk song would necessarily be a contrived, inferior, corrupt imitation of the real thing. In the mid-1970s, Tüfekçi had ascended to a position of power sufficient to enforce his belief. He had overseen a reorganization of TRT's Folk Music Division, in the process helping to establish a repertoire committee that oversaw the content of TRT folk music programming.

Members of the committee claimed to be able to hear the difference between a composed, contrived türkü and an anonymous one, and they sought to sniff out any imposters. Others, however, would later claim that they had deceived the committee, submitting original compositions under the guise that they had collected them from villages. Demirsipahi was one such artist who had composed songs in the style of folk music. Furthermore, he loudly demanded copyright royalties from TRT for the performance of these and other original works on the airwaves. Tüfekçi seems to have found this outrageous.

One context for these events is that, around the same time, international scholars were describing supposedly essential differences between orality and literacy as modalities of human communication and expression. Epic poetry scholars Albert Lord and Millman Parry, for example, had theorized techniques of oral composition, artifacts of which could be detected through analysis of the texts so produced (Lord 2000). Building on such work, scholars began to view the oral and the literate as distinct stages of human evolution (W. Ong 1982). One common theory was technological determinism: the introduction of writing, the printing press, or electronic communication media were thought to revolutionize human societies, radically transforming patterns of thought and modalities of verbal creativity (W. Ong 1982; McLuhan 2013). Other scholars soon critiqued

Copyright and Traditionalism in Broadcasting **109**

such ideas, often by attending to facts on the ground that revealed complex interactions between literate and oral modalities, which themselves turned out to be more varied phenomena than the grand generalizations often assumed (Feld 1986; Finnegan 1988, 1990; Sterne 2011). Yet the story I tell here reveals a less studied consequence of these debates. Versions of these ideas circulated beyond the academy. For actors who took the supposedly radical difference between orality and literacy for granted, the sea changes wrought by technology might represent desirable progress, but they might also provoke a nostalgia or even a defense of the oral modalities—such as anonymous folkloric creativity—whose viability seemed to be endangered. Copyright, as a legal regime that facilitates the production and monetization of print and electronic media, might represent a harbinger and an agent of this shift. How do actors respond to this situation?

In this chapter, I argue that Tüfekçi and other traditionalists viewed Demirsipahi's early copyright activism as part of a larger set of developments that looked like a commercialization threatening folk music. Afforded an opportunity to react against these developments as they ascended to power at a moment of restructuring within state broadcasting, they initiated a number of policy interventions aimed at preserving folk music's authenticity, understood in terms of anonymity. While it is impossible to assess the degree to which the policy approaches I discuss can be attributed to reactions against copyright activism specifically, it is also impossible to disentangle copyright from the larger set of social changes that were reshaping music-making at the time, including mass urbanization and technological developments in music recording and distribution. In the wake of these developments, at least by some accounts, the insistence within state broadcasts that folk music was anonymous seems to have shifted from an ideal invoked as a matter of practical convenience to a firm principle enforced more strictly as a matter of policy. One implication of the history I describe here is thus that it complicates the widespread sense I encountered in Turkey's music sector that copyright had been largely irrelevant until the era of reform beginning in the late 1980s. Furthermore, scholarship on music in Turkey has long tended to focus on the cultural reforms of the early republic, failing to account for how policies in folk music institutions after 1950 have also been crucial in shaping the genre. Here, I document key shifts in how folk music specialists have conceptualized anonymity and folkloric authenticity, particularly since the 1960s.

These observations support and fill out my larger story of copyright consciousness in turn. By presenting folk music as an anonymous national heritage that must not be commoditized or claimed for individual profit, traditionalists at

TRT shaped how audiences—not to mention the many performing artists who passed through the radio and television studios—understood the genre. Specifically, this framing contributed to an emergent sense of legality in folk music when copyright law began to be enforced more effectively in the late 1980s, as I describe in chapter 5. Furthermore, the anonymity idea shaped the documentary record of authorship in folk music, as even those who were skeptical of the idea sometimes presented their original türküler as anonymous to access the airwaves. Such practices complicated the implementation of folk music in the genre in turn. In other words, in this chapter I clarify the role that state broadcasting played in the highly contingent process through which copyright legality emerged in Turkey's music sector. My account draws upon oral history interviews as well as archival documents, especially transcripts from the meetings of the TRT Art Music and Folk Music Special Advisory Committees (TRT 1974, 1990, 1991), which periodically gathered leading musicians and experts who offered nonbinding guidance to the agency on its policies toward programs featuring these genres.

THE BACKGROUND OF THE CONFLICT

Nida Tüfekçi (1929–1993) was a protege of Muzaffer Sarısözen (1899–1963), who is often celebrated as the founding father of folk music in Turkey. Sarısözen spearheaded folk music collecting expeditions around Anatolia from the late 1930s to the early 1950s, overseeing the preservation of the resulting recordings from his post as the head of the Ankara State Conservatory archive (N. Yılmaz 1996; Elçi 1997; Şenel 2018b). The leadership at state-run Ankara Radio also recruited Sarısözen to appear on radio programs and teach their ensembles the folk music he had collected on his expeditions (Şenel 2010, 2:84; Tör 1976, 54–55).[4] Sarısözen began by appearing as a guest on radio shows featuring a Turkish art music ensemble. He would teach the radio ensemble how to perform the folk songs that he and his collaborators had collected on their expeditions. Partly because of Sarısözen's frustration with the art music ensemble's tendency to play in a style he considered appropriate to art music but not to folk music, the station founded a now-famous folk music program called "Voices from the Homeland" (*Yurttan Sesler*), which featured its own regular lineup of folk music specialists under Sarısözen's direction. Sarısözen taught the ensemble by writing notations on a blackboard. Members of the ensemble—iterations of which were later founded at regional radio stations around Turkey—copied these notations into their notebooks, using them as lead sheets during broadcast performances.

Copyright and Traditionalism in Broadcasting 111

In addition to performances by the ensemble, such radio programs also featured guest artists: individual representatives of the regional traditions that made up the larger body of folk music. Tüfekçi began his career as a regional musician from Yozgat, receiving invitations to perform as a guest on Ankara radio broadcasts beginning in 1947. He joined Sarısözen's ensemble as a regular member in 1953 (Duygulu 2019).

Prior to the 1960s, state radio broadcasts were run out of regional stations with limited broadcast range. The stations operated independently of each other. Each station had a music division with committees that oversaw broadcast content (Yücel Paşmakçı, interview, March 11, 2014).[5] Folk music was one element of programming at each of the local radio stations. In the mid-1960s, the state expanded into television broadcasting and set up TRT as an umbrella institution governing all the regional radio stations in addition to television. TRT set up a Folk Music Division to centralize oversight of folk music programming in broadcasts around the country. While a private record industry existed outside the reach of TRT's growing bureaucracy, the agency held a monopoly on broadcasting that made it a gatekeeper with the power to control which music might be promoted on radio and television.

Sarısözen's career at the radio ended in 1960, while Tüfekçi moved to Istanbul in 1959, becoming the director of the Istanbul Radio Folk Music Division in the mid-1960s. Tüfekçi was called upon to return to Ankara to head the new TRT Folk Music Division in 1972. When he arrived, he instituted a number of reforms. One of these involved forming a repertoire committee to consolidate and standardize the body of music performed in folk music broadcasts around the country. The handwritten lead sheets held by members of the "Voices from the Homeland" ensemble—which often differed from each other—were reviewed and edited, then printed as official, standard notations. These made up the core of the official TRT Turkish Folk Music Repertoire that began to grow as the committee reviewed newly collected folk music, selectively adding items to be performed in official programs. Tüfekçi was later made interim director of the larger Music Division before leaving his official post at TRT in 1976 to help found the new Turkish Music State Conservatory, now based at Istanbul Technical University (ITU). But he continued to wield an outsized influence at the agency, advising those who remained in charge and continuing to participate in committees and programs while passing on his ideas to the next generation of musicians at ITU (see Duygulu 2019).

The TRT Folk Music Repertoire Committee had a slightly different set of con-

112 *Copyright Consciousness*

cerns than Sarısözen had had when collecting and teaching the music. According to Sarısözen, the purpose of radio folk music broadcasts was to promote the idea of national folk music by introducing regional türküler and tunes to a national audience, and by extension to foster solidarity among the country's population around the idea of a shared heritage of folk music (Çeren 1944). In most parts of the country at the time when Sarısözen began his work, citizens might have been familiar with a few local examples of türküler, yet most citizens did not yet understand these to be part of a national heritage, nor did they constitute a kind of mass-mediated music that was widely consumed.

By the time Sarısözen's protege Tüfekçi took on his leadership role within the newly formed TRT Folk Music Division in the early 1970s, however, music of the Anatolian countryside had begun to fascinate mass audiences. In part this was the result of Sarısözen's efforts, but in part it may have reflected a growing nostalgia for the countryside in the context of mass urbanization (from the 1950s on) as well as migration to Germany (from 1961), trends that were reshaping Turkey's demographics. Concurrent with the folk revival that was peaking in the 1960s in North America and the United Kingdom, popular Turkish acts known for performing localized versions of Western popular music began adapting türküler, spinning them into hits sold on the private record market (And 1984, 223). The trend developed into a rock genre known as Anadolu Pop (see Meriç 2006, 239–61; Skoog 2012). While this genre waned in popularity after the 1970s, popular artists of various genres have continued making hits out of türküler.

Part of the context for the story I tell in this chapter, then, is this shift in the popular position of folk music. While Sarısözen had seen his role as promoting folk music in order to bolster a nation-building effort in the early decades of the Turkish Republic, Tüfekçi rose to power at a time when popular musicians were taking up folk music enthusiastically. In the process, they often interpreted it in ways not envisioned by official approaches to folk music within the broadcasting agency. Tüfekçi thus seems to have been more concerned with preserving tradition as he understood it than with promoting the music as had his mentor. He was also known for his stern personality that some saw as particularly suited to the task.

Cemil Demirsipahi (1933–2013), who tried to have Tüfekçi put in jail, had also performed in Sarısözen's radio programs. He was an accomplished composer working with a number of popular recording artists. At the same time, he researched folk dances, publishing a massive book on the subject (Demirsipahi 1975), and he began a long career as a university folk music instructor at about the time of his confrontation with Tüfekçi. He was also a trained copyright lawyer who had opened some of the first lawsuits over music copyright in Turkey (see chapter 1). While most musicians I spoke with recalled copyright going largely ignored until the formation of collecting societies in the 1980s, Demirsipahi was an early copyright activist who sought to have the law enforced. He later spearheaded ultimately unsuccessful efforts to form a copyright collecting society in the 1970s (MÜZKO 1978).

THE ANONYMITY POLICY

One of TRT's folk music policies under which Demirsipahi and others bristled was the agency's traditional insistence that folk music does not have known authors, and songs with known authors should not be included in the official TRT Folk Music Repertoire. Notably, notations in the TRT Repertoire list a collector (*derleyen*), source (*kaynak kişi* or *alınan*), region of origin (*yöre*), and transcriber (*notaya alan*), but they do not credit composers.[6] Items not included in the official TRT Repertoire have long been allowed in broadcasts, particularly if performed by a visiting guest artist. However, songs that are to be performed must be approved for broadcast by the supervisory office (*denetim*); the TRT Repertoire has a special importance because its constituent songs and tunes are pre-approved for airplay, and the agency's regular broadcast ensembles primarily draw their setlists from it. Many musicians claim, however, that türküler with known authors are in fact played regularly in TRT folk music broadcasts or are even included in the TRT Repertoire but are presented as anonymous.[7] Others complain that türküler that belong in such broadcasts are excluded because false authorship claims have been made on them, while many musicians and other commenters contest the very idea that folk music must be anonymous.[8]

Tüfekçi and his fellow reformers loudly asserted the anonymity policy at the time of TRT's restructuring in the early 1970s. At one meeting of the newly formed Repertoire Committee, they reportedly removed about 1500 items from the official TRT broadcast repertoire. Yücel Paşmakçı, then director of folk music at Istanbul radio, recalls traveling to Ankara for the meeting.[9] According to his recollection, he drew on his recent experience working in the record industry to identify those songs and tunes he strongly suspected of having known composers, works he characterized as "contrived [*uyduruk*]" (interview, March 11, 2014; Şenel 2009, 102).[10] Some radio artists objected to having these works stricken from the TRT Repertoire. "They got very angry and gossiped," Paşmakçı recalled,

114 *Copyright Consciousness*

chuckling, when I asked him about it. According to Şenel, the affected artists appealed (apparently unsuccessfully) to parliament over the matter (pers. comm., June 19, 2018; Şenel 2009, 103).

The traditionalists on the Repertoire Committee seem to have understood such interventions as a response to a perceived corruption of folk music programming in recent years. Several musicians who were working at TRT in the 1960s and 1970s related to me that with the departure of Sarısözen in 1960 and his subsequent death in 1963, the monitoring of folk music programming at the radio had become lax for a brief period during the 1960s, particularly at Ankara Radio. During this period, radio musicians who also had outside performing careers would return from their tours around the country with türküler they had collected during their travels, and they would add them to the notebooks of lead sheets and perform them on the radio. But some of these musicians were also composing original music that attempted to approximate the formal features and sound of anonymous türküler.[11] These newly composed folk songs are often referred to as *beste türkü*, drawing on a general term for a musical composition (*beste*) that had a negative connotation in folk music contexts, at least for traditionalists like Tüfekçi (Markoff 1986, 151).

According to a narrative that was critical of these developments, under Sarısözen's watch such items would never have received airplay, or at the very least, would not have been accepted into the performance repertoire of the official radio ensembles. Not only were their composers known, but they were also viewed as aesthetically poor imitations made by radio musicians insufficiently immersed in a rural tradition. These musicians were said to be seeking airplay for their own works in order to boost record sales on the private market (TRT 1974, 24).

Under the principles of Sarısözen, the radio was a place for promoting folk music, not one's own career. He even reportedly had a policy according to which radio folk music artists who left for careers as performers in entertainment venues, especially nightclubs (*gazino*), could not return to perform on the radio again (N. Yılmaz 1996, 44). Some viewed the increasingly popular practice of performing composed songs in folk music programming as one manifestation of a breakdown of discipline in Sarısözen's absence in the 1960s. By the early 1970s, a number of radio artists' own songs, songs of dubious authenticity in the eyes of traditionalists like Tüfekçi, had worked their way into the performing repertoire of the broadcasting ensembles.

Tüfekçi framed the anonymity policy, like other policies on which he and

Copyright and Traditionalism in Broadcasting **115**

his cohort doubled down during the restructuring of the 1970s, as a reassertion of principles from the Muzaffer Sarısözen era. Sarısözen, for example, did not record (or apparently even inquire about) authorship credits when he collected folk music during his numerous expeditions for the Ankara State Conservatory in the 1930s to 1950s (see chapter 3). At TRT advisory committee meetings where the anonymity policy was discussed, Tüfekçi also occasionally summoned evidence from Sarısözen's personal papers to support his position.[12] At one meeting, he read from a letter that Sarısözen had apparently written to a regional musician who had sent the notation for a türkü he hoped to have performed on the radio:

> "Dear Aziz Çekirge," Aziz Çekirge the artist from Urfa. "I received the letter and the notation, thank you for reminding me. Let me immediately make [my] perspective clear, that yours or another's composed work [*bestelediği eser*] is not a *halk türküsü* [folk, i.e., anonymous, türkü]. Those are not the property of the people but of individuals. For example, tunes like "Urfalıyam dağlıyam, derde kerem" [I'm from Urfa, I'm from the mountain, be kind to my sorrow] that the people sing without being able to know who the author is, are considered folkloric music. As I have said on the radio several times, please do us a favor and do not send us türkü lyrics or notations; as a point of principle we cannot perform these." (TRT 1991, 42)

This letter seems to suggest that Sarısözen not only maintained something like an anonymity policy in his own broadcast programs, but that he also did so in response to repeated attempts by listeners to have authored works performed on the air, listeners to whom it perhaps seemed not as obvious that folk music had to be anonymous.[13]

However, as far as I can tell, Sarısözen never directly addressed the idea of anonymity in published books or articles about folk music.[14] Furthermore, Demirsipahi insisted that Sarısözen knowingly allowed composed türküler in his broadcasts. In one published interview, for example, he recalled, "On 'Voices from the Homeland,' I found it difficult to constantly repeat the same, simple pieces, and I asked the esteemed Sarısözen, 'Master, I can make better compositions than these. May I do so?' And he said to me, 'Try it but don't tell anyone that it is an original composition [*beste*]. I will say it was 'taken from Cemil Demirsipahi' [i.e., collected from], which means the same thing" ("Cemil Demirsipahi ile söyleyiş" 2005).[15] Demirsipahi furthermore recalled how regional musicians occasionally came to the radio and performed his original compositions, pretending they were türküler from their home regions. In one such case Demirsipahi

116 *Copyright Consciousness*

described, Sarısözen reportedly questioned a visiting musician about a song he had performed in a broadcast, asking, "This is a türkü from your region?" The musician replied, "It's Mr. Cemil [Demirsipahi]'s composition but if we don't play it, they won't invite us to play at weddings there" ("Cemil Demirsipahi ile söyleyiş" 2005). The anecdote—if we are to take it at face value—not only works to contradict Tüfekçi's account of Sarısözen's stance on anonymity, but it also highlights how regional musicians' priorities differed from those of Sarısözen's nation-building and Tüfekçi's traditionalism.[16]

How do we reconcile Tüfekçi's and Demirsipahi's apparently conflicting versions of Sarısözen and his stance toward anonymity in folk music? Mehmet Özbek, director of the TRT Folk Music Division from 1982 to 1986, offered one explanation that seemed to make sense of the apparent contradiction. Özbek speculated to me that Sarısözen's anonymity policy was more a matter of practical strategy than of ironclad principle. He argued that Sarısözen had knowingly admitted composed türküler on occasion, but he used the principle of anonymity as a strategy for diplomatically denying unwanted submissions to the TRT Repertoire. In his view,

> If TRT had directly admitted that original compositions were being broadcast, everyone would start applying to submit quite contrived and simple things into the Repertoire. . . . Let's say I'm the director of the TRT Music Office. Someone brings a very simple melody that they want played on the air. In fact, before they came to me, they went to a member of parliament. In fact, if they are close [with him], they'll go to the Prime Minister. The Prime Minister calls the director of the TRT Music Office on the phone. "A friend of ours has a composition, let's put it in the Repertoire," he says. . . . So, for example, it was in order to prevent this sort of thing. . . . They would say that at the TRT [in Folk Music] there are no composed works. Because you can't say "no"; you can't offend them. (Interview, March 29, 2015)

This is a speculation on Özbek's part, but it comes from someone who has stood in Sarısözen's shoes, who has been in charge of Turkish Folk Music on state radio and knows firsthand the kinds of scenarios such an individual faces. The speculation also reconciles these two versions of Sarısözen we have encountered: that of the letter who refuses to accept the composition from the Urfa regional artist and that of the Demirsipahi anecdote, who encourages his own ensemble member, whose talent he knows, to go ahead and compose türküler but to lie about it.

Elsewhere, Özbek has explained why he thought Sarısözen might add such

Copyright and Traditionalism in Broadcasting **117**

items to the radio repertoire. Sarısözen's main concern, he points out, "was to bring into being a shared language, to bring about a shared heart [*gönül*] and a shared musical language. [But] having started from this idea, Sarısözen never introduced or applied a definitive principle of performing authentic music in the ensemble that he founded. I think it is a historical inaccuracy for those connected to folk music [to think that he held such a strict principle of anonymity]" (TRT 1996, 10).[17] Özbek may be right about the man held up as the founding father of Turkish folk music, or Tüfekçi—who was quite close to Sarısözen—may be right. Perhaps Demirsipahi's anecdotes were fabricated or exaggerated.[18]

However impossible it is to know with certainty what was going through Sarısözen's mind at the time, Demirsipahi and Özbek were not alone in sensing that something had changed in the Tüfekçi era. Some saw Tüfekçi's stern personality as exactly what was required to establish and maintain discipline and integrity in folk music. But musicians I spoke with who were around TRT in the 1970s often complained that Tüfekçi's positions could seem oppressive or excessively conservative. One folk music artist and outspoken critic I encountered on this issue felt that Tüfekçi had created "an incredible chasm" (*muhtiş bir uçurum*) by separating so strictly the anonymous from the composed. He told me he did not think Sarısözen had had the same anxiety about anonymity, not at the same level. When it came to anonymity, he described Tüfekçi as "excessively religious" (*aşırı dindar*), "a fanatic" (*taassup*), and completely uncompromising.

CONCEPTUALIZING ANONYMITY AND AUTHENTICITY

The rigid distinction Tüfekçi drew between the purportedly individualized nature of creativity in art music and the collective, anonymous nature of creativity in folk music aligned with other ways in which he sought to sharply delineate the sometimes-fuzzy boundaries of the folk music genre (see chapter 3). Like others involved in the project of musical nation-building at the time, he viewed folk and art musics as two branches of a larger Turkish national music. These also corresponded to two bureaucratic divisions at TRT: the Art Music Division and the Folk Music Division. Tüfekçi was serious about enforcing a strict divide between folk music and art music. In a 1973 meeting of the periodically convened TRT Turkish Art and Folk Music Special Advisory Committee, a heated discussion erupted because the art music staff wanted to be able to perform anonymous türküler, especially those from Istanbul that had traditionally been played quite commonly by art music performers. Members of the art music camp complained that there was an "iron curtain" at the radio forbidding them from doing so. Tüfekçi defended the need for this strict separation, invoking the historical issue of radio art musicians performing folk music with an urban art music style, which Sarısözen had sought to correct by forming a separate folk music ensemble. In the end the issue went to a vote, which fell heavily in favor of tearing down the "iron curtain." Tüfekçi objected forcefully (TRT 1974, 249–61).[19]

Songs from the repertoire of âşıklar, which Tüfekçi and others grouped with folk music despite this tradition's emphasis on individualized authorship (see chapter 3), presented particular complications for the anonymity policy. Tüfekçi was known to especially admire âşık music among folk music's sub-genres, and a number of people I spoke with credited him with increasing the number of âşıklar and âşık songs appearing in TRT broadcasts. This created a tension between Tüfekçi's and others' assertions that folk music was anonymous and the reality that remembered authorship held an important place in at least one of its sub-traditions. This tension seemed to have been partially resolved through shifting and inconsistent policies toward âşık music at TRT.

Paşmakçı suggested that âşıklar were sometimes allowed to perform their own original songs in broadcasts, but these would not be taken into the official TRT Repertoire for regular performance (interview, March 25, 2015). Another approach was to allow original compositions by âşıklar or famous regional masters if they were dead, but not while they were alive (Stokes 1992, 56). According to folklorist Süleyman Şenel, who studied under Tüfekçi at ITU, the latter often simply felt that türküler needed to age before they could be taken into the TRT Repertoire. He used the metaphor of tea: just as tea needed time to steep, Tüfekçi thought that folk music needed time to steep. When confronted with a newly composed türkü that seemed otherwise attractive and appropriate to the TRT Repertoire, whether penned by an âşık or another kind of folk music performer, he might decline it in order to allow time for it to further age. This, Şenel thought, was a matter of preference (*tercih meselisi*; interview, May 23, 2014). Şenel and others also pointed out that in many cases, Tüfekçi or the Repertoire Committee ended up taking a song by a living âşık into the TRT Repertoire but removing the final verse, in which âşıklar refer to themselves by name, thus avoiding referencing the living, known author. Sometimes the pen name of the living âşık was changed to that of an older, long dead âşık or to a different word altogether.[20] One of my bağlama teachers, Şendoğan Karadeli, who had worked with Tüfekçi at ITU, thought that

Copyright and Traditionalism in Broadcasting 119

Tüfekçi simply made a general exception for âşık music in his prohibition on original compositions in folk music (pers. comm., November 10, 2015).

These shifting and seemingly ad hoc interpretations of the anonymity policy may make more sense if we consider how Tüfekçi and his cohort on the Repertoire Committee seem to have conceptualized anonymity, as suggested by the fact that they claimed to be able to detect it as an audible trait of the music. The term "anonymity" most often refers to an epistemic status: a song may be anonymous because we simply don't know who composed it. But the theory of folkloric anonymity, according to which türküler are thought to express the shared feelings and ideas of a regional folk, contain poetic and musical elements recycled among many instances of regional folkloric repertoire, and become reworked over time in a collective process of oral transmission and re-creation (see chapter 3), suggests anonymity not only as an epistemic status but also as an ontological one. Anonymity is not so much a matter of what we know about the türkü's origins as it is a matter of the nature of türküler themselves. In this understanding, an anonymous türkü has emerged out of a creative process different from that of art or popular works composed by individuals; an anonymous türkü might also bear audible traces of this distinct status.

This understanding of anonymity affords another rationale by which âşık songs with acknowledged authors might be allowed despite the anonymity policy. Tüfekçi's daughter Gamze Tüfekçi Yazıcı discussed the famous Sivas âşık Veysel, who is credited with writing some now iconic original songs central to the folk music canon. She told me, "In Veysel's time, I asked my father a lot—is âşık music anonymous or not? The man writes his own lyrics, the music is also his own. My father would say, yes, but he sings that region's music. Veysel sings the music of Sivas that he heard for years. He was nourished on that region's music; he heard it there. You won't hear some kind of Zeybek [a genre common in western Turkey] from Veysel. So âşıklar bring together the regional tradition and their own style [üslup] such that, yes, it's their own, but since they reflect that region [bölge] we consider it anonymous" (interview, May 5, 2015).[21] If Yazıcı's account is accurate, Tüfekçi resorted to a seemingly self-contradictory logic to justify his absolutism about anonymity. Anonymous music reflects regional characteristics. Veysel writes music that reflects regional characteristics. Ergo, Veysel composes anonymous music.[22] It also highlights a slippage I sometimes encountered between the concepts of anonymity and regionality. For example, at one TRT Special Advisory Committee Meeting at which those in attendance discussed terminology to distinguish anonymous folk music from newly composed folk music, Aegean regional folk music specialist Özay Gönlüm proposed "Regional Folk Music" or "Local Folk Music" (*Yerel Halk Müziği*) for the former, reasoning that this makes sense because "the term 'local' is equivalent to 'anonymous'" (TRT 1991, 138; see also 19). Likewise, in my conversations with Paşmakçı, I asked him how he and the other members of the Repertoire Committee could tell if a newly collected türkü they were vetting for inclusion in the TRT Repertoire was anonymous or not. He told me, "We have regional artists. For example, Keskinli Hacı Taşan. I can carefully learn something that he plays. I can play it. But it has a particular scent [*koku*] such that—I'm not from Kırşehir [Hacı Taşan's home region]; I can't convey that same scent."

At this response, I felt that he was straying from the topic of anonymity and authorship, describing performing style, perhaps minute aspects of interpretation like expressive timing, rather than compositional elements. "I was asking about whether a folk song is anonymous or not," I said, trying to redirect him. "That also emerges from this point," he said. "Does it have the regional style [*yörenin üslubu*] or not?" The answer seemed to suggest that for Paşmakçı (and others) the concept of regionality mediated perceptions of anonymity: where the performance of a türkü resembled other türkü performances from a given region, it sounded anonymous.

While the aim of the anonymity policy would seem to be to safeguard the authenticity of folk music by excluding individually composed imposters, it also overlapped with a concern for an authenticity understood in terms of regional character and distinctiveness.[23] Thus Tüfekçi introduced further policies that aimed to preserve regional distinctiveness in folk music. For example, the newly organized TRT Folk Music Division of the 1970s firmly distinguished salaried TRT staff musicians from regional musicians (*mahalli sanatçılar*). While the former would play in ensembles on regular programs, the latter would appear periodically as guests. Staff musicians would have to be able to play türküler and tunes from every region of the country with proper style according to a system of stereotyped regional instrumental techniques that Sarısözen had standardized (Markoff 1986; Stokes 1992, 76–81). They also had to have other skills, such as sight-reading staff notation. Regional musicians, by contrast, should perform exclusively the repertoire traditional in their region, modeling the proper regional style in the process. They were discouraged from spending too much time at TRT, where they might be overly exposed to styles from other regions of the country as mediated by urban artists, as this might begin corrupting their own performance style (TRT 1974, 183–85).[24]

Copyright and Traditionalism in Broadcasting **121**

This separation of regular staff and regional guest musicians—and regimentation of their roles in representing regional authenticity—suggests that there was an increasing anxiety around preserving a purported traditionality understood in terms of regional stylistic distinctiveness. Radio and television exposed regional musicians to broadcasts containing music from other regions, and when they were invited to perform on the radio, to musicians from other regions as well as to urban musicians who synthesized styles from a variety of sources. This anxiety paralleled a wider-spread fear of what American ethnomusicologist Alan Lomax—writing around the same time as the TRT reorganization—called "greyout": a homogenization of musical taste and style that he thought would result from the new forms of mass media ascendant in the mid-twentieth century (1972; 1978, 8). But given that such broadcasts in Turkey arose from the self-conscious efforts to promote national folk music at TRT rather than from private broadcasters' promotion of commercial popular music (as in the cases that concerned Lomax), and especially given the tendency to understand folkloric authenticity in terms of regional distinctness, there was perhaps a special irony to the Turkish case.[25] It helps further explain Tüfekçi's staunchly traditionalist approach, however controversial it proved to be.

CONTESTING THE ANONYMITY POLICY

The anonymity policy—along with the general idea that folk music must be anonymous—was sometimes hotly contested, as suggested by Demirsipahi's dramatic confrontation with Tüfekçi. Indeed, Demirsipahi was perhaps the first to speak out against it. In the midst of his massive tome on genres of folk dance and folk music in Turkey (1975), he sets aside a few pages to critique the anonymity theory:

> [A work's] performance by other people does not remove the composer. Just as a poem's becoming famous all over Turkey does not remove the poet, when a musical composition becomes widespread the composer does not disappear. ... Whose right is it to change a composer's product, whether out of ignorance, an insufficiently trained ear, or the pursuit of personal interest, to obtain a profit, to win fame by concealing the composer, to change the work through insufficiency of performance because one's voice is not strong enough? ... Isn't it disrespect toward the creator of the work? Just as changing a poem by Tevfik Fikret,[26] damaging it as a result either of beautification or corruption,

adding thoughtless contributions, will not turn it into the property of society, we must feel obligated to bear the same respect toward a composer's work. . . . The work is removed further from its value and originality with every addition. . . . Nowadays to think that a painting by someone famous like Goya should be subject to additions in an effort to beautify it is a mistaken idea. . . .

Besides, how is a work with a known author, for example a beste by Âşık Veysel, going to be worked on by the folk? When will the traces of Veysel be erased? How will they be erased? Who can measure this, by what criteria? What will be the form of this erasure of individual traces? Who is going to decide this? What will be achieved by separating it from other individual works? (160–61)

Demirsipahi thus challenges the Romantic assumption that a collective process of re-creation in oral transmission will enhance the value of folk music and render it the shared property of the people. He leverages the language of the copyright doctrine of moral rights, according to which authors hold a right to prevent alterations to their works, to negatively valence the reshaping process that purportedly anonymizes türküler.[27] Furthermore, comparing Veysel and other first creators of türküler with Goya and the Ottoman poet Fikret, he seems to deny an essential difference between authorship and the "burning" of a türkü (cf. Fossum 2023a).

Yet in my interviews with folk music experts and in my archival research, I found that these objections were not the most common ones. Indeed, Demirsipahi himself also hints at a more typical objection to the anonymity idea, one that hinges on a particular temporality: "Today it is no longer anyone's right to have the power to erase the creator. The law gives the appropriate punishments to those who do this. Writing and notation have done away with the ongoing uncertainty. We have reached a conclusion. Finally we have attained a guarantee that the composition and the lyrics are the property of their creator" (1975, 161). Here, Demirsipahi seems to assert that a discursive rupture has occurred, marking off a past era in which the vagaries of orality were at play from a present in which writing and notation (and, we might suppose, audio recording technology) have allowed for musical works to be fixed, their authors documented.

While Demirsipahi seems to frame this epochal shift in positive terms, others—even those who set themselves to the task of composing new türküler—seemed to embrace the change ambivalently, with a nostalgia for the imagined condition of orality (see also Öztelli 1972, cited in Atılgan 1992, 165). This theme emerged at the 1991 TRT Turkish Art and Folk Music Special Advisory Committee Meeting, where the idea of ending the anonymity policy and allowing newly composed folk songs with acknowledged authors (so-called beste türküler) was debated. Here, the composer Ertuğrul Bayraktar declared, for example:

> What is affecting our current day? The growth of mass communication media. Nowadays we are in an era when recordings take a türkü and, without letting it live [i.e., spread and change through traditional oral transmission], impose them directly on people. In other words, when a türkü is burned in some region, connected to some event [*olay*], in connection to some setting, in connection to some love, it is beginning to no longer go through the process of taking on the form of something shared among the people. Why? Because the moment it is taped [is] the moment it sheds the characteristic of being the common property of society, and this is what we are living through today. (TRT 1991, 25)

Even more dramatically, folk music artist İhsan Öztürk claimed that not only had the anonymization process involved in oral transmission ceased, but so had the initial "burning" of türküler itself:

> I was born and grew up in the town of Şarkışla in Sivas district and I am someone who got his music culture from that place.[28] I have seen myself how türküler are burned. In the old days *imeceler* [traditional events during which neighbors provide mutual assistance with agricultural labor] would happen, for example an *imece* to harvest bulgur wheat. We were little then; the women would gather, lay out a *kilim* [flat-woven carpet], and there the girls would tease each other with *maniler* [a traditional rhyming verse form], and since we were little we were allowed to be there among them.[29] . . . These were the best circumstances for burning türküler. But now when I return to my hometown [*memleket*] I see that there is no tradition of burning türküler; it's over. While people are hoeing in the fields they put a stereo tape player with huge speakers on top of the tractor. They put some artist's tape in and do their work while they listen to it. That means the tradition of burning türküler is disappearing, and we can say this for all of Turkey in general. (38)

While most proponents of allowing beste türküler in TRT broadcasts—including Bayraktar and Öztürk—seemed to express some nostalgia for the imagined lost age in which the folk purportedly burned and anonymized türküler, they also leveraged the assertion that a discursive rupture had occurred to bolster their arguments that it would now be appropriate and even necessary for individuals to compose new ones.

124 *Copyright Consciousness*

Advocating for named authorship of türküler furthermore entailed a belief that it was possible to compose folk music in a way that was not "contrived" (*uyduruk*), as the beste türkü skeptics asserted it would necessarily be. Özbek was one who opined to me that it was possible to create a beste türkü that listeners—including the expert members of the Repertoire Committee—could not distinguish from old, anonymous ones; indeed, this was why so many had reportedly made it into the TRT Repertoire. Özbek cited a few examples, including Sadettin Kaynak's "Batan gün kana benziyor" (The setting sun looks like blood) and one of his own original songs, "Gözleri fettan güzel" (Her eyes are enticingly beautiful), claiming that these had the same character as anonymous türküler. He predicted that if he didn't tell me "Gözleri . . ." was his own song, I wouldn't be able to pick it out from among similar, anonymous türküler that he proceeded to sing for me on the spot (interview, March 29, 2015).[30] A number of anecdotes furthermore circulate about folk music artists slipping original compositions by the Repertoire Committee by presenting them as anonymous türküler they had collected from a village (Stokes 1992, 55).

That such voices favoring authorship in folk music emerged when they did was not, I argue, an accident. The idea of allowing and acknowledging beste türküler in broadcasts was proposed at several Special Advisory Committee meetings throughout the late 1980s and early 1990s, a period that coincided with the state's turn toward neoliberal economic policy and with the era of copyright reform that I describe in chapter 1.[31] Turkish composers, to whom TRT had long resisted paying copyright royalties, had won a key legal victory when a 1981 court decision required the agency to begin compensating them for the broadcast of their works (Beşiroğlu 1999, 313–29; Avcı 2021, 70). Meanwhile, several people with knowledge of TRT policy in this period recalled that the agency would often remove türküler from the TRT Repertoire to avoid paying royalties when an individual claimed the rights in them.[32] MESAM, the first of Turkey's copyright collecting societies for musical authors, was founded in 1987, furthermore creating a mechanism that promised to allow türkü composers to register their works and begin accruing royalties. Meanwhile the state had begun defunding TRT, liberalizing media in the early 1990s in a move that introduced new competition for the agency as listeners and viewers could turn to other outlets to find broadcast music.

While the musicians who claimed to have composed türküler did not usually mention the copyright context in their arguments, they did invoke authors' rights in ethical terms. Addressing those who had enforced the anonymity policy, the Alevi bağlama virtuoso Yavuz Top declared:

Copyright and Traditionalism in Broadcasting **125**

You personally drove me to crookery and fraud; I was driven to it and I have eight or ten or twenty beste and I'll tell you which ones they are. I found someone else and I taught them the türkü, and after that I had them sing it for a recording, and I wrote the notation from that and sent it to the supervisory office [*denetim*]. You made me into a fraud! You can't do that sort of thing. Didn't Âşık Veysel compose original songs? . . . Our friend İhsan Öztürk here and I did it together, the türkü "Gam Elinde Benim Zülfü Siyahım," he composed it himself, and I wrote the notation. "Yarım Senden Ayrılalı" is my own beste. "Erbahi Ezelde Levli Kalemde," which Nida Tüfekçi transcribed, is my own beste; who is going to claim it? Why should I make some beste of mine someone else's property? Isn't it a shame? I am a mortal and I'm going to die one day, but I'm saying let my name pass into history. (TRT 1991, 6)

In addition to decrying this scenario in which türkü composers had to conceal their authorship and thus fail to be recognized for it, Top and others furthermore blamed the situation for the departure of musical talent from the culturally important folk music genre in favor of commercially popular genres such as arabesk, which those involved in musical nation-building often viewed as inferior and degenerate: "İbrahim Tatlıses was a Folk Musician. His records went to arabesk and his listeners went with him. Orhan Gencebay, Ferdi Tayfur were Folk Musicians;[33] we could say that all artists engaged with arabesk have their roots in Folk Music. . . . Those creative people might have made more beautiful, more listenable, more national products in the mold of folk music. But unfortunately they were forced to make arabesk" (TRT 1991, 6–7).

If it weren't for the anonymity policy, so the argument goes, gifted musicians such as Tatlıses, Gencebay, and Tayfur might have poured their energies into composing new türküler that would have drawn listeners toward the supposedly more edifying genre. Folk music's vitality could only be sustained by an infusion of new türküler that would only be created by authoring them. As Öztürk put it, "For those of us who love Folk Music, who are going to be alive in the year 2000, these three thousand or so türküler [that we have now] won't be enough to satisfy our musical taste. I don't think there will be this common sharing, this shared feeling. Therefore, I am a person who looks favorably on the idea of the TRT making space for besteler in the style of folk music" (38). The proponents of beste türküler also explicitly referenced the effects of the state's neoliberal turn. Zihni Derçin, who as director of the TRT Music Office presided over the 1991 meeting, pointed out, "Furthermore, there is no more financial support

126 *Copyright Consciousness*

coming to the TRT from the state. The cost of our broadcasts is going to be met by advertising and this will keep the Institution alive and serving people. The general director . . . has told us not to spend so much; the administrators are constantly warning us. An important source of our income is advertising" (49). Derçin joins the voices opposing the anonymity policy, viewing the broadcast of newly composed türküler as an attraction that might help draw in audiences and advertising revenue in the environment of this newly transformed economic and cultural policy.

Traditionalists like Tüfekçi held their rhetorical ground in the face of these attacks on the anonymity policy. They denied the idea that the old modalities of türkü production had died. As Tüfekçi's wife—the prominent singer and long-time conservatory instructor Neriman Altındağ Tüfekçi, herself a staunch traditionalist—had put it at the 1990 Special Advisory Committee meeting: "The riverbed of folk production will not dry up. . . . It is such a waterfall that if we dry up the waterfall, it will find other branches and emerge somewhere else. . . . But if beste music gets put into the folk production, if we try to spread our own personal expressions and call them folk music, in that case we will dry it up, we will dry up the spring" (TRT 1990, 31). At the 1991 meeting, where those in attendance ultimately voted to allow newly composed türküler into folk music programming, Nida Tüfekçi pronounced ominous warnings.

> You know that [the results of] this meeting will be written and published, and as a historical document all of our names will be there, and in the decision we make, how on target are we going to be? I'm filled with worry about whether we are doing something good or something bad, and I feel this historical responsibility in my conscience, in my mind. I am a person who believed in Folk Music, and I have lived my life that way. My worry is, can this issue be exploited? If it is exploited and beste music and Folk Music become mixed up with each other, how will we be able to sort them out? And second, are we making a decision that will kill *derleme* and *derlemecilik* [folk song collection and its craft]? By way of conclusion, is it possible that because the royalties are greater, more than the payment for a derleme, real, collected Folk Music melodies will be claimed as composed works and pass over to the other category? (TRT 1991, 142)

On this last count, Tüfekçi was perhaps right to be concerned, as we shall see in chapter 5. He punctuates his concerns with an ominous assertion, invoking the ghost of (his version of) the master himself: "Yesterday evening in our dinner meeting we had Muzaffer Sarısözen amongst us. Without our inviting him, without our knowing it, without our being conscious of it, but he came himself, he made his presence felt there and he said, 'For heaven's sake, be careful!' That's what I felt" (142).

THE LEGACY OF THE ANONYMITY POLICY

The Turkish newspaper *Milliyet* published an article several days after the 1991 meeting with the headline: "Reform in Folk Music: Two Extremes Come Together at the TRT Folk Music Advisory Committee." The article was by Dedeoğlu, the veteran journalist who had documented the clash between Tüfekçi and Demirsipahi in the 1970s. "Composed works will now be accepted into the TRT Turkish Folk Music Repertoire," it announced (Dedeoğlu 1991). A photo shows Demirsipahi and Tüfekçi posing casually with a few other members of the committee. The caption reads, "TRT Music Office Director Zihni Derçin oversaw the rapprochement of Nida Tüfekçi, known within Folk Music as a conservative, and lawyer Cemil Demirsipahi, known for his progressive efforts in music."

In retrospect, the article was perhaps misguided in some of its enthusiasm. The decisions of TRT's Special Advisory Committee meetings were never binding. During my dissertation fieldwork (2013–2016), the Repertoire Committee still was not allowing works with known authorship into the TRT Repertoire. That said, Erkan Sürmen, another longtime musician-bureaucrat active in the TRT Folk Music Division, claimed to me that during the early 1980s the division's leadership had intentionally allowed an increasing number of türküler composed by âşıklar into the TRT Repertoire (interview, February 5, 2015). Unofficially, the policy's application relaxed still further in the 1990s. I commonly heard complaints, even from members of the pro-beste camp, that the 1990s had seen the entry or reentry of countless items into the TRT Repertoire, including aesthetically inferior, "contrived" items that did not belong there. To make matters worse, they continue to appear as anonymous, failing to document their authors, at least in the TRT Repertoire notation and catalogs.

For proponents of newly composed folk music, TRT's anonymity policy had had some painful consequences. For believers in TRT's reformist agenda of preserving and promoting folk music, the instances of composed türküler presented as anonymous in broadcasts deceived the public and blighted the integrity of the TRT Repertoire itself. In addition to ethical concerns about publicly acknowledg-

128 *Copyright Consciousness*

ing authorship, there were legal and financial concerns. For active TRT artists, some of whom valued performance on TRT over and above any career they might have had in the private sector, the notation submitted to the TRT Folk Music Repertoire Committee might be the earliest documentation of a given türkü, and it documented the türkü as anonymous. Öztürk told me that he no longer submits his own besteler to the Repertoire Committee because once in the TRT Repertoire, record producers on the private market would hold it up as evidence that he had not composed it, using this to justify denying him royalty payments (interview, May 12, 2015).[34]

In other cases, another musician might register the türkü under their own name and start collecting royalties from commercial recordings on it. The actual composer may have a difficult time sorting the issue out during a long and potentially expensive legal process. Folklorist and folk music artist Halil Atılgan—with whom I struck up a friendship during my many visits to consult with him on the topics discussed in this chapter—grew exasperated as he animatedly recalled such an experience in one of our early conversations. Atılgan claims to have composed "Gide gide bir söğüde dayandım" (As I went along I leaned against a willow), a gorgeous, brooding türkü about a heartbreak.[35] According to his account, he wrote the song in the style of a genre of women's songs called *henk havaları* found in the Adana/Karaisalı region. Atılgan performed the song on a TRT television broadcast in 1977, passing it off as a folk song he had collected because otherwise he would not have been allowed to perform it under the anonymity policy. Atılgan recalls that Tüfekçi, who had been on the program with him, apparently liked the song and subsequently transcribed it off the tape of the show, adding it to the official TRT Repertoire. The TRT notation shows Atılgan as the türkü's source musician and Tüfekçi as its collector. This created an early record documenting the song as an anonymous work. About a decade later, when MESAM had been recently formed, affording the possibility of accruing ongoing royalties from composition rights, another artist recorded the song, and it suddenly became a high-selling hit. When Atılgan went to MESAM to collect royalties on the song, he found that a record producer had claimed the composer credit himself. The burden of proof fell on Atılgan to show that he had authored it, despite the record producer's claim. Some thirty years later, Atılgan was still fighting to claim his rights in a lawsuit, but the documentary record was working against him. In the end, he only succeeded in contesting the record producer's claim, but the song ended up with an anonymous/public

Copyright and Traditionalism in Broadcasting **129**

domain credit. Atılgan still receives no royalties from the many recordings and performances of the song.

Some of my interlocutors dismissed such complaints. Traditionalists I spoke with often doubted musicians' claims to have composed a türkü in the TRT Repertoire, suspecting that they were only out to profit from the royalties. One whom I asked about "Gide gide bir söğüde dayandım" doubted Atılgan's claim, opining that if he had composed it, the lyrics would have sounded more "literary" (*edebi*) and the Repertoire Committee would have known it immediately. Bağlama virtuoso and former MESAM president Arif Sağ minimized the extent of the issue as "100–150 türküler out of 15,000" (interview, June 9, 2015). By contrast, Atılgan's 2003 book *Revolt of the Türküler* (Türkülerin İsyanı) offers a five-hundred-page compendium of examples of purported erasures of authorship and other errors in the TRT Repertoire. Most of my interlocutors, however, expressed greater concern about the opposite problem: false claims of authorship over anonymous türküler rightly in the public domain; this is an issue I consider in detail in chapter 5.

CONCLUSION

In this chapter, I have documented how actors in official state broadcasting responded to the dramatic developments of the mid- to late twentieth century—the history of commercial recording artists taking up folk music, technological novelties including broadcasting and recording, mass migration and urbanization, neoliberal cultural policy, and early copyright activism—that threatened to disrupt the creative processes and the noncommercial ethos thought to have produced folk music. While international scholarship was debating whether orality and literacy represented essentially different modalities of human communication that belonged to radically distinct epochs of social evolution, versions of these debates played out among folk music artists and experts in Turkey. Was anonymous, folkloric creativity still viable? Might musicians from a literate milieu legitimately contribute to the country's body of folk music? What should be the status of any such newly composed folk songs? As an extensive musicological literature on Turkey has repeatedly discussed, in its early days radio had functioned as a tool for disseminating localized musical traditions, reframing them as national heritage. Here, I have examined a shift that such literature has neglected: as the music became more popular through increasingly mass-mediated channels, it was used in ever new contexts by individuals with varying understandings of its boundaries. The music's construction as noncommercial heritage gave it a quasi-sacred status, motivating traditionalists to defend it through such mechanisms as the renewed anonymity policy. For the purposes of my own argument, the most important legacy of the story I have told here is how these developments shaped the emergent sense of copyright legality in folk music. With the rise of a more effective copyright infrastructure in the 1990s and 2000s, there would be new stakes to the contestation of legality in the genre.

FIVE

When Copyright Meets Folk Music

In 2005, MESAM—the larger of Turkey's two copyright collecting societies for musical authors[1]—organized a two-day symposium of leading experts on folk music. Some of the participants were academic folklorists or musicologists, some were composers, some were recording artists, and some were lawyers (MESAM 2005). MESAM had been in operation for nearly twenty years, and yet there were a series of unresolved issues with implementing copyright in the folk music genre specifically. Many asserted that it was too easy for ill-intentioned individuals to falsely claim authors' rights in anonymous folk music. The copyright system offered no good way to halt what many participants considered to be corruptive or inappropriate uses of folk music heritage. Some participants felt there should be a copyright for collectors of folk music, while others objected to this idea (see chapter 6). Finally, where ownership of türküler might be contested, the system for resolving these conflicts was unsatisfactory, especially because both folk music institutions and the record industry had left a spotty and questionable documentary record of authorship.

It is hardly surprising that the genre of folk music presented special problems for the copyright system. Worldwide, much ink has been shed about how copyright laws leave traditional culture unprotected (for a few examples of scholarship in this area, see Dutfield 2003; Robinson, Abdel-Latif, and Roffe 2017). The mechanisms of copyright were not designed for scenarios where authors are unknown or where creators partake in dynamic cultural practices rather than fixing artistic expressions in a tangible medium of expression. In fact, in the same year that MESAM held its symposium, the World Intellectual Property Organization (WIPO) published the first in a series of booklets addressing these issues in an international context (WIPO 2005). While the Turkish state has not responded by creating *sui generis* protection regimes for traditional cultural expressions as have some other countries, the discourse about applying copyright in folk music focused on a similar set of issues.

I began researching copyright in Turkey more than eight years after the MESAM symposium. I had not initially intended to research the topic. While working on other aspects of folk music in Turkey, I found myself in MESAM's office in March 2014, almost on a lark. When I mentioned my interest in folk music to two lawyers working for the society, they began describing a litany of challenges the genre presented for them, and they generously handed me a copy of the symposium's proceedings. By 2014, the copyright environment in Turkey was changing rapidly. A new revision to the statute was in the works. Streaming platforms were poised to dramatically reshape musical distribution. And yet, as I was to discover in the coming months in interviews and conversations with folk music artists and experts—including those who had spoken at the symposium—the issues raised in 2005 persisted. The lawyer who handed me the proceedings remarked that these issues "come up at every meeting of the board of directors," and "since our members come in frequently to ask for [these proceedings], very few copies are left."

In interactions with many people in Turkey—especially nonexperts or people with only an everyday knowledge of folk music—I often encountered the idea that copyright simply had nothing to do with the genre. Türküler were anonymous and in the public domain, so how could they be subject to copyright? But individuals active in the music industry or the legal system understood that the situation was more complex. Some folk songs had known authors or were at least subject to claims of authorship that had to be taken seriously. Even where no one claimed authorship, one could claim rights in an arrangement of a türkü or profit from neighboring rights in a folk music recording. The copyright system would somehow have to negotiate the complexities the genre presented.

In this chapter, I argue that the construction of folk music as anonymous, noncommercial heritage, outlined in chapters 3 and 4 of this book, mediated this negotiation by shaping the legal consciousness of those involved. That is, it motivated and informed how actors participated in constituting copyright legality in the folk music sector. Here, I offer an ethnographic account of these dynamics. Folk music's quasi-sacred status as national heritage charged the purportedly false authorship claims over türküler with a particular ethical valence. It animated the debate over objectionable uses of folk music that the copyright system afforded no mechanisms to prevent. Finally, it colored how copyright

When Copyright Meets Folk Music **133**

administrators, courts, and recording artists alike perceived and evaluated the creativity involved in contemporary arrangements of public domain folk music. I analyze a policy implemented during the main period of my fieldwork: from 2001 to 2021, Turkey's copyright collecting societies for musical authors (MESAM and MSG) offered only a limited (10 percent) royalty on such arrangements. This policy diverged from common international practice, and it presented an imperfect solution to the problem of how to value contemporary creativity in the folk music genre. I document a range of kinds of arrangement in folk music, showing how folk music experts' and copyright officials' assessments that often minimize the value of these arrangements are motivated by ideologies of creativity that attended folk music's construction as national heritage. The policy therefore reveals how localized discourses of creativity and national belonging shape copyright legality, though music sector politics, legal doctrine, and bureaucratic convenience are also key factors.

THE THEFT OF FOLK MUSIC

> Now ever since copyright [*bu telif haklarından sonra*], quite a few people's son or daughter or grandchild has started to say "this was my grandfather's composition [*beste*]." It's not a composition! It's an anonymous work from that region. [They're saying that] because money will come from it.
>
> *Daughter of a renowned folk music artist*

When I broached the topic of copyright in my many conversations and interviews with folk music artists, scholars, and enthusiasts, the most common issue they raised was the recent history of individuals using the copyright system to claim the rights in anonymous türküler. While there were cases of individual musicians composing türküler (see chapter 4), the complaints focused on the many cases in which those knowledgeable about folk music felt the authorship claims to be false. The outrage such individuals expressed revealed how the construction of folk music as heritage shaped perceptions of legality around such claims.

In some cases, popular recording artists performed arranged or popularized versions of türküler and claimed the composition rights in them because they had recorded them despite the fact that according to copyright doctrines merely performing, arranging, or recording a song does not make one its author. There is a long history of such arrangements in Turkey, but they particularly increased in popularity in the 1960s and 1970s, when urban youth took up an interest in their roots and began performing türküler with rock instruments, sometimes also incorporating traditional Anatolian instruments such as the long-necked lute bağlama or the end-blown flute *kaval*, in a genre that came to be known as Anadolu Pop (Meriç 2006; Skoog 2012; Baysal 2018). Many of the türküler such groups performed were staples of TRT folk music programming, while others were songs by politically outspoken âşıklar whose lyrics appealed to leftist youth in the polarized environment of the era (Sharpe 2019).[2] Arabesk performers have also frequently recorded türküler, rendering them with the melodramatic vocal delivery, Arab-inspired beats, and spectacular string sections that mark the genre. While many popular musicians were and are conscientious about crediting such songs as public domain or the work of an âşık or other musician, I did hear of cases when recording artists had quietly registered such songs as their own to collect royalties (cf. Seeman 2019, 292). In some cases, record companies may have credited a recording artist as composer against their own will; the widow of the Anadolu Pop icon Cem Karaca asserted that this had happened in several cases where Karaca had recorded Armenian folk songs with newly composed Turkish words (Yıldız 2018, 138).

In another kind of scenario, folk music performing artists who engaged in their own folk song collection efforts might claim the composition rights in the türküler and tunes they had learned from musicians in the Anatolian countryside. In fact, as I describe in greater detail in chapter 6, folk music experts and other actors in the IP system debated whether a copyright for such collectors should in fact be recognized. Sometimes it was rural musicians themselves who claimed the rights in türküler in their own performing repertoire, which urban folk music performers and enthusiasts felt were anonymous. As suggested by the quote in the epigraph above, it was also frequently the heirs to the estates of rural twentieth-century source musicians who claimed that their testators had composed a türkü they had recorded. Âşıklar often are the composers at least of the lyrics of the türküler they record, and they traditionally value distinguishing these works from the works of prior masters (*usta malı*) that they nonetheless perform in order to honor these forebears. One folk music performer complained about the "ignorance" of the descendants of such âşıklar or other rural source musicians, heirs who "think everything the âşık sang belonged to them."

Given the popularity of âşık songs on the wider market for a variety of genres, the composition rights in âşık songs with known composers might also be claimed by recording artists inhabiting more powerful positions in the industry. In particular, the revival of music of the Alevi religious minority since the 1980s has exacerbated this dynamic. Some cases of purported theft involved famous Alevi performers who had popularized religious songs (*deyişler*) composed or transmitted by rural *dedeler* (spiritual leaders; sing. *dede*), whose recordings often circulate on informal tapes created by amateur documentarians devoted to Alevi ritual and music. Such rural sources sometimes reportedly received no compensation. When I asked one âşık what he thought âşıklar should do in such situations, however, he responded that they should say nothing because commercial concerns had nothing to do with being an âşık. One recording artist speculated that Alevis may refrain from protesting these situations because of the traditional Alevi value around being the master of one's tongue (*diline sahip olmak*). Several âşıklar did complain to me, however, about recording artists who failed to sing the final verse of their poems, which contain the âşık's pen name and function to credit the lyric's author. In another kind of scenario that likely predates the modern recording industry, they also decried cases when âşıklar might appropriate the poems of other âşıklar by replacing the original lyric with their own pen names in this final verse.[3]

Many in the folk music industry referred to such questionable authorship claims as "theft" (*hırsızlık*). As one performer and music scholar put it, "I used to play ball on a field that belonged to all of us. Now it belongs to someone else. It's being usurped [*gasp ediliyor*]." At the conclusion of a talk I gave to an audience of Turkish music scholars in which I considered whether aspects of the international integration of the country's copyright system represented a form of neocolonialism, one audience member promptly asked, "What about when musicians claim the rights in anonymous türküler? Is that colonialist?" In another case, I managed to secure a brief interview with a rock recording artist and board member from one of the collecting societies, only to find myself spending the bulk of the time responding to his string of questions about the issue of false authorship claims in folk music.

One metaphor I repeatedly encountered compared the claiming of anonymous türküler to urban migrants' construction of illegal squatter settlements (*gecekondu*) on public lands on the outskirts of Turkey's major cities in the mid-twentieth century. Politicians eager to woo these populations famously offered to grant them deeds on this land in exchange for their votes if elected (see Karpat 1976, 65).[4] Beyond the anger at this appropriation of public lands, established urban populations resented the cultural differences these migrants brought with them, including their taste for the popular musical genre arabesk, which traditionalists at official music institutions disdained and censored (Stokes

136 *Copyright Consciousness*

1992). I was thus never sure that the comparison didn't carry a whiff of elitism, an alarmist fear of cultural degradation.

Accusations could be particularly fraught when the alleged theft transgressed communal lines. For example, among the many allegations leveled at iconic Abdal folk music artist Neşet Ertaş (more below) are a few that accuse him of stealing the melodies of Kurdish-language songs, setting Turkish lyrics to them, and claiming the composition rights. One YouTube poster, for example, juxtaposes a 1968 recording called "Min Te Ditibû" (I had seen you) by Risteme İsko and Ciwan Haco's 1970 recording of "Rêya'm dûr e" (My road is long), both in Kurdish, with Neşet Ertaş's later songs "Gönül Dağı" (Mountain of the heart) and "Tatlı Dile Güler Yüze" (Sweet tongue, smiling face) respectively (see Tirk'an 2018; Beki 2015). The melodic similarity of each pairing is striking. The resemblance could be naturalized by taking it as a sign of "the closeness of the [Kurdish and Turkish] peoples to each other" and by asserting the similarity of many Anatolian folk melodies to each other, as one commenter on the YouTube video has done. Yet for some Kurds I spoke with, such cases seemed inseparable from the painful history of the erasure of Kurdish culture and language by the Turkish state, which often involved replacing Kurdish-language song texts with Turkish ones (see O. Aksoy 2018; Yıldız 2018).

The rumors on the topic of stolen türküler swirled. My fieldnotes are littered with examples my interlocutors reported to me. I often found these hard to confirm or unethical to publish, yet the sense of injustice I encountered was real. I heard from multiple musicians who had recorded what they thought to be an anonymous türkü on an album only to later receive a threatening phone call from a lawyer representing a recording artist who had claimed the song's rights through a collecting society. In other cases, musicians discovered such rights claims by checking with MESAM or MSG before releasing a recording but found themselves facing the distasteful prospect of negotiating an authorization fee for what they considered a public domain work.[5] One recording artist in this situation confronted the young woman who had claimed the rights in a türkü he wanted to record, and she became embarrassed. The recording artist had a recording of the türkü from before the woman had been born. He thought the situation was common, and he had little fear of being sued. "They know what they're doing," he told me, "and if they objected, the truth would come out."

When Copyright Meets Folk Music **137**

THE CHALLENGE OF ADDRESSING TÜRKÜ THEFT

There were several ways in which the legal system seemed to afford questionable authorship claims. In observing this dynamic, a variety of actors voiced a critical legal consciousness, critiquing how a system designed to protect authors' rights could be exploited in unjust ways that could not always be successfully countered through the legal system itself. When recording an album, labels or recording artists report composer, lyricist, and arranger credits to MESAM or MSG. The collecting societies then create database records on the basis of this prima facie claim, and they begin distributing royalties according to these database records. Royalty distributions can proceed for some time before someone challenges the authorship claim. Legal experts (and the societies) emphasize that these initial assignments of authors' rights are provisional (*karine*), but the system puts the burden of proof on the person who contests the claim. A common form of evidence used to contest authorship claims are credits on old vinyl or gramophone records or a published notation or lyric. However, many in the industry viewed these old forms of documentation with suspicion. In the lax copyright environment in which many of these records were produced and which predated the IP reform of the 1980s and 1990s, there might have been little incentive to research composer credits carefully or to contest someone's claim to have authored a türkü. Many old records also fail to note a date of publication, making it difficult to compare the relative age of conflicting evidence of authorship. While some old records list composer/lyricist credits for a given song, others name someone only as the performer (*okuyan*), while still others provide an ambiguous credit that simply lists the recording artist's name without specifying a relationship to the song. There were also stories that circulated about record producers who would sign an authorization agreement with a composer to allow a recording artist to perform a song, but then the label would credit the performing artist as songwriter on the record. There seem to have been a few publishing companies in the 1960s and 1970s monitoring records released on the market and attempting to keep record labels honest; these included MESAM founder Nevzat Sümer's company FİSAN (see chapter 1). But FİSAN specialized in Turkish classical music, and in my research I did not encounter any records or memory of a publisher working in folk music.

Those wishing to contest an authorship claim can appeal to their collecting society's Technical Expertise Committee (*teknik bilim kurulu*). Both MESAM and MSG have such committees, each staffed with a rotating cadre of knowledgeable musicians elected from the society's membership and advised by lawyers the society employs. Here too, I documented a series of complaints, however. One musician with a large record collection told me he had made a list of türküler he considered anonymous but that were registered under individuals' names in one of the society's databases. He told me he had sent the list, along with photocopies of old records crediting the works as anonymous, to the society, but the society had purportedly done nothing. I was unable to confirm the story with the society's staff, who told me they had no significant backlog of challenges to authorship credits at the moment. One musicologist thought the societies were sometimes granting a composition right to the first recording artist to perform a türkü on a record. However, when I discussed this with staff at one of the societies, they emphasized that the record must credit a composer/lyricist (*söz/müzik*) and not a performer (*okuyan*). A common perception was that an ill-intentioned recording artist might change a single word in a türkü or in its title and claim rights over the song in this way. Again, collecting society staff viewed this as a kind of urban legend; conceivably, the recording artist in question might have a right over the change itself if it was original enough (but not, by extension, over the underlying work). Altering a word might be a strategy for slipping one's false claim over a work into the database without notice, but it could be challenged, and the Technical Expertise Committee would deliberate over this carefully. Finally, there was always the recourse of appealing to the courts, though this would mean relying on similar sorts of evidence to those the Technical Expertise Committees used. When I spoke with judges during a phase of my research in which I was visiting courts to request documents related to case law, some of them raised further issues with the process of determining copyright ownership. In one case involving Kurdish musicians, a court ordered new expert witness reports because they didn't trust the initial reports drawn up by Turkish musicologists, whom they suspected did not know the relevant repertoires as well as Kurdish musicological experts would. In another case, the Court of Cassation—the highest appeals court—had overturned a lower court ruling on the basis of evidence that the lower court did not think should be accepted in court (a photocopy, which might be easily doctored, of an old record).

I did hear of instances in which false authorship claims were successfully challenged through this system. The daughter of a well-known, now deceased folk music recording artist who had been accused of falsely claiming a number of türküler even told me that the family had initiated transactions through MESAM when they realized, on the basis of their own collection of her father's records, that he had been credited incorrectly. In another case, Hasan Saltık, the late owner of the influential label Kalan Müzik, told me that he had met with MESAM officials together with Neşet Ertaş, who was signed to the label and who was frequently accused of stealing türküler (including those thought to have been composed by others; see Fossum 2023b). In the meeting, they removed Ertaş's name from many of these database entries. In Saltık's account, many of these cases had actually resulted from other recording artists who incorrectly credited Ertaş when they recorded their own versions of songs that he had performed but not authored.

I also heard about the reverse complaint: works with known authors being credited as anonymous. In one case, a folk music artist who had composed a türkü discovered that someone else had recorded it and claimed that it was anonymous by reporting it under a different title. The folk music artist only became aware of the issue when one of his students noticed it and told him about it. While the folk music artist got the registration corrected, the experience jaded his view of the collecting society. He told me, "This is not a serious way to work. You need to have an expert in charge. When you submit the list of works on an album, you should have to include the sheet music for the works. The expert should look at the notations. The notation goes into the computer. They should look to see whether or not it is the same name or the same melody, and only after that give permission [to make the recording]. [Instead,] they put some bureaucrat over there who doesn't understand music or notation."

A number of folk music experts, especially those familiar with TRT and its top-down, bureaucratic approach to regulating and promoting folk music on the airwaves, made similar complaints. They thought there should be some academic mechanism, perhaps a panel of musicological experts, who would proactively determine and assign the rights in folk music, policing false authorship claims on türküler. Some viewed the system in place to be haphazard and easily manipulated. Some thought the societies should carefully consult the official TRT Folk Music Repertoire as an authoritative source on authorship and anonymity. One folk music scholar and performer suggested, for example, that MESAM should bring in a panel of folk music experts annually to review türküler that had been claimed by individuals and examine them, analyzing how they were constructed melodically and lyrically, to determine if they were anonymous or not. The proposed committee sounded something like the TRT Turkish Folk Music Repertoire Committee, which reviews submissions to be added to the agency's programming repertoire (see chapter 4). The calls for such a mechanism

140 *Copyright Consciousness*

thus reveal how the experience of the older cultural policy regime shapes some actors' engagements with the copyright system in turn.

The problem with such suggestions was that collecting society officials are limited by the copyright statute itself, which requires no copyright registration and stipulates that claims to copyright rights as inscribed on published copies must be accepted until valid evidence of an older claim contradicts them (see Turkey's Law on Intellectual and Artistic Works, article 11). When one of the collecting societies generously allowed me to observe their Technical Expertise Committee at work, I was struck that—contrary to some of the critiques I encountered in conversations with many people in the industry—the committee was made up of top-notch musicians who were adept at analyzing musical similarities. A trained lawyer also attended the meeting to consult on the bases the law afforded for determining authorship. However, the committee's hands seemed clearly tied to written documentary forms of evidence, and all they could do if they doubted an authorship claim was to call knowledgeable individuals to see if they had compelling forms of evidence, such as an old record, that might overturn the claim. Furthermore, the society's staff told me they no longer used the TRT Repertoire as a form of evidence because of the numerous cases of türküler with known authors being represented as anonymous at TRT.

One of the Technical Expertise Committee's members described a final challenge they struggled with: the many cases when folk musicians such as âşıklar had created a version of a traditional melody (see chapter 6). Often it was unclear whether the version constituted a new composition altogether or a variation on an old anonymous one. Such rural musicians often perceived a tune to be their own work where urban specialists viewed it as an insignificant variation on a well-documented anonymous one. One example from a paper by folklorist Süleyman Şenel was read aloud in a presentation at the 2005 symposium: "We remember it like it was yesterday. It was August 1983. In a village of Dirmil, a folk artist named Necat, who was participating with his *saz* in a musical gathering, before singing a türkü said, 'This is my composition,' and played a 'Teke zortlatması' that was not at all unfamiliar to our ears. Taşköprülü Fikriye Yurtseven performs some hymns and says some of them are his compositions but doesn't realize that these are hymns in the style of Sufi lodges and, taking Sufi poems and putting them to melodies without knowing to whom they belong, calls this composition" (Ergüner 2005, 75).[6] The example highlights how rural concepts of creativity may diverge from more widely circulating understandings of authorship and ownership, a further dynamic that those implementing copyright in folk music must navigate.

When Copyright Meets Folk Music 141

PROTECTING FOLK MUSIC HERITAGE

Türküler, folk türküler, are something sacred that has been entrusted to us. It
is not only the duty of those connected with Folk Music to protect
this trust; it is a whole nation's responsibility. It is a responsibility
that cannot be renounced.

Folk music doyen Nida Tüfekçi speaking at a meeting of a TRT *special
advisory committee on folk music (*TRT *1991, 47)*

Like all folklore goods, folk music, which is an important part
of our folklore, has been created by the folk, our "folk products," which
have been brought forward and are the heritage of our ancestors to our
nation. The owner of this treasury that is called Turkish Folk Music is
the Turkish nation. The Turkish nation lives with the Turkish state
and will live even if the world stops. This rich fortune that belongs
to our nation can only be and must be claimed by the state.

MESAM *founder Nevzat Sümer (Sümer 2005, 72)*

As these two epigraphs—one from someone powerful in institutions of musical
folklore and one from a prominent music copyright activist—suggest, much of
the rhetoric around copyright in folk music focused on the fact that the legal
regime left public domain folk songs and tunes unprotected. The problem wasn't
only that ill-intentioned individuals seemed to be appropriating the public heritage of folk music by claiming authors' rights in it; a few loud voices complained
about some of the *ways* folk music was used. Where musical works had known
authors, rightsholders could leverage their rights to stop uses that didn't suit
their taste (see chapter 2). But no one could stop objectionable uses of türküler
in the public domain. The alarm bells that certain traditionalists raised about
folk music's vulnerable status highlight how the genre had been constructed as
a sacred national heritage. For some, copyright's failure to offer any mechanism
for protecting this heritage represented a moral failure with the legal regime.
This apparent failure both shaped their narratives about the law and informed
how they sought to change it, such as by calling for the state to claim ownership
of the public domain.

What did türküler need protection from? Several folk music experts I interviewed, especially those who had participated in TRT's traditionalist approach
to folk music, complained about the use of türküler in advertising jingles or

142 *Copyright Consciousness*

television program theme music, which they characterized as "corruption" (*bozulma* or *yozlaşma*). These uses often involved altering or re-writing the türkü's lyrics to sell a product or fit the theme of a show. Even more often, traditionalists objected when recording artists performed türküler in popular music styles. They often complained about "arabeskified" (*arabeskleşmiş*) versions of türküler, but there were examples beyond the controversial arabesk genre as well. Sometimes these involved altering lyrics or losing the spirit of the emotions the türkü is thought to express. Musicologist Sadi Yaver Ataman once complained about a case when a popular recording artist set a türkü with the sorrowful lyric, "I've fallen into pain without a cure, doctor please give me a cure" to a cha-cha beat (TRT 1974, 53).

At the time of my fieldwork, the genre that most rankled folk music traditionalists was *Ankara havaları* (see Satır 2012; Tan 2013; also known as *Ankarabesk*). Here, performers at seedy dance clubs called *pavyon* incorporate Ankara regional folk tunes and songs into their repertoire, accompanying themselves with electrified bağlama, synthesizer, and drum kit or drum machine and often interpolating (sometimes lewd) new lyrics. In 2012 one such performer, Ankaralı Coşkun (Direk), scored a nationwide smash hit with his version of the türkü "İp attım ucu kaldı" (I threw a rope and the end stayed), into which he had inserted an infectious lyric refrain referencing Ankara's tangled street grid and someone too drunk to raise their arms. Yet the story of irreverent popular arrangements was an old one. Consider Barış Manço's erotically charged 1973 psychedelic rock classic "Lambaya püf de" (Blow out the lamp). The music is based on a gramophone recording of a folk tune performed by Osman Pehlivan (1847–1942), a staple of 78 RPM records and early folk music radio programming in Istanbul and Ankara. Manço's version adds drums, bass, and an electrosaz filtered through a wah-wah pedal in addition to the traditional bağlama. It starts out by significantly relaxing the tempo of the original before jumping to higher tempo partway through the track. Throughout, Manço softly recites his lyric in a quasi-spoken delivery over top of the traditional tune. The lyric depicts his attempt to seduce an imagined woman, coaxing her to put out the light and darken the room.[7]

Critiques of these uses of folk music often rely on an enduring (if problematic) binary constructed between "commercial" (*piyasa*) and noncommercial music. Various organs of the state, including TRT, promoted official versions of folk and traditional art music by supporting some artists with regular salaries to perform on the airwaves or in regular ensembles. The traditionalists running these state organizations often viewed the "commercial" world of the private

When Copyright Meets Folk Music **143**

recording industry and entertainment venues such as *gazinolar* (nightclubs) with suspicion (see also Beken 1998, 15–39; Seeman 2019, 185–87). As the debate over allegedly corrupt uses of folk music reveals, traditionalists seemed to believe that makers of folk and art music should be motivated purely by an expressive urge; the feelings the music expressed should furthermore be feelings proper to an imagined, idealized image of the nation (see Balkılıç 2009, 2018). The use of türküler in advertising jingles made them tools for commercial pandering, while setting a sad türkü to a cha-cha beat or performing one in the morally questionable environment of an Ankara *pavyon* would distort its expressive power and intent. In the heyday of TRT's broadcasting monopoly, committees at the agency carefully censored programming to filter out such ostensibly "corrupt" takes on folk music. In particular, an older generation who had participated in such projects tended to view it as the state's responsibility to protect folk music heritage from the vagaries of market-driven uses.

The liberalization of broadcast media, which accompanied IP reform in the early 1990s, defanged the old censorship mechanisms. Why hadn't the state done anything to reassert a form of control over folk music and prevent such corruptive uses?[8] Folklorist Nail Tan, who had organized an (ultimately ineffective) petition to revise the copyright statute to empower the Cultural Ministry to claim rights in and protect public domain türküler, suggested a cynical theory: that Cultural Ministry bureaucrats simply didn't want to create more work for themselves (2013, 8). Yet there were a host of other factors that might explain the state's abandonment of the public domain of folk music. The traditionalists clamoring for statist interventions into culture perhaps represented a vocal minority. During the height of state control over the airwaves in the 1970s to 1980s, for example, the pages of the youth culture magazine *Hey* were filled with critiques of TRT's censorship. Younger generations of folk music enthusiasts meanwhile often found official productions stilted and boring. Multiculturalist approaches to folk music furthermore critiqued traditionalist folklore for the nationalist filter that excluded or misrepresented aspects of the ethnically complex origins of the country's folk music heritage. The prospect of state control would introduce a new dimension into these already fraught issues: if the Turkish nation-state were made the owner of works in the public domain, would it be given control of Kurdish, Laz, or other minority heritage?

Ultimately, any push for state policing of folk music went against the tide of the state's neoliberal approach to culture since the 1980s. Furthermore, that so many musicians were appropriating public domain türküler for advertising jingles or interpolating new ideas into them to make pop hits suggests that some musicians were rather inclined to treat the public domain of folk music as a creative resource to be reused and remixed. This inclination aligns with the ideas of many international IP scholars who critique what they frame as various encroachments on the public domain such as bright line rules against unlicensed sampling in the United States or ever-expanding terms of copyright protection (e.g., Vaidhyanathan 2003; McLeod 2005; Boyle 2008; Lessig 2016).[9] Nonetheless, the unprotected status of public domain türküler continued to fuel narratives that depicted the legal system as ineffective at addressing injustices toward folk music heritage.

VALUING ARRANGEMENTS OF ANONYMOUS TÜRKÜLER

The state may have refused to take legal ownership of the public domain and so protect anonymous folklore from objectionable appropriations, but there were also more subtle ways that the old construction of folk music as national heritage seemed to inform actors' legal consciousness and affect copyright policy in turn. In the rest of this chapter, I highlight this dynamic through an intriguing example that I often encountered in my research: the problem of how to assess the originality and quantify the financial value of arrangements of public domain works such as anonymous türküler.

The problem came up relatively unprompted in an interview that I conducted with an executive for a music publishing firm in 2016, for example. We had spoken for over an hour in which he generously and patiently described many details of what he does as a music publisher to advocate for the composers he represents. Such composers often arrange public domain works and collect royalties on the performance of such arrangements via MESAM or MSG. While we had mostly spoken generically about situations that apply to almost any genre of music, as the interview wound down, I turned to the genre that interested me most:

DF: As a last thing, actually my dissertation project has to do with folk music especially. . . . Does folk music in particular cause you any problems, as a genre?

PUBLISHER: Aaah, one of the problems we quite frequently encounter actually is this. . . . If a work is anonymous, there's no one who can restrict you from

When Copyright Meets Folk Music **145**

making an arrangement. You can do it. But in other countries, when you arrange [an anonymous] work the [arranger] can become the owner of 100 percent of the performing right.

DF: Mmm hmm.

PUBLISHER: In Turkey, very unfortunately, in this area, you can't get more than 10 percent of the right as an arranger. So there's this problem that arises.

Here, the publisher offered by way of example a türkü of unknown authorship that was arranged by a composer he represents who used the song as part of a film score. I'll call the composer "composer X" and the song "türkü X" here.

PUBLISHER: When [composer X] arranges [türkü X], because it goes through MESAM, 90 percent [of the royalty share is] anonymous—in other words this share is divided up among [all the other members of MESAM]—and he gets a 10 percent portion as his share. He can't get the other 90 percent. Whenever a . . . member of [German copyright collecting society] GEMA arranges [türkü X], they can take 100 percent of the [performing right]. Even [if the performance is] in Turkey. So unfortunately, we have this loss of our right, our [arrangers] do.[10] [Composer X's] arrangement of "Jingle bells" gets a 10 percent share [of the performing right], but a GEMA member . . . let's say a [British collecting society] PRS member, a member of any collecting society, when a [member] arranges "Jingle Bells" they can take 100 percent. So with Turkish [arrangers], members of MESAM and MSG, we can talk about a 90 percent loss of the right. So for example, [türkü X] was used in [film X]. [Composer X] arranged it. It was very serious music that was widely acclaimed, and it took on a completely different form. Here, let's say our [arranger] earned 1,000 lira from the song. If the [arranger] had been a member of GEMA, they would have earned 10,000 lira. . . . So we're talking about a quite serious loss for our local [arrangers].

In this conversation, the publisher is referencing a policy established by MESAM and MSG: for many years, beginning in the early 2000s, the societies granted only a 10 percent royalty share on arrangements of public domain works (as we shall see, the policy was revised in 2021). The 10 percent policy interests me in part because for many copyright stakeholders, it appeared unjust. They felt that a 10 percent royalty share did not fully recognize the creativity and hard work they had put into arranging a public domain melody. It might seem unfair that when composer X's arranged version of türkü X aired on the radio, for example, 90 percent of the performing royalties the radio station sends to MESAM go into a general pool that is divided among all MESAM members.[11]

However, the alternative scenario that the publisher describes, in which an arranger might earn 100 percent of the performing royalties accrued when their arrangement is performed, could also seem unfair:

> DF: Why did they do it like this? . . .
>
> PUBLISHER: . . . Unfortunately there's this other situation that also arises. With-out making any kind of arrangement, without changing a note, someone is just playing it anew, just doing a re-recording . . . , they can register them-selves as the arranger. Actually, all you've done is had someone perform it again. You haven't added or changed any notes. You haven't done anything. It's the same melody and the same tone [ton]. But unfortunately we can claim that we've made an arrangement, and we earn a royalty on this. In other countries we see that people are much more honest [dürüst] about this. Because in our library catalogue music, people who make a new arrangement of a work by Beethoven, if they haven't changed anything in the notation, they make the performing right 0 percent. . . . But when it happens with us/here [bizde olduğunda], even when it's the same notation, the same notes, they claim that they have made an arrangement and they take 10 percent. So the collecting societies' perspective is this: if we allow [a 100 percent royalty on arrangements of public domain works], everyone is going to do this with anonymous works. So they don't want to grant a royalty for this.

As the publisher's reported experience suggests, the 10 percent policy repre-sented an imperfect solution to an intriguing problem. Copyright is supposed to reward creators for their creativity. Yet there are no clear criteria for measuring the value of this creativity or *how* creative a work is. When a musical work is not in the public domain, when it has a known owner, an arranger must nego-tiate with this owner for permission to make a derivative work—the musical arrangement—over which the arranger will own rights in turn. When this ar-ranged version of the work is broadcast over the radio or performed in another medium, it accrues performing royalties. The proportions according to which the owner(s) of the rights in the underlying work share these royalties with the arranger are determined by the negotiation among them. In effect, instead of measuring the value or amount of the arranger's creative contribution, it mea-

When Copyright Meets Folk Music **147**

sures a power relation between the arranger and the owners of the rights in the underlying work. Arrangers who have a track record of making arrangements that are successful in the market might be able to demand a higher royalty share because the rightsholders may hope that the new arrangement will increase the frequency with which the song is performed. In the case of public domain works, there are no rightsholders for the arranger to negotiate with. Therefore, some other logic must determine how much of a share the arranger can take from the performing royalties. But what should this logic be?

Evident from the publisher's account is that publishers, collecting society officials, and composers are often quite aware of the solutions collecting societies in other countries have chosen. Many such individuals I interviewed believed that arrangers of public domain works in other countries could claim a 100 percent royalty share; this included collecting society officials who had control over this policy point. The situation begged an explanation. Why had MESAM and MSG chosen to grant only 10 percent to these arrangers, especially if they assumed societies in other countries granted 100 percent?

While I asked a number of knowledgeable people about the 10 percent policy, I never got a satisfying answer. I suggest that there is no single answer; rather, to make sense of the 10 percent policy, we have to consider several factors. In the rest of the chapter, I will provide some context by first offering some examples of arrangements of folk music in Turkey to give a sense of the range of the kinds of originality involved. Then I will describe a series of factors that together help to make sense of the 10 percent policy.

Among these factors, however, there is one I particularly aim to highlight and that supports my overall argument that recurring narratives about Turkey's specific history, and especially the construction of folk music as national heritage, informs actors' legal consciousness and shapes policy in turn. If the 10 percent policy diverged from practice in other countries, this suggests that policymakers might justify their choice in terms of imagined differences between the situation in Turkey and that in other countries. The publisher I cite above, for example, who had access to a database that showed the royalty shares foreign arrangers of public domain works earned on their arrangements, assumed that these foreign rightsholders were more "honest" in their rights claims than were Turkish rightsholders. In my research, I found that other such social imaginaries also seemed to inform discussions of copyright policy. In particular, I argue that the historical framing of Turkey's folk music as a noncommercial body of national heritage imbued the genre with a Romantic aura. As a result of this framing—and likely in response also to the issues I have described as "the theft of türküler" above—policy makers may see it as their role to guard this heritage from excessive commercial exploitation. Limiting the royalty share an arranger can earn on an anonymous work may be a strategy for inhibiting such exploitation.

Arranging Public Domain Works in Turkey

So what sorts of creativity are involved in arranging folk music in Turkey? As catalogued for example in Martin Greve's book *Makamsız* (2017), in the past several decades there has been a huge variety of ways that performing artists have interpreted Turkey's traditional music, whether *makam*-based urban art music or rural folk music (see also Bates 2016). In this section, I analyze several approaches to arranging folk songs and tunes in order to illustrate the range of creative approaches to arranging folk music. I intend this discussion to be suggestive but not exhaustive in its presentation of the great variety of kinds of arrangement happening today.

One kind of arrangement involves virtuoso performers of the bağlama and other traditional instruments. During my fieldwork in Turkey, I studied bağlama with several different teachers, including the late Ümit Şimşek, who worked at the music school of his brother-in-law, the bağlama virtuoso Erdal Erzincan. I was fortunate to see Erzincan at work in a variety of environments. I saw him teach classes of advanced bağlama students. I saw him practicing blisteringly fast improvisations as he sat around the music school's kitchen area. I saw him give concerts, including several with Iranian *kamancheh* master Kayhan Kalhor. I observed him working in the recording studio, laying down tracks on his own albums as well as on one of Alevi *dede* Dertli Divani's albums. He also generously gave me an interview in which he described how he had developed some of his playing techniques.

Along with bağlama artists like Hasret Gültekin, Arif Sağ, and Erol Parlak, Erdal Erzincan has been part of a cadre of musicians who have pioneered new techniques since about the 1970s, generally pushing the limits of what is possible on the instrument. Setting down the plectrum that has long been a standard tool for urban bağlama players, Erzincan and these other artists developed an approach called *şelpe*, which involves different ways of strumming and plucking the strings with the fingers or tapping on the instrument's fingerboard (Parlak 2000; Baysal 2013; Çalışkan 2018; Baysal and Altınbüken 2019). As Erzincan explained to me in our interview, this process involved traveling around Anatolia

When Copyright Meets Folk Music **149**

and finding inspiration in rural musicians, especially Alevi *dedeler*, who were using such techniques to a limited extent. He also borrowed some ideas from guitarists. Erzincan perfects, expands upon, and deploys these techniques in combination in a way that one would not encounter in traditional Anatolian contexts. He wows audiences with pyrotechnic displays in his renditions of such tunes and songs as "Çeke Çeke," a classic deyiş attributed to sixteenth-century Alevi revolutionary Pir Sultan Abdal and set to a driving 5/8 melody. Another well-known example of how he uses these techniques to reinterpret a folk tune is his well-known recording of "Sinsin halayı," from one of his early albums titled *Anadolu* (2000).

"Sinsin halayı" is a dance tune that was collected and transcribed by Muzaffer Sarısözen from Adnan Türköz (1925–1982), a Kayseri-born âşık and bağlama artist who long performed on Istanbul radio and taught at Istanbul Municipal Conservatory (see "Bünyanlı harbi" 2009). This version appears in TRT's Dance Tune (*Oyun Havaları*) Repertoire, number 110. As one of my bağlama teachers, Şendoğan Karadeli, demonstrated for me, this version would have been played as a straightforward, relatively unadorned single melodic line on a long-necked bağlama. Erzincan plays on the short-necked version of the instrument in a different tuning (*bağlama düzeni*) that affords a different set of sonorities and fingering patterns when strumming across the strings. His version elaborates the tune into a stunning series of variations; for example, where the original features a simple stepwise descending line of quarter notes, Erzincan inserts a rapid-fire series of finger-tapped arpeggios whose peaks sketch out the original melodic contour. While it is traditional to ornament melodies, to borrow a famous line from US case law on arrangements, these were hardly "cocktail pianist variations"[12] that would have been standard fare for bağlama performers, at least at the time of the album's release. The recording is also layered with multiple tracks of bağlama, creating a lush chorus effect. Low in the mix, a sparse bassline outlines a simple but effective counterpoint that suggests harmonic movement, while a frame drum punctuates this wall of sound and holds down the pace as the track drives climactically forward. The track strings the tune together with two others that receive a similar treatment: "Elmaların yongası" and "Kıyılı halayı." With the recording, Erzincan took a fairly obscure tune and turned it into a modern classic that bağlama enthusiasts and the larger folk music listening public now associate most closely with him.

A second kind of arrangement involves adapting folk music to a Western art music idiom. This tradition of arrangement can be traced back at least to the early republican era, when faculty at Istanbul Municipal Conservatory, including Mahmut Ragıp Gazimihal, began collecting folk music with the intention of incorporating it into symphonies and other classical genres in an effort to a create a modernized national Turkish music (Gazimihal 2006; Türkmenoğlu 2021). Early republican composers who participated in this project included Ahmet Adnan Saygun, Cemal Reşit Rey, and Ulvi Cemal Erkin, all of whom were trained in Europe and were influenced by European composers such as Liszt, Chopin, and Dvorak, who similarly incorporated national folk musics into their own works. Rey's "Turkish scenes" (*Türk sahneleri*) arranges a series of folk tunes including *Zeybek* melodies for symphonic orchestra, while "Ten Anatolian Türkü" (*10 Anadolu Türküsü*) recasts a series of türküler for piano. A few composers of later generations have continued working in such an idiom. One such composer is Yalçın Tura, who presented at MESAM's 2005 symposium, arguing passionately that public domain folk music needed to remain available for such artists to arrange in a Western art music style. In his talk, Tura emphasizes how the work that goes into such arrangements is effectively equivalent to creating a new composition altogether:

> While a composer may generally content themselves with such humble characterizations as "harmonized by [*armonileyen*], arranged for multiple voices by [çokseslendiren], [or] arranged by [*düzenleyen*]" before their names when they write a piano accompaniment for a folk tune or arrange it for a multi-part chorus, when they take up a folk melody as a raw material and turn it into an enormous symphonic production by putting it into various guises, at some point we consider them the creator of the entire work without paying too much attention to how they have used folk melodies or putting too much weight on the degree to which some of the themes in the production they have put forth actually originate [as folk melodies]. (Tura 2005, 62–63)

Orchestral arrangements of folk music often appear in television show soundtracks or TV commercials, which are some of the most lucrative arenas for composers in Turkey today.

A third kind of arrangement involves performing türküler with instruments common to international popular music forms. One popular genre that provides a number of examples is the aforementioned Anadolu Pop of the 1960s and 1970s. The tradition continues with performers in various popular genres turning to türküler to expand their repertoire today. Popular arrangements often involve not only choices of instrumentation and style, but also harmonizing the primarily monophonic or heterophonic textures of folk music. As musicologist Ozan Baysal points out, at least in the genre of Anadolu Pop, musicians often experimented with non-standard or non-functional harmonic progressions that fit the distinctive traditional Anatolian melodies they were arranging (2018, 210).

A classic example of Anadolu Pop arrangement is leftist rocker Cem Karaca's famous 1970 song "Dadaloğlu," which was a version of the eponymous nineteenth-century bard's lyric "Kalktı göç eyledi Avşar elleri" (The Avşar people have picked up and moved). Musically, Karaca created a rock arrangement apparently based on the version recorded by leftist folk music icon Ruhi Su, itself likely based on the Abdal master Muharrem Ertaş's own rendition. Karaca's recording opens with an improvised bağlama introduction before his voice dramatically enters with a declamatory "Ay dooooost!"; both are gestures toward the traditional central Anatolian free meter genre *bozlak*, which Ertaş exemplifies. Where Su had more literally translated Ertaş's version for his trademark operatic baritone voice, in Karaca's recording a rock band drops in after the introduction to recast the tune into a driving duple meter that builds to a climax under Karaca's soaring vocal delivery. Dadaloğlu's poem, a statement of defiance on the part of the pastoral Avşar Türkmens against the Ottoman state that sought to forcibly settle them, resonated with the leftist activism of Karaca's own time.

As a second, slightly different example, consider the aforementioned "Lambaya Püf De," which Barış Manço assembled by laying original spoken lyrics over an arrangement of a classic Anatolian bağlama tune. The public MESAM and MSG databases list Karaca and Manço, respectively, as arrangers of the songs, which have public domain credits (aside from Manço's lyricist credit).[13] According to publicly available news items, however, Manço's publisher seems to have petitioned or sued MSG for composition rights, which the society appears to have denied (see "Barış Manço lambaya" 2017).

Accounting for Arrangements

So how should we assess the value of these various forms of arrangement? During my conversations and interviews with musicians and copyright officials, one fact that surprised me was how many individuals seemed to find the 10 percent policy natural. Considering the many sorts of creativity involved in assembling the kinds of arrangements I have described here, I was struck by how musicians often minimized the value of arrangement, finding a 10 percent royalty share to be fair. In fact, Erzincan told me specifically that he had not even claimed the 10 percent arranger's right on his well-known recording of "Sinsin Halayı / Elmaların Yongası / Kıyılı Halayı."[14] Arrangements of this kind were often characterized as "instrumentation" (çalgılama) to distinguish them from forms of arrangement that were more highly valued as such. Many performers of traditional instruments tended not to think of themselves as making arrangements at all, and thus, like Erzincan, they never claimed even a 10 percent right. For example, Recep Ergül, a folk music artist who was president of MESAM when I spoke with him in 2022, does not claim any arranger credits on the türküler he performs. When I asked him about this, he told me he did not consider himself an arranger (though he has composed a number of original songs in the folk music genre).

One IP court judge told me that he thought the derivative right in a musical arrangement really was meant for orchestral arrangements. Yet staff at one of the collecting societies suggested to me that even composers of such orchestral arrangements were awarded only a 10 percent royalty share. While in some of these cases, where the public domain tune seems relatively incidental to the larger orchestral work, composers control full composition rights, in other cases it appears that they control only arranger rights.[15] As one collecting society staffer told me, "[Composer Y] has very serious works of this kind. [Composer Y] takes an anonymous melody and creates almost a twenty-page work from it. Now, what this person has done, to even call this an arrangement is incorrect. So we definitely have to come up with a solution for this problem."

For those arrangers who object to being awarded only a 10 percent royalty share for their arrangement, a recourse is to appeal to their collecting society's Technical Expertise Committee. During a phase of my research in 2014–2015 when I focused on this issue, one of the societies was piloting a modification to the policy, according to which an arranger of a public domain work could appeal to the committee and be awarded as much as a 55 percent royalty share, partly to address situations such as that of "composer Y." In the Technical Expertise Committee meeting I was able to observe, the committee members deliberated on several cases in which arrangers were appealing for a share greater than 10 percent. This included an album of dance-y pop versions of türküler in which the arrangement principally involved choices of instrumentation. One of the members declared, "It's not an arrangement; it's just instrumentation [çalgılama]"; another playfully began singing, "Ten percent, 10 percent [yüzde on yüzde on]," to the tune of one of the türküler. The moment seemed to me to vividly illustrate the extent to which the committee members had come to accept 10 percent as a standard assessment of an arrangement's value. In my debriefing with members

When Copyright Meets Folk Music **153**

of the committee after I had observed their meeting, they emphasized their objectivity in assessing the value of arrangements. They described a recent case in which one of the committee's members had appealed over one of his own arrangements, passionately advocating for the value of the many creative choices and interventions involved in the arrangement. Yet the other members were not swayed, and even he had walked away with only a 10 percent share.

The challenge arrangers faced when appealing for more than 10 percent was the problem of defining objective and quantifiable criteria for assessing the financial value of one's arrangement. During an interview, one former member of a Technical Expertise Committee recalled to me that a musician had once requested a 60 percent share for arranging the famous türkü "Katibim." As this interviewee put it:

> It's sung and played all the time on all twelve of our islands, in Greece, all over the Aegean, something that's leapt to other places in the world and become well-known. How correct can this be within folk culture, this 60 percent? What can you do? Can you change the melody? You've written a bass part under it. Written a few parts. I mean, how much could it be? I don't know, to give 60 percent on this work. We talked about it a lot at the time, how much could it be, how much shouldn't it be. The examples from the West were a little different. There you can give those kinds of shares. But to tell the truth, we couldn't come to a decision. We left it as 10 percent.

Note that this interviewee remarked on how widespread "Katibim" is, as if to suggest that even the choice of song was unoriginal. Such a consideration should be irrelevant to evaluations of the copyrightability of an arrangement, but it perhaps exemplifies a wider-spread tendency to minimize the creativity involved in arranging türküler. One explanation for this tendency may lie in the sense, described in chapter 4, that a discursive rupture has occurred and that the old modalities of anonymous, folkloric creativity have ceased. Current performers tend not to think of themselves as contributors to the ongoing development of türküler but rather as performers of songs that have emerged from such a process that no longer continues.

Collecting society staff and Technical Expertise Committee members both suggested that to earn more than 10 percent an arranger would have to add original interpolations measurable in terms of track time, not in terms of notes appearing simultaneously with the arranged melody. Staff at the collecting society did describe to me a case in which they had granted a 16 percent share, for

154 *Copyright Consciousness*

example, but this was because 6 percent of the track constituted original material (such as an improvised instrumental introduction), with the other 10 percent made up of the standard arranger's share. In another case in which a musician had composed two new verses for a public domain türkü, they had told the musician they could apply for a greater royalty share, but the musician hadn't bothered.

While this solution of measuring arrangement value in terms of track time had the benefit of presenting a quantifiable metric for assessing the arranger's contribution, it fails to account for many other creative choices an arranger might make involving harmony, timbre or instrumentation, and rhythmic accompaniment to the public domain melody. The publisher I cited above, for example, recalled a rare case in which one of his composers *had* been granted greater than a 10 percent royalty share, but this was because the composer had made a track involving an original composition, only part of which incorporated a public domain melody. Thus, the publisher did not feel that arrangements were truly being valued even in exceptions to the 10 percent policy.

So where did the 10 percent policy come from? I interviewed several people whom I thought might have knowledge of the policy's history; these included former staff, lawyers, and elected officials from MESAM. One former MESAM lawyer recalled that the society had at first granted no royalties at all for arrangements, but the general assembly had later voted to grant them. This was likely the result of arrangers' lobbying; one former MESAM staffer even recalled that arrangers had at one point discussed forming their own society to enforce their rights. But why 10 percent? I encountered only educated guesses even from those with good institutional memory. Some speculated that it may have been borrowed from another country's society. While this explanation seemed at odds with the frequent acknowledgement that in other countries the societies grant 100 percent, it is also true that some societies grant less (in the United States, ASCAP grants a 10 percent royalty share for arrangements of public domain works, while BMI awards 20 percent).[16]

The most convincing explanation I encountered was that 10 percent represented the default share an arranger would receive for a work still under copyright. If no contractual agreement establishes a specific royalty share, the Turkish collecting societies' regulations stipulate the following shares: 45 percent for the composer, 45 percent for the lyricist, and 10 percent for the arranger. By analogy, if the composer and lyricist are unknown (or the work is past the term of protection), all that remains is a 10 percent arranger's share. Thus 10 percent may represent a starting point from which debates about granting a larger share

When Copyright Meets Folk Music 155

would have launched. Ten percent may have stuck because of the impossibility of identifying some other satisfying metric. As an answer to why this number would seem so natural to many musicians, however, especially in the face of many objections from arrangers and their publishers, this explanation seems hardly satisfying. In the following sections, I provide additional context that may help make further sense of the policy.

Legal Perspectives on Valuing Arrangements

One important context for considering the 10 percent policy is legal doctrine. In my conversations with legal experts in Turkey, they emphasized that the threshold for legally protectable originality is high in their system relative to that in some other countries. In the United States, for example, landmark cases such as *Feist Publications vs. Rural Telephone Service Co.* have established that only a modicum of creativity is necessary for an expression to be copyrightable.[17] That is, originality may be found even in a quite modest difference between a work and others it resembles. Turkish copyright law establishes the principle of hususiyet, according to which a work must also express something distinct to the author's personality to be copyrightable (Yavuz, Merdivan, and Türkay 2013, 64). In practice this often translates to a relatively higher threshold of originality. In one conversation on the topic, a legal expert raised the example of photographs. Whereas in the United States any photograph is often understood to be subject to copyright because of the creative choices a photographer is assumed to make (in choosing subject matter, angle, lighting, etc.),[18] in Turkey family photographs are often not subject to copyright because they are not considered an artistic expression in the way a famous photographer's work hanging in a museum is.

Turkish case law seemed to implement this higher threshold of originality through findings that minimized the originality involved in many musical arrangements. While describing a recent case in which a client had been denied even a 10 percent derivative right as an arranger, one lawyer commented to me that rights in musical arrangements in Turkey were virtually nonexistent ("yok gibi bir şey"). As mentioned above, the Turkish copyright system often relies heavily on the opinions of musicological experts. One legal scholar handed me an expert witness report from a case in which a well-known musician had prepared the music for a film score. Some of these were original compositions, but in several cases they were performances of public domain works, including anonymous türküler and compositions from traditional urban art music repertoire. The musician claimed derivative rights as the arranger of these works, which he had performed in his own, highly recognizable, individual style, which included ornamenting the melodies in original ways, performing improvised introductions, and making some choices in instrumentation. However, he was denied these derivative rights in the arrangements when the expert musicologists found that the level of creativity in the arrangement was low; they characterized them as mere performance rather than arrangements.

Legal doctrine about the threshold of originality therefore represents one important context for understanding the 10 percent policy: it could be that, attending to the findings of courts and the opinions of musicological experts, collecting society officials and staff may have internalized Turkey's legal doctrines that establish a high threshold for originality. In many cases, this might mean characterizing someone's version of a public domain work as merely a performance rather than an arrangement deserving derivative rights as a work in itself. But such legal doctrine might further fuel a tendency to minimize the originality involved in musical arrangements through granting this limited, 10-percent royalty share even where a version meets the criteria for a protectable arrangement.

Complicating the issue, however, is the fact that Turkey's system reflects widespread legal approaches found across continental Europe; Turkey's law (including its doctrine of hususiyet) was modeled on the German statute. Yet actors in the Turkish copyright system, including the publisher I cite above, asserted that in Germany arrangers were granted a 100 percent share on public domain works. Meanwhile, even in the United States, where the threshold of originality is generally low compared to that in Turkey, legal scholars have argued that musical arrangements represent an area where case law seems oddly to implement a higher threshold than that applied in other kinds of derivative works (Brandstetter 1997; Evans 1997; Fishman 2021). These facts make it unsatisfying to point to distinctive Turkish legal doctrines as an explanation for the 10 percent policy.

Utilitarian Perspectives

Another context to consider in understanding the 10 percent policy is a utilitarian perspective on the purpose of copyright law. As described in chapter 2 of this book, copyright laws are sometimes justified in terms of authors' natural rights, where authors are accorded a right because works express their personality or embody their intellectual labor. But they may also be justified in utilitarian terms, as a way to incentivize creators to put their ideas out into the public sphere and

When Copyright Meets Folk Music **157**

thus contribute to culture. Accordingly, copyright also features mechanisms aimed at preserving public access to this culture.[19] Statutes limit the terms of protection of a work, and doctrines such as fair use in the United States, fair dealing in the United Kingdom, or statutory exceptions in many continental jurisdictions ensure that some uses of copyrighted works do not require a license.

Some of my interlocutors offered explanations for the 10 percent policy that seemed to resonate with such utilitarian or public interest perspectives on the law. One possibility, for example, is that if an arranger could show that it was their own arrangement of a türkü that others were performing, they might be able to obstruct people from performing the türkü. Furthermore, one collecting society staffer opined that if everyone were granted a 100 percent royalty on arrangements of public domain works, no one would write new songs; they would just perform türküler, especially given how popular folk music is in Turkey. Thus the 10 percent policy might incentivize people to create new works. Another collecting society official and a former Technical Expertise Committee member both explained meanwhile the subsequent adaptation to the 10 percent policy—granting up to a 55 percent share for arrangements of public domain works—in similarly utilitarian terms. They told me they thought the aim of this updated policy was to incentivize musicians to make particularly creative reinterpretations that might popularize lesser-known türküler.

The utilitarian reading of the situation can cut both ways, however. Several people, including a collecting society board member and a former staffer, commented that they thought the 10 percent policy led record producers to encourage their artists to record anonymous türküler because they would save money on the mechanical royalties they owe on the sale of recordings. Thus, if the 10 percent policy had been made with utilitarian motives in mind, it may have had perverse or unintended outcomes.

The Politics of Royalty Shares for Arrangers

Another crucial factor to consider in making sense of the 10 percent policy is the often-opposed interests of different actors involved. Here, it may be instructive to consider an international example, that of Ireland. In contrast to what I encountered in Turkey during my fieldwork, the Irish performing rights society IMRO has long taken the approach of granting a 100 percent performing royalty share on arrangements of public domain works.[20] As detailed in ethnomusicologist Anthony McCann's account (2002, 71–99), in the late 1990s IMRO was attempting to legitimate its right to collect royalties on music performed at traditional Irish sessions, the semi-formal gatherings of musicians stringing together sets of traditional tunes, often at public houses. The organization faced some resistance from musicians who felt strongly that copyright had nothing to do with traditional music and that IMRO should not be collecting licensing fees from pubs and festivals where traditional music was performed. IMRO eventually legitimated its presence in such contexts in part through an agreement with the traditional music organization Comhaltas Ceoltoiri Eireann (CCE). According to the agreement, CCE would pay a nominal licensing fee at its events in exchange for generous support for traditional music from IMRO.

Reading between the lines of McCann's account, however, it also appears that IMRO's policy of granting a 100 percent royalty on arrangements of public domain works may have been aimed at incentivizing traditional musicians to join the organization. In contrast to the Turkish collecting societies, IMRO seems to have strategically declined to minimize the originality involved in performing traditional tunes. As an IMRO representative put it, "If [Irish traditional fiddler] Frankie Gavin is playing in a pub, he's a member, so it's copyright music. It's his copyright. If you're playing music in a pub and you're a member, therefore you turn it into copyright music" (96). In other words, the difference between a mere performance of a public domain work and a performance of an arrangement warranting derivative rights was simply whether the performer was a member of IMRO or not. There would be no musicological experts assessing the originality of the interpretation. IMRO members were furthermore encouraged to log the tunes they performed and send the list in to the society at the end of the year in order to claim royalties on the arrangements they had performed (97). By offering a 100 percent performing royalty on such arrangements of traditional works, then, IMRO could incentivize traditional musicians to join its ranks, increasing the numbers of copyrighted works being performed and thus the licensing fees they could demand from traditional venues in turn.[21]

So why hadn't MESAM or MSG taken a similar tack in Turkey? One possibility is that in Turkey there was not the same need to incentivize folk musicians to join the society. Based on my conversations with MESAM staff and leadership, folk music artists were active in the society from its early days (note that the bulk of folk music rightsholders are members of MESAM rather than MSG). There could be several reasons for this. Important portions of the folk music repertoire consist of türküler with known authors. A prime example is âşık music, where traditional âşıklar compose their own lyrics and sometimes set these to original

When Copyright Meets Folk Music **159**

melodies as well. There is also a well-established practice of folk music artists setting old âşık poems, preserved in handwritten notebooks called *cönk*, to new musical compositions that could be copyrighted.

There were also those who might benefit from the 10 percent policy. Consider that the 10 percent mechanical royalty on public domain works allows record producers to pocket the other 90 percent, for example. From the mid-1990s, record producers also became influential within MESAM because some of them simultaneously functioned as publishers (or were themselves songwriters) and were thus also members of the society.[22] Additionally, while I never heard anyone mention this, if the remaining 90 percent share on performing rights in public domain works is distributed among all of the society's membership, this represents a windfall or subsidy for the bulk of the society's members. It thus offers them a reason to support the 10 percent policy.

In sum, MESAM may not have had much need to incentivize folk music performers to join the society, and record producers meanwhile may have resisted paying mechanical licensing fees on public domain music. These explanations are not fully satisfying, however, since surely there remain many folk music artists who could be lured to the society by the prospect of 100 percent royalty shares on their performances of folk music.[23] Furthermore, the issue of record label resistance can only account for the policy as it applies to mechanical royalties and not to performing royalties. All of this begs consideration of an additional factor.

Ideologies of Creativity and National Belonging

Perhaps what best helps explain the 10 percent policy is the role of ideologies of creativity and national belonging. As I have described at length in chapter 3, narratives attending the genre of folk music constructed it as a realm of practice where creativity works in ways that are essentially different from modern authorship. Folk music artists and experts often imagine that modern technology and copyright laws have triggered a discursive rupture: where rural türkü-makers and transmitters once cared little for authorship claims and had no way to monetize them in any case, commercialization had radically changed this landscape. As I described in chapter 4, while some bemoaned this epochal shift and others embraced it as a fait accompli that required some modernizations of practice, a body of folk music survived from the past as a collective heritage. *Whose* heritage it is remains a point of contention. For nationalists, it belongs to the Turks; for multiculturalists, to a more ecumenical vision of society. Yet the anti-commercial

160 *Copyright Consciousness*

strain of folk music's narrative construction connects such contrasting visions of heritage. Compare traditionalists' distaste for the use of türküler in advertising jingles, or how individuals claiming authors' rights in türküler seemed to resonate with the history of urban migrants building shanty towns on public lands. Consider also the former Technical Expertise Committee member for whom 60 percent for an arrangement of a well-known türkü was unthinkable. "How correct can this be within folk culture, this 60 percent? . . . The examples from the West were a little different. There you can give those kinds of shares." Consider the publisher who made the culturally intimate assertion that "In other countries . . . people are much more honest about this. . . . But when it happens with us/here [*bizde olduğunda*], even when it's the same notation, the same notes, they claim that they have made an arrangement and they take 10 percent." Such explanations of the 10 percent policy sometimes seemed to assume that the conditions in Turkey were different from elsewhere, that creators needed to be incentivized to come up with something new, and that a divergent policy might be necessary (note how IMRO's liberal granting of 100 percent arranger shares to traditional performers troubles the assumption that elsewhere musicians would not claim arrangers' rights over mere performances). The 10 percent policy perhaps makes sense as an imperfect attempt to halt an exploitation that appears incongruent with the genre's anti-commercial aura and yet inevitable according to certain pessimistic imaginings of the state of Turkish society.

In 2021, under new leadership, MESAM and MSG revised their policies, finally choosing to grant a 100 percent share on all arrangements of public domain works. The international federation of musical authors' collecting societies, CISAC, had reportedly proposed this change to the societies' distribution directives along with a few others. On the one hand, this would bring the Turkish societies' policies into alignment with the most common international practices, and on the other hand, there was a legal argument for doing so: where an arrangement warranted rights in a derivative work, those rights belonged 100 percent to the arranger. MESAM's board of directors had presented the revised distribution directive, which included the new policy on royalties for arrangements of public domain works, to the general assembly of the society's membership in 2021, and (I was told) the new directive had been approved unanimously. Yet a member of the current Technical Expertise Committee whom I interviewed the following year maintained a sense that the share should be lower. "The lyric doesn't belong to me. The composition isn't mine either," he said, imagining an example of an anonymous türkü. "I just process it [*işliyorum*]. I arrange it [*düzenliyorum*]. And I take the whole rights over [the work]. If you ask me, this is a huge injustice," he told me.

The societies' policies on the value of arrangements of public domain works—whether they grant 10 percent or 100 percent—exemplify how copyright legality emerges from a shifting negotiation among actors informed by international legal forms and practices (like CISAC's recommended distribution policies) and motivated by the competing interests of various stakeholders (like arrangers and record producers). Histories of institutionalization and the construction of folk music as national heritage furthermore forged socially shared values around creativity and ownership. These histories thus feed critical reflections on the law, as expressed for example in the anxieties about the theft or inappropriate use of türküler. They also shape legality by informing individuals' actions, such as the tendency for musicians to decline to view their own performances as arrangements.

THE THEFT OF TÜRKÜLER, DIGITAL REDUX

In October 2020, the Turkish newspaper *Hürriyet* published a story alleging that the major international music company Universal Music Publishing Group (UMPG) was illegally siphoning off composition royalties from YouTube streams of recordings posted by Turkish music companies, including on a number of tracks featuring anonymous türküler (İ. Yılmaz 2020). The independent label Kalan had noticed the issue because the YouTube music clips listed the publishers and collecting societies who licensed the composition rights involved in each clip. Because different societies and publishers may license a given song in different territories, and because the songwriting shares may be split among several individuals (for publisher, composer, lyricist, and arranger rights), YouTube's system allows multiple parties to claim these rights simultaneously (note that Kalan also functions as a publisher through its affiliate company Kalan Ses). Somehow, UMPG seemed to have claimed a share of the overseas composition royalties over songs produced by Kalan and other companies where Kalan alleged they had no right to do so. UMPG reportedly withdrew its claims when Kalan questioned them, characterizing the claims as the result of a software error.

It remains unclear how much UMPG had collected in royalties from these songs during the period in which it had claimed a share (five years, according to Kalan's allegation). Also unclear is whether similar claims had been placed over tracks on other digital streaming platforms such as Spotify and Apple Music, which do not publicize the names of the agents licensing the tracks as YouTube did. Kalan's owner Hasan Saltık asserted that it was MESAM and MSG's role to take charge of the situation (İ. Yılmaz 2020). When I asked collecting society officials about the issue, they told me they did not think there was much substance to the allegation, and that it was up to the individual owners of the rights at issue to sue. Kalan faced the prospect of taking on an international major music company as a small independent publisher and may have seen it as the collecting societies' role to organize a class action among all the Turkish rightsholders affected. In fact, my suspicion is that Saltık alerted the press precisely to leverage public opinion to pressure MESAM and MSG to act. In his statement to the press, he foregrounded examples of anonymous türküler that UMPG had claimed in particular, a tactic that would appeal to the already widespread outrage at false claims to public heritage that I have described here.

As far as I can tell, MESAM may also have felt that because royalties were still coming to them for these tracks, it was not affecting their income. But others with knowledge of the situation questioned whether it was possible to know that UMPG hadn't in fact been able to claim a portion of the royalties, especially because royalty rates from YouTube are constantly in flux in any case. YouTube would have records of the exact royalty shares that had been doled out, but these would have to be subpoenaed during a challenging international lawsuit that might not turn out to be worth the expense. In a final twist, for reasons I have described in this chapter, no one would be able to sue over the claims to anonymous türküler. In most cases, because of the common reticence to claim arrangers' rights in performances of public domain türküler (which most of the recordings at issue exemplified), no one had legal standing to challenge UMPG's claims over a portion of the composition rights. Only if the performer(s) or an arranger had claimed an arranger credit could they sue. Nor could the Cultural Ministry or some other organ of the state sue, since the state had not been made the owner of works in the public domain. It remains to be seen whether these altered stakes involved in the digital streaming economy will start to shift attitudes toward claiming rights in arrangements of türküler or toward the state's role in guarding the public domain.

CONCLUSION

In this chapter, I have built upon my account of how folk music was constructed as noncommercial, anonymous collective heritage. My ethnographic data show that as copyright became more effectively applied in the music sector beginning in the 1980s, it stoked a series of debates that resonated with the larger international conversation about protecting traditional cultural expressions, especially as it plays out in fora such as WIPO's Intergovernmental Committee on Intellectual Property and Genetic Resources, Traditional Knowledge and Folklore. These international discussions tend to take it for granted that folklore and other traditional culture is incompatible with copyright, and that separate mechanisms must be developed to protect it from objectionable uses. As I argued in chapter 3, in Turkey this incompatibility had to be constructed through an essentializing account of creativity in folk music. Here I have further traced the implications of this constructivist account to show how folk music's framing as a noncommercial, collective heritage shaped the emergent copyright legality in the music sector. It motivated objections to certain commercial uses of türküler and especially to musicians' purportedly false claims to have authored them. But as my analysis of arrangers' rights in public domain music showed, it also mediated perceptions of originality. The line between original arrangement and mere performance is an ambiguous, subjective one. The mythology of anonymity locates the creative agency that forged folk music in a past epoch of collective, oral modalities of creation. This seems to lead many musicians to minimize their own creative agency by perceiving their arrangements as mere performance. For many years, it seems to have led the collecting societies to minimize the value of arrangements even where a right in the arrangement was claimed. Such examples highlight how localized discourses of creativity and national belonging shape a variety of actors' copyright consciousness, informing copyright legality as it emerges far beyond the walls of a courtroom or a legislature. In the next chapter, I further explore the relationship between this emergent, everyday legality and formal law itself. I examine how some copyright stakeholders sought to formalize a set of categories of creative contribution that institutional folklore had naturalized but which did not readily map onto legal categories laid out in the copyright statute.

SIX

Collectors, Copyright, "Kiziroğlu"
Formal Law and Everyday Legality

A thing which you have enjoyed and used as your own for a long time,
whether property or an opinion, takes root in your being and cannot
be torn away without your resenting the act and trying to
defend yourself, however you came by it.

Oliver Wendell Holmes (1897, 477)

In late December 2014, Turkey's ruling party (AKP) unveiled its new campaign song for the upcoming elections. It was a version of the well-known türkü "Kiziroğlu Mustafa bey," performed by the rock group Ayna and given new lyrics praising the party's prime ministerial candidate, Ahmet Davutoğlu. When Ayna's political version of "Kiziroğlu" aired, the popular press promptly erupted with sensational headlines about lawsuits over the song. Incredibly, the main opposition party had apparently planned to use the same song for its own campaign, and they contested the ruling party's right to use it.[1] The opposition party (CHP) took to the media, threatening to sue.[2] They had already signed an agreement with the presumed owners of the rights to the song, the heirs to the estate of Murat Çobanoğlu, the famous âşık with whom the song is closely associated in the public consciousness. One of the âşık's grandchildren happened to be a parliamentary candidate within the opposition party, and he also took to the press. He lobbed his own threats to sue on behalf of his family, who had not given the ruling party permission to use the song. However, these threats soon dissolved into mere protest. The ruling party had responded to the threats by claiming that the song was in the public domain, and they needed no permission to use it ("Habertürk TV 1" 2014). A few days later Çobanoğlu's grandson redirected his anger at the way the song had been dealt with by copyright administrators (Konuralp 2014). He had apparently consulted with MESAM, the copyright collecting society of which the family are members, and he had learned that his grandfather was registered as the song's collector, not its composer or even its arranger. Furthermore, as he would have been informed, this designation afforded no rights under current copyright law.

At the center of this chapter is the idea of the folk song collector, which has a particular history within Turkey's music industry and institutions of musical folklore. In the media uproar over "Kiziroğlu," the term *collector* appeared again and again. Furthermore, there was a slippage between the ideas of "collector" and "composer." For example, a written title in a report on the channel Flash TV identified "the composer's grandson" even as the announcer declared that in MESAM records the famous minstrel is registered as the song's collector. A Fox TV report stated (incorrectly) that according to the copyright collecting society MESAM, "both the song's collection and its composition belong to Çobanoğlu" ("Fox Tv Kiziroğlu Haberi" 2014).

The incident of the election and "Kiziroğlu" raised a series of questions that suggested the case might reward further research. Why did the opposition party sign an agreement with Çobanoğlu's estate in the first place if the latter didn't actually control the rights to the song? Why did Çobanoğlu's family at first seem so convinced that they had rights over the song? Why had copyright administrators officially registered Çobanoğlu as the song's collector when this designation affords him no rights anyway? And from the perspective of Turkish folklore, "collector" is an odd description for Çobanoğlu's relationship to the song. So why and how did he end up with this label?

The confusion over composers and collectors is more than a matter of layman misconceptions. In fact, throughout most of the period of my research the issue stood at the center of a legal debate surrounding revisions to Turkey's copyright statute. In this final chapter, I analyze this debate through the lens of "Kiziroğlu," examining why the idea of a copyright for folk song collectors seemed so compelling to many people in Turkey—and not just to the folklorists who would stand to profit—despite the unlikelihood that such a legal provision would ultimately materialize. As sociolegal scholars Austin Sarat and Thomas Kearns have argued, "Law is continuously shaped and reshaped by the ways it is used, even as law's constitutive power constrains patterns of usage. . . . Everyday life . . . is a mélange of social practices and normative commitments that stand, no doubt, in a wide variety of relations to law and legal materials" (1993, 55–56). What the "Kiziroğlu" case reveals, I argue, is just how complex and contingent is this co-constitutive interrelation between formal law and the messy social world of musical creativity and senses of ownership. This is particularly so in Turkey, where copyright doctrines intended to draw an ambiguous line between infringement and fair borrowing, between original expression and uncopyrightable or recycled ideas, meet a long history of lightly enforced formal law in the music sector (see chapter 1). The absence of regular assertions of formal law allowed the legalities of record industry contractual practice and creative production in folk music to evolve on their own . . . until it suddenly didn't.

FROM FOLK EPIC TO COPYRIGHT SAGA

"Bir hışmıyle geldi geçti!" (He came and went with a fury!) declares Çobanoğlu at the opening of "Kiziroğlu." Çobanoğlu punctuates the line with the infectious vocables "peh peh peh." The song relates an episode from the life of the legendary sixteenth-century hero Köroğlu, to whom the lyrics are often also attributed.[3] In one version of the story, Köroğlu has gotten into a turf war with Kiziroğlu Mustafa bey, another warrior. They battle each other for days, and even their horses wrestle each other. In the end, Kiziroğlu overwhelms Köroğlu. As Kiziroğlu is preparing to dispense with Köroğlu, the latter requests a brief reprieve to say goodbye to his wife. Kiziroğlu obliges, and Köroğlu returns home. The song "Kiziroğlu" is supposed to be the lyric Köroğlu composes as he sings of the greatness of his vanquisher to his wife. But Kiziroğlu, feeling that Köroğlu has dallied too long at home, goes to find him, and as it happens, he overhears the song. He is so touched by it that he spares Köroğlu's life.[4]

The song thus belongs to the Köroğlu legend that minstrels around the northeastern Turkish town of Kars have sung about for many years. In 1965 Çobanoğlu sang his rendition of the song at a nationwide âşık competition and took first prize with his performance. This victory brought nationwide acclaim and recognition from the state; the mayor's office of Kars even gave him a parcel of land to build a café where minstrels gather to sing and compete with each other (Erdener 1995, 34). It thus has a special significance for Çobanoğlu. The song became popular outside Kars after Çobanoğlu released a record of it.

Since Çobanoğlu's famous recording, "Kiziroğlu" has been covered by a number of artists. One of the better-known covers is that by the leftist operatic interpreter of folk songs Ruhi Su. In 1998 two popular groups recorded the song. One was Laçın, who released a light pop version with a mix of traditional and rock instrumentation. The other was the hard rock group Ayna (Mirror), whose grinding electric guitars the bookish prime minister would call into service for his campaign sixteen years later. Long before the group had spun their rock and roll paean to Davutoğlu, they had sung "Kiziroğlu" using the Köroğlu lyrics from Çobanoğlu's recording. It was the first hit from their high-selling album *Dön Bak Aynaya* (Turn and look in the mirror). Apparently, Çobanoğlu had sought financial compensation for their use of the song. From what I can piece together of the incident, the group seems to have signed an agreement with him, paying him a fee in exchange for permission to use it. But subsequently he did not receive ongoing royalties for it.

The resulting dispute over the song became a public spectacle when popular television talk show host Savaş Ay had both Çobanoğlu and Ayna's producer, Erol Köse, as guests on his program, clips of which were long available on YouTube.[5] On the show, Çobanoğlu makes a series of claims to "Kiziroğlu," some of which seem to contradict each other. First, he mentions being the popularizer of the song, starting with his performance at the competition in 1965. If he had not put out a record of the song on the market, he says, how would Ayna have heard it in the first place?[6] Second, Çobanoğlu claims to have composed the song. He calls it his own musical composition (*beste*). But in the ensuing discussion, this position appears to be compromised.

The fact emerges that before Çobanoğlu, the song had been collected from Âşık Dursun Cevlani, another, older minstrel from Kars. This is a reference to the version that we find in the official repertoire of the folk music division at TRT. Here the collector is listed as Muzaffer Sarısözen, the father of Turkish musical folklore. In response to this added information, however, Çobanoğlu claims that his own father, Âşık Gülistan, was singing the song before Dursun Cevlani. This statement seems to contradict his initial claim to have composed the song. Nonetheless, Çobanoğlu sticks to his guns, insisting he composed it. His reasoning is not entirely clear, but he appears to be asserting that he had created a unique version of the song, and that this version should be considered a composition.

What is unique about Çobanoğlu's version? Another âşık from Kars making an appearance on the show, Nuri Çırağı, specifies this. At the time, in the early 1960s, no one in Kars could sing it like Çobanoğlu could sing it, he says. In particular, Çobanoğlu had inserted the emphatic syllables "peh peh peh!" into the song. To my own ears, these vocables do in fact seem to lend the song a certain infectiousness.[7] One audience member objects that what Çobanoğlu has done is an âşık's duty, that he had "found the song, but others made it live." When Köse calls Çobanoğlu the song's collector and not its composer, another audience member objects: "But composer and collector are the same!"

Çobanoğlu, perhaps channeling his inner Köroğlu, seems to want to resolve the matter through an act of bravado. Audience member Mustafa Budan, a bağlama player, composer, and record producer, has a copy of the notation of the TRT version collected from Cevlani (see figure 6.1). Çobanoğlu challenges him to read along while he sings the song for comparison. After listening, Budan concludes that Çobanoğlu's version is essentially the same as the TRT version. The melody is basically the same, the words are the same. The TRT version doesn't have "peh peh peh" written into the notation, but there is a footnote stating that some minstrels in Kars like to insert these syllables sometimes.[8] The episode leaves the confusion unresolved. Köse tries to discuss the issue of a collector's legal right over a song, or rather, the lack thereof. On a previous episode of the show on which Köse had also appeared, authorities from MESAM had discussed this.[9]

Savaş Ay, the host, cuts him off, protesting: "That's a technical discussion! We discussed it for a whole program! We got a 2.5 rating! I'll never forget it as long as I live!" Ay instead manufactures an unconvincing rapprochement between Çobanoğlu and Köse, getting them to shake hands and make a show of mutual respect by way of ending the segment. One senses that behind the scenes, the feud boils on. During the segment, Çobanoğlu had poignantly posed a question that remains unanswered: "Why can I not get my rightful dues from the song?" Köse, meanwhile, has not had an opportunity to make his technical argument about why Çobanoğlu in fact has no legal rights in the matter.

A DISCUSSION WORTH A 2.5 RATING

So what is the technical discussion that Ay avoids on the program? During my fieldwork, there was an ongoing legal debate over whether collectors (*derlemeci* or *derleyen*) warrant copyright rights over türküler and folk tunes they have collected. As I have discussed at several points in this book, a key legal doctrine encoded in the copyright statute holds that to qualify as a copyrightable work, an expression must "[bear] the characteristic of its author" (Yavuz, Merdivan, and Türkay 2013, 64). The doctrine reflects the legal basis for copyright in continental European legal traditions, where the capacity of a work to embody an aspect of the author's personality grounds an author's rights over it. The term translated

Collectors, Copyright, "Kiziroğlu" **169**

here as "characteristic" (*hususiyet*) also encodes a notion of originality, since in practice, courts locate that which is specific to the author in a work's distinctiveness from other works. Turkey's court of last instance, the Court of Cassation (Yargıtay), has firmly established that a musician does not have a valid claim to lyricist or composer rights to an anonymous folk song simply by virtue of having collected it from a village—that is, if they did not in fact compose the words or music themselves. According to my conversations with ıp courts, this was tested in a series of cases in the early to mid-2000s, and since then such claims have ceased or slowed (see also Yavuz, Merdivan, and Türkay 2013, 128–29; Çolak 2008, 139–42). Yet the doctrine of hususiyet bore upon the "Kiziroğlu" case by posing the following question: in forging and promoting his version of the song, did Çobanoğlu reshape it through original contributions vested with some aspect of his personality? Writ larger, the question is whether folk song collectors contribute hususiyet when they collect and popularize a türkü.

Those arguing for Çobanoğlu's right over the song had to justify it in the terms the statute afforded. Most were drawn to article 6, which delineates rights to derivative or adapted works (*işleme eserleri*) and compilations (*derleme eserleri*). The article specifically lists musical arrangements among the types of derivative works it recognizes, raising the possibility that collectors might control rights over their version of a türkü if we can consider it a protectable arrangement. As I discussed in chapter 5, the question of what counts as a protectable arrangement of a türkü is surprisingly complicated and political: the line between arrangement and mere performance is drawn in the eye of the beholder. When adjudicating the question in court, it often boils down to how the expert musicologists summoned in the case see it.

Article 6 also appeals to advocates for collectors' rights because of its delineation of rights in compilations (*derleme eserleri*). The classic example of this kind of work is a literary compilation or anthology (items 6 and 7 of the article). In such a case, the assembler of the anthology merits rights over the assembly itself, having contributed a kind of originality in the process of curating the works that will go into the collection. However, each of the individual works within the anthology remains the property of its creator, and the editor does not then become the owner of the works within the volume. One of the oddities of the discussion over copyright for folk song collectors is that the Turkish word for folk song collection (*derleme*) is the same word that was used in article 6 to describe compilations or literary anthologies. This happenstance seems to have drawn advocates for folk song collectors' rights to this article for support. But does *derleme* in this context refer to folk song collection in addition to anthologies and the like?

Among those who take article 6's usage of *derleme* to refer to folk song collection is Sümer Ezgü, a popular folk song performer who has also done some folk song collecting himself. Ezgü has served on MESAM's Board of Directors and has been an active proponent of rights for folk song collectors. When Ezgü first became a member of MESAM in the early 1990s, he was surprised to learn that the society was not distributing royalties for folk song collection, and subsequently he worked to change the situation (interview, March 30, 2015). Ezgü enlisted the help of a MESAM lawyer in trying to change the society's internal distribution rules to initiate a system for administering copyright for folk song collectors. When I spoke with this lawyer, he gave me a similar reading of the law. He had also researched lawsuits over anonymous works, and he felt that in fact the courts had not come to a definite conclusion as to whether article 6 could apply to folk song collection or not (interview, April 15, 2015). Ezgü carried the matter to a general membership meeting at MESAM, and according to his recollection, the membership voted in favor of beginning to administer rights in folk song collection. He was incredulous as to why this decision was not being enforced.

In theory, if a collector could demonstrate how they have contributed originality in the process of collecting a folk song, such as if they added a lyric or some musical element, they might have rights over their collected version as a derivative work, warranting protection for the contributions they have added to the adapted version of the work but not for the collection of the folk song per se. Judge Uğur Çolak, who presided over Istanbul's 4th Intellectual Property Civil Court during the early years of my fieldwork, considered the legal status of folk song collectors within a larger, systematic examination of legal avenues for protecting anonymous folk music (2008). He points out the following problem: to demonstrate that a collector (or for that matter, the source person from whom a türkü is collected) has contributed something original and distinct to the türkü, we have to compare the collected version to some prior version. Yet the version a folklorist collects may be the first or only version documented; as such, making such a comparison may prove impossible (146–47).

When I spoke with Ezgü, I asked him: how does a collector contribute originality to the folk song? The example that he raised in response was "Kiziroğlu" and the signature "peh peh peh" that Çobanoğlu had supposedly added. But the courts can have high standards for judging originality in arrangements, and it remains to be seen whether "peh peh peh" would hold up in court as a protect-

Collectors, Copyright, "Kiziroğlu" **171**

able original contribution. Lawyers who have been involved with MESAM opined that for now the society does not have the legal authority to distribute royalties for folk song collection that does not qualify as an adapted work, and this is why they have not begun doing so despite the efforts of people like Ezgü.

Another possibility for recognizing a copyright in folk song collection would be to revise the statute to clarify or create such a right. One of the contexts for this debate over folk music collectors' rights was the negotiation of a revision to the statute, whose latest version dated to 2008.[10] Many of the copyright collecting society officials, lawyers, and judges I interviewed during my fieldwork were involved in these negotiations, proposing revised or added language and commenting on revisions others had suggested. By my 2022 follow-up fieldwork, these negotiations had failed, as stakeholders with opposing interests—collecting societies and the businesses to whom they sold licenses for performing rights, for example—proved unable to resolve their differences of opinion about the revisions. But during most of my fieldwork, the possibility that the revised statute might clarify or create a right for folk music collectors seemed plausible, even if unlikely. As the example of "Kiziroğlu" shows, MESAM has for some time held out enough hope that the law will someday recognize such a right that they have actually been registering collectors in their database for years. As impressively, an official from the Cultural Ministry's copyright office, which coordinates the negotiation of statutory revisions, confirmed for me that such changes were at one point put into the draft. These proposed changes included revisions to article 6, as far as this official could recall (interview, September 17, 2015).[11]

Lawyers and judges I spoke with who were involved in the negotiations remembered seeing the relevant proposed revisions, and some told me they had protested vehemently. They viewed folk song collection as different from the assembling of an anthology (see also Çolak 2008, 134–35). Note that the editor of a literary anthology controls the rights only over the assembled collection of a set of works, whereas a folk song collector stands to control the rights over an individual work that others might wish to use. It is perhaps this difference that makes legal authorities view the two differently. However, my sources at the Cultural Ministry and at MESAM also recalled that according to some of the proposals, a provision for folk song collectors might not have entailed the same rights that composers and lyricists have. There could have been a shorter term of protection than authors have in their works (currently until seventy years after the death of the author). The collector might also have exercised a nonexclusive right of remuneration in their collections: they might have been granted some royalties from the profits others gained by using folk music they had collected, but they might not have had the right to deny permission for uses they opposed. In this scenario, Çobanoğlu's family presumably would not have been able to stop the ruling party from using "Kiziroğlu," for example, though they might have received some royalties for the use of the song.

"EVERYONE'S GOING TO TRY TO GET IN ON IT"

If most legal authorities saw folk song collection as different from the sorts of creative acts that warranted copyright rights, why was the idea of granting rights so appealing to some folk music artists and experts, enough so that MESAM was in fact tracking collectors in their database? An obvious answer has to do with the incentives of those involved. Opponents often saw the idea of granting a copyright to folk song collectors as greed driven. One folk music artist I spoke with opined that folk song collection should be academic work, work that you do for the glory of it (*ihtisam*). His view was that in the 1980s people undertaking derleme started to say that folk song collectors needed rights. Money started to come in from copyright with the formation of MESAM, and they wanted to get in on it. "There's money there," he told me. "Even the most foolish person, when they see this money getting distributed, everyone's going to come and try to get in on it." Meanwhile administering a right for the collectors of anonymous türküler would provide a new income stream for MESAM and MSG, significantly expanding the catalogue of works whose rights they manage.

If critics viewed a copyright in derleme as corrupt commercialization, there were other ways to view the situation. One folk song collector and recording artist I spoke with read the situation in the opposite way: what represented corrupt commercial influence on folk music was the *denial* of copyright to folk song collectors. According to this perspective, the profiteers were those who stood to benefit from derleme remaining *unprotected*. And indeed, according to my conversations with officials involved in the statutory revisions, the opponents of collectors' rights include some record producers who would have to pay mechanical royalties to collectors of anonymous türküler that their recording artists wished to record.

Another folk music artist I spoke with had seen a recording of a song that he had collected from a rural village explode in popularity. He recounted how other people—the record producers and the media outlets broadcasting it—were making a huge profit off the song. And yet he wasn't seeing a penny of royalties from the composition rights. He ended up registering the song as his own composition, and he quietly split the royalties fifty-fifty with the rural musician who had served as his source. This artist became a vocal proponent of copyright for folk song collectors (and for rural source musicians), partly because of this experience. His desire was to see the song properly registered as a collected folk song, but also to get what he viewed as his just deserts for collecting it.

Some actors thus identify collectors seeking a copyright as profit-seeking, greedy, and corrupt. Yet some see it as unjust when record producers, media companies, and performers profit from a song in whose popularity the collector has played a key role that goes unrewarded. "Kiziroğlu" illustrates the situation well: do Çobanoğlu's contradictory claims to the song represent a greedy grasping at legally unjustified profits? Or is his gripe legitimate? Çobanoğlu is arguably most responsible for the song's popularity, its emergence as a profit-producing hit, and this role is not recognized or compensated by the copyright system.

"HOW MANY DERLEME DO YOU HAVE?"

If it seemed to some that collectors should have a copyright, it might also have to do with how the figure of the collector has been celebrated and valorized in Turkey. TRT's bureaucrats—in a project also involving government institutions such as the Cultural Ministry and educational ones like Istanbul Technical University's State Conservatory—had sought to promote a national Turkish music with two branches: Turkish Folk Music and Turkish Art Music. These genres were defined along a series of mutually contrasting dimensions, one of which was creative modality: where art music compositions were usually attributed to named authors, folk melodies and texts were believed to emerge from a collective, anonymous creative process, passed down by rural transmitters until a trained folk music collector such as Muzaffer Sarısözen came around to document them (see chapter 3).

In the world of art music, composers and lyricists were praised for their creative contributions to Turkish musical heritage, their works incorporated into the TRT Art Music Repertoire with their names at the top of the official notation. The notations of the TRT Folk Music Repertoire, in a way that paralleled the credits given to composers of Turkish Art Music, recorded the collector, source person (*kaynak kişi*), and region of origin (*yöre*) of its constituent musical pieces. These figures were then announced during broadcasts of the music. This approach was either established or affirmed at the 1973 TRT Turkish Art and Folk Music Special Advisory Committee Meeting, where participants discussed "the need to present works in such a way that the person who has brought the artistic work into being is at peace economically and morally" (TRT 1974, 233). Several participants suggested a need to credit the collectors of folk music just as the composers of art music were credited. The poet and folk literature specialist Turgut Günay said: "In the section of your proposal about copyright, there's a benefit to saying authors' [telif] and collectors' [derleme] rights, because particularly those working in the field of folk music may also be characterized as collector." While Günay insisted that the two figures (author and collector) play distinct roles that merit different sorts of rights, he and others at the table also seemed to take it as natural that the two belong side by side in a discussion of copyright. No one objected to the language of the eventual policy proposal, which mandated observing both "proper author's [telif] and collectors' [derleme] rights and performers' fees" (233–34). There were also other ways that the figure of the derleyen was celebrated. It is common in folk music programming or even in informal conversations among folk music artists to ask, "How many songs have you collected [Kaç derlemeniz var]?" and biographies of folk music artists often mention the songs they have collected. In my interviews with folk music artists, they often proudly recalled the stories of how they had collected individual türküler. I argue that, in part due to such approaches at TRT and elsewhere, the folk song collector was valorized in a way that paralleled the status of art music composers. This status may in turn have led folk music industry actors to conceptualize the collector as a figure deserving rights that parallel the rights of authors.

"BUT COMPOSER AND COLLECTOR ARE THE SAME!"

What exactly do we mean by folkloric collection (derleme)? This is a question with a complicated answer. But the legal debate over copyright in folk song collection turns on the question of whether collectors contribute originality, hususiyet, in the process of collection; this matter depends in turn on how we view the role of the collector. Two competing impulses seem to drive folkloric collection. The first is a purely documentarian impulse. In one presentation on the topic, for example, folk music artist and researcher Mansur Kaymak stresses the need to make sound or video recordings of the source musician when collecting folk songs in order to document "the originality of the source" (2005, 35). Can Etili, a folk music artist who also holds a law degree, writes that "in folkloric collection there is no element of personal creativity. The collector is making a recording of a situation [durum tespiti]" (2005, 271). In his article on the subject, Judge Çolak likens the folk song collector to an archeologist who uncovers ancient works in the course of an excavation. Such an archeologist has not contributed hususiyet, and Çolak suggests that they might turn not to copyright law but to unfair competition law to prevent others from publishing photographs and sketches of the recovered works (2008, 142).[12]

Yet there is a second, corrective or editorial impulse in folkloric collection. I commonly encountered collectors who spoke about this in relation to lyrics; it was common for source musicians to transmit old texts that included archaic vocabulary the source musician may not actually understand. In such cases, the words could also become corrupted, and it was the task of the collector to research them and attempt to recover the text as it had existed prior to such corruptions. Given how collectors often undertook their work with an eye toward promoting national culture via mass media and especially official state broadcasting, there are also many cases of published and performed versions of türküler being sanitized or otherwise revised to better fit official images of Turkish national character (see Balkılıç 2009). (Of course, the collector might also distinguish such instances from other kinds of changes that may be deemed to enrich the text or represent new variants that are not necessarily corrupt).

In an idealized, documentarian notion of derleme, folk song collectors operate under the auspices of an official institution such as a university or TRT. It is a duty they perform as part of their jobs, and their efforts are rewarded through professional esteem and, of course, the salaries they receive from their institutions. Folk music is made primarily in rural areas, often by minstrels called âşıklar or *ozanlar*, and trained folklorists go out from their urban posts to document folk music and make it more available to a general public. Sarısözen did this by arranging the music he collected for the radio ensemble and broadcasting it over the airwaves. Sometimes TRT would also bring in such source musicians to play on a broadcast. Or folklorists might publish notations of songs they had collected in a book. Collectors often strive to maintain a strict separation between themselves—the urban, institutional collectors—and those contributing to regional traditions from their positions as local insiders.

In practice, much derleme diverges from this idealized notion. We could also identify any number of ways that even the most documentarian folk music collectors intervene in the tradition: selecting source musicians; presenting an example of a fluid genre with interchangeable verses as a relatively fixed-looking poem by publishing it as such in a book or recording; standardizing intonation; distilling a skeletal melody from a more ornamented or irregular performance;

176 *Copyright Consciousness*

and so on.[13] In other cases, the collection may not be undertaken in its ideal setting in situ in a village. Former TRT Folk Music Division director Yücel Paşmakçı even recalled to me how he had collected a türkü while getting a haircut in Istanbul when he realized that his barber, who hailed from another region of the country, was singing something he had never heard (pers. comm., May 13, 2014). Alternatively, some actors even considered transcribing and re-arranging a work found on a record to be a kind of derleme.

In some of these cases, collectors may also make creative contributions that diverge from the non-interventionist, idealized notion of derleme. Mehmet Özbek, former director of the TRT Folk Music division, for example, told me:

> Let's say a record has come into your hands, but on that record there are some insufficiencies, mistakes, corruptions. [Doing derleme from a record means] by arranging these anew, by correcting the mistakes, by filling in the insufficiencies, to put forth a new, sounder [*daha sağlam*] work. . . . Let me give an example. There's a record with a türkü called "Kapıyı çalan kimdir" [Who is at the door]. It's an Urfa türkü. I have known the original version of that türkü since I was a child. In order to learn it even better, I listened to the record. But the instrumental interludes [between verses or lines of verse; *ara sazı*] aren't clear at all; the melody is unclear. You put an instrumental part in there, you insert an instrumental fill [between the sung lines; *aranağme*]. This is also a derleme. The singer sang it in a broken way; you can repair it. They sang the lyric wrong; you can correct the lyric. This is derleme. (Interview, March 29, 2015)

Conceptually, then, the non-interventionist approach and Özbek's interventionist example represent two opposing approaches to the derleme concept. One strain of thought views derleme as a matter of scholarly documentation. At its extreme, in the other, interventionist strain of thought, the concept of derleme may even get entangled with the concept of composition.

Recall that during the "Kiziroğlu" debate on Savaş Ay's television program, one audience member declared, "Collection and composition are the same!" In fact, this was not the only place that I heard such an assertion. For example, I once spoke with a former record seller who had worked at Doğu Bank İşhanı in Istanbul's Sirkeci neighborhood, the main distribution hub for the record industry from the 1930s to 1960s. He recalled that when he had been working in the industry, collectors were treated as if they had an economic right over songs they collected. In fact, this appeared natural to him. He told me the collector (*derleyen*) was "the one who brought forth the work [*ortaya çıkaran*], the

Collectors, Copyright, "Kiziroğlu" **177**

composer [*bestekar*]." The collector "found it and made it [*bulmuş yapmış*]" (field note, October 22, 2015). In my conversation with him, Nevzat Sümer likewise asserted that when he had been working as a publisher on the private market prior to founding MESAM, record labels were compensating folk song collectors financially for the use of türküler they had collected (interview, September 12, 2015). In fact, Halit Kakınç, founding member of the group Dönüşüm, which covered "Kiziroğlu" in the 1970s, told me the group considered Çobanoğlu the owner of the song, and they paid several thousand lira for permission to record it (field note, July 13, 2018). On Çobanoğlu's commercial recordings of the song, he is also listed as composer and lyricist. Thus, a slippage between the concepts of derleme and composition may even have motivated financial practices on the private record market prior to the copyright reform of the 1980s. This would mean that collection was a recognized mode of creative contribution, one even met with financial rewards similar to those for composition.

Another slippage sometimes occurs between the concept of collector and source musician (*kaynak kişi*). Consider the case of "Kiziroğlu," which MESAM decided to categorize as Murat Çobanoğlu's derleme. Çobanoğlu hardly fits the category of an institutionally based, trained folklorist. Rather, he is himself an âşık, a minstrel, trained through master-disciple lineages in a traditional context in Kars. There is actually a larger tradition of such minstrels or other source musicians positioning themselves as folk song collectors of the traditional songs they learn in such contexts. In one extreme example, Âşık Mahzuni Şerif is listed in the TRT Repertoire as the source person for the song "İşte gidiyorum çesm-i siyahım." On the record he made of the song on the private market however, he is credited as the derleyen, the collector of the song. Yet the song also contains his own pen name, marking it as his own original composition (cf. Atılgan 2005, 22).

In these cases, âşıklar or other source musicians had enough skill and appeal as a performer that they were able to successfully introduce songs to the market themselves through their own performances without the mediation of TRT ensembles or another popularizer. In other cases, popular urban performers in the folk music market undertook collection as private individuals, performing a türkü in a way that would sell in the urban folk music industry. Based on my conversations with copyright administrators, it seems that this latter form of folk song collection is often what advocates of collectors' rights have in mind. It is not primarily a question of granting royalties to the Muzaffer Sarısözens of the folk music world.

I asked Arif Sağ, the famous folk music artist who was president of MESAM at the time of our conversation, about a specific problem that might arise if copyright were granted for folk song collections. What would they do in cases when the same folk song was collected by multiple individuals from different rural sources? His answer was telling: "One of those collections will have become popular. Let's say three or four versions of the same folk song have been collected. But among these, one of them will have attracted interest. . . . Whichever version sells well, that's the version the rights go to. That's the version that gets the money" (interview, June 9, 2015). Implicit in this solution is the idea that what deserves rewarding is the ability to find or present a version of a folk song in such a way that it becomes popular. And this is exactly what we see in "Kiziroğlu." Despite having been collected by Sarısözen from Âşık Dursun Cevlani, the song was rarely played; it languished in obscurity until Çobanoğlu came along and refashioned it into a national hit.

WHAT'S IN A "PEH"?

So what did Çobanoğlu contribute to "Kiziroğlu"? How original was his version? Where did it lie on the spectrum of documentarian and interventionist approaches to derleme, or on that of performance and (re-)creation?

It is telling to compare the Cevlani and Çobanoğlu versions alongside the TRT notation, credited to Sarısözen. Cevlani's recording, captured on a 78 RPM record released in 1941, eluded me for years until someone posted it on YouTube in 2018. Sitting down with the recording, my bağlama, and the TRT notation, I struggled to reconcile the notation with what I heard in Cevlani's recording. I brought the issue to my bağlama teacher Şendoğan Karadeli, who set the TRT notation to the side, began playing snippets of the recording, and eagerly began scrawling out notes on some staff paper. He promptly worked out the problem, eventually producing impeccable notations of both the Cevlani and Çobanoğlu versions. Comparing them reveals a number of differences, including the oft cited "peh peh" Çobanoğlu is said to have inserted.

The instrumental introductions contain similar motifs such as the variable, repeated G–F–G or G–F♯–G figure; the number of repetitions of the motif seems flexible, as if it represents what Albert Lord, in his classic analysis of oral epic, had called a "formula" (2000). The introductions also trace distinct melodic paths in a gradual downward descent. While Çobanoğlu begins around g' and eventually alights on A, nearly an octave below, Cevlani explores a narrower melodic range, descending from g' only down to C before leaping to a high

Collectors, Copyright, "Kiziroğlu" **179**

FIGURE 6.1 The official TRT notation for "Kiziroğlu."

FIGURE 6.2 Comparative transcription of the introduction to Çobanoğlu's and Cevlani's versions of "Kiziroğlu," after a transcription courtesy of Şendoğan Karadeli. Çobanoğlu's version is represented on the upper staff. The superscript "2" next to the B♭ in Çobanoğlu's staff indicates a neutral second scale degree between B♭ and B♮. The superscript "3" next to F♯ indicates a slightly lower sharp than an equal tempered F♯. The transcription combines vocal and instrumental (*saz*) lines on the same staff; during singing, the saz doubles the vocal line.

c' to cue his vocal. There are also intonational differences: Çobanoğlu plays F and B♭ higher than Cevlani does. These differences in pitch and range reflect a more radical difference: the signature G–F–G figure of the introduction turns out to trace different scale degrees for each of the musicians. For Çobanoğlu it centers on the 7th scale degree, but for Cevlani, it outlines the 4th scale degree. Once the singers sing the first verse, it becomes clear that—at least as Karadeli

Collectors, Copyright, "Kiziroğlu" **181**

FIGURE 6.3 *above and opposite* Comparative transcription of Çobanoğlu's and Cevlani's versions of "Kiziroğlu," after a transcription courtesy of Şendoğan Karadeli. Çobanoğlu's performance is represented on the upper staff.

has transposed the respective recordings—for Çobanoğlu the tonic is A, while for Cevlani it is D. It was no wonder I had been thrown off by viewing the TRT notation while listening to Cevlani: despite crediting Cevlani as the source musician, the TRT notation in fact resembles Çobanoğlu's in that the tonic is A and the G–F♯–G figure thus centers on the 7th scale degree.

In the vocal section, the melodic rhythm of each version is similar, while there are slight differences in the melodic contour and lyric; for example, Cevlani sings

"Bir *hışmınan* geldi geçti," while Çobanoğlu sings "Bir *hışmiyle* geldi geçti" ("a furious one came and went" as opposed to "he came and went with a fury"). The "peh peh" and "hey hey" vocables represent another important difference. In the Cevlani/TRT version, syllables within the name "Kiziroğlu Mustafa bey" are held: "Kiziroğlu MustaFAAAA BEEEEY." But Çobanoğlu spits out Kiziroğlu's name, rushing ahead to the playful vocables with which he fills the ensuing measures: "Kiziroğlu Mustafa bey HEY HEY HEEEEY."

The vocal section of the TRT notation resembles what Cevlani sang, except that Sarısözen has transcribed much of it in 3/8 rather than 6/8, with sections of it in 10/8, an interpretation I struggled to reconcile with the Cevlani record-ing. Though Sarısözen may have worked from a field recording rather than the commercial record, it was also hard to imagine that Cevlani had performed it *so* differently for Sarısözen.

So how should we evaluate these differences between Çobanoğlu's version and other, prior versions? Many folk music experts shared the view articulated by Mustafa Budan, the guest on Savaş Ay's television program who had minimized the differences between Çobanoğlu's performance and the version captured in the TRT notation. Other interpretations were possible, however. One contrasting perspective I encountered was that of Âşık Mürsel Sinan, a long-time apprentice of Çobanoğlu who had lived in the latter's house for nearly a decade.

Sinan cuts an impressive figure, exuding confidence and a meticulously cul-tivated manner of self-presentation. He is clearly an enormously gifted âşık, one who prides himself on self-discipline and a musical training that surpasses that of many other âşıklar, since he is fluent with staff notation and could rely on these skills—bursting into solfege several times—as we discussed and ana-lyzed Çobanoğlu's iconic take on "Kiziroğlu." Sinan had heard Cevlani perform, although, when I first interviewed him in 2015, he could not recall ever having heard Cevlani's version of "Kiziroğlu." This changed when the Cevlani record-ing was posted to YouTube in 2018. I subsequently sent Sinan the clip and we discussed it both over the phone and in an additional interview in 2023.

In our initial interview, Sinan and I took a careful look at the TRT notation, and he made a few observations that Budan, the dismissive TV audience member, seems to have missed, including some of the same differences I have noted above. Most importantly, while Çobanoğlu sings the song in a consistent 6/8 meter, Sinan pointed out the stretches of 3/8 and 10/8 in the TRT notation. To him, these indicated that Cevlani's version did not have the same catchy, consistent, driving pulse that helps make Çobanoğlu's version so infectious. Sinan also emphasized the "peh peh" section and the refrain (*nakarat*), saying that he had never heard anyone else who sang it like Çobanoğlu. "If you had heard Murat Çobanoğlu in person, you'd say, 'That's not a normal person.'" His instrumental skill was much higher than that of other âşıklar. He had an enthusiasm, a particular creativity, Sinan told me. "He'd add something to a song and you'd think, where did that come from? He'd take a rhyme, and others would do something with that rhyme, but Çobanoğlu would do something more his own [*kendine has*], more lyrical." Sinan even ventured a guess at what percentage of the popular version of the song constituted Çobanoğlu's contribution (we both agreed that later cover versions were clearly referencing Çobanoğlu's iconic take on the song). He initially guessed about 30 percent, and later revised this upward as we continued to talk. If he were in a position to assess the percentage of the right that Çobanoğlu should have to the song, he would call it 50 percent, he thought. In fact, the TRT version seemed to him to be lacking in some way (*eksik geliyor*). "Çobanoğlu's style [üslup] and this style [üslup]," he said, pointing to the TRT notation, "his exuberant way of singing, this is the difference in my opinion."

When I later heard the Cevlani recording, I was surprised to find that on first impression it resembled Çobanoğlu's more than I had expected. There was no "peh," but the consistent 6/8 was there, even if a notch more relaxed. To my surprise, for Sinan, hearing the Cevlani recording only seemed to confirm or amplify his earlier opinion. In fact, he further revised his estimate of Çobanoğlu's contribution upward to 70 percent. When I pressed him to explain this, he expanded on his discussion of Çobanoğlu's performing style.

"Kiziroğlu" exemplifies a subgenre of âşık songs, known as *koçaklama*, found in northeastern Turkey and Azerbaijan. The genre is used to praise a mythical hero for bravery and prodigious deeds. In my many conversations about "Kiziroğlu," knowledgeable folk music experts would point out how Çobanoğlu was simply performing a well-known song that exemplifies this established genre. Some of these individuals pointed out how *koçaklama* songs also belong to a common melodic type, and they pointed to the purportedly limited melodic variability of the genre to minimize the originality involved in performing a *koçaklama* song as Çobanoğlu had done.

Sinan flipped this logic on its head, emphasizing the creativity and skill involved in *conforming* to the genre. He described how some musicians—including Cevlani—sang "Kiziroğlu" like they would any türkü. "I'm not saying [Cevlani's version] is bad," Sinan told me, "but that's not how you do *koçaklama*." To illustrate the contrast, he sang the song in a timid way, one that focused on savoring the melodic contour and holding out notes as Cevlani had done ("Mustafaaaaa beeeeey"). He sang a well-known dirge, "Red Roses in Bunches" (Kırmızı gül demet demet), in the same manner to drive home his point. Then, puffing out his chest and projecting his voice, he suddenly transported me to the world of epic recitation, regaling me with a colorfully exaggerated anecdote about Köroğlu's famous horse Kırat leaping over the lake of Van. He sang "Kiziroğlu" in his best Çobanoğlu impression, leveraging this more punctuated take on the lyric to fill the room with a warlike masculine energy. I briefly forgot that I was conducting an interview.

Collectors, Copyright, "Kiziroğlu" **185**

"It's as if the âşık has become Köroğlu," Sinan told me. "The âşık lives it. . . . If the âşık is passive, it won't do." But when the âşık embodies the persona of the epic hero, "it's immediately apparent . . . that it's *koçaklama*." As I listened, I found myself dubious, sensing that these aspects of Çobanoğlu's version would not likely square with copyright doctrines that might warrant the âşık a right in the song. But when I brought the topic back to MESAM's decision to categorize Çobanoğlu only as the song's collector, Sinan replied: "I agree, but there's something they don't know. Çobanoğlu contributed at least 50 percent to this work." He seemed to link his entire discussion of performing style to more compositional elements of Çobanoğlu's version: "Anyway, if we transcribe Çobanoğlu's version and these other versions, it will become apparent . . . " He told me:

> Sometimes they put Çobanoğlu on television. Now, Çobanoğlu can't explain himself there. It's like asking a bee, "Bee, how do you make honey?" The bee can't explain it. . . . Çobanoğlu made such a contribution—I mean, if I said 70 percent, that's correct—he made such a contribution that he can't explain it himself. On TV they ask him. They say: "This isn't yours." . . . He couldn't say, "It's mine," but he also didn't know how to say, "I made a contribution." Anyway, it's not his. It's an anonymous work. But Çobanoğlu made close to a 70 percent creative contribution. He picked the work up off the ground, from the dirt and dust, and he sent it up to the sky. . . . It was there at the TRT, but it didn't ascend to the sky. It's sung on the market, in the cafés, but no one is listening to it. But after Çobanoğlu sang it, the whole world listened. Why did they listen? Because his contribution was so well composed [*derlitoplu*]. He made such a contribution that everyone liked it.

Ayna's album *Dön Bak Aynaya* had been released in early June 1998. The matter of the rights to "Kiziroğlu" was decided by MESAM's Technical Expertise Committee in late July.[14] The committee seems to have found that the lyrics and music should be registered as written by Köroğlu (and thus in the public domain, since the legendary Köroğlu lived centuries previously), and that Çobanoğlu was the song's collector. At the time, the Technical Expertise Committee featured a member, Şeref Taşlıova, who was perhaps uniquely qualified to resolve the case. Taşlıova and Çobanoğlu are probably the two most famous representatives of the Kars school of âşıklar. Taşlıova knew Çobanoğlu well, and his authority on Kars âşık repertoire, including Köroğlu songs, was unparalleled. Taşlıova discussed the committee's decision during a presentation seven years later (2005, 70). While he appears to have been in the majority opinion, he complained about where this left Çobanoğlu. His assessment was that when Çobanoğlu added such elements as the vocables "peh peh peh," the song had been adapted and in the process it "had been gained for society" (*işlenerek . . . topluma kazandırılmış*). Taşlıova decried the fact that despite the decision, "which makes Murat Çobanoğlu the rightsholder as collector," Çobanoğlu has still not earned any royalties from the song because there was no protection in the copyright statute for someone who had played such a role in a song's popularity. Taşlıova called this a major gap or oversight (*boşluk*) in the law.

It appears that Çobanoğlu's family appealed the decision, as Tolga Çobanoğlu claimed he would do during the fallout from the ruling party's use of the song. Later iterations of the Technical Expertise Committee reportedly reconsidered the matter, consulting outside experts who argued that the famous interjections like "hey hey" and "peh peh" were traditional in Kars and not unique to Çobanoğlu, and that he thus had no claim to more than the status of collector and performer of the song.[15]

COLLECTORS' RIGHTS AND BABY SHARKS

While legally recognizing a copyright for folklore collectors would be unusual, the idea was in fact a throwback to older, internationally circulating ideas. The Austrian lawyer and musician Johann Vesque von Püttlingen, in the first legal commentary on music copyright, proposed calling the first publishers of anonymous folk songs authors, since the publisher "first recognized the aesthetic, historic, or ethnographic value of the musical piece in its artistic significance . . . ; through his own intellectual activity he [*sic*] has rescued it from hiddenness or forgottenness and truly recreated it for the musical audience" (Dommann 2019, 24). Music historian Matthew Gelbart points out how notions of authorship have changed over time, and in the eighteenth century, "the author was still generally conceived as the *presenter* – the assembler or relayer of the material that itself was basically God-given and in the public domain"; accordingly, "copyright and 'authorship' often represent[ed] the most recent source rather than a primary '*Ur-source*'" (2007, 22; emphasis in the original). In 1957 the International Folk Music Council issued a statement arguing that folklore collectors deserve copyright in the works they collect (Karpeles 1963), though their recommendations do not seem to have resulted in legal revisions. In Bolivia, meanwhile, folkloric works of cultural heritage are protected under the country's copyright statute; the state collects a royalty on uses of these works, of which a 10 percent share goes to the collector and 10 percent to the community of origin, if they can be identified (see Bigenho 2002, 220–25; Title XI of Bolivia's Law on Authors' Rights [Ley No. 1322 de 13 de Abril de 1992]).

There have also been cases in which a folklorist or first publisher has successfully leveraged the copyright system to control the rights in songs they have collected. In a well-known, notorious example of racialized exploitation, the American folk music documentarian John Lomax claimed copyright in the songs he collected from Black prisoners such as Huddie "Leadbelly" Ledbetter, whom he and his son Alan also promoted by appealing to demeaning stereotypes; they furthermore hoarded the concert earnings from his performing tours, during which he was treated as their personal servant and chauffer (Filene 1991, 610–11; Stewart 2016, 91–119). By virtue of such efforts, the Lomaxes have even wound up with hip-hop songwriting credits via byzantine chains of sampling that involve songs they collected (McLeod and Dicola 2011, 95–98). In fact, the Lomax example figured prominently in a debate among 1960s folk revivalists over the ethics of collectors claiming rights in folk music (Dommann 2019, 170–73).

The "Kiziroğlu" saga also resembles a few other cases of songs with attributed authorship that nonetheless bear an ambiguous relationship to prior existing musical ideas and traditions. One of the most extensively discussed cases is that of Solomon Linda, who was eventually credited as the composer of the song "Mbube," on which the international hit "The Lion Sleeps Tonight" was based, although his initial assignment of the rights in the song to the record company Gallo Africa characterized the work as an "arrangement of the traditional folk song" (Erlmann 2022, 79). Commentators often describe "Mbube" as derived from a preexisting song circulating among musicians who were pioneering the South African genre *isicathamiya* in the 1920s and 1930s (Erlmann 1990, 212; Lafraniere 2006; Shabalala 2021). Pete Seeger—whose group, The Weavers, recorded a well-known version of the song, called "Wimoweh"—reportedly requested that royalties be sent to Linda, though the latter benefitted little from the songwriting credit during his lifetime (Erlmann 2022, 82). Ethnomusicologist Veit Erlmann's close reading of the more recent legal efforts to win proceeds from Disney's use of "The Lion Sleeps Tonight" for Linda's family highlights how colonial era law still shapes the terms in which the sides had to argue the case and how racial divides persist in a post-Apartheid era of reconciliation (106–7). Most relevant to my own discussion is how stakeholders dealt with the indeterminate status of the originality of "Mbube" by assigning it to categories the law recognizes ("traditional/arranged"; "composed by") in order to establish its copyright. Had they lived in the weird universe of the "Kiziroğlu" case, Linda—or Seeger—might have styled himself the collector of the song, then become caught up in a campaign to gain recognition for this status.[16]

Interestingly, courts have sometimes affirmed the copyright claims of folklore collectors. In the 1953 US copyright case *Wihtol v. Wells*, an appeals court overturned a district court ruling that had invalidated the plaintiff's copyright claim in a version of a Russian folk song. In its decision, the appeals court drew a parallel to an earlier case (*Italian Book Company, Inc., v. Rossi*), in which a Sicilian sailor had sung and played Sicilian folk songs from memory, filling in the gaps in his recollection with original elements. As the *Italian Book Co.* court had put it, "There must have been something which [the sailor] added which brought the old song back into popularity with his own people in this country, and sufficient, I think, to support his claim of copyright."[17] It is striking to see a copyright court contemplate popularity as evidence for the originality or value of a performer's version of a folk song—a logic that also seemed obvious to Çobanoğlu's advocates.

In more recent, similar cases, courts have viewed the role of such popularizers differently. A documentary filmmaker wishing to use the civil rights anthem "We Shall Overcome" sued a publishing company that had long controlled the copyright. The publisher claimed derivative rights in a few small changes relative to preexisting, public domain versions of the song. The district court in the case found the copyright not to be valid, judging the differences between Pete Seeger's version (whose rights the publisher controlled) and the prior versions to be trivial, lacking requisite originality. The differences included a few altered words ("shall" in place of "will," "deep" instead of "down") and a few small variations in the melody. In declaring its judgement, the court explicitly refused to contemplate Seeger's role in popularizing the song, stating, "popularity does not equate with originality."[18] In a contrasting case, *Sawkins v Hyperion Records, Inc.*, however, a UK court found that musicologist Lionel Sawkins did have a copyright in his performing edition of a set of out-of-copyright works by the baroque composer Richard de Lalande; the decision emphasized both the low threshold of originality required by the law and the labor and skill that Sawkins had put into his three thousand editorial interventions aimed at helping contemporary performers interpret the baroque scores (Sher 2005).

The most uncanny parallel to the "Kiziroğlu" case may be that of the children's song "Baby Shark," a ubiquitous earworm that accrued billions of hits on YouTube when a Korean children's entertainment conglomerate produced a version of it in 2016 (see Kinos-Goodin 2019; Lim 2021; Paskin 2019). The song had circulated as a camp sing-along of unknown authorship until children's entertainer Johnny Only recorded a version of it in 2011. Only made a number of interventions as he arranged the camp sing-along, most notably sanitizing it to remove its references to a shark attack. One of the striking parallels to "Kiziroğlu" is that the "Baby Shark" lawsuit originated when a right-wing Korean political party used a version of it as a political campaign song, and Pinkfong, the brand behind the viral clip, threatened to sue the party, who defended itself by saying that Only had granted them permission. Only had viewed the song as a public domain work over which he held no rights—at least until Pinkfong's decision to sue made him reconsider whether he had a claim in his arrangement, to which the Pinkfong version bore a resemblance. A Korean court eventually rejected his claim that Pinkfong's version infringed upon his own.[19] With his failure to capitalize on his own contributions to a song that enriched a more powerful industry actor, Only's position resembles that of Çobanoğlu, who found his own inability to leverage copyright to claim a portion of the "Kiziroğlu" rights so exasperating.

IT CAME AND WENT WITH A FURY . . .

When the dustup over the AKP's campaign song hit the news in late 2014, I watched with keen interest. If only for the sake of my research project, I hoped that the public conversation would go on for a while. It didn't. By March 2015 I had resigned myself to tuning out the tinny loudspeakers of the ruling party campaign trucks as they made their rounds through my neighborhood, blaring Ayna's distorted guitars and throaty salute to the politician Davutoğlu. Nonetheless, my research into the case turned out not to be in vain. It revealed how contingent is the relationship between formal law and everyday legality: "The meanings, sources of authority, and cultural practices that are commonly recognized as legal, regardless of who employs them or for what ends" (Ewick 2015, 471). The debate over folk song collectors' rights and the example of "Kiziroğlu" reveal several aspects of this contingent relationship.

First, actors positioned both inside and outside the legal profession apply categories and concepts from the legal sphere to interpret experiences and assert perceived rights. Sometimes they do so in ways that might not hold up in court.

Çobanoğlu's sense of ownership over "Kiziroğlu" resembles some other examples of informal property claims that bear such an ambiguous relationship to the law. Susan Silbey has described how residents of northeastern US cities put chairs and other household objects out on the street to stake a claim on parking spots they have cleared of snow. They justify the practice through Lockean logics in which their quasi-property rights are warranted by the labor put into the snow shoveling (2012). Another example comes from the world of knitting communities, where knitters assert a series of norms around the ownership and use of patterns, invoking the authority of IP law in the process. The norms "sometimes fit with IP statute and case law, but often they exceed its protections" (Robertson 2014). Often such normative assertions result when "people actually *choose* to understand the law through information and opinion gathered from friends, strangers, coworkers, and the media," whose understandings of the law may diverge from those of courts (Murray, Piper, and Robertson 2014, introduction; emphasis in the original). While Çobanoğlu's claim to "Kiziroğlu" is highly contested, he and his defenders often invoke more widely circulating understandings of copyright doctrine to support their assertions. Çobanoğlu calls himself the song's "composer," while Sinan engages in musicological analysis to compare Çobanoğlu's and prior versions of the song, locating original, individual contributions in the differences. The indeterminacy of copyright doctrines—where the line between infringement and permissible borrowing, between original (re-)creation and mere performance, is often fuzzy—likely contributes to the contingency of how people take them up in such informal contexts. Yet, Çobanoğlu's claims ultimately exceed what the case law—which has established that collectors do not have a right over folk songs they have collected—will back up. Interestingly, however, it does appear that in the long years in which the recording industry's contractual practices received little oversight from copyright authorities, collectors were recognized as copyright owners and apparently controlled some sort of ownership over the songs they collected. In this, too, the issue of collectors' claims to songs otherwise in the public domain resembles that of the parking chairs, where it was clear that while the practice was illegal, legal authorities were complicit in it through their lack of enforcement and their failure to offer an alternative system of snow removal (S. Silbey 2012, 146).

This brings me to a second point about the contingent relationship between the law and everyday legality: how extralegal norms and customs can become encoded into formal law (Bohannan 1973). One of the striking features of the "Kiziroğlu" case is how "collector" may seem an odd category in which to place Çobanoğlu. Yet it seemed right to actors such as MESAM leadership and Çobanoğlu's fellow âşıklar Taşlıova and Sinan. This probably has to do with the decades in which TRT and other official institutions were able to naturalize a set of categories for imagined creative roles—collector and source musician—through which folk music reached wider audiences. Individuals contested how they were categorized, with actors such as Çobanoğlu and Mahzuni Şerif positioning themselves as collectors rather than source musicians (even where they might also feel themselves to be authors). Yet the categories themselves went largely uncontested despite the messy reality of the overlapping roles they named. In other words, categorizing folk music's creative contributors as "collector" and "source" became a custom to which the actors were habituated enough that some sought to have them encoded into the law in the new world of more robust copyright enforcement developing in the 1990s. While they ultimately failed to do so, they did succeed in having the idea seriously debated in the context of revisions to the copyright statute, and MESAM continues to track collectors in its database. A few international examples such as Bolivia's provision for collectors' rights to remuneration in folk music, or older case law such as *Wihtol v. Wells*, suggest that the outcome of Turkey's debate was not a foregone conclusion.

Why, then, did the efforts to create a copyright for collectors fail? This brings me to a third point about the contingent relationship of formal law to the everyday legality contested beyond the courts. Over the years that I researched the debate over collectors' rights, I carried a sense that recognizing such a right was a long shot. I had spent many afternoons immersed in Turkish legal scholarship at Bilgi University's law library in Istanbul, internalizing the same ideas that drove most of the IP experts I interviewed to oppose collectors' rights to the fundamental principles of copyright law. While some individuals saw collection and composition as similar, they tended not to be the legal professionals with a strong voice in the negotiations over a statutory revision (though they did rank among collecting society leadership). The legal professionals tended to be in greater touch with current international copyright laws and practices, where a provision for collectors' rights would be an anomaly, albeit not unheard of (indeed, this was the reason I found myself—as a researcher interested in all things particular to Turkey's copyright story—eagerly watching to see if such a right would be recognized). The international parallels I have discussed were not only relevant to me as an American working on the topic. In my interviews with them, I found that the often-European-trained judges presiding over Turkish courts attend to legal doctrines from abroad, including the United States.

In one music copyright case, for example, the Court of Cassation referred to an American legal test for determining the similarity of two musical works: the ordinary lay observer test.[20]

Judge Çolak points out that the definition of "collection" in article 6 of the Turkish statute derives ultimately from the Berne Agreement's article 2(5), which concerns encyclopedias and anthologies, and he concludes from this fact that the tantalizing word *derleme* of article 6 does not refer to folkloric collection (2008, 134; see also Ateş 2007, 293). Çolak's argument illustrates how legal authorities whose frame of reference is international models may resist locally divergent readings and revisions of the law. An argument could be made that the Berne Agreement does not preclude adding provisions to those it defines; it only bars subtracting from the provisions it stipulates. It could be possible to argue that Turkey could expand the definition of "collection" to explicitly include folk song collection (there is also the example of Bolivia). However, legal professionals tended to seek greater harmony with international practice—especially as it plays out in Europe—rather than creative solutions for adapting copyright doctrines to localized creative concepts and practices.

In chapter 5, I was interested to identify the role that courts, copyright collecting societies, and expert musicologists played in shaping Turkish copyright legality in ways that fit localized traditions of musical practice and ideologies of creativity. In my case study of the rights in arrangements of public domain türküler, for example, I described how a long-standing tendency to locate folkloric creative agency in an imagined anonymous collective seemed to lead some folk music performers to dismiss their own contributions as arrangers and collecting society officials to minimize the value of such arrangements even where someone did claim an arranger's right. The "Kiziroğlu" case—and the ultimate failure to create or recognize a statutory provision for collectors' rights—highlights the constraints on this adaptability of IP to such extralegal frames for understanding creativity. Accommodations of copyright legality to localized ideologies of creativity tend to occur on the margins. Reviewing several recent histories of copyright that link developments in IP law to larger social trends and that highlight the contingencies of copyright legality, legal scholars Shyamkrishna Balganesh and Taisu Zhang offer a correction through their concept of "legal internalism." Legal internalism, in their formulation, refers to "the internal point of view that regular participants in a legal practice usually develop toward it that sees it as normative, epistemologically self-contained, and logically coherent" (2021, 1071). The argument builds on Robert W. Gordon's classic analysis of

Collectors, Copyright, "Kiziroğlu" **193**

critical legal histories, in which he emphasized how "the legal forms we use set limits on what we can imagine as practical options: Our desires and plans tend to be shaped out of the limited stock of forms available to us" (1984, 111, cited in Balgananesh and Zhang 2021, 1117).

In the end, the result of the debate over rights for folk music collectors may have been overdetermined, since the larger efforts to revise the copyright statute foundered on the inability to reconcile stakeholders' competing interests. Yet the case nonetheless seems to exemplify the dynamic of legal internalism, since the legal experts and authorities most engaged in reading and recrafting the copyright statute seem to find such a provision unthinkable in the terms the law affords. Consider, for example, how Judge Çolak struggles to reconcile the act of folk song collection with the legal concept of hususiyet, and how he resists a creative (mis)reading of the statutory provision for anthologies by referring to that article's origins in the Berne Convention. As Balgananesh and Zhang argue, "The ascendancy of law as the dominant system of sociopolitical ordering, coupled with escalating levels of legal complexity that elevate legal knowledge to the status of true expertise, will likely lead to the widespread embrace of internalism among legal professionals" (1104). Turkey's IP reform represents just such a case of the ascendency of law as the dominant system of sociopolitical ordering within the music sector. The shifting position of folk song collectors from the effective equivalent of authors to the bearers of a legally unrecognized status may simply be an artifact of this sea change.

Conclusion

In the introduction of this book, I identified three questions that had emerged as I began my research. The first had to do with creativity. Since copyright can be viewed as a cultural policy regime for regulating creativity, I wondered how IP reform might involve reconciling the concepts of authorship and ownership underlying copyright laws with potentially contrasting ideas prevalent within Turkey's musical traditions. Where there were tensions between localized and more broadly circulating understandings of creativity, in what ways might copyright prove adaptable enough to accommodate localized practice, and how might indigenous approaches to authorship and ownership change because of the efforts to shore up the copyright system? Second, I wondered about the relationship between IP reform and older cultural reform projects. In contrast to older, nationalist cultural reform projects, IP reform was ostensibly identity-blind, and it was not clear how it bore upon processes of subject formation and identity construction, if at all. How, I asked, might copyright mediate sociality, belonging, and understandings of the self? Third, I wondered what relation Turkey's copyright regime bore to the international IP infrastructure or to the national systems of other countries. The general historical relationship was easy enough to see, since Turkey's laws were modeled on continental European laws, and its IP reform process was driven by international agreements and ultimately by its political-economic relationships with other countries. Yet these frameworks left room for actors operating in a national jurisdiction to shape a domestic legal regime in all sorts of ways. What might be distinct to Turkey's system, and what values and politics might account for features specific to the domestic regime?

Answering these questions, I have argued, requires taking a broad view of copyright—not just as it exists "on the books" or in the courts, and not even only as an administrative system for managing rights. Rather, I have focused on copyright *legality*, the law as a cultural practice shaped by a broad range of actors from judges to industry executives to working musicians. I took up the sociolegal term *legal consciousness* to describe how this range of actors bring their own frames, values, and agendas to the process of contesting and enacting legality. I argued that, because of the emergent, contingent, and intersubjective nature of this process, copyright legality is co-constitutive with concepts of personhood and senses of self and belonging. Having explored these themes through six chapters, let me review how my data help answer my three research questions and how they support my overall argument in turn.

By way of addressing my first question, I have offered an extended examination of the folk music genre. In chapter three, I showed how the genre had been constructed in terms of an imagined creative modality that was contrasted with that of Turkish or post-Ottoman art music. Viewing the situation from another angle, we can say that the genre is constructed in terms of a particular legal consciousness: folk music is understood as that to which copyright should not apply. In chapter four, I showed how this legal consciousness shaped how the genre was framed and presented at official institutions, especially Turkish Radio and Television, prior to the years of IP reform. I have argued that the agency's policy toward anonymity in folk music may have been a response to early copyright activism among certain folk music artists who advocated for and claimed original authorship in some folk songs and tunes. The idea of anonymity seems also to have shaped the documentary record upon which courts and collecting societies rely today to determine authorship and apportion rights. In chapter five, we saw how this legal consciousness also informed the discourse surrounding the application of copyright in folk music in the era of IP reform. It drove a variety of musicians and other industry stakeholders to decry allegedly false claims of authorship; meanwhile, IP reform afforded an opportunity for others to assert such claims, perhaps by motivating them to reimagine their roles in the production of folk music. This last point was particularly evident in chapter six, where actors claimed and contested the status of "collector," which bore an ambiguous relationship to the forms of authorship recognized by copyright doctrine. In answer to my first question, then, focusing on legality reveals the crucial role that copyright has played in shaping ideas of creativity and ownership: it has motivated some folk music artists to make claims in terms of such legal categories of authorship and rights. Yet it has also stoked a sense of collective ownership that motivates a contest over the boundaries of the public domain and the interpretation of copyright doctrines.

Here, we are not far from the theme of my second question, since the story of folk music also reveals how copyright legality is co-constitutive of concepts of personhood and identity. Perhaps easiest to see is the parallel to what Chua and Engel call the "identity school" of legal consciousness research, which documents how legal categories may provide the terms in which citizens self-identify and advocate for themselves (2019, 338). Where actors make and contest authorship claims in folk music or claim and debate the status of the collector, they are taking up legal categories in just this way. However, because the idea of folk-lore's anonymity underwrote the twentieth-century collection and promotion of folk music, which was central to the state's cultural nation-building project, it is also clear that copyright consciousness within folk music is entangled with larger narratives about Turkish identity and citizenship. To assert or contest how copyright is applied in folk music is to participate in a larger negotiation of what it means to belong to Turkish society, since what is at stake is the nature of citizens' relationships with collective heritage. Copyright also turns out to reshape concepts of national heritage; in chapter 4, for example, I showed how, along with a few other developments, copyright was imagined to have triggered a discursive rupture, ending the traditional modes of folkloric production and necessitating modernized approaches to creativity in folk music. Chapters one and two furthermore revealed how copyright shapes senses of self and belonging in ways that transcend the framings of a particular genre. I highlighted a reflexive aspect of legal consciousness in the arena of Turkish IP, one that results in part from how copyright is national in jurisdiction and in part from how the project of developing this system seems to have stakes for Turkey's larger geopolitical standing. These factors result in a group status awareness that emerges in several of the cultural schemas according to which actors constitute legality. Informed by common understandings of Turkish history, they may interpret some of their experiences of the copyright system in terms of a critical narrative about IP as a form of cultural imperialism that puts Turkey in a quasi-colonial position, for example. In what I call the intimate dimension of legal consciousness, the domestic copyright system's apparent failures may make sense in terms of—and therefore inflect or reproduce—familiar self-stereotypes tied to longstanding narratives about what it means to be a citizen of Turkey.

Turning to my third question, which focuses on the particularities of Turkey's copyright regime and its relationship to international models and agreements, it should be clear that oral history and ethnography offer an ideal method for understanding this aspect of copyright legality. Within my account are several

Conclusion **197**

examples of particularities of Turkey's national regime, and the historical and ethnographic context reveals the contingencies that have produced these. For example, that Turkish copyright law is modeled on Germany's is the result of historical events apparently unrelated to IP itself: a German Jewish émigré fleeing the political situation in his homeland in the 1930s took refuge in Turkey, where he wound up in a position to draw up the statute. In a few cases, I have focused on the story of such contingencies at length. In chapter two, I discussed the challenges of licensing new recordings or re-releases of previously published musical works, a situation that seems to result from a combination of factors: rightsholders seeking to secure income streams in a low-royalty environment, songwriters seeking to perpetuate an older model of remuneration, the bundled nature of copyright rights that afforded collecting societies a mechanism to leave authorizations in the hands of members, and so on. In chapter five, I inquired why the collecting societies long offered only a limited (10 percent) royalty on arrangements of public domain works, an approach that diverged from practice in most countries. Here too, several factors seemed to be at play, but the case seemed to powerfully illustrate how longstanding ideologies about creativity and national heritage may motivate policy. Chapter six took on this theme most directly, as the debate over rights for folk song collectors revealed the contingent relationship between copyright doctrines and statutes, with their grounding in international models and standards, and older customs in the domestic music industry (in this case those regarding the value and status of derleme). Where the history of nationalist musical folklore motivated some actors to valorize and claim the status of collector, advocating for its legal recognition, legal forms also seemed to constrain the possibilities for accommodating local practice in this way.

SIGNIFICANCE

I also wish to highlight the significance of these findings both for this book's primary audience—(ethno)musicologists—and for other audiences who will find it relevant (especially scholars in sociolegal studies or Middle East studies). Following an era in which copyright appeared only occasionally within and usually on the fringes of music scholarship, (ethno)musicologists are beginning to grapple with the topic more deeply, especially in contexts beyond the global North. That it has taken so long probably relates to the challenges of getting a grasp on IP law's technicalities and sometimes esoteric doctrines (something music scholars aren't necessarily trained to do) and accessing data about money flows, legal cases, and rights management. Focusing on legality and legal consciousness addresses some of these challenges by identifying an object of analysis that is relatively available to ethnography as a mode of empirical inquiry. Ethnography is also particularly well suited to the project of understanding not just copyright doctrines and case law but also the broader lived experience of copyright among those implicated in the systems it sets up. Some of the richest (ethno)musicological research into copyright has critiqued its potentially chilling effects on creativity, or the unjust apportioning of royalties, or its failure to offer a mechanism for preventing ethically questionable appropriations of traditional culture. Yet more recently, scholars have also acknowledged how even musicians working in genres not always associated with canonical forms of authorship may take a pragmatic tack, making ownership claims, pursuing copyright-related income, and affirming the coeval-ness of traditional with modern, mass-mediated culture. I have also contributed to such studies: where music scholarship often assumes the incompatibility of copyright and traditional knowledge systems such as folklore, my folk music genre study shows how this incompatibility had to be constructed.

All of these are worthy lines of inquiry in themselves. Yet the multidimensional model of legal consciousness that I sketch in chapter two provides a framework for contextualizing such phenomena as part of a more complex picture in which there exist necessary tensions between the ideal and reality of the law, tensions that actors find several strategies for making sense of. Through such an approach, we can document how actors affirm the normative basis of the law, take it up as a cultural practice, reflect on it critically or resist it, and also find in the negotiation of legality and the project of developing a national copyright infrastructure an intimate space for integrating frustrations and failures into larger narratives about what it means to be a citizen of such a country. Such an account can highlight the contingencies inherent in copyright legality but also show how recurring cultural schemas pattern the process. That these cultural schemas emerge from localized histories points to the need for further research into copyright legalities around the world, since such research might further clarify both their contingent nature and also the ways a globalized IP law may constrain their adaptability. Such a research focus also offers novel links to older, larger, and emerging concerns of ethnomusicology, such as music's relationship with identity, citizenship, and coloniality. Where ethnomusicologists have often described the cultural intimacy surrounding embarrassing, mass-mediated musical genres (Stokes 2023), the intimate dimension of legal consciousness represents a less often observed way that music forges intimate sociality. My folk

Conclusion **199**

music case study, meanwhile, suggests how legal consciousness can play a key role in constructing the boundaries of a genre.

I also hope that sociolegal scholars will find in my account a significant contribution to a field where ethnographic data on copyright legality remain scarce. I intend my theoretical approach to legal consciousness to inflect existing paradigms such as Ewick and Silbey's influential (1998) approach. Most notably, I highlight how the cultural schemas according to which actors constitute copyright legality are shaped both by the specific categories and bureaucratic structures through which IP organizes its world and by the (quasi-)postcolonial stakes involved when countries on the margins of the global North implement IP reform. In particular, the culturally intimate dimension to legal consciousness is a novel observation that likely has parallels elsewhere. For musicologists and historians of Turkey, I intend my study to highlight a long-neglected aspect of the fraught story of cultural reformism in the country, one that helps account for the dramatic transformations that have occurred since the country's neoliberal turn in the 1980s.

FUTURE DIRECTIONS

While I intend these contributions to invite further, similar inquiry elsewhere, my account is not comprehensive, and it is worth considering which aspects of the topic might reward further research—both in Turkey and in other countries. Perhaps most obviously, I have chosen to focus on folk music at length, while giving the experiences of musicians and industry actors working in other genres shorter shrift. How might copyright consciousness look in a genre whose canons of authorship contrast less dramatically with those underlying copyright laws? There also remains much room for archival work and oral history to fill out the historical account of legal consciousness before the era of IP reform. Further research might also draw copyright users more fully into the ethnographic account. And in my account of folk music, I found it easier to document the perspectives of actors positioned within official institutions than those of rural source musicians who created and passed on the repertoire now framed as a national heritage of folk music. Deeper research into such individuals' perspectives on authorship and ownership are in order, though data that haven't been filtered through the frames of institutionalized folklore can be hard to come by.

———

During the years that I researched this topic, copyright changed in myriad ways. Digital streaming, which initially seemed to portend the drying up of royalty streams and the dethroning of the major multinational music companies, has been integrated into the music sector to such an extent that the recording industry's copyright-related income streams have almost recovered to the historical highs of the peak CD era. MESAM and MSG saw a complete changeover in their leadership in the last years of my research, and there were signs that the societies were becoming better organized and more effective at collecting and distributing licensing income. Even as I draw up my final thoughts in this book that represents the culmination of more than ten years of research, I continue to attend to the latest relevant developments. I have a Google Alert that feeds me daily links to news items related to copyright. I sit in departmental meetings in which we grapple with how to incorporate artificial intelligence into our teaching, and I find myself eager to get my work into print before the technology potentially transforms how we approach copyright.

And yet I also have a lingering sense that the more things change, the more things stay the same. For example, the Turkish Cultural Ministry's website recently featured a news item about a workshop at which the head of the Copyright Statute and Collecting Societies Office declared that "work was being undertaken with the goal of establishing an effective copyright system in our country by directing administrative implementation [and] developing statutory revisions that will strengthen and meet the needs of the culture and arts sector."[1] The summary seems to frame "establishing an effective copyright system" as a yet unrealized goal. There is, in other words, a nagging sense that IP reform is incomplete and ongoing: the practice of the law remains far from the imagined ideal.

Writ larger, however, the situation also makes sense because the tensions between the ideal and practice of the law may be a necessary feature of legality, which actors constitute in a complex, multidimensional, seemingly contradictory way. There will always be a need, then, to understand how actors negotiate such tensions, how the music plays on in the face of copyright legality's contingencies.

Conclusion **201**

APPENDIX

The Basics of Turkish Copyright

The basis of Turkey's copyright law is Law No. 5846 on Intellectual and Artistic Works (*Fikir Sanat Eserleri Kanunu*, abbreviated as LIA in English and as FSEK in Turkish). The statute, which was originally modeled on Germany's copyright law, was accepted in 1951 and has been amended several times since 1983, with notable updates to conform to the TRIPs agreement, European Union law, the Paris text of the Berne Convention, and the Rome Convention for the Protection of Performers, Producers of Phonograms, and Broadcasting Organizations.

What Is Protected?

Articles 1–6 of the LIA enumerate the kinds of works accorded protection, listing these under the following categories: Literary and Scientific Works, Musical Works, Works of Fine Arts, Cinematographic Works, and Adaptations and Collections. Musical works are defined as "all types of musical compositions, with or without lyrics" (art. 3). Art. 6 explicitly lists "musical arrangements" as one type of protectable adapted work (provided the rights of the author of the underlying work are reserved). Art. 80 of the LIA establishes the "neighboring" or "related" rights of phonogram producers in sound recordings made of performances of musical works and the rights of performers of musical works whose performances are fixed in phonograms.

What Are the Requirements for Protection?

Turkish legal scholarship often discusses the LIA's so-called *subjective* and *objective conditions* for protection (e.g., Ateş 2007). The objective condition requires that the work fall under one of the categories of protectable work listed in art. 1–6. The subjective condition, equivalent to the originality requirement described in other jurisdictions, requires that a work bear "the characteristic [*hususiyet*] of its author." This sometimes leads to a higher threshold of originality than that established in the United States, for example, by case law such as *Feist Publications, Inc., vs. Rural Telephone Service Co.*, which held that only "a modicum of creativity" is required. According to Turkish case law, if a party to a suit challenges whether or not a work meets the originality requirement, courts must assign expert witnesses specializing in the relevant field to determine whether the work warrants protection (Okutan Nilsson 2012, 1034).

Phonogram producers' related rights in a sound recording may prejudice neither the rights of the author of the works fixed in the phonogram nor the rights of the performers in the recording (art. 80/A). The LIA also requires that a performer interpret "a work in an original manner [*biçim*] with the permission of its author" (art. 80/A).

While registration is not required as a qualification for protection (see discussion of presumptive authorship below), producers of films and phonograms are required to register their fixations with the Cultural Ministry for purposes of anti-piracy tracking via "banderoles" mandatorily affixed to commercial reproductions; however, the law specifies that this registration is done "without the aim of creating any rights" (LIA art. 13).

Who Owns the Copyright in a Work?

The LIA defines the author as the person who has created the work (art. 8) and grants the author the exclusive right to exercise moral (art. 14–17) and economic rights (art. 18) in the work. The term translated as *author* in the English version of the LIA is *eser sahibi*, literally "master" or "owner of the work." The law also provides for joint authorship (art. 9) and stipulates some exceptions to who controls the rights in a work; for example, a publisher may exercise the rights in works on which the author's name is not given (art. 12). The LIA also stipulates a presumption of authorship for the person whose name is given as the author on published works or whose name is customarily announced as the author in performances and broadcasts (unless a different author is named in publications; art. 11).

What Rights May a Copyright Holder Exercise?

Authors are accorded both moral and economic rights over a work. Moral rights include the following:

- The right of public disclosure (LIA art. 14)
- The right to determine how authorship is attributed on copies or adaptations (or, for works of fine art, displayed with the original; LIA art. 15)
- The right to prohibit modifications to the work (LIA art. 16)

- A right of temporary access to and a right to prevent damage or destruction of the original of a work an author has sold to someone else. Such originals include the handwritten scores of composers (LIA art. 17)

Economic rights include the following:

- The right of adaptation (LIA art. 21)
- The right of reproduction (LIA art. 22)
- The right of distribution (LIA art. 23)
- The right of performance ("on public premises either directly or by means of devices enabling the transmission of signs, sounds, or images"; LIA art. 24).
- The right of communication to the public by devices enabling the transmission of signs, sounds, and/or images (such as television, radio, and digital transmission; LIA art. 25)
- The right to a share of proceeds from sales of the original of a work of art, including the handwritten scores of composers (LIA art. 45)

Without prejudice to the moral and economic rights of the author whose works they perform in a sound recording, performers also exercise similar moral and economic rights to their recorded performances to those that authors exercise in their works (LIA art. 80). After acquiring from the author and performer an authority to exercise economic rights, producers of phonograms have rights of reproduction, distribution, sale, rental, lending to the public, and communication to the public.

In the music industry, the rights of reproduction and distribution, which are involved in making and distributing physical copies such as CDs or vinyl records, are commonly referred to as mechanical (*mekanik*) rights, while the rights of performance and communication to the public, which are involved in live performances, broadcasts, digital streams, and playing recorded music over speakers on public premises, are often called performing (*temsil*) rights.

How Long Does the Copyright in a Work Subsist?

The term of protection for copyrighted works is the life of the author plus seventy years. For works published after an author's death, works whose authorship is not established and whose rights are exercised by a publisher, or whose author is a legal person (such as a corporate entity), the term is seventy years from the date of first publication (LIA art. 12, 18, 19, and 27). For phonogram producers' and performers' related rights, the term of protection is seventy years from the date of first fixation (art. 82).

Appendix **205**

Can Ownership of the Copyright in a Work Be Transferred or Licensed to Someone Else?

Authors or their heirs may transfer (*devretmek*) their economic rights to others, and they may also restrict the duration of the transfer, limit it to use in specific territories, or transfer only a portion of the right or limit its purpose (LIA art. 48). The holder of economic rights may grant an exclusive license (*tam ruhsat*) to only one person, or they may grant a non-exclusive license (*basit ruhsat*), in which case they may grant the same license to others (LIA art. 48).

Moral rights may not be transferred, but authors may appoint someone to exercise their moral rights on their behalf; after death, the authority to exercise these rights passes to an executor of the estate or to legal heirs according to an order of succession stated in the law (LIA art. 19).

Provisions for the transfer of related rights in sound recordings and recorded performances are not addressed in the LIA, but a separate regulation, the Directive on Neighboring Rights, extends the LIA's stipulations for transfer of an author's economic rights to the holders of neighboring rights by analogy (Öngören 2010, 313–14).

Can I Use Someone's Work Without Their Permission?

In contrast to jurisdictions such as the United States where a doctrine of fair use provides a set of abstract factors to consider in determining whether authorization is required for a use, the LIA enumerates a set of statutory limitations or exceptions to the rights of the copyright holder. These include reproducing speeches by public officials in news broadcasts; performing published works for face-to-face educational purposes; quoting previously published works within new literary and scientific works; "incorporating certain elements of a published composition, at the most such as themes, patterns, passages, or ideas, into an independent musical work"; or reproduction for personal, noncommercial use (art. 30–40). Most of these statutory limitations include qualifications such as that the use may not "prejudice the legitimate interests of the author" or "conflict with the normal exploitation of the work" and that the author be credited.

What Remedies Are Available to the Copyright Owner?

For violations of moral rights such as the failure to properly credit the author on reproductions of a work, an author may force the infringer to cease reproduction, correct copies already in circulation to properly credit the author, and pay for publication of the court judgement in newspapers (LIA art. 67). An author may also sue for compensation for moral damages suffered (LIA art. 70). For infringements of economic rights, rightsholders may sue to have infringing copies handed over or destroyed; in cases of unauthorized copying, they may also sue for compensation up to three times the amount that could have been granted by contract (LIA art. 68). Rightsholders can also get an injunction to stop unauthorized public performance of music (Okutan Nilsson 2012, 1039). They may also sue to prevent a probable infringement (LIA art. 69). Infringers of authors' moral or economic rights or of related rights are also liable for criminal action resulting in jail time or judicial fines (LIA art. 71).

Further Reading in English

Law No. 5846 on Intellectual and Artistic Works Dated 5/12/1951. Available at https://wipolex-res.wipo.int/edocs/lexdocs/laws/en/tr/tr001en.pdf.

Okutan Nilsson, Gül. 2012. "Turkey." In *Balancing Copyright: A Survey of National Approaches*, edited by Reto Hilty and Sylvie Nérisson, 1029–45. New York: Springer.

GLOSSARY

Abdal: A member of a minority group sometimes defined in ethnic (Türkmen) and sometimes in Sufi/religious (Bektashi) terms; also an ascetic, wandering dervish. Abdals are known for specializing in music among other trades

Anatolia: Asia Minor, the peninsula making up the bulk of modern Turkey's territory

ağıt: A folk song of lament, a dirge (pl. *ağıtlar*)

Alevi: A follower of a form of Sufism that comprises a large, historically marginalized and oppressed non-Sunni religious minority in Turkey (often estimated at 15–20 percent of the population)

arabesk: A melodramatic popular musical genre synthesizing elements of mid-twentieth-century Egyptian film music with sounds indigenous to Turkey; associated with the culture of urban migrants particularly during its popular peak around the 1970s

âşık: A singer-poet belonging to a tradition that involves composing in standard verse forms and instrumentally accompanying oneself, usually with the bağlama; often glossed as "bard" or "minstrel" in English (pl. *âşıklar*)

bağlama: A long-necked lute commonly used in rural Anatolian musical practices and mass-mediated folk music; also commonly referred to as *saz*

banderole: A holographic anti-piracy seal affixed to copyrighted products in the Turkish marketplace

beste: Musical composition; in folk music contexts refers to a newly composed musical work as opposed to an anonymous one (pl. *besteler*)

CISAC: The International Confederation of Societies of Authors and Composers, a non-profit organization that coordinates among national copyright collecting societies for musical composers, lyricists, arrangers, and publishers

collecting society: An organization that collectively manages the licensing of copyrights on behalf of rightsholders, redistributing licensing income as royalties

composition rights: The copyright rights in a musical composition; in my usage the term includes the rights in song lyrics and arrangements

derleme: The Turkish term for the documentation (lit. "collection") of folklore

deyiş: A form of sung poetry produced by âşıklar; most often refers specifically to Alevi religious songs (pl. *deyişler*)

folk music (*halk müziği*): A genre label applied to a variety of historically mostly rural musical practices; often framed as "Turkish" or "Anatolian" folk music

GEMA: Gesellschaft für musikalische Aufführungs- und mechanische Vervielfältigungsrechte, a copyright collecting society for musical composers, lyricists, arrangers, and publishers in Germany

IMRO: Irish Music Rights Organization, a copyright collecting society for musical composers, lyricists, arrangers, and publishers in Ireland

IP: Intellectual property; refers broadly to property rights in creations of the mind. Areas of law include copyright, patent, trademark, and trade secrets, among others.

ITU: Istanbul Technical University, home to the Turkish Music State Conservatory, the oldest conservatory focused on music native to Turkey (founded 1976)

makam: A melodic modal type; part of a system of such modes central to (post-)Ottoman (also called Turkish) classical or art music

MESAM: Türkiye Musiki Eseri Sahipleri Meslek Birliği (Musical authors' professional union of Turkey), the oldest and largest of Turkey's collecting societies for composers, lyricists, arrangers, and publishers

MSG: Musiki Eseri Sahipleri Grubu Meslek Birliği (Musical authors' group professional union), the second largest of Turkey's collecting societies for composers, lyricists, arrangers, and publishers

MÜ-YAP: Bağlantılı Hak Sahibi Fonogram Yapımcıları Meslek Birliği (Phonogram producers' collecting society of Turkey), a professional organization and collecting society managing record producers' phonogram rights

MÜYORBİR: Müzik Yorumcuları Meslek Birliği (Musical performers' professional union), a collecting society managing recording artists' rights in their recorded performances

neighboring rights: An umbrella term for the rights of record producers in their sound recordings and of performers in their performances fixed in sound recordings; see also *related rights*

phonogram rights: The copyright rights in a sound recording (as opposed to those in a song or performance fixed in such a sound recording); also called "master rights" or "sound recording rights"

post-Ottoman art (or classical) music: my preferred term for a genre that incorporates a set of musical practices historically centered at the Ottoman court, in Sufi lodges, and in other urban contexts; also called Turkish or Ottoman classical (or art) music

related rights: Another term for neighboring rights (see above)

SACEM: Société des Auteurs, Compositeurs et Éditeurs de Musique, a French collecting society for musical composers, lyricists, arrangers, and publishers

saz: A general term for musical instrument, often used to refer to the bağlama

TRT: Turkish Radio and Television, Turkey's state-owned broadcasting agency

Turkish art (or classical) music: See *post-Ottoman art music*

Turkish folk music: See *folk music*

türkü: A general term for folk song (pl. *türküler*)

WIPO: World Intellectual Property Organization, a United Nations agency coordinating IP policy internationally

NOTES

Introduction

1. "Türkiye'de telif hakları telef hakkı olmuş durumunda."

2. Literally, "the system hasn't sat down," which I took to mean that it hasn't been firmly established yet, that its rules are still being settled, and that it has yet to fully acquire an aura of legitimacy among those who engage with it.

3. The "eight-measure rule" that I encountered in Turkey appears to be a version of a more widely circulating urban legend, often formulated as a *six*-bar rule. The six-bar myth may have its origins in the US copyright case *Marks v. Leo Feist, Inc.*, which found the borrowing of a six-measure phrase within a 150-measure composition not to be an infringement (though the decision did not in fact establish six measures as a generally applicable guideline for non-infringing borrowing; see Moser and Slay 2011, 32–33).

4. See Tunalı 2019 for an excellent study of this issue as it plays out in Turkey.

5. A great deal of scholarship on copyright and music has been written by scholars working in the United States or United Kingdom, where the primary rationale for copyright is a utilitarian one: copyrights are granted to authors as a way to temporarily monopolize their works so that they can monetize their creations and thus be incentivized to contribute to culture and public discourse. Scholars of this Anglo-American approach have often voiced concern that the growth and expansion of copyright has begun to inhibit access and thus undermine this public-benefit purpose of the law. Turkey's copyright laws, however, are modeled on continental European ones, whose primary rationales are to protect the natural rights of authors: creators deserve rights over their creations because they have brought them into being. Authors have a moral investment in their works because the latter embody some aspect of their creator's personality. Thus, when considering Turkish copyright as a regime for regulating and valuing creativity, while the economic rationales are not irrelevant, the fundamental normative questions are most often framed as a matter of whether authors' rights are sufficiently respected and rewarded.

6. For example, in their classic book, Wallis and Malm locate their copyright case

studies within a pattern they call *cultural imperialism*, in which "cultural dominance is augmented by the transfer of money and/or resources from the dominated to the dominating cultural group" (1984, 299). Legal scholar Graham Dutfield (2008) described the trade agreements of the 1990s and 2000s (a key context for the present book) as founded on an "IP fundamentalism" that equated copying with piracy and threatened to deny developing countries the same benefits of loose protection for foreign IP that wealthier countries had enjoyed (given the history of the United States itself benefitting from looser IP protections). In a study that resonates in many ways with my own, Eve Darian-Smith argues that globalizing IP law entails "new forms of imperialism and new forms of colonialization" (2002, 294). See also the section "Why Folk Music?" later in this chapter, where I discuss how scholars critique the requirements for copyright protection that often leave cultural practices and products of the global South available for exploitation by more powerfully positioned actors in the music industries, particularly in the global North.

7. There exist two additional, smaller societies for the owners of neighboring rights in sound recordings (MÜZİKBİR and MÜYA-BİR), and in the late stages of my research, a new society was formed to administer the rights of backing performers in sound recordings (TSMB).

8. Focusing on the semiotics of digital textuality, Dent's theoretical approach differs from mine, but his account incorporates a similarly broad range of actors and is likewise set against a backdrop of national anxieties about piracy and IP. Silbey's books document the perspectives of creators and business professionals in the United States, but she leverages her data toward a normative critique that the stated purposes of US IP law are out of sync with the realities of creative production and how people use the law, especially in the digital era. Erlmann's account of South African copyright perhaps parallels my own book most closely, and he takes up several of the same theoretical points from the sociolegal literature that I do. He similarly focuses on copyright law in its many manifestations beyond the courtroom, problematizes the law/society dichotomy (while also leveling a Latourian critique of the "society" construct itself), and likewise highlights something like Robert W. Gordon's (1984) contingency or indeterminacy thesis as an answer to the failures of "instrumentalist" legal scholarship that approaches the law as a means to achieve some social end. Mann's book documents how Jamaicans' creative practices often defy norms of authorship and ownership encoded in copyright laws and constitute a space for contesting coloniality. Boatema Boateng's *The Copyright Thing Doesn't Work Here* (2011), published just prior to my fieldwork and focusing on traditional textiles in Ghana rather than on music, models yet another approach.

9. See for example Cornut St-Pierre's (2019) account, informed by actor-network theory, which argues that "legal technique" is how lawyers bridge the gap between the law on the books and law in action, producing law in the process. As another example, Erlmann

214 *Notes to Introduction*

(2022, esp. chapter 2) tracks how lawyers and other actors take up the law, whose form constrains and affords their actions.

10. The scholarly literature has catalogued countless cases of similar appropriations across differences of power (e.g. Harris 2005; McNally 2017; Springer 2007; Taylor 2003; Theberge 2003).

11. One other recently recurring sort of argument complicates these examples of marginalized actors taking up copyright, however: critical analyses of the victories they have won in court frame these wins as pyrrhic. After the Marvin Gaye estate prevailed in the famous "Blurred Lines" case, critics warned that "the decision did a disservice to the goal of radical racial equality in copyright, in part because one remedial outcome cannot repair a history of racial injustice" (Vats 2020, 18). Similarly, Erlmann argues that the outcome of the "Mbube" case, which awarded the family of Solomon Linda proceeds from Disney's use of a derivative of the song in *The Lion King*, "risks forestalling more sustained scrutiny not only of copyright law's colonial roots but also the persistence of the very colonial concepts and structures the democratic order set out to undo" (2022, 66).

12. It should be said that industry executives and IP experts could also be critical of the US copyright system, of whose quirks—such as the lack of a broadcast performing right for sound recordings—they were often aware.

ONE *Copyright Reform and Cultural Modernization*

1. This last sentence is my loose translation of a proverbial saying that Tez invoked: "aynı tas aynı hamam," which literally means "it's the same bowl, the same bathhouse." The proverb conjures the image of an aging Turkish bathhouse, where patrons scoop water out of sinks with a bowl (*tas*).

2. For a discussion of some of these issues as they stood at the time in a global context, see Marshall 2015.

3. At the time, the two societies for composers were operating under a common licensing protocol together with MÜ-YAP, the organization that administers record producers' phonogram rights, and MÜYORBİR, the organization that administers recording artists' rights in their performances captured in recordings. However, since 2012 labels have negotiated deals with digital service providers independently of MÜ-YAP.

4. Ironically, European military bands were themselves an appropriation from the Ottoman *mehter* model, part of a fashion for "alla turca" that had previously spread through Europe (Popescu-Judetz 1996).

5. For further discussion of Gökalp's role, see Behar 1987; Feldman 1990/1991; Stokes 1992; O'Connell 2016; Gill 2017.

6. There is a long-running debate as to the reasons for the relatively late adoption of

the printing press in the Ottoman Empire. According to one view, conservative Islamic authorities' suspicion of printing books had held back the Ottoman Empire's development. This argument implies that religiosity accounts for Turkey's backwardness and thus supports a certain secular-nationalist discourse. Other arguments emphasize economic reasons: some say that the Sultan's scribes resisted the printing press, for example, which they viewed as threatening their livelihood (see Mardin 2006, 98–100).

7. For more recent examples, see *Fikri ve Sınai* 2005, 241; MESAM 2007, 24.

8. As a matter of legal history, most historians trace the development of copyright in Turkey to the late Ottoman Empire (see Deligöz 2010, 71–97; Gemrik 2008, 12–13; Karlıdağ 2010, 161–80; Öztrak 1971, 11–14; Suluk 2004, 25–29; Surmeli 2011, 42–67). A series of limited, piecemeal regulations concerning issues in copyright in the empire were instituted in 1850, 1857, and 1870. The most comprehensive Ottoman regulation, the Copyright Law (*Hakk-ı Telif Kanunu*) of 1910, arose in the final years of the empire. Where previous regulations had mostly focused on book printing, the 1910 law protected a variety of kinds of intellectual works, including musical compositions. This law continued to obtain after the founding of the Turkish Republic in 1923.

9. The history of capitulations, privileges granted to European merchants operating in Ottoman territory, added to this semi-colonial dynamic (see İnalcık and Quataert 1994, 189–95). European creditors furthermore leveraged Ottoman debt to forward their own interests via the Ottoman Public Debt Administration, founded in the 1880s (Liebisch-Gümüş 2019, 20).

10. This approach followed the thinking of Gökalp, discussed above for his role in developing ideologies that informed the state's early approaches to cultural nation-building. For Gökalp, the international order, as embodied by the League of Nations, was equivalent to European civilization: where the nation was the community of people who shared a common culture, internationalism represented the community of nations who shared a common civilization (Liebisch-Gümüş 2019, 35).

11. Such characterizations of authors' rights as essential to modern civilization drew on discourse originating within western Europe itself (see Dommann 2019, 23; Hemmungs Wirtén 2004, 14–37).

12. Another point in the debate concerned the idea that a mania for translation (*tercüme hastalığı*) might ensue if rights were not granted to foreign authors. In this imagined scenario, Turkish authors would not be incentivized to create original works because it would be easier simply to translate foreign works (Hirsch 1985, 305).

13. Hirsch had drawn up a draft as early as 1941, but, as he recalls in his memoir, it had been "forgotten in a desk drawer at the National Education Ministry" (1985, 431).

14. The 1951 law afforded limited rights in translation but stipulated that foreign works could be freely translated if an authorized Turkish translation had not yet appeared within the first ten years of publication of the original (Öztrak 1970, 6–7; Hirsch 1985, 427–34).

216 *Notes to Chapter One*

This debate over limiting the rights of foreign authors also reflected a broader debate within other developing countries—especially former colonies of European empires—who acceded to Berne (see Olian 1974; Ricketson and Ginsburg 2022, vol. 1, §3.64). Hirsch was dismissive of those in Turkey who advocated denying rights in translations in foreign works altogether, claiming that they were interested in personally gaining from translating such works and passing them off as their own (1985, 305).

15. Ottoman *Hakk-ı Telif Kanunu*, article 29, as reproduced in Çakmak 2007, 227.

16. MESAM founder Nevzat Sümer recalled, however, that İsmail Kemal Elbir, a legal scholar and older brother of his own collaborator Halit Kemal Elbir, had attempted to found a collecting society for composers together with some other prominent individuals during the initial six-month window afforded by the passage of the 1951 statute but had not been able to do so (interview, September 12, 2015).

17. So-called "servitude contracts" (*kölelik sözleşmeleri*) often involve not only granting a license to record and distribute the works recorded on the album; performing artists signing such contracts sometimes even agreed to pay a percentage of income from concert performances. One lawyer described to me a contract she had seen in which a well-known artist who also wrote their own works had transferred all rights to the label rather than granting only permission to use the works on the recording in question. Most frustratingly for artists bound by one of these contracts, they agreed not to work with any other label until a set number of albums had been produced under the contract; if the label decided to stop working with an artist because of a lack of success, the artist would be unable to switch to another label and their career would effectively end (see Çakmur 2001, 247–54, for one account).

18. Binboğa also recalled signing waivers when he appeared on TRT, signing away all rights to make a copyright claim over the use of his works on the broadcast.

19. See chapter 4.

20. Interestingly, a hip-hop adaptation of this song, recorded by Halodayı and Azer Bülbül, brought it back to the top of the charts in 2023.

21. The Court of Cassation's decision in the case (Yargıtay 4. Hukuk Dairesi E. 1961/11099 K. 1962/8799) established such principles as a recording artist's liability in cases of unauthorized duplication (Sevimli 2007, 116; Akyüz 2009, 88–89).

22. The full Turkish name translates to Firm for the Formation of a Union of Musical Lyricist, Composer, and Publishing Organizations and the Protection of Creators' Rights.

23. Another of Kaya's films, *Arabeks*, also links the proliferation of new musical talent in the arabesk genre to the growth of the domestic film industry at this time (see Bulut and Kaya 2010).

24. While industry actors framed such unauthorized reproduction of records as piracy (*korsanlık*), it is worth noting that the 1951 copyright statute did not actually recognize a copyright in sound recordings; it only protected rights to compositions captured in sound

Notes to Chapter One **217**

recordings. The legal status of sound recordings was perhaps irrelevant given the lack of enforcement at the time, though recording industry lawyers I spoke with posited that record producers could theoretically have asserted rights through unfair competition law.

25. Legal studies scholars have pointed out that a number of countries, including the United States, have similarly refrained from enforcing foreign IP rights as a matter of protectionist economic policy that fosters domestic industry (e.g. Beukelauer and Frederiksson 2019, 463; Dutfield 2008; Karaganis 2011).

26. Demirsipahi reported that in a meeting with what he called "the International Composers' Union" (possibly CISAC?), they reproached him (*beni ayıpladılar*) for not doing enough to raise awareness of copyright among Turkey's composers ("Cemil Demirsipahi ile söyleyiş" 2005, 292).

27. Unfortunately, I wasn't able to follow up on this issue and find out the exact capacity in which Özdemiroğlu appeared at such a meeting. He was ill during my research and passed away in 2016.

28. These additions recognized rights required by the 1961 Rome Convention for the Protection of Performers, Producers of Phonograms and Broadcasting Organisations, though Turkey did not join the convention until 2004.

29. While the rights of producers and performers were recognized in the 1995 statute, they did not organize as collecting societies until 2001. In the meantime, MÜ-YAP operated as a professional organization, but not a collecting society.

30. During my research, much of this income was distributed, however, according to analogy with broadcasting, meaning that the collecting societies distributed royalties for performing rights in public spaces on the basis of radio and television playlists. This was because of the difficulty of tracking the music played in public spaces, though in some cases they were able to use software to do so, and venues hosting live performances often submit setlists of repertoire performed.

TWO *Constituting Legality in the Music Sector*

1. These normative and pragmatic dimensions of legality loosely correspond to some categories other scholars have discussed, such as Tyler's (2006) instrumental and normative perspectives on why people obey the law.

2. Özyürek describes how, in the late 1990s and early 2000s, locating modernity in Europe became complicated for Kemalist citizens, who felt that the country's sovereignty was threatened by EU critiques of Turkish statist interventions that sustained the hegemony of Kemalism. Faced with the resurgence of Islamist political parties, however, neither could they locate modernity in the present or future of Turkey; they thus began to locate modernity in a nostalgic vision of 1930s Turkey (2006, 10–11). Such complexities may have contributed to the vagueness of the international imaginary that

I describe here, particularly considering the impossibility of locating an ideal copyright system in 1930s Turkey.

3. The US constitution, for example, grants Congress the power to "promote the Progress of Science and Useful arts, by securing, for limited Times, to Authors and Inventors, the exclusive Right to their respective Writings and Discoveries" (U.S. Const. art. I, § 8, cl. 8).

4. *Eser sahibi*, literally "master/owner of the work," could also be translated as "rightsholder." I have rendered this as "author" in this context, as it often is, but in some contexts the term refers also to arrangers and publishers.

5. The status of publishers within the societies has apparently changed several times over the years, but this official saw those periods when publishers had full voting membership as times when the societies' bylaws conflicted with how the copyright statute positioned authors vis-à-vis publishers. At the time of our interview, publishers were not full, voting members of the societies. The membership categories have also since changed, and society members are now classified as "ordinary" (*olağan*) or "full" (*tam*) members.

6. As discussed in the book's introduction, this musician uses the term "copyright consciousness" (*telif bilinci* in Turkish) in a sense overlapping with but distinct from the scholarly, sociological term "legal consciousness."

7. Unlike in the US system that was more familiar to me, where defendant and plaintiff each bring in their own expert witnesses to testify in their own favor (cf. Leo 2021, 15), expert witnesses in the Turkish system are expected to be neutral.

8. While the collecting societies generally do not force performers to get an authorization from rightsholders to perform their works live as they do for making sound recordings (see later in the chapter), a 2004 revision of article 41 of the copyright statute allowed rightsholders to get a court injunction to block public performances of copyrighted repertoire (see Okutan Nilsson 2012, 1039). A few composers have exploited this right, most famously when the songwriter Kayahan blocked recording artist Nilüfer from performing his songs after the two had a falling out (Denker 2006).

9. It is worth noting that legal experts and professional administrators play key roles within the societies. For example, while the MESAM board and president are all elected society members, at present the general secretary, who advises the president closely, is a lawyer.

10. The historical reasons for this disproportionate representation are usually traced to traditionally negative Sunni attitudes toward music coupled with the centrality of music to Alevi belief and practice.

11. As Walton points out, the literature on political intimacy à la Herzfeld overlaps with another strain of the anthropology of intimacy that other scholars of Turkey have taken up to show how state power and public discourse mediate private citizens' intimate relationships, affect, and subjectivity (2015, 62; cf. Sehlikoğlu 2016; Stokes 2010).

Notes to Chapter Two **219**

12. When I shared this passage with Baydur as I was revising my manuscript, he did, however, modify his comments by naming several Turkish firms that he perceived to be well-functioning and successful.

13. See US Copyright Office circular 73, https://www.copyright.gov/circs/circ73.pdf, accessed May 13, 2024. US Code Title 17 § 115 specifies that the work must "have previously been distributed to the public in the United States under the authority of the copyright owner of the work." Strictly speaking, most compulsory licenses are arranged through the private Harry Fox Agency, though the availability of the statutory mechanism ensures that these licenses are granted at the statutory rate.

14. Per Ricketson and Ginsburg (2022), Germany, Austria, Bulgaria, the United Kingdom, and Switzerland created compulsory licensing for mechanical reproduction of works, while Italy, Belgium, and Czechoslovakia did not. The United States, India, and Taiwan seem to be among those who maintain compulsory licensing for mechanical reproduction for this use (Kwee-Tiang 2010, 440, 456), while some countries who established such a regime later abolished it (Elton 2011, 30).

15. Here there are important differences among various jurisdictions. In the United States and the United Kingdom, for example, there are separate collecting societies managing performing rights (ASCAP, BMI, and SESAC in the United States, PRS in the United Kingdom) and mechanical rights (The Harry Fox Agency and MCPS, respectively). In other jurisdictions, a single society handles all of these rights, as is the case for example with GEMA in Germany and MESAM and MSG in Turkey.

16. Here I wish to credit Professor Gül Okutan Nilsson, who first explained this mechanism to me.

17. One lawyer cited an anecdote to explain MESAM's decision to return the right of distribution to authors: a composer reportedly objected to the frequent use of one of his compositions as a dramatic backdrop for news reports covering disasters. He found this contrary to what he had meant to express in the piece but had been unable to prevent such uses under MESAM's original policies. While this anecdote seems to involve a synchronization right rather than distribution (*yayma*), the Turkish copyright statute does not specify a distinct synchronization right. MESAM appears to consider synchronization to fall under the heading of distribution rights; thus, by returning the right of distribution to members, this type of issue could be addressed. On MESAM categorizing synchronization rights as *yayma hakkı*, see http://www.mesam.org.tr/Uyelik-SSS, accessed October 9, 2016.

18. This 1986 law was later revoked, but its stipulations were incorporated into article 13 of the 2004 revision of the copyright statute.

19. When the ministry established its registration system, labels were allowed to declare their rights to old recordings for a period of time, often simply on the basis of a copy of the old record, whose printed label states the name of the company that produced it.

But not all recordings were registered in this way, and, in many of the remaining cases, controlling the rights to the recording comes down to one's ability to provide evidence in court documenting that one has acquired all the necessary permissions related to works on the album. In some cases, the phonogram rights to the recording itself could even be in question if a label has acquired them from another label (which may have long since gone out of business).

20. Öngören suggests that there remains a debate as to the validity of the pre-1986 agreements, since relying on older forms of consent documentation (such as the *eser işletme belgesi*) is common industry practice and case law has affirmed the validity of some of them. It also seems clear that rightsholders can authorize the reproduction of their works "in all formats," but where an agreement stipulates a specific format, it throws into question whether the producer is authorized to release the recording in other formats (2010, 324, 326–27).

21. Article 640 of the Turkish Civil Code offers a provision that a set of heirs can appoint a representative to administer the rights in a shared inheritance such as a copyright in a work, which would streamline the negotiation of a mechanical license, but absent the formal appointment of such a designated representative, a prospective licensee would have to come to terms with each heir individually. On the other hand, per article 10/2 of the copyright statute, an individual heir can take legal action against an alleged infringer on behalf of all the heirs if it is in their collective interest (see Ateş 2020, 49).

THREE *Essentializing Creativity: Authorship and Anonymity*

1. Cevdet Çağla (1900–1988) was a violinist, composer of *makam*-based art songs, and long-time administrator at Istanbul radio. He was present at the 1973 meeting where Tüfekçi made these comments.

2. Compare my chapter 2 discussion of the reflexive aspect of copyright consciousness in Turkey, according to which actors contrast the condition of copyright in Turkey with that as they imagine it elsewhere.

3. My concept draws some inspiration from Perlman's (2019) discussion of "focalized" and "peripheralized" authorship. We swapped drafts of our respective papers on this topic and had many conversations about it.

4. In my fieldwork I found that the available names for this genre were contested and unsatisfactory to just about everyone involved. Gill (2017) settles on "Turkish classical music" in her ethnography of the genre. Here I also frequently use "Turkish art music," since this is the longstanding official name at TRT (see later in this chapter). But "Turkish art music" is also a label sometimes specifically applied to mid-twentieth-century light classical song repertoire. Meanwhile many musicians use other labels as well, such as

Notes to Chapter Three **221**

Türk musikisi, which translates simply to "Turkish music" but specifically uses the older Greek cognate for music (*musiki*) rather than the French cognate (*müzik*) introduced in the republican era (on the differing valences of these cognates see Gill 2017, 31–33).

5. For a general overview of the introduction of Western notation into Turkish *makam*-based music, see Ayangil 2008.

6. Note that such terms used on these manuscripts often differ from the folklore key-word *anonim*, perhaps signaling that anonymity in post-Ottoman art music is understood as an epistemic status, not an ontological one (see chapter 4).

7. This comparison highlights the wider-spread nature of distinctions between notions of originality that demand relative autonomy of works and those that accommodate or celebrate intertextual relationships. The latter include African American practices involving repetition with a difference that Henry Louis Gates Jr. theorized as "signifyin" (2014) or that copyright scholars have sometimes discussed as "remix" (Lessig 2008). Writer Robert Macfarlane argues that literary critical discourse has historically swung back and forth between two different visions of literary creation. Certain periods have been dominated by what he calls he calls *creatio*: the aforementioned Romantic idea of the autonomous creator bringing forth original works ex nihilo. Accordingly, within such a milieu any sign of literary resemblance may be judged "unoriginal," and the greatest sin is plagiarism. At other times critics and authors have embraced what he calls an *inventio* aesthetic, acknowledging and even celebrating how creativity involves appropriation and intertextual reference (2007, 1–7). It is worth emphasizing that the *inventio* creativity of the Ottoman lyric tradition did involve a strong concept of individual authorship, as evidenced by the appearance of an author's name in the final verse of a poem and the presence of collected works (*divan*) of single authors.

8. Other scholars have occasionally discussed individually-identifiable stylistic differences among composers of earlier eras (e.g., Feldman 1996, 370).

9. Legal experts occasionally complained to me about this casual usage of the term, insisting on a distinction between "anonymous works" and "works past their terms of protection" (*koruma süresi bitmiş eserler*).

10. For assertions and discussions of this theory, see Boratav 1942, 81–83; Çolak 2008, 103; Emnalar 1998; Fossum 2023a; Güney 1953, 9–13; Özbek 2005; Öztelli 1972, 10–11; Özürküt 2005; TRT 1991, 101; 1996, 15.

11. Most histories of Turkish folklore focus on this nationalist paradigm, perhaps for good reason, since it produced the core of the folk music repertoire most often performed and heard today. However, it is worth highlighting traditions of folklore collection that predated and contrasted with the early republican nationalist approach. Notably, examples of folkloric genres (türkü and *varsağı*) were performed at the Ottoman court and are even recorded in the seventeenth-century manuscripts of Ali Ufki. In 1905, the musician and folk song collector Georgios Pachtikos published a compendium of Greek folk songs

that included examples from Anatolia and Thrace; the priest and composer Gomidas Vartabed likewise collected folk music from the Armenian populations of Anatolia prior to the founding of modern Turkey (see M. Erol 2015, 140–46; Yıldız 2016, 101–23). In the late Ottoman era, researchers and early commercial record companies also recorded examples of folk music by Kurdish performers (Reigle 2013) and Greek musicians in Smyrna (Pappas 1999). Counter-nationalist folklore projects, such as much of the work of the record label Kalan (see Yıldız 2018, 134) or the *radikal folklor* of the group Kardeş Türküler (Bates 2008, 63–67) have also emerged more recently.

12. Asserting the anonymity of folk music also positioned it in the public domain, making it available for these composers to freely incorporate into their compositions. As I discuss in chapter 5, subsequent composers in this tradition such as Yalçın Tura have argued passionately for keeping folk music in the public domain for this reason.

13. See Saltık and Taş 2016, 56, which includes a photo of Sılemano Qız playing for a national Victory Day celebration in Tunceli in 1937.

14. Feminist and other critical legal scholarship has further shown how IP laws often privilege masculine-associated genres of practice (see Bartow 2006; Kraut 2011).

15. When he made field recordings on his folk music collection trips, Sarısözen recorded metadata on a standard collection form (*derleme fişi*) that does not include a line for noting an author, but does include a place for recording from whom, when, and where the source musician had learned the song or tune ("kimden-ne zaman, nerede oğrendiği"). Şenel 2018b provides examples of these forms. In many cases source musicians responded that they had learned the music "from the ancients" of their village (*eskilerden*); in other cases, the line is blank; and in a few cases, it names a specific individual such as "Burdurlu Hacı Mustafa" (853). In what reads intriguingly like an oblique authorship claim, some informants responded "myself" (*kendi kendim*), though this might also mean simply that the musician is self-taught and has absorbed popularly circulating songs (900–901).

16. Similar practices are sometimes described as "melodized speech" rather than song; see de la Bretèque 2016.

17. The term *deyiş* can refer generally to the poems of âşıklar, as I use it here, though it often refers more specifically to the religious poems of âşıklar from the Alevi minority.

18. Some folklorists divide folk music repertoire into anonymous and âşık components (e.g., Albayrak 2012).

19. For a relatively early example of an âşık claiming a tune, see Tulunay 1930, 169, where both lyrics (*güfte*) and composition (*beste*) of a deyiş are ascribed to Âşık Ahmet, an âşık featured in the article. However, it is not clear whether Âşık Ahmet made such a melodic authorship claim himself, or whether the writer of the article assumed that his claim to have authored the poem also entailed a claim to have composed the tune.

20. Similarities among Âşık Veysel's tunes are a commonly discussed example (e.g.

Notes to Chapter Three **223**

Şenel 2018a, 40–41). However, I would note that one could evaluate creativity in relation to the constraints of conforming to generic expectations in multiple ways. One could point to the narrowness of the regional repertoire to minimize an individual's creativity, but people tend not to make the opposite argument: that the narrow range of regional style might constitute a set of constraints within which individuals must be all the more creative or original to operate (cf. Sawyer 2003, 152).

21. Some of my interlocutors expressed doubt that all of Neşet Ertaş's attributions of melodies to his father were reliable, citing a purported increase in such claims after copyright became better enforced. The documentary record of Abdal authorship prior to Muharrem Ertaş's generation is weak, and it is possible that some of these tunes were orally transmitted, older tunes or variants derived from older tunes. However, Abdals do maintain distinctions between new and long-standing tunes (using the term *usta malı* or "property of masters" for the latter; e.g., Parlak 2013, 1:277).

22. Laing's example of Copland's use of Shaker melodies in "Appalachian Spring" is one that complicates this idea (2002, 180); others include many of Bartok's works or, in Turkey, many of the works of Ahmet Adnan Saygun.

FOUR *Copyright and Traditionalism in State Broadcasting*

1. Despite an exhaustive search, I have been unable to locate the story and photograph Dedeoğlu describes. However, the April 30, 1975, issue of *Hey* features a report that Demirsipahi opened such a lawsuit against Tüfekçi. The story confirms several details of Dedeoğlu's recollection (see "C. Demirsipahi tarafından . . ." 1975). The August 20, 1975, issue furthermore reports that the two men were vying to take over the leadership of the larger TRT Music Division from recently departed director Cüneyd Orhon at the time (Tüfekçi had been made interim director; see "TRT Müzik Dairesindeki Başkanlık . . ." 1975). It seems possible that this competition heightened the stakes of their rivalry, though two of my consultants who were knowledgeable about TRT history doubted that Demirsipahi was a serious candidate.

2. Dedeoğlu related another anecdote in which Demirsipahi, who had been experimenting with adding frets to his bağlama in order to afford extra intonational possibilities, left his instrument at the offices of the radio. Tüfekçi, finding it there and learning that it was Demirsipahi's, is said to have cut the extra frets off with a knife. Demirsipahi reportedly refused to perform on the radio after this (see Dedeoğlu 2016).

3. One of the stories in *Hey* reports that Tüfekçi furthermore complained that Demirsipahi was overpaid for his work on the program, which was called *Dünden Bugüne* (From yesterday to today; see "C. Demirsipahi tarafından . . ." 1975).

4. While Şenel characterizes the invitation to Sarısözen to appear on radio programs as filling a void left by Sadi Yaver Ataman, who had directed folk music programs until

being called up for military service, Tör recalls inviting Sarısözen to rectify the poor quality of the performance of türküler in broadcasts at the time.

5. Much of the information in the following paragraphs is synthesized from interviews with Paşmakçı and Mehmet Özbek as well as Şenel 2009 and Duygulu 2019. See Kocabaşoğlu 1980 for a more detailed account of the changing institutional structures in broadcasting leading up to the founding of TRT in 1964.

6. See figure 6.1 in chapter 6 for an example of TRT Folk Music Repertoire notation.

7. One of my favorite examples is "Fırat Kenarının ince Dumanı" (Fine mist of the banks of the Euphrates), collected by Mehmet Özbek, TRT Turkish Folk Music Repertoire item number 2387. The song is also included in a published and edited volume of türküler and folk dance melodies from Urfa, where the source person has provided a long anecdote (öykü) to describe the story behind this supposedly anonymous türkü (Doruk 1977, 50–51, 99). But the same song is also included in the official TRT Art Music Repertoire, listed as a composition by the great twentieth-century singer and composer Sadettin Kaynak. Two other examples of türküler in the TRT Folk Music Repertoire that are registered elsewhere as original compositions by Kaynak: "Yeşil yaprak arasında kırmızı gül goncesi" (Red rosebud between green leaves), region: Elazığ; source person: Adnan Çilesiz; collected by: Salih Turhan; TRT Repertoire no. 4045; and "Çıkar Yücelerden Yumak Yuvarlar," region: Erzincan; source person: Erzincanlı Şerif; collected by: Nida Tüfekçi (elsewhere registered as a composition by Kaynak, lyrics by Vecdi Bingöl). Halil Atılgan alerted me to these examples.

8. It is worth noting that the anonymity policy applies only to certain regular programs, and in particular on the radio as opposed to the agency's television stations, which seem to have eluded the reach of the Folk Music Division headquarters in Ankara and its aspirations to control the broadcast content of folk music programming. On the other hand, the official Folk Music Repertoire has an additional importance, since it serves as a kind of de facto folk music canon that researchers take as a key reference and whose notations many musicians commonly use as lead sheets in many contexts beyond broadcast programs.

9. Note that in the particular instance of the removal of the 1500 türküler, Tüfekçi was apparently not present (Şenel 2009, 103), but he does appear to identify with those who participated (TRT 1991, 110).

10. When I asked Paşmakçı to name some of these songs, he recalled a few of Demirsipahi's songs, including "Şenola düğün şenola" and "Ana beni eversene," along with songs by other composers (pers. comm., April 19, 2015).

11. An academic presentation on tunes from the Çukurova region suggests a few names of such artists: Aziz Şenses, Ali Limoncu, Abdurrahman Yağdıran, Dr. Çetin Ünal Özülkü, and Halil Atılgan (Seyhan 1990, 525).

12. Tüfekçi may have had access to Sarısözen's personal documents, since he married Sarısözen's former wife, Neriman Altındağ, and raised his son Memil.

Notes to Chapter Four **225**

13. In fact, we can read the letter as evidence of Sarısözen's views but also as evidence that regional artists like Çekirge composed original works that they thought would be appropriate to folk music radio programming.

14. See for example Şenel's massive compendium of writings by and about Sarısözen (2018b).

15. Demirsipahi claims elsewhere that "the term 'taken from' [alınan] used to be used in place of the term 'composer.' In even earlier broadcasts, Mesut Cemil would name the *makam*, the form, the *usul* [metrical genre], composer, and lyricist, one by one. . . . We contrived a few lies, every state does such things, every society lies. But later we ourselves believed these lies" (TRT 1991, 161; see 158–66 for further such anecdotes from Demirsipahi). Coming later in the same meeting at which Tüfekçi read from Sarısözen's letter cited above, these examples appear to be cited in direct response to Tüfekçi. It is worth noting that there is reason to doubt some of Demirsipahi's claims; Süleyman Şenel found, for example, that "Tutam yar eline tutam," a türkü Demirsipahi claimed to have collected, had been previously published in a 1953 issue of *Türk Folklor Araştırma Dergisi* (pers. comm., June 19, 2018).

16. The example also parallels international cases in which folklorists have acted on a different sense of what repertoire is appropriate to folk music than have the musicians who served as their sources; John and Alan Lomax, for example, worked to keep Leadbelly from performing popular songs (Filene 1991, 612–13).

17. Here Özbek is likely alluding to Sarısözen's statements in the journal *Radyo* that the aim of "Voices from the Homeland" was to bring the country into a state of feeling the same feeling (Çeren 1944).

18. One folk music expert who admired Sarısözen and Tüfekçi and to whom I related Demirsipahi's anecdotes about Sarısözen doubted their veracity, speculating, for example, that Demirsipahi may have invited the musicians from Urfa onto the program to play his song.

19. It is unclear whether this vote precipitated a change in policy; the advisory committee's decisions were not binding. While art music programming today features occasional türküler, their presence may not date to this moment. The incident also exemplifies how post-Ottoman art musicians often seem more relaxed in how they delineate folk and art than are some folk music traditionalists like Tüfekçi.

20. A famous example is Muhlis Akarsu's "Bu yarayı dosttan aldım ezeli" (I got this wound from a friend long ago). The final verse contains the line "Akarsuyum böyle böyle çamurlu yolda" (I am a stream [akarsu] along the muddy road), which cleverly plays on the meaning of the âşık's name. The identity of the author is hidden and the clever wordplay is lost in the official TRT version, which reads "Bir garibim böyle böyle çamurlu yolda" (I am a stranger on the muddy road).

21. See also Tüfekçi 1992, where he argues that "when âşıklar sing their deyişler, they don't

make new compositions [*besteler*]. They stay within the musical style and manner [*tarz ve tavır*] of the region where they were trained and they set their texts to old tunes" (242). In my interview with him, Özbek countered this argument with examples from âşıklar who seem to have composed new melodies that he had never encountered in older recordings.

22. Note the contradiction in this logic, according to which a known composer composes something anonymous. One possible resolution is to argue that there is something inherently different about this sort of composition, such as that it is "unconscious," isn't "rule-based," or carries regional and not individual characteristics, some of the arguments I describe in greater detail in Fossum 2023a.

23. Other scholars have also commented on the salience of regionality in Turkish nationalist folklore, especially to critique its role in erasing markers of ethnic difference (e.g. Bates 2016, 29–34; Seeman 2019, 174–80).

24. While this distinction between staff musicians and regional guest performers was grounded in older radio ensemble practices dating to the Sarısözen era, it was now further bureaucratized through exams and committee reviews. There were separate exams for both staff musicians and for regional musicians to qualify to play on the Radio regularly. The artist exam reports for 1972, for example, show that the (now quite famous) Muhlis Akarsu applied both as a staff musician for Diyarbakır radio and to be able to perform as a regional artist, presumably representing his hometown of Sivas/Kangal. He was rejected on both counts because he was unable to properly reflect specific regional styles and was deemed to be "imitating" other artists (TRT 1972b, 7).

25. See Solmaz 1999 for a critique of such perceived effects of TRT's broadcasting.

26. Pen name of the influential late Ottoman poet Mehmet Tevfik (1867–1915).

27. This negative assessment of oral transmission also seems to echo what American folklorist Alan Dundes called "the devolutionary premise in folklore theory" (1969).

28. For Turkish folklore specialists (and many average citizens), this name would have rung a loud bell as a place especially known for its rich tradition of âşık music, having most famously produced Âşık Veysel and Âşık Ali İzzet Özkan, among many others.

29. I.e., if they had been older, they would have been excluded according to the rules of gender separation that begin to apply as children approach puberty.

30. Interestingly, even beste türkü proponents often maintained a distinction between such well-composed türküler and "contrived" ones. Folklorist and folk music artist Halil Atılgan and I discussed one example: Konya regional artist Rıza Konyalı's song "58 modelli araba" (1958 model automobile), a tongue-in-cheek, commercially produced hit lament about a car that constantly breaks down. While in the style of a türkü and performed by a regional musician, the song's title and recurring hook offer an obvious clue that it had been composed at least since a 1958 car would have become unreliable; topically it also appeared to Atılgan to diverge from the themes of authentic folk music in a way that marked it as "commercial."

Notes to Chapter Four **227**

31. The issue provoked heated arguments and even led to a committee vote at a meeting in 1988, according to several people I spoke with who were present (the pro-beste side apparently won the vote, but the proposed policy change was subsequently not implemented). Unfortunately, I was unable to get my hands on the transcripts from this meeting. The issue was again discussed at the 1990 meeting, and it was the main item on the agenda at the 1991 meeting.

32. To name one example, the türkü "Varıp neğlemeli sılağı gayrı" was accepted into the TRT Repertoire in 1975 (Rep no. 1190), where it shows the collector as Kenan Şele, the source person as Adanalı İboş Ağa, and the transcriber as Tuğrul Şan. Subsequently when the türkü started to be played on TRT, according to Halil Atılgan, a dentist from Adana named Çetin Özükül wrote to TRT claiming to have composed it and demanding royalties. Per Atılgan, Özükül had sung the song to Tuğrul Şan in 1970. Şan had notated it and given it to the Repertoire Committee. Şan also played it on an LP. Upon receipt of Özükül's letter, TRT removed it from the TRT Repertoire (1992, 166–67; field note, June 12, 2015; see Demirel 2005, 47, for further examples).

33. Tatlıses, Gencebay, and Tayfur are among the best-known recording artists in the arabesk genre, though Gencebay has resisted this genre label.

34. Seeman (2019, 292) likewise notes that record labels often sought to register songs as anonymous so that they could avoid paying mechanical royalties even where Roman musicians claimed to have composed the songs.

35. See Atılgan 2005, 16, for another account of the song's history.

FIVE *When Copyright Meets Folk Music*

1. As described elsewhere in this book, the Turkish term for the members of this society is "authors" [*eser sahipleri*, lit. "work owners"], which includes composers, lyricists, arrangers, publishers, and the heirs to such authorship rights. This is contrasted with the owners of "neighboring rights" in sound recordings or in the performances captured in these recordings.

2. On TRT folk music programming, see chapter 4. On the âşık tradition, see chapter 3.

3. For an example, see Özkan and Başgöz 1979, 43–44. Here, Başgöz reports an incident in which the iconic Âşık Veysel calls out a younger âşık for claiming one of Âşık Ali İzzet Özkan's poems as his own.

4. One example came from Turkish art music composer Yalçın Tura's presentation at the 2005 MESAM symposium (Tura 2005, 63). For a published example in English, see Tunalı 2019, 42.

5. The Cultural Ministry requires recording artists or their labels to submit a proof of authorization (*muvafakatname*) for each work recorded on an album, and MESAM and MSG provide the contact information for the rightsholders whose authorization is

required. As described in chapter 2, because there is no compulsory licensing system in Turkey, rightsholders can demand any fee they like in return for their authorization. For public domain works, the recording artist or label pays a nominal registration fee to the ministry in place of a licensing agreement.

6. Süleyman Ergüner, then director of the TRT Music Office, read this quote during his presentation. He cites Şenel's paper "Türk Halk Müziği'nde 'Beste', 'Makam' ve 'Ayak' Terimleri Hakkında," V. Milletlerarası Türk Halk Kültürü Kongresi, Ankara, 1997, 372–73. "Saz" here is another name for the bağlama. "Teke zortlatması" refers to a type of instrumental tune found in the Aegean region of Turkey.

7. For further analysis of Anadolu pop examples, see Baysal 2018 and Skoog 2012. For analyses of a popularized version of folk music outside the Anadolu pop genre, see Stokes 2010, 107–45. The rock group Ayna's version of "Kiziroğlu," discussed in chapter 6 of this book, provides yet another example.

8. As far as I can tell, in Turkey proposals for a *sui generis* legal regime to protect traditional culture have not advanced beyond the publication of a few academic research papers, such as those by Judge Uğur Çolak (2008) and entertainment lawyer Oğuz Müftüoğlu (2005).

9. There is also the cautionary tale of Ghana, where the state claimed ownership of public domain folklore, but then leveraged this ownership to charge musicians a tax on their own ancestral traditional music they performed (Collins 2006).

10. In several places the publisher used the term "author/rightsholder" (*eser sahibi*) to refer generally to members of MESAM and MSG. In translation, the term creates some confusion in this case, so I have made a choice to translate this as "arranger" in several places that I have indicated with brackets.

11. From what I can tell, the case of mechanical rights—the royalties that accrue when physical recordings are sold—might appear even more unfair. In the case of such mechanical royalties, which are normally paid by the record label, while composer X might be granted a 10 percent share of the royalties on sales of the physical recording of türkü X, the other 90 percent could simply be absorbed as profit by the label.

12. Woods v. Bourne Co, 60 F.3d 978 (2d Cir. 1995).

13. The database entry for "Dadaloğlu" actually lists the nineteenth-century bard as the author of both words and music, though his death date puts the song in the public domain anyway.

14. In our conversation, he named "Kıyılı halayı" and "Sinsin halayı" individually, but I assume he was referring to the recording on his *Anadolu* album. MESAM's publicly available database records seem to confirm his claim, as "Sinsin halayı / Elmaların yongası / Kıyılı halayı" appears with a public domain credit and no arranger; see https://www .mesam.org.tr/eser-arama/search, accessed April 27, 2022. However, Erzincan is listed as the arranger for other recordings of "Sinsin Halayı."

15. MESAM's public database lists Rey as the *composer* of "12 Anadolu Türküsü," a setting of twelve Anatolian folk songs for piano and voice, for example, while Muammer Sun is credited only as arranger for his orchestral and choral setting of the public domain march "İzmir'in dağlarında çiçekler açar" (Flowers will bloom in the mountains of İzmir), which notably appeared in the epic 1994 mini-series *Kurtuluş* and a 2020 ad for the gasoline distributor Petrol Ofisi.

16. See https://www.ascap.com/~/media/files/pdf/members/payment/drd.pdf, accessed April 27, 2022, and https://www.bmi.com/creators/royalty_print, accessed February 22, 2022.

17. Feist Publications, Inc., vs. Rural Telephone Service Co., 499 U.S. 340 (1991).

18. See for example the 9th circuit case *Ets-Hokin v Skyy Spirits, Inc*, referenced in Fishman 2021, 914.

19. One argument against the United States' low threshold of originality, for example, is that particularly in the digital era, if copyright protections are accorded too liberally, it may inhibit meme culture and other appropriative forms of cultural expression that have a value as public discourse (Fishman 2021, 914).

20. An official FAQ document prepared by IMRO states: "Traditional works arranged by you are afforded exactly the same standard of payment as those that you have composed." See http://www.songwritingessentials.com/wp-content/uploads/2013/03/Irish MusicRightsOrganisation-IMRO.pdf, p. 5, accessed January 22, 2022.

21. McCann quotes one IMRO representative who explicitly notes that they hoped to recruit perhaps twenty-seven thousand of CCE's thirty-seven thousand members, for example (108). McCann notes that some venues negotiated lower licensing tariffs from IMRO because performances featured a large share of traditional music outside copyright (71). By the same logic, I assume that IMRO might try to demand higher tariffs if they can claim that much of this music is copyrighted as arrangements belonging to its members.

22. Longtime MESAM president Arif Sağ, for example, has many composition credits to his name and also ran his own record label.

23. In fact, the founding of MSG would have provided a context in which it would have been particularly logical to try to draw in additional members through such policy choices, since the legal provision that allowed the formation of an additional society in the same rights area stipulated that founding a second society required attaining membership numbers equal to or greater than one-third the number of members in MESAM.

SIX *Collectors, Copyright, "Kiziroğlu"*

1. Meanwhile, the right-wing Nationalist Movement Party (MHP) had already used it in 1999 and felt that the right to use it belonged to them. Oktay Vural, a representative of the MHP, also appeared on news outlets to condemn the AKP: "When someone has the will [*irade*] to use [a song] and you say, 'Let me use it too,' that is an infringement." *Show*

TV, December 30, 2014, https://www.youtube.com/watch?v=HjSQwAyo9O8, accessed April 3, 2017.

2. Pop singer Yusuf Güney, whom they had contracted to perform their revised version of the song, was already in the studio at the time working on the recording. In media appearances CHP general secretary Gürsel Tekin threatened lawsuits of his own.

3. The MESAM database, for example, lists Köroğlu as the song's author. Versions of the Köroğlu story can be found across the Caucasus and Central Asia. However, Turkish scholars debate whether this local version of the legendary hero Köroğlu may be based on a figure who participated in the sixteenth- and seventeenth-century Celali rebellions and whether he may be the same as a well-known, roughly contemporary singer-poet of the same name who is mentioned in Evliya Çelebi's writings (see Öztelli 1974, 124–25).

4. See www.turkuler.com/hikayeler/kiziroglu.asp, accessed April 26, 2023; see also Öztelli 1974, 58–59.

5. https://www.youtube.com/watch?v=oxcxdWzhpIE, accessed September 29, 2014, and https://www.youtube.com/watch?v=wOaP8YCh488, accessed September 29, 2014. These had been removed from YouTube due to copyright infringement complaints as of April 2017. Unfortunately, I was unable to find the date that the episode originally aired.

6. Köse claims he heard the song from Ruhi Su, but this thread goes nowhere and comes across as disingenuous.

7. See also Taşlıova 2005, which also attributes these syllables to Çobanoğlu and suggests that this contribution is what made it so popular.

8. The footnote on the TRT notation states that "artists in Kars insert the words 'peh peh peh' in order to try to portray the extraordinary speed with which Kiziroğlu comes and goes; then they return to the song." However, while Sarısözen is credited as the collector of the song, the TRT notation is an edition dating from 1973, ten years after Sarısözen's death and eight years after Çobanoğlu had made the song famous. The footnote may thus date from 1973 and actually reference Çobanoğlu's version.

9. To my own frustration, I have been unable to locate this previous episode that they reference.

10. The statute has been modified in some ways in the meantime by court decisions and by a few separate laws that made alterations to the language of several statutes (see appendix 2420–28 to the copyright statute as posted at https://www.telifhaklari.gov.tr/re sources/uploads/2021/12/28/Fikir-ve-Sanat-Eserleri-Kanunu.pdf, accessed April 24, 2023).

11. Another less discussed option would be to revise article 12. Article 12 allows the first person to publicly present or publish a work whose author is unknown to provisionally exercise rights over it until someone makes an evidence-based claim to be its creator. At present this is a little applied article of the statute, but there were proposals to insert language here to specify collector alongside first publisher or presenter as categories of people who could exercise such provisional rights over a work of unknown authorship.

Notes to Chapter Six **231**

12. Other legal experts I spoke with doubted whether competition law should apply, and I never heard of a case of a collector pursuing this legal avenue.

13. See Balkılıç 2009; Bates 2016, 66–71, for further discussion of folk song collectors' interventions.

14. The Technical Expertise Committee's decision is published in Şenel 2018a, 31. It reads: "The work known as (Kiziroğlu) performed by Ayna Group and belonging to the *ozan* Köröğlu known from our folk literature by everyone was further developed by Murat Çobanoğlu and presented to the people. Murat Çobanoğlu is its rightsholder as its collector [*derlemeci sıfatı ile hak sahibidir*]."

15. It should be noted that the label on Çobanoğlu's original record of the song credits him as composer of both the words and music. In the current MESAM database, however, entries for recordings of the song either credit Köroğlu as the owner of words and music or they simply list a public domain credit (without mentioning Köroğlu). And while it seems clear that in most if not all cases artists covering the song have drawn on Çobanoğlu's version, the rights in the arrangements belong to the arranger on each recording, and Çobanoğlu does not have any arranger credits in the database. His family thus apparently receives no royalties on sales or performances of versions of the song, excepting perhaps royalties for the related rights in his own performance on his own recording.

16. Wallis and Malm describe two further examples that (imperfectly) parallel the Lomax, "Mbube," and "Kiziroğlu" cases: Seeger's registration of the Cuban song "Guantanamera" under his own name and Harry Belafonte's claim to "Banana Boat Song/Day O," both of which had a prior existence in the form of variable lyrics set to tunes that could (arguably) be characterized as "traditional." Both were claimed as original compositions by local musicians in Cuba and Jamaica, respectively, and in the Jamaican case, as a folkloric collection by a local first publisher of the song as well (Wallis and Malm 1984, 188–99; cf. Manuel 2006). Singer-songwriter Oscar Brand catalogs a host of further parallels from his experience in the North American folk music sector (1962, 201–15).

17. Italian Book Company, Inc., v. Rossi et al., 27 F.2d 1014 (1928), cited in Wihtol v. Wells, 231 F.2d 550 (1956).

18. We Shall Overcome Foundation v. Richmond Org., Inc., 221 F. Supp. 3d 396 (2016).

19. Credits on the YouTube clip suggest that Pinkfong claimed rights in the arrangement, calling the underlying composition "traditional" (https://www.youtube.com /watch?v=XqZsoesa55w, accessed March 20, 2023).

20. For background on the intended audience or ordinary lay observer tests (and differences between them) in US law, see Grinvalsky 1992. The tests parallel other "reasonable person" tests in US law; according to such tests, findings of "substantial similarity" in cases of alleged copyright infringement in music should be decided by impressions of similarity on lay listeners rather than on expert analysis. Decision E. 2005/3742, K. 2006/3428 (April 3, 2006) by the 11th civil law chamber of the Turkish Court of Cassation

(Yargıtay) appears to invoke a similar lay listener test: "In musical works, the presence of an author's original contribution must be determined according to the impression it creates on an ordinary listener [*sıradan bir dinleyici*]" (as cited in a subsequent decision, E. 2015/13399, K. 2017/1106 of February 27, 2017). Thanks to Semin Tunalı for directing my attention to this decision.

Conclusion

1. See https://telifhaklari.ktb.gov.tr/TR-332836/fikri-mulkiyet-hukuku-calistayi-16-18-mayis-2022-tarihlerinde-antalya39da-gerceklestirildi.html, accessed August 13, 2024.

WORKS CITED

Ahıska, Meltem. 2003. "Occidentalism: The Historical Fantasy of the Modern." *South Atlantic Quarterly* 102, no. 2–3 (Spring/Summer): 351–79. https://doi.org/10.1215/00382876 -102-2-3-351.

————. 2010. *Occidentalism in Turkey: Questions of Modernity and National Identity in Turkish Radio Broadcasting.* London: Tauris Academic Studies.

Ahmad, Feroz. 1993. *The Making of Modern Turkey.* London: Routledge.

Akman, Haşim. 2006. *Gönül Dağında Bir Garip: Neşet Ertaş Kitabı* [A stranger on the mountain of the heart: The book of Neşet Ertaş]. İstanbul: Türkiye İş Bankası Kültür Yayınları.

Aksoy, Bülent. 1981. "Tanzımat'tan Cumhuriyet'e Musiki ve Batılılaşma." [Music and Westernization from the Tanzımat to the republican era]. In *Cumhurriyet Dönemi Türkiye Ansiklopedisi.* Vol. 5. Istanbul: İletişim Yayınları.

————. 2008. *Geçmişin Musiki Mirasına Bakışlar* [Perspectives on the musical heritage of the past]. Istanbul: Pan Yayıncılık.

Aksoy, Ozan E. 2018. "Kurdish Popular Music in Turkey." In *Made in Turkey: Studies in Popular Music,* edited by Ali C. Gedik, 149–66. New York: Routledge.

Akyüz, Burcu. 2009. "Müzik Eseri ve Müzik Eseri Sahibinin Mali Hakları ile Korunması." [Protecting the musical work and the musical author with economic rights]. MA Thesis, Başkent Üniversitesi Sosyal Bilimler Enstitüsü Özel Hukuk Ana Bilim Dalı.

Albayrak, Nurettin. 2012. "Türkü." In *Türk Diyanet Vakfı İslâm Ansiklopedisi.* Istanbul: TDV İslâm Araştırmaları Merkezi. https://islamansiklopedisi.org.tr/turku#1.

Aliverti, Ana. 2019. "Law, Nation and Race: Exploring Law's Cultural Power in Delimiting Belonging in English Courtrooms." *Social and Legal Studies* 28, no. 3 (June): 281–302. https://doi.org/10.1177/0964663918776486.

Altınay, F. Reyhan. 2000. "Cumhuriyet Döneminde Türk Halk Müziği Alanında Yapılan Bilimsel Çalışmalar." [Scholarly work on Turkish folk music in the republican era]. PhD diss., Ege Üniversitesi.

And, Metin. 1984. "Atatürk and the Arts, with Special Reference to Music and Theater." In *Atatürk and the Modernization of Turkey*, edited by Jacob M. Landau, 215–32. Boulder, CO: Westview Press.

Andrews, Walter G. 2006. "Ottoman Lyrics: Introductory Essay." In *Ottoman Lyric Poetry: An Anthology*, edited by Walter G. Andrews, Najaat Black, and Mehmet Kalpakli, 3–23. Seattle: University of Washington Press.

Aracı, Emre. 2010. *Naum Tiyatrosu: 19. Yüzyıl İstanbul'unun İtalyan Operası* [Naum Theater: Nineteenth-century Istanbul's Italian opera]. Istanbul: Yapı Kredi Yayınları.

Aragon, Lorraine V. 2014. "Law versus Lore: Copyright and Conflicting Claims about Culture and Property in Indonesia." *Anthropology Today* 30, no. 5 (October): 15–19. https://doi.org/10.1111/1467-8322.12132.

Arel, Hüseyin Sadettin. 1969. *Türk Musikisi Kimindir* [Whose is Turkish music]. Istanbul: Milli Eğitim Basımevi.

Aslan, Ali. 2013. "Problematizing Modernity in Turkish Foreign Policy: Identity, Sovereignty and Beyond." *Uluslararası Hukuk ve Politika* 9 (33): 27–57.

Aslan, Mikail. 2010. "Müzik ve Kültürel Kökler Bağlamında Dersim Müziği." [Dersim music in the context of music and cultural roots]. In *Herkesin Bildiği Sır: Dersim* [The secret everyone knows: Dersim], edited by Şükrü Aslan, 197–220. Istanbul: İletişim Yayınları.

Ateş, Mustafa. 2007. *Fikri Hukukta* Eser [The work in intellectual law]. Ankara: Turhan Kitabevi Yayınları.

———. 2020. "Sahibi Ölen Fikir ve Sanat Eseri Üzerindeki Mali Hakların Mirasçılara İntikali." [An Examination on the Results of the Economic Rights on the Literary and Artistic Work of the Author After Death]. *Ticaret ve Fikri Mülkiyet Hukuku* 6 (1): 44–59.

Atılgan, Halil. 1992. "Halk Müziğinde Anonimlik ve Beste Meselesi." [The problem of anonymity and composition in folk music]. In *Türk Halk Musikisinde Çeşitli Görüşler*, edited by Salih Turhan, 163–73. Ankara: Kultur Bakanlığı.

———. 2003. *Türkülerin İsnyanı* [Revolt of the Türküler]. Ankara: Akçağ Yayınları.

———. 2005. "Halk Müziği Eserlerinde Hak Sahibi Tespit Ölçüleri Nasıl Olmalıdır?" [What should be the standards for rights ownership determination in folk music works?]. In *MESAM Halk Müziği Eserleri Sempozyumu* [MESAM symposium on folk music works], 14–23. Istanbul: MESAM.

Avcı, Mustafa. 2021. "Bestenin Anlam Dünyası: Yaratma, Hatırlama, Bulma, ve Keşfetme Ekseninde Müzik Üretimi." [The world of the composition's meaning: Musical production on the axis of creation, memory, finding, and discovery]. *Mustafa Kemal Üniversitesi Sosyal Bilimler Enstitüsü Dergisi* 18 (48): 54–78.

Avşar, Esin. 2008. *Yaşamımdan Esin'tiler* [Inspirations from my life]. Istanbul: İş Bankası Kültür Yayınları.

Ayangil, Ruhi. 2008. "Western Notation in Turkish Music." *Journal of the Royal Asiatic Society* 18, no. 4 (October): 401–47.

Ayata, Bilgin, and Serra Hakyemez. 2013. "The AKP's Engagement with Turkey's Past Crimes: An Analysis of PM Erdoğan's 'Dersim Apology.'" *Dialectical Anthropology* 37, no. 1 (March): 131–43. https://doi.org/10.1007/s10624-013-9304-3.

Aydın, M. Mehmet. 2005. "17.06.2005 Tarihli 1. Ulusual Sempozyum Sunuş Bildirimi." [June 17, 2005, opening statement for the first national symposium]. In *Fikri ve Sınai Mülkiyet Hakları ve Kültürü (1. Ulusal Sempozyumu): Sorunlar ve Kurumsal Çözüm Yolları.* İstanbul: İstanbul Barosu Yayınları.

Babül, Elif M. 2017. *Bureaucratic Intimacies: Translating Human Rights in Turkey.* Stanford, CA: Stanford University Press.

Balganesh, Shyamkrishna, and Taisu Zhang. 2021. "Legal Internalism in Modern Histories of Copyright." *Harvard Law Review* 134, no. 3 (January): 1066–1130.

Balkılıç, Özgür. 2009. *Cumhuriyet, halk ve müzik: Türkiye'de müzik reformu 1922–1952* [Republic, folk, and music: Musical reform in Turkey, 1922–1952]. Ankara: Tan.

———. 2018. "Music Reform in Turkey: On the Failures and Successes of Inventing National Songs." In *Made in Turkey: Studies in Popular Music*, edited by Ali C. Gedik, 63–72. New York: Routledge.

"Barış Manço Lambaya Püf De İlginç Gazete İlanı." [An interesting news announcement about Barış Manço's "Lambaya Püf De"]. 2017. *Dipsahaf Plak* (blog). June 10, 2017. http://www.dipsahaf.com/baris-manco-lambaya-puf-de-ilginc-gazete-ilani/.

Barlas, Dilek. 1998. *Etatism and Diplomacy in Turkey: Economic and Foreign Policy Strategies in an Uncertain World, 1929–1939.* Leiden: Brill.

Barron, Anne. 2006. "Copyright Law's Musical Work." *Social and Legal Studies* 15, no. 1 (March): 101–27. https://doi.org/10.1177/0964663906060985.

Bartow, Ann. 2006. "Fair Use and the Fairer Sex: Gender, Feminism, and Copyright Law." *American University Journal of Gender, Social Policy, and the Law* 14, no. 3 (January): 25.

Başgöz, İlhan. 2008. *Türkü.* Istanbul: Pan Yayıncılık.

Bates, Eliot. 2008. "Social Interactions, Musical Arrangement, and the Production of Digital Audio in Istanbul Recording Studios." PhD diss., University of California, Berkeley.

———. 2016. *Digital Tradition: Arrangement and Labor in Istanbul's Recording Studio Culture.* New York: Oxford University Press.

Bauman, Richard, and Charles L. Briggs. 1990. "Poetics and Performance as Critical Perspectives on Language and Social Life." *Annual Review of Anthropology* 19:59–88.

Baysal, Ahmet Ozan, and Eray Altınbüken. 2019. "Analytical Approaches to Harmonic Practices in Şelpe Performing of Saz/Bağlama." *Porte Akademik*, no. 18–19: 9–23.

Baysal, Ozan. 2013. "Performing Traditions of the Teke Region's Üçtelli and Bağlama without Plectrum: The Musical Change in Bağlama Music of Turkey Since the 1990s." Master's thesis, Istanbul Technical University.

———. 2018. "Reconsidering 'Anadolu Pop.'" *Rock Music Studies* 5 (3): 205–19. https://doi.org/10.1080/19401159.2018.1544357.

Behar, Cem. 1987. *Klasik Türk Musıkisi Üzerine Denemeler* [Essays on Turkish classical music]. Istanbul: Bağlam Yayınları.

———. 1998. *Aşk Olmayınca Meşk Olmaz* [Without love there is no *meşk*]. Istanbul: Yapi Kredi Yaynlari.

———. 2006. "The Ottoman Musical Tradition." In *The Cambridge History of Turkey*, edited by Suraiya Faroqhi, 3:391–407. Cambridge: Cambridge University Press.

———. 2013. "Text and Memory in Ottoman/Turkish Musical Tradition." In *Ottoman Intimacies, Balkan Musical Realities*, 3–11. Helsinki: Foundation of the Finnish Institute at Athens.

Beken, Münir Nurettin. 1998. "Musicians, Audience and Power: The Changing Aesthetics in the Music at the Maksim Gazino of Istanbul." PhD diss., University of Maryland, Baltimore County.

Beki, Akif. 2015. "Neşet Ertaş intihalcı miydi?" [Was Neşet Ertaş a plagiarist?]. *Hürriyet*, April 25, 2015, sec. akif-beki. https://www.hurriyet.com.tr/yazarlar/akif-beki/neset -ertas-intihalci-miydi-28831154.

Berkes, Niyazi. 1998. *The Development of Secularism in Turkey*. London: Hurst.

Beşiroğlu, Akın. 1999. *Düşünce Ürünleri Üzerinde Haklar* [Rights to intellectual products]. Ankara: Ankara Patent Büroso.

Beukelaer, Christian de, and Martin Fredriksson. 2019. "The Political Economy of Intellectual Property Rights: The Paradox of Article 27 Exemplified in Ghana." *Review of African Political Economy* 46, no. 161 (July): 459–79. https://doi.org/10.1080/030562 44.2018.1500358.

Bigenho, Michelle. 2002. *Sounding Indigenous: Authenticity in Bolivian Music Performance*. New York: Palgrave Macmillan.

Bilgin, Pinar, and Ali Bilgiç. 2012. "Turkey and EU/Rope: Discourses of Inspiration/ Anxiety in Turkey's Foreign Policy." *Review of European Studies* 4, no. 3 (July): 111–24. https://doi.org/10.5539/res.v4n3p111.

Birinci Türk Neşriyat Kongresi, 1–5 Mayis 1939: Raporlar, Teklifler, Müzakere Zabıtları [The first Turkish publishing congress, May 1–5, 1939: Reports, proposals, negotiation proceedings]. 1939. Istanbul: T. C. Maarif Vekilliği.

Blakeney, Michael. 1999. "What Is Traditional Knowledge? Why Should It Be Protected? Who Should Protect It? For Whom? Understanding the Value Chain." In *Copyright and Other Fairy Tales: Hans Christian Andersen and the Commodification of Creativity*, edited by Helle Porsdam, 108–28. Cheltenham, UK: Edward Elgar.

Blumenthal, Susanna L. 2012. "Of Mandarins, Legal Consciousness, and the Cultural Turn in US Legal History: Robert W. Gordon. 1984. Critical Legal Histories. *Stanford Law Review* 36:57–125." *Law and Social Inquiry* 37, no. 1 (Winter): 167–86.

Boateng, Boatema. 2011. *The Copyright Thing Doesn't Work Here: Adinkra and Kente Cloth and Intellectual Property in Ghana*. Minneapolis: University of Minnesota Press.

Bohannan, Paul. 1973. "The Differing Realms of the Law." In *The Social Organization of Law*, edited by Donald Black and Maureen Mileski, 306–17. New York: Seminar Press.

Boratav, Pertev N. 1942. *Halk Edebiyatı Dersleri: 1. Kitap* [Lessons in folk literature: Volume 1]. Ankara: Uzluk Basımevi.

Boyle, James. 1996. *Shamans, Software, and Spleens: Law and the Construction of the Information Society*. Cambridge, MA: Harvard University Press.

———. 2008. *The Public Domain: Enclosing the Commons of the Mind*. New Haven: Yale University Press.

Brand, Oscar. 1962. *The Ballad Mongers: Rise of the Modern Folk Song*. New York: Funk & Wagnalls.

Brandstetter, Jeffrey. 1997. "The Lone Arranger: Have the Courts Unfairly Singled Out Musical Arrangements by Denying Them Protection as Derivative Works?" *Entertainment and Sports Lawyer* 15 (1): 1–23.

Bretèque, Estelle Amy de la. 2016. "Self-Sacrifice, Womanhood, and Melodized Speech: Three Case Studies from the Caucasus and Anatolia." *Asian Music* 47, no. 1 (Winter): 29–63. https://doi.org/10.1353/amu.2016.0008.

Brisbin, Richard A. 2010. "Resistance to Legality." *Annual Review of Law and Social Science* 6:25–44. https://doi.org/10.1146/annurev-lawsocsci-102209-152904.

Brooks, Tim. 2005. "How Copyright Law Affects Reissues of Historic Recordings: A New Study." *ARSC Journal* 36, no. 2 (Fall): 183–203.

Brown, Michael F. 2003. *Who Owns Native Culture?* Cambridge, MA: Harvard University Press.

Bulut, Gökhan, and Cem Kaya, dirs. 2010. *Arabeks*. Potsdam, Germany: teamWorx Television & Film GmbH.

"Bünyanlı Harbi (Adnan Türköz)." 2009. *Bünyan* (blog). May 29, 2009. https://bunyan38.wordpress.com/2009/05/29/bunyanli-harbi-adnan-turkoz/.

Çakmak, Diren. 2007. "Osmanlı Telif Hukuku İle İlgili Mevzuat." [Legislation on Ottoman copyright law]. *Türkiyat Araştırma Dergisi*, no. 21: 191–234.

Çakmur, Barış. 2001. "Music Industry in Turkey: An Assessment in the Context of Political Economy of Cultural Production." PhD diss., Middle East Technical University.

———. 2002. "Türkiye'de Müzik Üretimi." [Musical production in Turkey]. *Toplum ve Bilim*, no. 94: 50–64.

Çalışkan, Faruk. 2018. "1980'lerden Günümüze Performans Pratiğinin Dönüşümü ve Etkileri: Bağlama Çalgısında El İle (Tezenesiz) Çalma Tekniği." [The transformation and effects of performance practice from the 1980s to today: Fingerstyle technique for bağlama]. *Porte Akademik* 17 (Spring): 7–29.

Caporal, Bernard. 1982. *Kemalizmde ve Kemalizm sonrasında Türk kadını: (1919-1970)* [The Turkish woman in and after Kemalism (1919-1970)]. Ankara: Türkiye İs Bankası Kültür Yayınları.

"C. Demirsipahi Tarafından Nida Tüfekçi Aleyhine Hakaret Davası Açıldı." [C. Demirsipahi has opened a defamation suit against Nida Tüfekçi]. 1975. *Hey* 5, no. 24 (April 30, 1975): 63.

"Cemil Demirsipahi Ile Söyleyiş." [An interview with Cemil Demirsipahi]. 2005. *Folklor/ Edebiyat* 11 (42): 291–98.

Çeren, Şerif Sait. 1944. "Muzaffer Sarısözenle Bir Konuşma." [A conversation with Muzaffer Sarısözen]. *Radyo*, June 1944.

Certeau, Michel de. 1984. *The Practice of Everyday Life*. Berkeley: University of California Press.

Chakrabarty, Dipesh. 2009. *Provincializing Europe: Postcolonial Thought and Historical Difference*. New Edition. Princeton, NJ: Princeton University Press.

Chander, Anupam, and Madhavi Sunder. 2004. "The Romance of the Public Domain." *California Law Review* 92, no. 5 (October): 1331–73. https://doi.org/10.2307/3481419.

Chua, Lynette J., and David M. Engel. 2019. "Legal Consciousness Reconsidered." *Annual Review of Law and Social Science* 15:335–53.

CISAC. 2022a. "Global Collections Report." October 27, 2022. https://www.cisac.org /Newsroom/global-collections/global-collections-report-2022.

———. 2022b. "Good News for Societies and Creators in Turkey as CMOs Achieve New Collaboration." April 27, 2022. https://www.cisac.org/Newsroom/articles/good-news -societies-and-creators-turkey-cmos-achieve-new-collaboration.

Clifford, James. 1988. *The Predicament of Culture: Twentieth-Century Ethnography, Literature, and Art*. Cambridge, MA: Harvard University Press.

Çolak, Uğur. 2008. "Türkülerde İşleme Eser Sahipliği ve Sui Generis Koruma Modeli Önerisi." [Derivative authorship of Türküler and a proposal for a sui generis protection model] *Ankara Barosu Fikri Mülkiyet ve Rekabet Hukuku Dergisi* 8 (2): 95–156.

Collins, John. 2006. "Copyright, Folklore, and Music Piracy in Ghana." *Critical Arts: A Journal of South-North Cultural and Media Studies* 20, no. 1 (July): 158–70.

Coombe, Rosemary J. 1998. *The Cultural Life of Intellectual Properties: Authorship, Appropriation, and the Law*. Durham, NC: Duke University Press.

Cornut St-Pierre, Pascale. 2019. "Investigating Legal Consciousness through the Technical Work of Elite Lawyers: A Case Study on Tax Avoidance." *Law and Society Review* 53, no. 2 (June): 323–52. https://doi.org/10.1111/lasr.12397.

Cowan, Dave. 2004. "Legal Consciousness: Some Observations." *The Modern Law Review* 67, no. 6 (November): 928–58. https://doi.org/10.1111/j.1468-2230.2004.00518.x.

Cowdery, James. 2005. "Kategorie or Wertidee? The Early Years of the International Folk Music Council." In *Music's Intellectual History: Founders, Followers, and Fads*, edited by Barbara Dobbs Mackenzie and Zdravko Blažeković, 805–11. New York: RILM.

Cummings, Alex Sayf. 2010. "From Monopoly to Intellectual Property: Music Piracy and the Remaking of American Copyright, 1909–1971." *Journal of American History* 97, no. 3 (December): 636–58.

Darian-Smith, Eve. 2002. "Myths of East and West: Intellectual Property Law in Postcolonial Hong Kong." In *Relocating Postcolonialism*, edited by David Theo Goldberg and Ato Quayson, 294–319. Oxford: Blackwell.

Dedeoğlu, Taner. 1991. "TRT Halk Müziği Danışma Kurulu'nda İki Ayrı Uç Bir Araya Geldi: Halk Müziğinde Reform." [Two extremes have come together at the TRT folk music advisory committee: Reform in folk music]. *Milliyet*, June 20, 1991.

———. 2016. "Rıfat Balaban: 'Cahil dönemimizde bağlamada nota olmaz diye bilirdik.'" [Rıfat Balaban: "In our ignorant age we thought you couldn't have notation for bağlama"]. *24 Saat Gazetesi*, April 3, 2016. https://www.24saatgazetesi.com/.

Deligöz, Halil. 2010. "Türkiye'de Fikri Mülkiyet Haklarının Gelişimi ve Sorunları." [The development of and problems with intellectual property rights in Turkey]. Expertise Thesis for the Office of the Prime Minister. Ankara: T. C. Başbakanlık.

Demers, Joanna Teresa. 2006. *Steal This Music: How Intellectual Property Law Affects Musical Creativity*. Athens, GA: University of Georgia Press.

Demirel, Altan. 2005. "Halk Türkülerinin Gerçek Sahipleri . . ." [The true owners of folk türküler . . .]. In *MESAM Halk Müziği Eserleri Sempozyumu*, 46–50. Istanbul: MESAM.

Demirsipahi, Cemil. 1975. *Türk Halk Oyunları* [Turkish folk dances]. Ankara: Türkiye İş Bankası Kültür Yayınları.

Denker, Sema. 2006. "Nilüfer'e 17 Şarkı Yasağı." [The forbidding of seventeen songs to Nilüfer]. *Hürriyet*, November 29, 2006, sec. kelebek. https://www.hurriyet.com.tr/kelebek/nilufer-e-17-sarki-yasagi-5521121.

Dent, Alexander Sebastian. 2020. *Digital Pirates: Policing Intellectual Property in Brazil*. Stanford, CA: Stanford University Press.

DiCola, Peter. 2013. "Money from Music: Survey Evidence on Musicians' Revenue and Lessons about Copyright Incentives." *Arizona Law Review* 55 (2): 301–70.

Dommann, Monika. 2019. *Authors and Apparatus: A Media History of Copyright*. Ithaca, NY: Cornell University Press.

Donovan, James M. 2007. *Legal Anthropology: An Introduction*. Lanham, MD: Altamira Press.

Doruk, Yaşar. 1977. *Urfa'dan Derlenmiş Türküler ve Oyun Havaları* [Türküler and dance tunes collected from Urfa]. Ankara: Başbakanlık Basımevi.

Dressler, Markus. 2008. "Religio-Secular Metamorphoses: The Re-Making of Turkish Alevism." *Journal of the American Academy of Religion* 76, no. 2 (June): 280–311. https://doi.org/10.1093/jaarel/lfn033.

Drott, Eric. 2018. "Music as a Technology of Surveillance." *Journal of the Society for American Music* 12, no. 3 (August): 233–67. https://doi.org/10.1017/S1752196318000196.

Dundes, Alan. 1969. "The Devolutionary Premise in Folklore Theory." *Journal of the Folklore Institute* 6, no. 1 (June): 5–19.

Dutfield, Graham. 2003. "Protection of Traditional Knowledge and Folklore." Issue Paper No. 1. Geneva, Switzerland: International Centre for Trade and Sustainable Development (ICTSD).

———. 2008. "Knowledge Diplomacy and the New Intellectual Property Fundamentalism." In *Interpreting and Implementing the TRIPS Agreement: Is It Fair?*, edited by Justin Malbon and Charles Lawson, 31–45. Cheltenham, UK: Edward Elgar.

Duygulu, Melih. 2019. "Tüfekçi, Mehmet Nida." İn *TDV İslâm Ansiklopedisi*, Ek-2:614–15. https://islamansiklopedisi.org.tr/tufekci-mehmet-nida.

Edwards, Lee, Bethany Klein, David Lee, Giles Moss, and Fiona Philip. 2015. "'Isn't It Just a Way to Protect Walt Disney's Rights?': Media User Perspectives on Copyright." *New Media and Society* 17, no. 5 (May): 691–707. https://doi.org/10.1177/1461444813511402.

Elçi, Armağan Coşkun. 1997. *Muzaffer Sarısözen: Hayatı, Eserleri, ve Çalışmaları* [Muzaffer Sarısözen: His life, works, and endeavors]. Ankara: Kültür ve Turizm Bakanlığı.

Elton, Serona. 2011. "The Origins of Mechanical Licensing of Musical Compositions." *Journal of the Music and Entertainment Industry Educators Association* 11 (1): 13–38.

Emnalar, Atınç. 1998. *Tüm Yönleriyle Türk Halk Müziği ve Nazariyatı* [Turkish folk music and its theory from every aspect]. İzmir, Turkey: Ege Üniversitesi Basımevi.

Engel, David M. 1998. "How Does Law Matter in the Constitution of Legal Consciousness?" In *How Does Law Matter?*, edited by Bryant Garth and Austin Sarat, 109–44. Evanston, IL: Northwestern University Press.

Engel, David M., and Frank W. Munger. 2003. *Rights of Inclusion: Law and Identity in the Life Stories of Americans with Disabilities*. Chicago: University of Chicago Press.

Erdener, Yıldıray. 1995. *The Song Contests of Turkish Minstrels: Improvised Poetry Sung to Traditional Music*. Milman Parry Studies in Oral Tradition. New York: General Music.

Ergüner, Süleyman. 2005. "TRT ve Anonim Eserler." [TRT and anonymous works]. In *MESAM Halk Müziği Eserleri Sempozyumu*, 74–79. Istanbul: MESAM.

Erkmen, T. Deniz. 2018. "Stepping into the Global: Turkish Professionals, Employment in Transnational Corporations, and Aspiration to Transnational Forms of Cultural Capital." *Current Sociology* 66, no. 3 (May): 412–30. https://doi.org/10.1177/0011392116653236.

Erlmann, Veit. 1990. "Migration and Performance: Zulu Migrant Workers' Isicathamiya Performance in South Africa, 1890–1950." *Ethnomusicology* 34, no. 2 (Spring–Summer): 199–220. https://doi.org/10.2307/851683.

———. 2022. *Lion's Share: Remaking South African Copyright*. Durham, NC: Duke University Press.

Erol, Ayhan. 2009. "Marketing the Alevi Musical Revival." In *Muslim Societies in the Age of Mass Consumption*, edited by Johanna Pink, 165–84. Cambridge: Cambridge Scholars.

———. 2012. "Music, Power and Symbolic Violence: The Turkish State's Music Policies

During the Early Republican Period." *European Journal of Cultural Studies* 15, no. 1 (February): 35–52. https://doi.org/10.1177/1367549411424947.

Erol, Merih. 2015. *Greek Orthodox Music in Ottoman Istanbul: Nation and Community in the Era of Reform*. Bloomington: Indiana University Press.

Ertür, Başak. 2022. *Spectacles and Specters: A Performative Theory of Political Trials*. New York: Fordham University Press.

Etili, Can. 2005. "Türk Halk Müziğinin Fikir ve Sanat Eserleri Kanununun Karşısındaki Konumu." [The place of Turkish folk music in relation to the law on intellectual and artistic works]. In *Halk Kültürlerini Koruma-Yaşatma ve Geleceğe Aktarma Uluslararası Sempozumu Bildirileri*, 254–74. Kocaeli, Turkey: Kocaeli Üniversitesi.

Evans, Roy. 1997. "Musical Arrangements: The Unprotected Intellectual Property." *Media Law* 5 (3): 23–36.

Ewick, Patricia. 2015. "Law and Everyday Life." In *International Encyclopedia of the Social and Behavioral Sciences*, edited by James D. Wright, 468–73. Amsterdam: Elsevier. https://doi.org/10.1016/B978-0-08-097086-8.86050-X.

Ewick, Patricia, and Susan S. Silbey. 1998. *The Common Place of Law: Stories from Everyday Life*. Language and Legal Discourse. Chicago: University of Chicago Press.

Eyüboğlu, Ali. 2009. "Marşlar Albümüne Bürokrasi Darbesi." [A bureaucratic blow to an album of marches]. *Milliyet*, May 14, 2009, sec. Cafe Yazarları. http://www.milliyet.com.tr/marslar-albumune-burokrasi-darbesi/ali-eyuboglu/cafe/yazardetay/15.05.2009/1094866/default.htm.

Feeley, Malcolm M. 1976. "The Concept of Laws in Social Science: A Critique and Notes on an Expanded View." *Law and Society Review* 10, no. 4 (Summer): 497–523. https://doi.org/10.2307/3053295.

Feld, Steven. 1986. "Orality and Consciousness." In *The Oral and the Literate in Music*, edited by Yosihiko Tokumaru and Osamu Yamaguti, 18–28. Tokyo: Academia Music.

———. 1994. "From Schizophonia to Schismogenesis: Reflections on the Discourses and Commodification Practices of 'World Music' and 'World Beat.'" In *Music Grooves: Essays and Dialogues*, edited by Charles Keil and Steven Feld, 257–89. Chicago: University of Chicago Press.

———. 2000. "A Sweet Lullaby for World Music." *Public Culture* 12, no. 1 (Winter): 145–71.

Feldman, Walter. 1990/1991. "Cultural Authority and Authenticity in the Turkish Repertoire." *Asian Music* 22, no. 1 (Autumn–Winter): 73–111.

———. 1996. *Music of the Ottoman Court: Makam, Composition and the Early Ottoman Instrumental Repertoire*. Intercultural Music Studies 10. Berlin: VWB-Verlag für Wissenschaft und Bildung.

———. 2015. "The Musical 'Renaissance' of Late Seventeenth Century Ottoman Turkey." In *Writing the History of "Ottoman Music,"* edited by Martin Greve, 87–138. Würzburg: Ergon-Verlag.

Ficsor, Mihaly. 2010. "Collective Management of Copyright and Related Rights from the Viewpoint of International Norms and the Acquis Communautaire." In *Collective Management of Copyright and Related Rights*, 2nd ed., edited by Daniel Gervais, 29–74. Alphen aan den Rijn, Netherlands: Wolters Kluwer.

Fikri ve Sınai Mülkiyet Hakları ve Kültürü (1. Ulusal Sempozyumu): Sorunlar ve Kurumsal Çözüm Yolları [Intellectual and industrial property rights and culture (first international symposium): The problems and the paths to institutional solutions]. 2005. Istanbul: İstanbul Barosu Yayınları.

Filene, Benjamin. 1991. "'Our Singing Country': John and Alan Lomax, Leadbelly, and the Construction of an American Past." *American Quarterly* 43, no. 4 (December): 602–24. https://doi.org/10.2307/2713083.

Finnegan, Ruth. 1988. *Literacy and Orality: Studies in the Technology of Communication*. Oxford: Blackwell.

———. 1990. "What Is Orality—If Anything?" *Byzantine and Modern Greek Studies* 14:130–49.

Fishman, Joseph P. 2021. "Originality's Other Path." *California Law Review* 109, no. 3 (June): 861–916. https://doi.org/10.15779/Z386Q1SH9P.

Fossum, Dave. 2015. "Westernizing Reform and Indigenous Precedent in Traditional Music: Insights from Turkmenistan." *Ethnomusicology* 59, no. 2 (Spring–Summer): 202–26. https://doi.org/10.5406/ethnomusicology.59.2.0202.

———. 2017. "Principles of Transmission and Collective Composition in Turkmen Dutar Performance." *Analytical Approaches to World Music* 5 (2): 1–37.

———. 2023a. "Authors and Burners: Imagining Creative Agency in Turkey's Musical Folklore." *Ethnomusicology Forum* 32 (1): 1–21.

———. 2023b. "Neşet Ertaş and the Ontologies of Turkey's Folk Music." *Asian Music* 54, no.1 (Winter/Spring): 28–59.

———. 2024. "The Frictions of IP and the Schism in Turkey's Collective Management of Music Copyright." *Journal of Popular Music Studies* 36, no. 2 (June): 52–75.

Foucault, Michel. 2003. "What Is an Author?" In *The Essential Foucault: Selections from the Essential Works of Foucault, 1954–1984*, translated by Josue V. Harari, 377–91. New York: New Press.

"Fox Tv Kiziroğlu Haberi." 2014. Clip from a December 2014 Fox News report. YouTube. December 31, 2014. https://youtu.be/V3sw9i7vdlk.

Gates, Henry Louis. 2014. *The Signifying Monkey: A Theory of African-American Literary Criticism*. Twenty-Fifth-Anniversary ed. Oxford: Oxford University Press.

Gazete Duvar. 2022. "MESAM ile Alman meslek birliği GEMA telif nedeniyle mahkemelik oldu." February 15, 2022. https://www.gazeteduvar.com.tr/mesam-ile-alman-meslek -birligi-gema-telif-nedeniyle-mahkemelik-oldu-haber-1553321.

Gazimihal, Mahmut R. 2006. *Anadolu Türküleri ve Musikî İstikbâlimiz* [Anatolian türküler and our musical future]. Edited by Metin Özarslan. Istanbul: Doğu Kütüphanesi.

Gelbart, Matthew. 2007. *The Invention of "Folk Music" and "Art Music."* Cambridge: Cambridge University Press.

Gemrik, Sevil. 2008. "Fikri Mülkiyet Hakları Bağlamında Korsan Yayıncılığın Ekonomi Politiği." [The political economics of pirate publishing in relation to intellectual property rights]. Master's thesis, Süleyman Demirel Üniversitesi.

Gennep, Arnold van. 1924. *Le folklore: croyances et coutumes populaires françaises.* Paris: Stock.

Gervais, Daniel, ed. 2010. *Collective Management of Copyright and Related Rights.* 2nd ed. Alphen aan den Rijn, Netherlands: Wolters Kluwer.

Gill, Denise. 2017. *Melancholic Modalities: Affect, Islam, and Turkish Classical Musicians.* New York: Oxford University Press.

Ginsburg, Jane C. 1990. "A Tale of Two Copyrights: Literary Property in Revolutionary France and America." *Tulane Law Review* 64, no. 5 (May): 991–1031.

Goehr, Lydia. 2007. *The Imaginary Museum of Musical Works: An Essay in the Philosophy of Music.* Rev. ed. Oxford: Oxford University Press.

Gökalp, Ziya. 1959. *Turkish Nationalism and Western Civilization.* Translated by Niyazi Berkes. New York: Columbia University Press.

Gökdemir, Sevgi. 1987. *Ahmet Kutsi Tecer.* Ankara: Kültür ve Turizm Bakanlığı.

Göle, Nilüfer. 1996. *The Forbidden Modern: Civilization and Veiling.* Ann Arbor: University of Michigan Press.

Gönlübol, Mehmet. 1975. "NATO and Turkey." In *Turkey's Foreign Policy in Transition: 1950–1974*, edited by Kemal H. Karpat, 13–50. Leiden: E. J. Brill.

Gordon, Robert W. 1984. "Critical Legal Histories." *Stanford Law Review* 36, no. 1/2 (January): 57–125. https://doi.org/10.2307/1228681.

Gordon, Wendy. 2003. "Intellectual Property." In *The Oxford Handbook of Legal Studies*, edited by Peter Can and Mark Tushnet, 617–46. New York: Oxford University Press.

Gould, Jon B., and Scott Barclay. 2012. "Mind the Gap: The Place of Gap Studies in Sociolegal Scholarship." *Annual Review of Law and Social Science* 8:323–35. https://doi.org/10.1146/annurev-lawsocsci-102811-173833.

Greenhouse, Carol J. 1988. "Courting Difference: Issues of Interpretation and Comparison in the Study of Legal Ideologies." *Law and Society Review* 22 (4): 687–708.

Greve, Martin. 2017. *Makamsız: Individualization of Traditional Music on the Eve of Kemalist Turkey.* Würzburg, Germany: Ergon Verlag.

Grinvalsky, Paul. 1992. "Idea-Expression in Musical Analysis and the Role of the Intended Audience in Music Copyright Infringement." *California Western Law Review* 28 (2): 395–429.

Güney, Eflatun Cem. 1953. *Halk Türküleri* [Folk songs]. Istanbul: Yeditepe Yayınları.

Gusterson, Hugh. 1997. "Studying Up Revisited." *Political and Legal Anthropology Review* 20, no. 1 (May): 114–19.

Güven, Merdan. 2013. "Anadolu Ağıtlarının Türküleşme Süreci." [The process of türküfication in Anatolian ağıtlar]. *Folklor/Edebiyat* 19 (75): 117–28.

"Habertürk TV 1." 2014. Clip from a December 2014 Habertürk TV 1 report. YouTube. December 31, 2014. https://youtu.be/yZwHRaH4w_k.

Hale, William. 1981. *The Political and Economic Development of Modern Turkey*. New York: St. Martin's Press.

Halk Bilgisi Derneği, ed. 1928. *Halk Bilgisi Toplayacılarına Rehber* [Guide for collectors of folklore]. Ankara: Türkiye Büyük Millet Meclisi Matbaası.

Halliday, Simon. 2019. "After Hegemony: The Varieties of Legal Consciousness Research." *Social and Legal Studies* 28, no. 6 (December): 859–78.

Halliday, Simon, and Bronwen Morgan. 2013. "I Fought the Law and the Law Won? Legal Consciousness and the Critical Imagination." *Current Legal Problems* 66 (1): 1–32. https://doi.org/10.1093/clp/cut002.

Handke, Christian, and Ruth Towse. 2007. "Economics of Copyright Collecting Societies." *IIC International Review of Intellectual Property and Competition Law* 38 (8): 937–57.

Harris, Rachel. 2005. "Wang Luobin: Folk Song King of the Northwest or Song Thief? Copyright, Representation, and Chinese Folk Songs." *Modern China* 31, no. 3 (July): 381–408.

Hassan, Aisha, and Dan Kopf. 2018. "The Reason Why Your Favorite Pop Songs Are Getting Shorter." *Quartz*. October 27, 2018. https://qz.com/quartzy/1438412/.

Hemmungs Wirtén, Eva. 2004. *No Trespassing: Authorship, Intellectual Property Rights, and the Boundaries of Globalization*. Studies in Book and Print Culture. Toronto: University of Toronto Press.

Hertogh, Marc, and Marina Kurkchiyan. 2016. "'When Politics Comes into Play, Law Is No Longer Law': Images of Collective Legal Consciousness in the UK, Poland and Bulgaria." *International Journal of Law in Context* 12, no. 4 (December): 404–19.

Herzfeld, Michael. 2005. *Cultural Intimacy: Social Poetics in the Nation-State*. New York: Routledge.

Hesmondhalgh, David, and Leslie M. Meier. 2018. "What the Digitalisation of Music Tells Us about Capitalism, Culture and the Power of the Information Technology Sector." *Information, Communication and Society* 21 (11): 1555–70. https://doi.org/10.1080/13 69118X.2017.1340498.

Hesmondhalgh, David, Richard Osborne, Hyojung Sun, and Kenny Barr. 2021. "Music Creators' Earnings in the Digital Era." Newport, UK: The Intellectual Property Office. https://www.ssrn.com/abstract=4089749.

Hirsch, Ernst. 1985. *Hatıralarım* [My memories]. Ankara: Türkiye İş Bankası Vakfı.

Holmes, Oliver Wendell, Jr. 1897. "The Path of the Law." *Harvard Law Review* 10, no. 8 (March): 457–78.

Holston, James. 2013. "Spaces of Insurgent Citizenship." In *The Anthropology of Citizenship: A Reader*, edited by Sian Lazar, 93–98. Hoboken, NJ: Wiley-Blackwell.

———. 2022. "What Makes Democratic Citizenship Democratic?" *Citizenship Studies* 26 (4–5): 491–504. https://doi.org/10.1080/13621025.2022.2091231.

Hughes, Justin. 1988. "The Philosophy of Intellectual Property." *Georgetown Law Journal* 77, no. 2 (December): 287–366.

IFMC. 1953. "General Report." *Journal of the International Folk Music Council* 5:9–35.

———. 1955. "Resolutions." *Journal of the International Folk Music Council* 7:23.

İnalcık, Halil, and Donald Quataert. 1994. *An Economic and Social History of the Ottoman Empire, 1300–1914*. Cambridge: Cambridge University Press.

İşyerleri İçin Müzik Eserlerinde Telif Hakkı Uygulamaları: Panel, 28.10.2004 [Implementation of copyright in musical works for workplaces: Panel, 10/28/2004]. 2004. İstanbul: İstanbul Ticaret Odası.

Jäger, Ralph. 2015. "Concepts of Western and Ottoman Music History." In *Writing the History of "Ottoman Music,"* edited by Martin Greve, 33–50. Würzburg: Ergon Verlag.

Jaszi, Peter. 1991. "Toward a Theory of Copyright: The Metamorphoses of 'Authorship.'" *Duke Law Journal* 1991 (2): 455–502.

Johns, Adrian. 2009. *Piracy: The Intellectual Property Wars from Gutenberg to Gates*. Chicago: University of Chicago Press.

Kapczynski, Amy. 2008. "The Access to Knowledge Mobilization and the New Politics of Intellectual Property." *Yale Law Journal* 117, no. 5 (March): 804–85.

Kaplan, Ayten. n.d. "Cemil Demirsipahi'nin El Yazması Defterinde Yer Alan Bestelerinde Müzikal Unsurlar." [Musical elements of compositions in Cemil Demirsipahi's manuscript portfolio]. Accessed July 24, 2023. https://www.academia.edu/37330284/.

Karaca, Dursun. 2005. *Telif Hakları Üstüne Ticari ve Siyasi Oyunlar and MESAM Gerçeği* [Economic and political games with copyright and the reality of MESAM]. Istanbul: Ten Basım Yayım.

Karaganis, Joe, ed. 2011. *Media Piracy in Emerging Economies*. New York: Social Science Research Council.

———. 2012. "The Bellagio Global Dialogues on Intellectual Property." PIJIP Research Paper no. 2012-12. American University Washington College of Law. http://digital commons.wcl.american.edu/research.

Karlıdağ, Serpil Konrapa. 2010. *Fikirlerimizin Sahibi Kim? Türkiye'de Müzik Endüstrisinde Telif Hakları Politikaları* [Who owns our thoughts? The politics of copyright in Turkey's music industry]. İstanbul: Kalkedon.

Karpat, Kemal H. 1975. "Turkish Soviet Relations." In *Turkey's Foreign Policy in Transition: 1950–1974*, edited by Kemal H. Karpat, 73–107. Leiden: E. J. Brill.

———. 1976. *The Gecekondu: Rural Migration and Urbanization*. New York: Cambridge University Press.

Karpeles, Maud. 1951. "Some Reflections on Authenticity in Folk Music." *Journal of the International Folk Music Council* 3:10–16.

———. 1963. "Communication on Copyright." *Western Folklore* 22, no. 3 (July): 187–89.

Kaya, Cem, dir. 2015. *Remake, Remix, Rip-off: About Copy Culture and Turkish Pop Cinema.* Potsdam, Germany: UFA Fiction GmbH.

Kaymak, Mansur. 2005. "Türkü Değil, Kürtü Diyenlere Ne Diyeceğiz?" [What do we say to those who say "kürtü" instead of "türkü"?]. In *MESAM Halk Müziği Eserleri Sempozyumu*, 32–45. Istanbul: MESAM.

Kemal, Yaşar. 2014. *Ağıtlar: Folklor derlemesi* [Ağıtlar: Folkloric collection]. Istanbul: YKY.

Keyder, Virginia Brown. 1996. *Intellectual Property Rights and Customs Union.* İstanbul: InterMedia.

Kinos-Goodin, Jesse. 2019. "The Long, Complicated History of Baby Shark—and the Artist Fighting for Credit." CBC Radio, January 24, 2019. https://www.cbc.ca/radio/q/.

Kirişci, Kemal. 2008. "Migration and Turkey: The Dynamics of State, Society and Politics." In *Turkey in the Modern World*, in vol. 4 of *The Cambridge History of Turkey*, edited by Reşat Kasaba, 173–98. Cambridge: Cambridge University Press. https://doi.org/10.1017/CHOL9780521620963.008.

Kjus, Yngvar. 2019. "The Use of Copyright in Digital Times: A Study of How Artists Exercise Their Rights in Norway." *Popular Music and Society* 44 (3): 1–17. https://doi.org/10.1080/03007766.2019.1698206.

Kocabaşoğlu, Uygur. 1980. *Şirket Telsizinden Devlet Radyosuna: TRT Öncesi Dönemde Radyonun Tarihsel Gelişimi ve Türk Siyasal Hayatı İçindeki Yeri* [From corporate wireless to state radio: The radio's historical development and place in Turkish political life prior to the TRT]. Ankara: Ankara Üniversitesi Siyasal Bilgiler Fakültesi.

Konuralp, Okan. 2014. "Kiziroğlu savaşı." [The Kiziroğlu war]. *Hurriyet*, December 30, 2014, sec. Gündem haberleri. https://www.hurriyet.com.tr/.

Koşay, Hamit Zübeyir. 1939. *Etnografya ve Folklor Kılavuzu* [Guide to ethnography and folklore]. Ankara: Ulusal Matbaa.

———. 1974. *Makaleler ve İncelemeler* [Articles and studies]. Ankara: Ayyıldız Matbaası.

Köymen, Erol. 2022. "Listening for Secular Bodies: Western Art Music, Occidentalism, and Belonging in Neo-Liberal Istanbul." PhD diss., University of Chicago.

Kraut, Anthea. 2011. "White Womanhood, Property Rights, and the Campaign for Choreographic Copyright: Loïe Fuller's Serpentine Dance." *Dance Research Journal* 43, no. 1 (Summer): 3–26.

Kreger, Alex. 2023. "The Stringed Qur'an: Post-Islamic Reform and Musical Revival among Alevis in Turkey and Europe." PhD diss., University of Texas at Austin.

Krueger, Alan B. 2019. *Rockonomics: A Backstage Tour of What the Music Industry Can Teach Us about Economics and Life.* New York: Crown.

Kural, Sadife Karataş. 2005. "Kullanım İzni ve Meslek Birlikleri." [Permissions for use and collecting societies]. In *Fikri ve Sınai Mülkiyet Haklari ve Kültürü (1. Ulusal Sempozyumu)* [Intellectual and industrial property rights and culture: First national symposium], 244–59. İstanbul: İstanbul Barosu Yayınları.

Kwee-Tiang, Ang. 2010. "Collective Management in Asia." In *Collective Management of Copyright and Related Rights*, 2nd ed., edited by Daniel Gervais, 409–65. Alphen aan den Rijn, Netherlands: Wolters Kluwer.

Lafraniere, Sharon. 2006. "In the Jungle, the Unjust Jungle, a Small Victory." *The New York Times*, March 22, 2006, sec. World. https://www.nytimes.com/2006/03/22/world/africa/in-the-jungle-the-unjust-jungle-a-small-victory.html.

Laing, Dave. 2002. "Copyright as a Component of the Music Industry." In *The Business of Music*, edited by Michael Talbot, 171–94. Liverpool: Liverpool University Press.

Landau, Jacob M. 1984. *Ataturk and the Modernization of Turkey*. A Westview Replica ed. Boulder, CO: Westview Press.

Lazar, Sian. 2013. *The Anthropology of Citizenship: A Reader*. Hoboken, NJ: Wiley-Blackwell.

Leach, James. 2007. "Creativity, Subjectivity and the Dynamic of Possessive Individualism." In *Creativity and Cultural Improvisation*, edited by Elizabeth Hallam and Tim Ingold, 99–116. Oxford: Berg.

Leo, Katherine M. 2021. *Forensic Musicology and the Blurred Lines of Federal Copyright History*. New York: Lexington Books.

Lessig, Lawrence. 2008. *Remix*. London: Bloomsbury Academic.

———. 2016. *Free Culture*. Raleigh, NC: Lulu Press.

Lewis, Bernard. 1961. *The Emergence of Modern Turkey*. New York: Oxford University Press.

Liebisch-Gümüş, Carolin. 2019. "Intersecting Asymmetries: The Internationalization of Turkey in the 1920s and the Limits of the Postcolonial Approach." *AUC Studia Territorialia* 19 (1): 13–41.

Lim, Chang-won. 2021. "American Toddler Music Entertainer Loses Legal Battle against Korean Baby Shark Video." *Aju Business Daily*, July 23, 2021, sec. Hobby. https://www.ajudaily.com.

Lindahl, Carl. 2004. "Thrills and Miracles: Legends of Lloyd Chandler." *Journal of Folklore Research* 41, no. 2/3 (May): 133–71.

Litman, Jessica. 1990. "The Public Domain." *Emory Law Journal* 39, no. 4 (Fall): 61.

———. 2006. *Digital Copyright*. Amherst, NY: Prometheus Books.

Lomax, Alan. 1972. "Appeal for Cultural Equity / Plaidoirie Pour Une Égalité Culturelle / Allen Kulturen Gleiches Recht." *The World of Music* 14 (2): 3–17.

———. 1978. *Cantometrics: An Approach to the Anthropology of Music*. Berkeley: University of California Extension Media Center.

Lord, Albert Bates. 2000. *The Singer of Tales*. Cambridge, MA: Harvard University Press.

Macfarlane, Robert. 2007. *Original Copy: Plagiarism and Originality in Nineteenth-Century Literature*. New York: Oxford University Press.

Mann, Larisa Kingston. 2022. *Rude Citizenship: Jamaican Popular Music, Copyright, and the Reverberations of Colonial Power*. Chapel Hill: University of North Carolina Press.

Manuel, Peter. 1993. *Cassette Culture: Popular Music and Technology in North India*. Chicago: University of Chicago Press.

———. 2006. "The Saga of a Song: Authorship and Ownership in the Case of 'Guantanamera.'" *Latin American Music Review / Revista de Música Latinoamericana* 27, no. 2 (Fall/Winter): 121–47.

Mardin, Şerif. 1962. *The Genesis of Young Ottoman Thought*. Princeton, NJ: Princeton University Press.

———. 2006. *Religion, Society, and Modernity in Turkey*. Syracuse, NY: Syracuse University Press.

Markoff, Irene Judyth. 1986. "Musical Theory, Performance and the Contemporary Bağlama Specialist in Turkey." PhD diss., University of Washington.

Marshall, Lee, ed. 2013. *The International Recording Industries*. New York: Routledge.

———. 2015. "'Let's Keep Music Special. F— Spotify': On-Demand Streaming and the Controversy over Artist Royalties." *Creative Industries Journal* 8 (2): 177–89. https://doi.org/10.1080/17510694.2015.1096618.

McCann, Anthony. 2001. "All That Is Not Given Is Lost: Irish Traditional Music, Copyright, and Common Property." *Ethnomusicology* 45, no. 1 (Winter): 89–106.

———. 2002. "Beyond the Commons: The Expansion of the Irish Music Rights Organisation, the Elimination of Uncertainty, and the Politics of Enclosure." PhD diss., University of Limerick.

McDonagh, Luke. 2018. "Protecting Traditional Music under Copyright (and Choosing Not to Enforce It)." In *Non-Conventional Copyright: Do New and Atypical Works Deserve Protection?*, edited by Enrico Bonadio and Nicola Lucchi, 151–73. Cheltenham, UK: Edward Elgar Publishing. https://doi.org/10.4337/9781786434074.

McLeod, Kembrew. 2005. *Freedom of Expression: Overzealous Copyright Bozos and Other Enemies of Creativity*. New York: Doubleday Religious.

McLeod, Kembrew, and Peter DiCola. 2011. *Creative License: The Law and Culture of Digital Sampling*. Durham, NC: Duke University Press.

McLuhan, Marshall. 2013. *Understanding Media: The Extensions of Man*. Berkeley, CA: Gingko Press.

McNally, James. 2017. "Favela Chic: Diplo, *Funk Carioca*, and the Ethics and Aesthetics of the Global Remix." *Popular Music and Society* 40 (4): 434–52. https://doi.org/10.1080/03007766.2015.1126100.

Meier, Leslie M., and Vincent R. Manzerolle. 2019. "Rising Tides? Data Capture, Platform Accumulation, and New Monopolies in the Digital Music Economy." *New Media and Society* 21, no. 3 (March): 543–61. https://doi.org/10.1177/1461444818800998.

Meintjes, Louise. 2003. *Sound of Africa! Making Music Zulu in a South African Studio.* Durham, NC: Duke University Press.

Melville, Caspar. 2017. "Valuing Tradition: Mali's Jeliw, European Publishers and Copyright." *Journal of World Popular Music* 4 (1): 10–44.

Meriç, Murat. 2006. *Pop Dedik: Türkçe Sözlü Hafif Batı Müziği* [Light/pop music with Turkish words]. Istanbul: İletişim Yayınları.

Merry, Sally Engle. 1990. *Getting Justice and Getting Even: Legal Consciousness among Working-Class Americans.* Chicago: University of Chicago Press.

MESAM. 2005. *MESAM Halk Müziği Eserleri Sempozyumu* [MESAM symposium on folk music works]. Istanbul: MESAM.

———. 2007. "MESAM Nasıl Kuruldu?" [How was MESAM founded?]. *Vizyon*, January 2007.

Miller, Ruth A. 2000. "The Ottoman and Islamic Substratum of Turkey's Swiss Civil Code." *Journal of Islamic Studies* 11, no. 3 (September): 335–61.

Mills, Sherylle. 1996. "Indigenous Music and the Law: An Analysis of National and International Legislation." *Yearbook for Traditional Music* 28:57–86.

Moser, David J., and Cheryl Slay. 2011. *Music Copyright Law.* Boston: Course Technology.

Müftüoğlu, Oğuz. 2005. "Anonim Eserelerle İlgili Yasal Zemin Arayışları ve Ülkemizdeki Yasa Boşluğu." [Searches for a legal foundation for anonymous works and a gap in our country's law]. In *MESAM Halk Müziği Eserleri Sempozyumu*, 5–9. Istanbul: MESAM.

Murray, Laura J., S. Tina Piper, and Kirsty Robertson. 2014. *Putting Intellectual Property in Its Place: Rights Discourses, Creative Labor, and the Everyday.* New York: Oxford University Press. https://doi.org/10.1093/acprof:oso/9780199336265.001.0001.

MÜZKO. 1978. *MÜZKO: Müzik Söz Yazarları Besteci Yayımcı Odalar Birliğini Kurma ve Yapıtçı Haklarını Koruma Şirketi.* [Istanbul?]: Türkofon Universal Müzik Yayınevi.

Nader, Laura. 1974. "Up the Anthropologist—Perspectives Gained from Studying Up." In *Reinventing Anthropology*, edited by Dell Hymes, 284–311. New York: Vintage Books.

Nardella, Federica. 2023. "Singing Poems, Reading Songs: Performing Pre-Reform Turkish; The Şarkı and the Nineteenth Century Language Debate." PhD diss., King's College.

Negus, Keith. 2019. "From Creator to Data: The Post-Record Music Industry and the Digital Conglomerates." *Media, Culture and Society* 41, no. 3 (April): 367–84. https://doi.org/10.1177/0163443718799395.

Neubauer, Eckhard. 1997. "Zur Bedeutung der Begriffe Komponist und Komposition in der Muzikgeschichte der Islamischen Welt." [Toward the meaning of the concepts "composer" and "composition" in the music history of the Islamic world]. *Zeitschrift für Geschichte der Arabischen-Islamischen Wissenchaften* 11:307–63.

Nooshin, Laudan. 2003. "Improvisation as 'Other': Creativity, Knowledge and Power: The Case of Iranian Classical Music." *Journal of the Royal Musical Association* 128 (2): 242–96.

———. 2015. *Iranian Classical Music: The Discourses and Practice of Creativity.* Burlington, VT: Ashgate.

Noyes, Dorothy. 2011. "Traditional Culture: How Does It Work?" *Museum Anthropology Review* 5 (1–2): 39–47.

O'Connell, John Morgan. 2000. "Fine Art, Fine Music: Controlling Turkish Taste at the Fine Arts Academy in 1926." *Yearbook for Traditional Music* 32:117–42.

———. 2005. "In the Time of Alaturka: Identifying Difference in Musical Discourse." *Ethnomusicology* 49, no. 2 (Spring/Summer): 177–205.

———. 2016. *Alaturka: Style in Turkish Music (1923–1938).* London: Ashgate.

Okutan Nilsson, Gül. 2012. "Turkey." In *Balancing Copyright: A Survey of National Approaches,* edited by Reto Hilty and Sylvie Nérisson, 1029–45. New York: Springer.

Olian, Irwin A. 1974. "International Copyright and the Needs of Developing Countries: The Awakening at Stockholm and Paris." *Cornell International Law Journal* 7, no. 2 (May): 81–112.

Ong, Aihwa, and Stephen J. Collier. 2005. *Global Assemblages: Technology, Politics, and Ethics as Anthropological Problems.* Malden, MA: Blackwell.

Ong, Walter. 1982. *Orality and Literacy: The Technologizing of the Word.* New York: Methuen.

Öngören, Gürsel. 2010. *Türk Fikir ve Sanat Eserleri Hukuku Açısından Müzik Eserleri* [Musical works from the perspective of Turkish law on intellectual and artistic works]. Istanbul: Öngören hukuk yayınları.

Oran, Baskın. 2007. "The Minority Concept and Rights in Turkey: The Lausanne Peace Treaty and Current Issues." In *Human Rights in Turkey,* edited by Zehra F. Kabasakal Arat, 35–56. Philadelphia: University of Pennsylvania Press.

Özbek, Mehmet. 2005. "Halk Müziğinde Eser Sahipliği." [Authorship in folk music]. In *MESAM Halk Müziği Eserleri Sempozyumu,* 58–61. Istanbul: MESAM.

Özdemir, Erdem. 2013. "Türkiye Örneğinde Âşıklarda Müzik." [The music of âşıks in the case of Turkey]. PhD diss., Sakarya Üniversitesi.

Özdemir, Urum Ulaş. 2015. "İstanbul Cemevlerinde Yürütülen Zakirlik Hizmetinin, Ritüel, Müzik İcrası ve Alevi Kimliği Bağlamında İncelenmesi." [An examination of *zakirlik* service, ritual, musical performance, and connection to Alevi identity as performed in Istanbul *cemevi*s]. PhD diss., Yıldız Teknik Üniversitesi.

Özkan, Âşık Ali Izzet, and İlhan Başgöz. 1979. *Âşık Ali İzzet Özkan: Yaşamı, Sanatı, Şiirleri* [Âşık Ali İzzet Özkan: His life, art, and poems]. Ankara: Türkiye İş Bankası Kültür Yayınları.

Özman, Aylin. 2010. "Law, Ideology and Modernization in Turkey: Kemalist Legal Reforms in Perspective." *Social and Legal Studies* 19, no. 1 (March): 67–84. https://doi.org/10.1177/0964663909346196.

Özsu, Umut. 2010. "'Receiving' the Swiss Civil Code: Translating Authority in Early

Republican Turkey." *International Journal of Law in Context* 6, no. 1 (March): 63–89. https://doi.org/10.1017/S1744552309990309.

Öztelli, Cahit. 1972. *Evlerinin Önü* [In front of their houses]. Istanbul: Hurriyet.

———. 1974. *Üç Kahraman Şair: Köroğlu, Dadaloğlu, Kuloğlu* [Three heroic poets: Köroğlu, Dadaloğlu, Kuloğlu]. Istanbul: Milliyet Yayınları.

Öztrak, İlhan. 1970. "Fikir ve Sanat Eserleri Üzerindeki Hakların Korunması Yönünden Pozitif Hukuktaki Tarihi Gelişim." [The historical development of positive law from the perspective of the rights to intellectual and artistic works]. *Ankara Üniversitesi Siyasal Bilgiler Fakültesi Dergisi* 25, no. 3 (March): 1–7.

———. 1971. *Fikir ve Sanat Eserleri Üzerindeki Haklar* [Rights to intellectual and artistic works]. Ankara: Ankara Üniversitesi Siyasal Bilgiler Fakültesi.

Öztürk, Veysel. 2016. "The Notion of Originality from Ottoman Classical Literature to Turkish Modern Poetry." *Middle Eastern Literatures* 19 (2): 135–61. https://doi.org/10.1080/1475262X.2016.1211405.

Öztürkmen, Arzu. 1993. "Folklore and Nationalism in Turkey." PhD diss., University of Pennsylvania.

Özürküt, Yaşar. 2005. "Türk Halk Müziği Üretim Sureci, Diğer Müzik Türleriyle Farkı (Olay-Ezgi-Söz Üçlemesi ve Bütünlüğü)." [The production process in Turkish folk music and its difference from other kinds of music (the event-tune-lyric trio and its unity)]. In *MESAM Halk Müziği Eserleri Sempozyumu*, 9–14. Istanbul: MESAM.

Özyürek, Esra. 2006. *Nostalgia for the Modern: State Secularism and Everyday Politics in Turkey*. Durham, NC: Duke University Press.

Paçacı, Gönül, ed. 1999. *Cumhuriyet'in Sesleri* [Voices of the republic]. Istanbul: Türkiye Ekonomik ve Toplumsal Tarih Vakfı.

Pappas, Nicholas G. 1999. "Concepts of Greekness: The Recorded Music of Anatolian Greeks after 1922." *Journal of Modern Greek Studies* 17, no. 2 (October): 353–73. https://doi.org/10.1353/mgs.1999.0031.

Parlak, Erol. 2000. *Türkiye'de El İle (Şelpe) Bağlama Çalma Geleneği Ve Çalış Teknikleri* [Fingerstyle (şelpe) bağlama tradition and playing techniques in Turkey]. Ankara: Kültür Bakanlığı.

———. 2013. *Garip Bülbül Neşet Ertaş: Hayatı, Sanatı, Eserleri*. 2 vols. Istanbul: Demos.

Paskin, Willa. 2019. "Baby Shark." Decoder Ring (podcast). Accessed March 20, 2023. https://slate.com/culture/.

Perlman, Marc. 2011. "From 'Folklore' to 'Knowledge' in Global Governance: On the Metamorphosis of the Unauthored." In *Making and Unmaking Intellectual Property: Creative Production in Legal and Cultural Perspective*, edited by Mario Biagioli, Peter Jaszi, and Martha Woodmansee, 115–32. Chicago: University of Chicago Press.

———. 2019. "Meta-Ideologies of Textuality: Authorship, Plagiarism, Copyright." *Signs and Society* 7, no. 2 (Spring): 245–87. https://doi.org/10.1086/702545.

Perullo, Alex, and Andrew J. Eisenberg. 2015. "Musical Property Rights Regimes in Tanzania and Kenya after TRIPS." In *The SAGE Handbook of Intellectual Property*, edited by Matthew David and Debora Halbert, 148–64. London: SAGE.

Pinkert, Melanie Terner. 2016. "A Voice of Their Own: Music and Social Cohesion in Turkish Alevi Life." PhD diss., University of Maryland, College Park.

Popescu-Judetz, Eugenia. 1996. *Meanings in Turkish Musical Culture*. Istanbul: Pan yayıncılık.

Pound, Roscoe. 1910. "Law in Books and Law in Action." *American Law Review* 44, no. 1 (January–February): 12–36.

Prey, Robert. 2016. "Music Analytica: The Datafication of Listening." In *Networked Music Cultures: Contemporary Approaches, Emerging Issues*, edited by Raphael Nowak and Andrew Whelan, 31–48. London: Palgrave Macmillan.

Quataert, Donald. 2000. *Consumption Studies and the History of the Ottoman Empire, 1550–1922: An Introduction*. Albany: State University of New York Press.

Ranasinghe, Prashan. 2010. "Ambivalence towards Law: Business Improvement Associations, Public Disorder and Legal Consciousness." *International Journal of Law in Context* 6, no. 4 (December): 323–42. https://doi.org/10.1017/S1744552310000273.

Reigle, Robert. 2013. "A Brief History of Kurdish Music Recordings in Turkey." *Hellenic Journal of Music Education, and Culture* 4, no. 1 (December).

Reinhard, Ursula, and Tiago de Oliveira Pinto. 1989. *Sänger und Poeten mit der Laute: Türkische Âşık und Ozan* [Singers and poets with a lute: Turkish âşık and ozan]. Berlin: Dietrich Reimer Verlag.

Richards, Sally. 2015. "Unearthing Bureaucratic Legal Consciousness: Government Officials' Legal Identification and Moral Ideals." *International Journal of Law in Context* 11, no. 3 (September): 299–319. https://doi.org/10.1017/S1744552315000166.

Ricketson, Sam, and Jane C. Ginsburg. 2022. *International Copyright and Neighbouring Rights: The Berne Convention and Beyond*. 3rd edition. 3 vols. New York: Oxford University Press.

Robertson, Kirsty. 2014. "No One Would Murder for a Pattern: Crafting IP in Online Knitting Communities." In *Putting Intellectual Property in Its Place: Rights Discourses, Creative Labor, and the Everyday*, edited by Laura J. Murray, S. Tina Piper, and Kirsty Robertson, 41–62. New York: Oxford University Press. https://doi.org/10.1093/acprof:oso/9780199336265.003.0003.

Robinson, Daniel F., Ahmed Abdel-Latif, and Pedro Roffe. 2017. *Protecting Traditional Knowledge: The WIPO Intergovernmental Committee on Intellectual Property and Genetic Resources, Traditional Knowledge and Folklore*. London: Routledge.

Röschenthaler, Ute, and Mamadou Diawara. 2019. *Copyright Africa: How Intellectual Property, Media and Markets Transform Immaterial Cultural Goods*. Wantage, Oxon: Sean Kingston.

Rosenblatt, Elizabeth L. 2019. "Copyright's One-Way Racial Appropriation Ratchet." *University of California Davis Law Review* 53, no. 2 (December): 591–661.

Said, Edward W. 1979. *Orientalism*. 1st Vintage Books ed. New York: Vintage Books.

Samuels, David William. 2004. *Putting a Song on Top of It: Expression and Identity on the San Carlos Apache Reservation*. Tucson: University of Arizona Press.

Saltık, Nilüfer, and Cemal Taş, eds. 2016. *Tertele: Ebe Şûara Tertelê 38i / Ağıtların Diliyle Dersim '38 / Dersim '38 in the Language of Laments*. Istanbul: Y / Kalan.

Sarat, Austin. 1985. "Legal Effectiveness and Social Studies of Law: On the Unfortunate Persistence of a Research Tradition." *Legal Studies Forum* 9 (1): 23–32.

Sarat, Austin, and Thomas R. Kearns, eds. 1993. *Law in Everyday Life*. Ann Arbor: University of Michigan Press.

Satır, Ömer Can. 2012. "Yeni Ankaralı Müzik Anlayışı ve Eğlence Geleneğinin Dönüşümü: Metâlaşma ve Tüketim Kültürü Bağlamında Bir İnceleme." [The new Ankara understanding of music and the transformation of the entertainment tradition: An examination of commercialization and consumption culture]. *İletişim: Galatasaray University Journal of Communication*, no. 45 (September): 203–14.

Sawyer, R. Keith. 2003. *Group Creativity: Music, Theater, Collaboration*. Mahwah, NJ: Taylor & Francis.

Scales, Amanda. 2005. "'Sola, Perduta, Abbandonata': Are the Copyright Act and Performing Rights Organizations Killing Classical Music?" *Vanderbilt Journal of Entertainment and Technology Law* 7, no. 2 (Spring): 281–99.

Scherzinger, Martin. 1999. "Music, Spirit Possession and the Copyright Law: Cross-Cultural Comparisons and Strategic Speculations." *Yearbook for Traditional Music* 31:102–25.

———. 2014. "Musical Property: Widening or Withering?" *Journal of Popular Music Studies* 26 (1): 162–92.

Seeger, Anthony. 1991. "Singing Other People's Songs." *Cultural Survival Quarterly* 15 (3): 36–39.

———. 1992. "Ethnomusicology and Music Law." *Ethnomusicology* 36, no. 3 (Autumn): 345–59.

Seeman, Sonia Tamar. 2019. *Sounding Roman: Representation and Performing Identity in Western Turkey*. New York: Oxford.

Sehlikoğlu, Sertaç. 2016. "Exercising in Comfort." *Journal of Middle East Women's Studies* 12, no. 2 (July): 143–65. https://doi.org/10.1215/15525864-3507606.

Semercioğlu, Cengiz. 2016. "Apple Music bu yaptığını Avrupa'da yapabilir miydi?" *Hürriyet*, February 7, 2016, sec. cengiz-semercioglu. https://www.hurriyet.com.tr/yazarlar/cengiz-semercioglu/apple-music-bu-yaptigini-avrupada-yapabilir-miydi-40050615.

Şenel, Süleyman. 1999. "Cumhurriyet Dönemi'nde Türk Halk Müziği Araştırmaları." [Turkish folk music research in the republican era]. *Folklor/Edebiyat* 5 (17): 99–128.

———. 2007. *Kastamonu'da Âşık Fasılları* [Âşık gatherings in Kastamonu]. Kastamonu: Kastamonu Valiliği Yayınları.

———. 2009. *Yücel Paşmakçı İle Türküler Üzerine* [On the topic of türküler, with Yücel Paşmakçı]. Istanbul: İTÜ Türk Musikisi Devlet Konservatuvarı.

———. 2010. *İstanbul Çevresi Alan Araştırmaları* [Field research in the environs of Istanbul]. 2 vols. Istanbul: İstanbul Avrupa Kültür Başkenti Ajansı.

———. 2015. "Ottoman Türkü." In *Writing the History of "Ottoman Music,"* edited by Martin Greve, translated by Efkan Oğuz, Martin Greve, and Onur Nobrega, 195–209. Würzburg: Ergon Verlag.

———. 2018a. *Bu Deyiş Kimindir? Mecnunum Leylamı Gördüm* [Whose lyric is this? I'm Majnun and I've seen my Leyla]. Istanbul: Siyah Kitap.

———, ed. 2018b. *Muzaffer Sarısözen: Türk Halk Müziği ve Oyunları Hakkında Yazılar, Röportajlar, Anılar, Ardından Yazılanlar, Belgeler, Notalar* [Muzaffer Sarısözen: writings, documentaries, memories on Turkish folk music and dances, and writings, documents, and notes about him]. Istanbul: Sivas Platformu.

Sevimli, Atahan. 2007. "Fikir ve Sanat Eserleri Kanunu Çerçevisinde Müzik Eserlerinin Korunması." [The protection of musical works within the framework of the law on intellectual and artistic works]. Istanbul: İstanbul Üniversitesi Sosyal Bilimler Enstitüsü Özel Hukuk Anabilim Dalı.

Seyhan, Özcan. 1990. "Çukurova'da Derlenen Kusurlu Halk Ezgileri." [Flawed folk melodies collected in Çukurova]. In *1. Uluslararası Karacaoğlan ve Çukurova Halk Kültürü Sempozyumu*. Adana, Turkey: Arif Ofset.

"Sezen Aksu: 'Telif hakkı insan hakları gibi demokratik bir haktır.' (1998 - Siyaset Meydanı)." 2015. Clip from a 1998 episode of the program "Siyaset Meydanı." YouTube. April 2, 2015. https://youtu.be/hvfN5WWbPOA.

Shabalala, Dalindyebo Bafana. 2021. "Do We Need Exit Rules for Traditional Knowledge? Lessons from Solomon Linda, and the Mbube/'The Lion Sleeps Tonight' Case." *SSRN Electronic Journal*. https://doi.org/10.2139/ssrn.3914377.

Sharp, Cecil James. 1965. *English Folk Song: Some Conclusions*. 4th rev. ed. Belmont, CA: Wadsworth.

Sharpe, Kenan Mikail Behzad. 2019. "Cultural Revolutions: Turkey and the United States During the Long 1960s." PhD diss., University of California, Santa Cruz.

Sher, Howard. 2005. "Copyright Originality and Performing Editions of Music out of Copyright." *Juta's Business Law* 13, no. 4 (January): 139–42.

Silbey, Jessica. 2014. *The Eureka Myth: Creators, Innovators, and Everyday Intellectual Property*. Redwood City, CA: Stanford University Press.

———. 2022. *Against Progress: Intellectual Property and Fundamental Values in the Internet Age*. Stanford, CA: Stanford University Press.

Silbey, Susan S. 2005. "After Legal Consciousness." *Annual Review of Law and Social Science* 1:323–68. https://doi.org/10.1146/annurev.lawsocsci.1.041604.115938.

———. 2012. "J. Locke Op. Cit.: Invocations of Law on Snowy Streets." In *Using Legal Culture*, edited by David Nelken, 120–52. London: Wildy, Simmons & Hill.

Silverstein, Michael, and Greg Urban. 1996. *Natural Histories of Discourse*. Chicago: University of Chicago Press.

Sipahi, Ali. 2021. "The Making of a National City: From Mezre to Elazığ." In *The Routledge Handbook on Contemporary Turkey*, by Joost Jongerden, 63–74. London: Routledge. https://doi.org/10.4324/9780429264030-6.

Skinner, Ryan Thomas. 2012. "Artists, Music Piracy, and the Crisis of Political Subjectivity in Contemporary Mali." *Anthropological Quarterly* 85, no. 3 (Summer): 723–54. https://doi.org/10.1353/anq.2012.0053.

Skoog, Gabriel. 2012. "On Strange Shepherds, Golden Microphones, and Electric Guitars: Genre, Scene, and the Rise of Anadolu Pop in the Republic of Turkey." PhD diss., University of Washington.

Solmaz, Metin. 1999. "Türkiye'de Müzik Hayatı: Başarısız Projeler Cenneti!" [The life of music in Turkey: A paradise for unsuccessful projects!]. In *Cumhuriyet'in Sesleri*, edited by Gönül Paçacı, 154–59. Istanbul: Türkiye Ekonomik ve Toplumsal Tarih Vakfı.

Somanawat, Kitpatchara. 2018. "Constructing the Identity of the Thai Judge: Virtue, Status, and Power." *Asian Journal of Law and Society* 5, no. 1 (May): 91–110. https://doi.org/10.1017/als.2017.32.

Sözcü. 2014. "Orhan Gencebay 11 milyon lira zarara soktu." March 21, 2014. https://www.sozcu.com.tr/mesam-wp473794.

Springer, Robert. 2007. "Folklore, Commercialism and Exploitation: Copyright in the Blues." *Popular Music* 26, no. 1 (January): 33–45.

Sterne, Jonathan. 2011. "The Theology of Sound: A Critique of Orality." *Canadian Journal of Communication* 36, no. 2 (August): 207–25. https://doi.org/10.22230/cjc.2011v36n2a2223.

Stewart, Catherine A. 2016. *Long Past Slavery: Representing Race in the Federal Writers' Project*. Chapel Hill: University of North Carolina Press.

Stobart, Henry. 2010. "Rampant Reproduction and Digital Democracy: Shifting Landscapes of Music Production and 'Piracy' in Bolivia." *Ethnomusicology Forum* 19 (1): 27–56.

Stokes, Martin. 1992. *The Arabesk Debate: Music and Musicians in Modern Turkey*. New York: Oxford University Press.

———. 2010. *The Republic of Love: Cultural Intimacy in Turkish Popular Music*. Chicago: University of Chicago Press.

———. 2023. *Music and Citizenship*. New York: Oxford University Press.

Street, John, and Tom Phillips. 2017. "What Do Musicians Talk about When They Talk about Copyright?" *Popular Music and Society* 40 (4): 422–33. https://doi.org/10.1080/03007766.2015.1126099.

Suluk, Cahit. 2004. *Yeni Fikir ve Sanat Eserleri Kanunu: Telif Haklari ve Korsanlikla Mücadele* [The new law on intellectual and artistic works: Copyright and the struggle against piracy]. Istanbul: Hayat.

Sümer, Nevzat. 2005. "Korunması Gereken Mirasımız; Halk Müziğimiz." [Our heritage that needs to be protected; our folk music]. In *MESAM Halk Müziği Eserleri Sempozyumu*, 71–72. Istanbul: MESAM.

Sunar, İkay. 1996. "State, Society, and Democracy in Turkey." In *Turkey Between East and West: New Challenges for a Rising Regional Power*, edited by Vojtech Mastny and R. Craig Nation, 141–54. Boulder, CO: Westview Press.

Sunder, Madhavi. 2012. *From Goods to a Good Life: Intellectual Property and Global Justice.* New Haven: Yale University Press.

Surmeli, Gungor. 2011. "The Enforcement of Intellectual Property Rights (IPR) in Turkey in the EU Accession Process: A Perception Analysis of the Police Officers Dealing with IPR Crimes." PhD diss., University of Durham.

Tan, Nail. 2008. *Folklor (Halk Bilimi): Genel Bilgiler* [Folklore: General information]. Istanbul: Özal Matbaası.

———. 2013. "Ankarabesk Tarzı Türkülerin Ankara Halk Müziğini Yozlaştırmasına Karşı Alınması Gereken Bazı Önlemler." [Some measures that need to be taken against Ankarabesk-style türküler's corruption of Ankara folk music]. In *2. Uluslararası Ankara-Kazan ve Çevresi Halk Kültürü Sempozyumu ve Uluslararası Sanat Çalıştayı*. Kazan, Turkey: T. C. Kazan Belediyesi Kültür ve Sosyal İşler Müdürü Kültür Yayınları. https://www.kahramankazan.bel.tr/files/sempozyum-2.pdf.

Taşlıova, Şeref. 2005. "Kaynaktan Anonime Geçiş." [The passage from the source to anonymity]. In *MESAM Halk Müziği Eserleri Sempozyumu*, 69–71. Istanbul: MESAM.

Taylor, Timothy D. 2003. "A Riddle Wrapped in a Mystery: Transnational Music Sampling and Enigma's 'Return to Innocence.'" In *Music and Technoculture*, edited by René T. A. Lysloff and Leslie C. Gay Jr., 64–92. Middletown, CT: Wesleyan University Press.

———. 2016. *Music and Capitalism: A History of the Present.* Chicago: University of Chicago Press.

ÖSYM. 2010. "T.C. Maliye Bakanlığı İç Denetçi Aday Belirleme Sınavı Genel Yetenek ve Genel Kültür Testi Alan Bilgisi Testi." Accessed April 17, 2024. https://www.osym.gov.tr/TR,6200/2010-ic-denetci-soru-kitapcigi-ve-yanitlari.html.

Tekelioğlu, Orhan. 1996. "The Rise of a Spontaneous Synthesis: The Historical Background of Turkish Popular Music." *Middle Eastern Studies* 32, no. 2 (April): 194–215.

———. 2001. "Modernizing Reforms and Turkish Music in the 1930s." *Turkish Studies* 2, no. 1 (Spring): 93–108.

Tez, Mehmet. 2015. "Apple Music neden bizde yok?" [Why don't we have Apple Music?]. *Milliyet*, July 5, 2015. http://www.milliyet.com.tr/.

Tirk'an, Diziya. 2018. "Neşet Ertaş'ın türkçeleştirdiği 2 KÜRTÇE eser." YouTube. October 7, 2018. https://youtu.be/tsoigUYFYoU.

Theberge, Paul. 2003. "'Ethnic Sounds': The Economy and Discourse of World Music Sampling.'" In *Music and Technoculture*, edited by René T. A. Lysloff and Leslie C. Gay Jr., 93–108. Middletown, CT: Wesleyan University Press.

Tomlins, Christopher. 2012. "What Is Left of the Law and Society Paradigm after Critique? Revisiting Gordon's 'Critical Legal Histories.'" *Law and Social Inquiry* 37, no. 1 (Winter): 155–66.

Tör, Vedat Nedim. 1976. *Yıllar Böyle Geçti* [Years passed like this]. Istanbul: Milliyet Yayınları.

TRT. 1972a. *Türkiye Radyo Televizyon Kurumu ile Ar-İş Sendikası Arasında İş Kolu Seviyesinde ve Müzik-İş Sendikası Arasında Ankara Radyosu İş Yeri Toplu Sözleşmeleri* [Professional agreements between the Turkish Radio and Television Institution and the Ar-İş Union and collective workplace agreements between Müzik-İş Union and Ankara Radio]. Ankara: TRT Merkez Müzik Dairesi Yayınları.

———. 1972b. *Türkiye Radyoları Türk Halk Müziği ve Türk Sanat Müziği Sanatçı Denetim Raporları 1969–1972* [Turkish radio Turkish folk music and Turkish art music artist examination reports, 1969–1972]. Ankara: TRT Müzik Dairesi Yayınları.

———. 1974. 2. *Türk Sanat ve Halk Müziği Özel Danışma Kurulu Toplantısı* [The second Turkish art and folk music special advisory committee meeting]. Ankara: TRT müzik dairesi yayınları.

———. 1990. *Türk Halk Müziği ve Türk Sanat Müziği 4. Özel Danışma Kurulu Toplantısı* [Turkish folk music and Turkish art music fourth special advisory committee meeting]. Ankara: TRT müzik dairesi yayınları.

———. 1991. *Türkiye Radio-Televizyon Kurumu Türk Halk Müziği 5. Özel Danışma Kurulu Toplantısı.* [Meeting of the Turkish Radio and Television Institution's fifth special advisory committee on Turkish folk music]. Istanbul: TRT.

———. 1996. *Türk Halk Müziğinin Dünü, Bugünü, Yarını Konulu Panel* [Panel on the topic of the yesterday, today, and tomorrow of Turkish folk music]. Ankara: TRT Müzik Dairesi Başkanı.

"TRT Müzik Dairesindeki Başkanlık Çekişmesi Hızlandı." [The competition for director of the TRT music office has accelerated]. 1975. *Hey* 5 (40): 62.

Tüfekçi, Nida. 1992. "Âşıklarda Müzik." [Âşıks' music]. In *Türk Halk Musikisinde Çeşitli Görüşler* [Various perspectives in Turkish folk music], edited by Salih Turhan, 227–43. Ankara: Kültür Bakanlığı.

Tulunay, Faik. 1930. "Âşık Ahmet." *Halk Bilgisi Haberleri*, September 1, 1930.

Tunalı, Semin. 2019. "Threshold of Music Plagiarism." Master's thesis, Istanbul Technical University Graduate School of Arts and Sciences.

Tungnirun, Arm. 2018. "Practising on the Moon: Globalization and Legal Consciousness of Foreign Corporate Lawyers in Myanmar." *Asian Journal of Law and Society* 5, no. 1 (May): 49–67.

Tura, Yalçın. 2005. "'Anonim' Müziklerden Yararlanarak Oluşturulan Kompozisyonlar." [Compositions that incorporate 'anonymous' musics]. In *MESAM Halk Müziği Eserleri Sempozyumu*, 61–64. Istanbul: MESAM.

Turino, Thomas. 2008. *Nationalists, Cosmopolitans, and Popular Music in Zimbabwe.* Chicago: University of Chicago Press.

Türkmenoğlu, Ömer. 2021. "Turkish Folk Songs Accompanied by Symphony." *Zeitschrift für die Welt der Türken / Journal of World of Turks* 13 (2): 277–86. https://doi .org/10.46291/ZfWT/130214.

Tyler, Tom R. 2006. *Why People Obey the Law.* Princeton, NJ: Princeton University Press.

Üngör, Uğur Ümit. 2011. *The Making of Modern Turkey: Nation and State in Eastern Anatolia, 1913-1950.* Oxford: Oxford University Press.

Ünlü, Cemal. 2004. *Git Zaman Gel Zaman: Fonograf—Gramofon—Taş Plak* [As time goes by: Phonograph—gramophone—78]. Istanbul: Pan Yayıncılık.

Üskül Engin, Zeynep Özlem. 2014. "Medeni Kanun ve Toplumsal Gelişim." [Civil law and social development]. In *I. Türk Hukuk Tarihi Kongresi Bildirileri*, edited by Fethi Gedikli, 31–44. Istanbul: On İki Levha Yayınları.

Vaidhyanathan, Siva. 2003. *Copyrights and Copywrongs: The Rise of Intellectual Property and How It Threatens Creativity.* New York: New York University Press.

Vats, Anjali. 2020. *The Color of Creatorship: Intellectual Property, Race, and the Making of Americans.* Stanford, CA: Stanford University Press.

Versan, Vakur. 1984. "The Kemalist Reform of Turkish Law and Its Impact." In *Atatürk and the Modernization of Turkey*, edited by Jacob M Landau, 247–50. Boulder, CO: Westview Press.

Wallis, Roger, Charles Baden-Fuller, Martin Kretschmer, and George Michael Klimis. 1999. "Contested Collective Administration of Intellectual Property Rights in Music: The Challenge to the Principles of Reciprocity and Solidarity." *European Journal of Communication* 14, no. 1 (March): 5–35.

Wallis, Roger, and Krister Malm. 1984. *Big Sounds from Small Peoples: The Music Industry in Small Countries.* London: Constable.

Walton, Jeremy F. 2015. "Labours of Inter-Religious Tolerance: Cultural and Spatial Intimacy in Croatia and Turkey." *Cambridge Journal of Anthropology* 33, no. 2 (Autumn): 59–76. https://doi.org/10.3167/ca.2015.330206.

Wang, Fei-Hsien. 2019. *Pirates and Publishers: A Social History of Copyright in Modern China.* Princeton, NJ: Princeton University Press.

Wilf, Eitan. 2014. "Semiotic Dimensions of Creativity." *Annual Review of Anthropology* 43:397–412. https://doi.org/10.1146/annurev-anthro-102313-030020.

Williams, Ralph Vaughan. 1953. "Opening Session Address." *Journal of the International Folk Music Council* 5:7–8.

Williamson, John, and Martin Cloonan. 2013. "Contextualizing the Contemporary Recording Industry." In *The International Recording Industries*, edited by Lee Marshall, 11–29. New York: Routledge.

Wiora, Walter. 1949. "Concerning the Conception of Authentic Folk Music." *Journal of the International Folk Music Council* 1:14–19.

WIPO (World Intellectual Property Organization). 2005. *Intellectual Property and Traditional Cultural Expressions/Folklore — Booklet No 1.* https://www.wipo.int/publications/.

Woodard, Kathryn. 1999. "Creating a National Music in Turkey: The Solo Piano Works of Ahmed Adnan Saygun." DMA thesis, University of Cincinnati.

Woodmansee, Martha. 1984. "The Genius and the Copyright: Economic and Legal Conditions of the Emergence of the 'Author.'" *Eighteenth-Century Studies* 17, no. 4 (Summer): 425–48.

Woodmansee, Martha, and Peter Jaszi, eds. 1994. *The Construction of Authorship: Textual Appropriation in Law and Literature.* Durham, NC: Duke University Press.

Wright, Owen. 1988. "Aspects of Historical Change in the Turkish Classical Repertoire." *Musica Asiatica* 5:1.

———. 1992. *Words Without Songs: A Musicological Study of an Early Ottoman Anthology and Its Precursors.* London: School of Oriental and African Studies, University of London.

Yavuz, Levent, Fethi Merdivan, and Alıca Türkay. 2013. *Fikir ve Sanat Eserleri Kanunu Yorumu* [Interpretation of the law on intellectual and artistic works]. Ankara: Seçkin Yayıncılık.

Yıldız, Burcu. 2016. *Experiencing Armenian Music in Turkey: An Ethnography of Musicultural Memory.* Würzburg: Ergon Verlag.

———. 2018. "Ethnic Spaces and Multiculturalism Debates on Popular Music of Turkey." In *Made in Turkey: Studies in Popular Music*, edited by Ali C. Gedik, 133–47. New York: Routledge.

Yılmaz, Adnan. 2008. *Kırşehir Örneklemesiyle Anadolu Abdalları.* Kırşehir, Turkey: Kırşehir Belediyesi Kültür-Tarih Yayınaları.

Yılmaz, İhsan. 2020. "Türkülere Kanca Atmışlar." [They've got their claws on folk songs]. *Hurriyet*, October 28, 2020. https://www.hurriyet.com.tr/yazarlar/ihsan-yilmaz /turkulere-kanca-atmislar-41647721.

Yılmaz, Niyazi. 1996. *Türk Halk Müziğinin Kurucu Hocası Muzaffer Sarısözen* [The founding teacher of Turkish folk music, Muzaffer Sarısözen]. Ankara: Ocak.

Yngvesson, Barbara. 1988. "Making Law at the Doorway: The Clerk, the Court, and the

Construction of Community in a New England Town." *Law and Society Review* 22 (3): 409–48.

Yönetken, Halil Bedi. 2006. *Derleme Notları* [Notes on folkloric collection]. Ankara: Sun Yayınevi.

Yurchak, Alexei. 2005. *Everything Was Forever, until It Was No More: The Last Soviet Generation*. Princeton, NJ: Princeton University Press.

Zemp, Hugo. 1996. "The/An Ethnomusicologist and the Record Business." *Yearbook for Traditional Music* 28:36–56. https://doi.org/10.2307/767806.

INDEX

10 percent policy, 26, 134, 146–48, 152–62, 188, 198, 229n11

45 RPM records, 9, 41

78 RPM records, 41, 143, 179

Abdal, Pir Sultan, 104, 150

activism, copyright, 25–26, 63, 85, 110, 114, 130, 142, 152, 196; and legality, 31, 35, 39–44, 50

administration, copyright, 7, 13, 26, 29–31, 134, 195, 201, 216n9, 221n1; and everyday legality, 166, 178; and legality, 57, 67, 79–80, 219n9. *See also* bureaucracies

advertising jingles, 65, 142, 144–45, 161

Aegean communities, 121, 154, 229n6

African musics, 18–19. *See also* Ghana

Ağa, Adanalı İboş, 228n32

agency, 8, 10, 20, 50, 55, 89, 106, 164, 193

ağıt (songs of mourning), 86, 89, 101–6

Ahıska, Meltem, 72–73, 87

Akarsu, Muhlis, 226n20

Aksoy, Bülent, 95

Aksu, Sezen, 59–60

alafranga style, 32

alaturka style, 32–33

Alevi communities, 22, 68, 86, 99–100, 125, 135–36, 149, 219n10

al-Farabi, 33

Ali, Çekiç, 105

amateur musicians, 20, 78, 97, 136

"Ana beni eversene" (song), 225n10

Anadolu Pop, 113, 135, 151–52

Anatolian communities, 33, 38, 54, 135, 137, 150–52, 230n15; and creativity, 83, 96, 99, 106, 109, 113

Andrews, Walter, 94

Ankara, Turkey, 21, 36, 112, 114, 143–44, 225n8

Ankara havaları (Ankarabesk), 143

Ankara Radio, 111–12, 115

Ankara State Conservatory, 33, 98, 111, 116

anonymity, 6, 16, 19–20, 24, 26, 193, 196–97; and creativity, 83–90, 93, 96–101, 103–7, 222n6, 222n9, 223n12, 223n18; and everyday legality, 170–71, 173–74, 186–87; and folk music, 132–37, 139–41, 145–47, 149, 153–58, 162–64; and traditionalism, 109–11, 114–31, 225nn7–8, 227n22, 228n34

Antalya, Turkey, 21

anti-imperialism, 28, 35, 46, 51, 70

Apple Music, 28–30, 45, 51, 163

appropriation, 4, 18, 24, 26, 66, 95, 199, 215n4, 215n10, 222n7; and folk music, 136, 142, 145, 230n19

Arab communities, 6, 31, 33, 71, 135

arabesk, 68, 126, 135–36, 143, 217n23, 228n33

Arel, Hüseyin Sadettin, 33

Armenian communities, 6, 91, 135, 223n11

arrangers, 3, 10, 26, 39, 47, 166, 193, 219n4, 232n15; and folk music, 138, 146–49, 152–64, 228n1, 229n10, 229n14, 230n15. *See also* 10 percent policy; burning; instrumentation âşıklar (traditional singer-poets), 38–39, 78, 102–5, 135–36, 151, 159–60, 223nn17–20, 228n2; and everyday legality, 165–69, 176–79, 184–86, 192; and traditionalism, 119–20, 123, 126, 128, 226nn20–21, 227n28

Ataman, Sadi Yaver, 143, 224n4

Atılgan, Halil, 129–30, 227n30, 228n32

Austria, 187, 220n14

authenticity, 17, 21, 26, 87, 110, 115, 121–22, 227n30

authority, 55, 64–65, 92–96, 172, 186, 190–91, 205–6, 220n13

authorization, 1, 10, 92, 137–38, 198, 206–7, 228n5; and legality, 57, 60, 64, 67, 75–81, 219n8, 221n20; and modernization, 37, 41, 45, 216n14, 217n21, 217n24

authorship, 1, 6–7, 12, 16–19, 26, 71, 195–200, 204–5, 214n8; and creativity, 87–106, 221n3, 222n7, 223n15, 223n19, 224n21; and everyday legality, 169–70, 175, 187–88, 190, 231n11; and folk music, 132–36, 138–41, 146, 160, 228n1; and modernization, 35–37, 40–42, 45–46, 49–50; and traditionalism, 111, 114, 116, 119–30

authors' rights (*telif hakları*), 1–3, 42, 86–89, 125, 157–58, 169, 188, 213n5, 216n11; and folk music, 132, 138, 142, 161; and legality, 50, 58–60, 76, 80

autonomy, 91, 94–96, 222n7

Avşar, Esin, 42

Avşar Türkmens, 152

Ay, Savaş, 168–69, 177, 184

Ayangil, Ruhi, 23

Aydın, Mehmet, 86

Aydoğdu, Hüsnü, 20–23

Ayna, 168, 186, 190, 232n14

Azerbaijan, 185

Babül, Elif, 72

"Baby Shark" (song), 190

backwardness, 24, 32, 42, 52–54, 71, 86, 88, 216n6. *See also* civilization

bağlama (instrument), 21–22, 34, 68, 103, 105, 169, 179; and folk music, 135, 143, 149–52, 229n6; and traditionalism, 109, 119, 125, 130, 224n2. *See also* saz (instrument)

Balganesh, Shyamkrishna, 193–94

banderole system, 45, 67, 77, 79, 204

Bartok, Bela, 98, 224n22

Başgöz, İlhan, 102–3

"Batan gün kana benziyor" (song), 125

Baydur, Dağhan, 47, 74, 220n12

Bayraktar, Ertuğrul, 124

Baysal, Ozan, 152

Beethoven, Ludwig van, 96

Behar, Cem, 92

Belafonte, Harry, 230n2

Belgium, 220n14

Bellagio Convention (1993), 18

belonging, 2, 6–7, 17, 26–27

Berlin, Germany, 42, 97–98

Berne Convention, 36–37, 50, 56–57, 193–94, 203, 217n14

Bilgi University, 24, 192

Binboğa, Ali Rıza, 38, 54, 72, 217n18

Boateng, Boatema, 214n8

Böhme, Jakob, 98

Bolivia, 188, 192

Boratav, Pertev Naili, 98

borrowing, 4–5, 65, 101, 150, 155, 167, 191, 213n3

Boyle, James, 18–19

Brand, Oscar, 232n16

British National Library, 74

broadcasters, 44, 54, 69, 122. *See also* radio; television; Turkish Radio and Television (TRT)

Budan, Mustafa, 169, 184

Bülbül, Azer, 217n20

Bulgaria, 56, 220n14

bureaucracies, 4, 11, 13, 21, 25–27, 50, 174, 200, 227n24; and folk music, 134, 140, 144; and legality, 53, 61–62, 72; and traditionalism, 118, 128. *See also* administration, copyright; policymakers

Burma, 19

264 *Index*

burning, 97, 99, 123–24. *See also* authorship; creativity

Bursa, Turkey, 21

"Bu yarayı dosttan aldım ezeli" (song), 226n20

Çağla, Cevdet, 89, 92, 221n1

Çakmur, Barış, 41

Cantemir, Demetrius, 92

capitalism, 31, 35, 42, 90

case law, 12–13, 65, 139, 150, 156–57, 189–92, 199, 204, 221n20

cassette tapes, 9, 41, 77

CDs, 77, 201

"Çeke Çeke" (song), 150

Çekirge, Aziz, 116

Çelik, Necati, 23, 93

censorship, 6, 22, 34, 136, 144

Cevlani, Dursun, 168–69, 179, 181–85

Chakrabarty, Dipesh, 31

Chander, Anupam, 18

China, 29

Chua, Lynette, 15

"Çıkar Yücelerden Yumak Yuvarlar" (song), 225n7

Çırağı, Nuri, 168

CISAC, 46, 48, 58, 68, 161

civilization, 35–36, 42, 53, 57–58, 74, 87, 89, 216nn10–11. *See also* backwardness

Clifford, James, 17

Çobanoğlu, Murat, 165–74, 178–87, 189–92, 231n7–231n8, 232nn14–15

Çolak, Uğur, 171, 175–76, 193–94, 229n8

Cold War, 36

collaboration, 6, 39–40, 48, 98, 101, 103, 106, 111, 217n16. *See also* collective practices

collecting, folk music, 27, 33, 97–100, 111–13, 116; and copyright, 132, 135, 139, 150–51, 166; and everyday legality, 166, 168–79, 186–94. *See also* derleme (folk music collection)

collecting societies, 1–4, 7, 10–11, 13–14, 18, 23–25, 196, 198, 201; and everyday legality, 166, 172, 192–93; and folk music, 132, 134, 136–41, 146–48, 153–55, 157–64; and legality, 52, 55–56, 58–64, 66–74, 76–77, 79–81;

and modernization, 28–30, 37–40, 43–44, 46–49, 51, 217n16; and traditionalism, 114, 125. *See also* CISAC; GEMA; MESAM (collecting society); MSG (collecting society); MÜ-YAP; MÜYORBİR; SACEM

collective management, 10, 48–49. *See also* collecting societies

collective practices, 6–7, 16, 19–20, 26, 160, 164, 174, 193, 196–97; and creativity, 85–90, 96–97, 100–103, 106; and legality, 56, 71, 73, 78, 82; and traditionalism, 109, 118, 120, 123. *See also* collaboration

Collier, Stephen J., 8

colonialism, 70–71, 87, 136, 188, 197, 199–200, 214n6, 214n8, 215n11, 216n9; and modernization, 31, 35, 43, 46, 49. *See also* imperialism; postcolonialism

Columbia (record label), 41

Comhaltas Ceoltoiri Eireann (CCE), 159

commercialism, 41, 48, 84, 173, 178, 184, 204, 206, 223n11, 227n30; and everyday legality, 133, 136, 143–44, 148–49, 160–61, 164; and legality, 63, 71, 76–80; and traditionalism, 110, 122, 126, 129–31

commercial use, 10, 25, 28, 44, 47–48, 69, 90, 164, 206

community, 2, 16, 21–22; and creativity, 94–95, 97–98

competitions, 167–68, 176, 218n24, 224n1, 232n12

composers, 4–5, 9–10, 17, 19, 25, 205; and creativity, 87–88, 92–98, 221n1, 222n8, 223n11; and everyday legality, 166, 169–75, 178, 188–91, 232n15; and folk music, 132, 135, 138–39, 145–48, 151–55, 162, 228n1, 228n4, 229n11, 230n15; and legality, 59–62, 66–68, 77–80, 219n8, 220n17; and modernization, 28, 34, 37–44, 47, 49, 51, 215n3, 217n16, 217n22, 218n26; and traditionalism, 113–15, 122–26, 129, 225n7, 225n10, 226n15, 227n22. *See also* songwriters; *individual composers*

compulsory licensing, 75–76, 80–81, 220n14, 229n5

Index **265**

concerts, 21–22, 48, 61, 95, 99, 149, 188, 217n17

conservatories, 4, 22, 33, 65, 78, 92, 97–98, 127, 150–51, 174; and traditionalism, 111–12, 116, 127. *See also* music schools; *individual conservatories*

consumption, 7, 9, 12, 28, 30, 39–40, 45, 90, 113

Coombe, Rosemary, 17

Copland, Aaron, 224n22

copyright consciousness (*telif bilinci*), 1, 5, 25, 110, 164, 197, 200, 219n6, 221n2; and creativity, 86, 89; and legality, 55–57, 60–62, 64–65, 72–73, 75, 81–82; and modernization, 30, 42, 50–51. *See also* legal consciousness

copyright reform. *See* intellectual property (IP) reform

corruption, 26, 45, 71, 109, 115, 121–22, 132, 143–44, 173–77

Coşkun, Ankaralı (Direk), 143

cosmopolitanism, 15, 62, 75, 94

Council of Europe, 37

courts, legal, 3–4, 11–14, 125, 195–96, 204, 206, 214n8, 215n11; and creativity, 86, 90; and everyday legality, 170–71, 189–93, 231n10, 232n20; and folk music, 134, 139, 153, 157, 164; and legality, 52, 54, 63–65, 73, 76, 219n8, 221n19; and modernization, 38, 42, 44, 48–49, 217n21. *See also* judges; lawsuits; lawyers; legal professionals; Turkish Court of Cassation (Yargıtay)

creativity, 3–13, 16–20, 25–27, 34, 195–99, 204, 213n5, 214n8; and authorship, 83, 85, 87–92, 95–107, 222n7, 224n20; and everyday legality, 167, 173–78, 184–86, 192–94; and folk music, 134, 141, 145–49, 152–58, 160, 162, 164; and legality, 66, 80; and traditionalism, 108–10, 118, 120, 126, 130

critical legal consciousness, 15, 51–56, 60, 64–73, 80–82, 89, 138, 162, 197–99, 215nn11–12, 222n7

critical legal scholarship, 7, 138, 194, 223n14

cultural intimacy, 15, 72–74, 199, 219n11

cultural policy, 6–7, 56, 127, 130, 141, 195. *See*

also cultural reform; intellectual property (IP) reform; Turkish culture

cultural reform, 6, 9, 13, 19, 82, 87, 110, 195, 200; and modernization, 31–34, 41

cultural schemas, 56–57, 60–61, 65–66, 69, 81, 197, 199–200

curation, 6, 20, 25–26, 85, 170

Customs Union, 44

Czech Republic, 46, 220n14. *See also* Prague, Czech Republic

"Dadaloğlu" (song), 152, 229n13

Darian-Smith, Eve, 214n6

databases, 3, 10, 47–48, 69, 172–73, 192, 229n13–230n15, 231n3, 232n15; and folk music, 138–40, 148, 152

davul (instrument), 99

Davutoğlu, Ahmet, 165, 168, 190

Dede, Zekai, 92

Dedeoğlu, Taner, 108–9, 224nn1–2

Deep Forest, 17

defamation, 108–9

de Lalande, Richard, 189

Demirsipahi, Cemil, 58, 70, 218n26, 224nn1–3, 225n10, 226n15, 226n18; and modernization, 40–43, 51; and traditionalism, 108–10, 113–18, 122–23, 128

democracy, 10, 59, 62, 215n11

Dent, Alex, 11, 214n8

Depression, the, 35

Derçin, Zihni, 126

derivative rights, 75, 96, 147, 153, 157, 159, 161, 170–71, 189, 215n11

derleme (folk music collection), 114, 127, 169–79, 193, 198, 223n15

deyiş (traditional poems), 86, 89, 103, 136, 150, 223n17, 223n19, 226n21. *See also* poetry

digital service providers, 3, 10, 13, 29, 31, 215n3. *See also* streaming services

Dirmil, Turkey, 141

disability, 16

Disney, 189, 215n11

distribution, 12–13, 28, 31, 40, 46, 110, 171, 177,

205, 220n17; and everyday legality, 133, 138, 161–62; and legality, 67–70, 77, 80–81

Divani, Dertli, 149

Diyarbakır, Turkey, 21, 227n24

documentary records, 26, 42, 78, 80, 85, 99–101, 106, 132, 196, 224n21; and everyday legality, 171, 176; and traditionalism, 111, 123, 129

Dommann, Monika, 87–88

Dönüşüm, 178

Dundes, Alan, 227n27

dutar (instrument), 20–21

Dutfield, Graham, 214n6

economics, 8, 35–36, 43, 50, 70, 125. *See also* protectionism

education, copyright, 63–64. *See also* activism, copyright; copyright consciousness (*telif bilinci*)

Efendi, Dede, 87–89

Efendi, Hafız Ahmet, 92

eight-measure rule, 4–5, 65, 213n3

Elbir, Halit Kemal, 39, 217n16

"Elmaların yongası" (song), 150

EMI, 41

Emre, Yunus, 87

enforcement, copyright, 5, 10, 25–26, 53, 66, 71, 91, 155, 218n24, 224n21; and everyday legality, 167, 171, 191–92; and modernization, 30, 37–44, 50; and traditionalism, 111, 114, 125

Engel, David, 12, 15–16

epic traditions, 99, 105, 109, 179, 185–86, 230n15

epistemology, 16, 120

"Erbahi Ezelde Levli Kalemde" (song), 126

Ergül, Recep, 1–3, 5, 69, 153

Ergüner, Süleyman, 229n6

Erkin, Ulvi Cemal, 151

Erlmann, Veit, 11, 73, 188, 214nn8–9, 215n11

Ertaş, Muharrem, 105, 152, 224n21

Ertaş, Neşet, 105, 137, 140, 224n21

Erzincan, Erdal, 22, 149–50, 152–53, 229n14

essentializing, 54, 72–73, 82, 90–91, 106, 164. *See also* Orientalism; stereotypes

etatism, 35, 37, 42

ethnography, 11, 14–17, 21, 25–27, 101, 187, 197–200, 221n4; and creativity, 54–55, 65, 71–72, 80–81; and folk music, 133, 164; and modernization, 30, 45, 51

ethnonationalism, 6, 16

Etili, Can, 175

Eurocentrism, 7–8, 18–19, 70. *See also* western European standards; westernization

European Union, 9, 44–45, 56, 70, 72, 203, 218n2

Eurovision, 38

everyday life, 3–4, 12–13, 55, 60, 81, 133, 164, 166–67, 190–92

Ewick, Patricia, 15–16, 55–56, 60, 66, 82, 200

Ezgü, Sümer, 171–72

false claims (authorship), 114, 130, 132–40, 164, 196

fees, 39, 54, 61, 67, 72, 75, 159–60, 175

Feist Publications vs. Rural Telephone Service Co., 156

Feldman, Walter, 94

Fersan, Refik, 92

festivals, 21, 159

feudal culture, 31, 86

Fikret (Mehmet) Tevfik, 123

film industry, 39–40, 75, 146, 156, 189, 204, 217n23

financial concerns, 7, 126, 129, 145, 154, 168, 178, 204, 213n5. *See also* 10 percent policy; royalties; value

"Fırat Kenarının ince Dumanı" (song), 225n7

First Turkish Congress on Publishing (1939), 35

FİSAN, 138

fixedness, musical, 17, 96, 103–4, 106, 123, 176, 203–4

folk literature, 16, 103, 175, 232n14

folklore, 16, 21–25, 198–200, 222n6, 222n11, 227n23, 227n27, 229n9; and creativity, 84–85, 88–91, 97–98, 101, 103, 105–6; and everyday legality, 166, 168, 187, 189; and folk music, 142–45, 164. *See also* folk music (*halk müziği*); türkü (folk songs)

Index **267**

Folklore Association, 98

Folklore Foundation (Folklor Kurumu), 22

folk music (*halk müziği*), 2–9, 16, 19–27, 132–64, 196–200, 229n7, 232n16; and creativity, 83–85, 89–90, 92, 96–101, 103–7, 222n11; and everyday legality, 167–68, 171–78, 184–88, 192–94; and legality, 69, 71, 78, 80, 82; and modernization, 33–34, 40, 217n18; and traditionalism, 108–31, 227n30. *See also* ağıt (songs of mourning); collecting, folk music (*halk müziği*); deyiş (traditional poems); folklore; folk music experts; türkü (folk songs)

folk music experts, 85, 89, 97, 123, 134–35, 140, 142, 184–85, 226n18. *See also* folk music (*halk müziği*)

foreignness, 35, 39–40, 44–47, 70–72, 92, 97–98, 148, 214n6, 218n25, 220n24; and authors, 36, 50, 216n12–217n14

Foucault, Michel, 87

France, 46, 51, 70. *See also* Paris, France

funerals, 99, 101–2. *See also* ağıt (songs of mourning)

Gallo Africa, 188

"Gam Elinde Benim Zülfü Siyahım" (song), 126

gaming: law as, 55, 57, 60–61, 80; progress as, 7, 14, 30, 74

gap-studies, 14

Gates, Henry Louis, Jr., 222n7

Gavin, Frankie, 159

Gaye, Marvin, 215n1

Gazimihal, Mahmut Ragıp, 97–98, 151

Gelbart, Matthew, 187

GEMA, 39–40, 43, 51, 69–70, 220n15

Gencebay, Orhan, 68, 126

gender, 223n14, 227n29

genres, 3, 6, 9, 16–26, 55, 68–69, 85, 89, 91, 99–100, 106, 111, 143, 188, 200, 221n4. *See also individual genres*

geopolitical position of Turkey, 56, 62, 71–72, 197

Germany, 36, 39, 46, 51, 57, 69–70, 113, 157, 198, 220nn14-15. *See also* Berlin, Germany

Ghana, 214n8, 229n9

"Gide gide bir söğüde dayandım" (song), 129–30

gift economy, 18

globalization, 7, 199, 214n6

Goehr, Lydia, 96

Gökalp, Ziya, 32–34, 97–98, 216n10

Gönlüm, Özay, 121

"Gönül Dağı" (song), 137

Gordon, Robert W., 193, 214n8

"Gözleri fettan güzel" (song), 125

Greek communities, 6, 74, 91, 94, 222n4, 222n11

Greve, Martin, 149

Gültekin, Hasret, 149

Günay, Turgut, 175

Güney, Yusuf, 230n2

Gusterson, Hugh, 21

Hacıbektaş, Turkey, 105

Haco, Ciwan, 137

Halodayı, 217n20

harmonization, musical, 150–52, 155

Harry Fox Agency, 220n13

Hatun, Hasibe and Telli, 102, 106

Hegelian theory, 58–59

hegemony, 15–16, 55, 64, 82, 218n2

heirs, 66–67, 78–80, 135, 165, 206, 221n21, 228n1

Hertogh, Marc, 56

Herzfeld, Michael, 72–73, 219n11

Hindemith, Paul, 33

hip-hop, 9, 64, 188, 217n20

Hirsch, Ernst, 36–37, 40, 49, 216n13

His Master's Voice, 41

Holmes, Oliver Wendell, 165

hospitality industry, 53–54, 60

Hugo, Victor, 87

human rights, 53, 58–60, 72, 87. *See also* authors' rights (*telif hakları*)

Hungary, 46

hususiyet, doctrine of, 59, 156–57, 170, 175–76, 194. *See also* originality ideals, legal, 54, 57–58, 82, 144

identities, 6–8, 15–16, 45, 56, 68, 72, 101, 195–99, 226n20

ideologies, 5–7, 18, 26–27, 56–58, 108–9, 193, 198, 216n10; and creativity, 83–84, 91, 96; and everyday legality, 134, 160; and modernization, 31, 36, 45

imperialism, 28–29, 31, 35, 43, 46, 51, 70, 96; cultural, 7, 69, 82, 89, 197, 214n6. *See also* colonialism

improvisation, 88, 93–94, 101, 103, 108, 149, 152, 155, 157

IMRO collecting society, 18, 158–59, 161, 230nn20–21

Indigenous musics, 16–19

individualism, 17, 20, 38, 49, 71, 82, 87–90, 95–96, 118–19

industrialization, 35, 43, 46, 86

industry executives, 3, 11, 25, 58, 61, 65, 69, 73, 196, 215n12; and modernization, 29–30, 47–48

informality, 24, 41–45, 136, 175, 191

infringement, 4, 65–66, 167, 191, 206–7, 213n3, 230n1, 231n5, 232n20; and modernization, 45, 48–49

injustice, 3, 7, 35, 54, 67–69, 82–84, 137, 145, 162, 215n11

instrumentation, 151, 153, 155, 157, 168. *See also* arrangers

Intellectual and Industrial Property Rights and Culture Symposium, 86

intellectual property (IP) expertise, 9, 44, 48, 53, 70, 85–86, 192, 215n12

intellectual property (IP) reform, 2, 9–14, 19, 23, 125, 178, 194–96, 200–201; and creativity, 85–87; and folk music, 138, 144; and legality, 53, 58–59, 69, 82; and modernization, 30, 34–46, 49–50

international copyright standards, 7–8, 19, 25, 27, 87, 161, 226n16; and legality, 52–53, 57–60, 63, 68, 80–81, 187, 193, 198–99; and modernization, 29–31, 42, 44, 46, 50–51. *See also* western European standards

International Federation of the Phonographic Industry (IFPI), 2, 43

International Folk Music Council, 18–19, 187

International Folk Music Council (IFMC), 98

internationalization, 36, 87

internet, 45, 48

intertextuality, 103, 222n7

"İp attım ucu kaldı" (song), 143

Iran, 88, 94, 149

Ireland, 158–59

Irish sessions, 159

Irish traditional music, 18

İsko, Risteme, 137

Istanbul, Turkey, 21–22, 41, 52, 70, 88, 112, 118, 143, 171, 177, 192

Istanbul Bar Association, 86, 88

Istanbul Conservatory, 33, 92

Istanbul Municipal Conservatory, 97, 150–51

Istanbul Radio, 39, 112, 114, 150, 221n1

Istanbul Radio Folk Music Division, 112

Istanbul Technical University (ITU), 22, 112, 119, 174

Italian Book Company, Inc., v. Rossi, 189

Italy, 46, 220n14

İzmir, Turkey, 21, 230n15

Jäger, Ralf Martin, 93

Janissary bands, 32

Japan, 46

jazz, 9, 94

Jewish communities, 91, 198

judges, 4, 8, 13, 23–27, 43–44, 108, 139, 153, 196, 206; and everyday legality, 171–72, 175, 189, 192–94; and legality, 52–54, 58, 63, 71–72, 75; and traditionalism, 86, 90–92, 229n8. *See also* legal professionals; *individual judges*

Justice and Development Party (AKP), 45, 165, 190, 230n1

Kakınç, Halit, 178

Kalan (music company), 79, 140, 162–63, 223n11. *See also* Saltık, Hasan

Index **269**

Kalhor, Kayhan, 149
"Kalktı göç eyledi Avşar elleri" (song), 152
kanun (instrument), 23, 38
"Kapıyı çalan kimdir" (song), 177
Karaca, Cem, 135, 152
Karaca, Dursun, 80
Karacaoğlan, 96–97
Karadeli, Şendoğan, 22–23, 119, 179, 181–84
Karakış, Nevzat, 22–23, 71, 78, 83
KardeşTürküler, 223n11
Karpeles, Maud, 98
Kars, Turkey, 167–69, 186–87
"Katibim" (song), 154
kaval (instrument), 135
Kaya, Cem, 40, 217n23
Kayahan, 219n8
Kaynak, Sadettin, 42, 125, 225n7
Kearns, Thomas, 81, 166
Kemal, Mustafa (Atatürk), 31, 34–36, 45, 84, 218n2
Kemal, Namık, 94–95
Kemal, Yaşar, 101
"Kırmızı gül demet demet"(song), 185
Kırşehir, Turkey, 105, 121
"Kıyılı halayı" (song), 150
"Kiziroğlu" (song), 104, 165–67, 170–74, 177–93, 229n7, 231n8, 232n14, 232n16
Konyalı, Rıza, 227n30
Korea, 190
Köroğlu, 104–5, 231n3, 232nn14–15
Koşay, Hamit Zübeyir, 97
Köse, Erol, 168–69, 231n6
Kurdish communities, 6, 100, 137, 139, 144, 223n11
Kurkchiyan, Marina, 56

Laçın, 168
"Lambaya Püf De" (song), 143, 152
Lausanne Agreement, 36
Law on Cinematic, Video, and Musical Works (1986), 44, 78
lawsuits, 3, 7, 13, 24, 114, 129, 163, 224n1, 231n2; and creativity, 63–66, 69, 78; and everyday

legality, 165, 171, 190; and modernization, 40, 42, 48–49
lawyers, 4, 13, 23, 25, 88, 90, 214n9; and everyday legality, 171–72, 187; and folk music, 132–33, 137, 139, 141, 155–56, 229n8; and legality, 52–55, 63, 66, 69, 71, 73, 77, 81, 219n9, 220n17; and modernization, 40, 43, 47–48, 217n17, 218n24; and traditionalism, 108, 114, 128. See also legal professionals; individual lawyers
Laz communities, 6, 144
lead sheets, 111–12, 115, 225n8
League of Nations, 216n9
Ledbetter, Huddie "Leadbelly," 188, 226n16
legal consciousness, 5, 8, 11–16, 25–26. See also copyright consciousness (telif bilinci)
legal internalism, 193–94
legality, 3–8, 12–16, 19, 24–27, 50–75, 196–201, 218n1; case study of, 75–82; everyday, 165–94; and folk music, 134, 162, 164; and traditionalism, 111, 131
legal professionals, 11, 21–23, 85, 138, 156, 192–94, 219n9, 222n9. See also judges; lawyers
liberalization, 9, 36, 43–44, 82, 95, 125, 144
licensees, 24–25, 47, 54, 221n21
licensing agreements, 29, 165–66, 195, 197, 203, 214n6, 221n20, 229n5; and folk music, 138, 155, 159; and legality, 64, 76, 79–81
licensing income, 1, 3, 13–14, 46–48, 53, 64, 67–69, 75, 80, 201
Linda, Solomon, 188–89, 215n1
"The Lion Sleeps Tonight" (song), 188. See also "Mbube" (song)
literacy, 26, 74, 109–10, 130
locality, 6–9, 21–27, 50, 58, 97, 103, 112–13, 130, 199; and creativity, 99, 105, 193, 195; and folk music, 134, 164; and modernization, 40–41, 50; and traditionalism, 121, 124. See also regionality
Locke, John, 191
Lomax, Alan, 122, 226n16
Lomax, John, 188, 226n16
London, England, 74

Lord, Albert, 109

lyricists, 10, 28, 39, 47, 170, 172, 174, 178, 226n15, 228n1; and folk music, 120, 135–39, 152, 155, 162

Macfarlane, Robert, 222n7

Magna Carta, 74

makam system, 91–92, 149, 221n1, 222n5, 226n15

Mali, 19

Manço, Barış, 143, 152

Mann, Larissa Kingston, 11, 214n8

marginalization, 6, 12, 15, 26, 29, 66, 68, 70, 215n11. *See also* minorities

Marks v. Leo Feist, Inc., 213n3

mass media, 9, 103–4, 113, 122, 124, 176, 199

master musicians, 20, 23, 135, 149, 152, 178, 204, 224n21; and creativity, 92–94, 103–5; and traditionalism, 116, 119, 127

"Mbube" (song), 188–89, 232n16, 215n11. *See also* "The Lion Sleeps Tonight" (song)

McCann, Anthony, 18, 158–59, 230n21

mechanical rights, 10, 37, 39, 75, 220n15, 229n11

media coverage: and copyright, 162, 165–66, 224n3, 230n1, 231n2; and modernization, 28–29, 51; and traditionalism, 68, 108, 128; and TRT, 144, 224n1

mediation, 3, 6–10, 16, 26, 30, 56, 82–84, 121, 178, 195, 219n11; and folk music, 133, 164; mass-, 104, 113, 130, 199

Meintjes, Louis, 58

melodic similarities, 66, 137, 224n20

melodies, 104–5, 185, 223n16

Melville, Caspar, 18–19

membership, collecting society, 10, 25, 29, 166, 171, 198; and folk music, 139, 146–47, 158–61, 228n1, 229n10, 230nn21–23; and legality, 53, 55, 60, 63, 67–69, 74–81, 219n5, 219n9, 220n17; and modernization, 39–40, 49. *See also* collecting societies

MESAM (collecting society), 1–3, 10, 25, 201, 217n16, 219n9, 220n15, 220n17; and everyday legality, 166, 169, 171–73, 178, 186,

192, 213n3, 232n15; and folk music, 132–34, 137–42, 145–48, 151–55, 159–63, 228nn4–5, 229n10, 229n14–230n15, 230n22–230n23; and legality, 52, 54, 58, 63–64, 67–69, 72–77, 80–81; and modernization, 28–29, 37–40, 43–44, 47–49; and traditionalism, 125, 129–30

meşk system, 92–93, 96. *See also* orality

metadata, 26, 223n15

methodology of book, 20–27

Mevlevi communities, 91

migrants, 33, 130, 133, 136, 161

militaries, 31–32, 100, 215n4

minorities, 7, 71, 93, 144, 223n17; religious, 22, 41, 68, 86, 99, 135. *See also* marginalization

"Min Te Ditibû" (song), 137

modernity, 25, 31–32, 35, 45, 72, 87, 218n2

modernization, 3, 6, 49–51, 53, 56–58, 72–74, 95, 151, 160, 197; and copyright reform, 25, 30–34. *See also* westernization

monopolies, 10, 26, 58, 70, 112, 144, 213n5; and modernization, 33, 39, 41, 44, 47

moral rights, 59, 80, 84, 89 123, 125, 204–6

MSG (collecting society), 10, 25, 173, 201, 220n15; and folk music, 134, 137–38, 145–46, 148, 152, 159–61, 163, 228n5, 229n10, 230n23; and legality, 52, 58, 67, 69, 74–77, 220n15; and modernization, 28–29, 37, 47–49

Müftüoğlu, Oğuz, 229n8

multiculturalism, 6, 144, 160

multinational corporations, 9, 41, 58, 70, 75, 201

Munger, Frank, 12

music companies, 9, 23, 41, 44–46, 50, 54, 58, 70, 162–63, 201. *See also* publishing, music; record labels

musicological experts, 65, 139–40, 156, 159, 170

music schools, 21, 32, 61, 99, 149. *See also* conservatories

Muslim communities, 34, 45, 52, 71, 94–95, 100, 218n2

MÜ-YAP, 10, 44, 47, 52–54, 71, 79–80, 215n3, 218n29

Index **271**

MÜYORBİR, 10, 44, 47, 67, 215n3
Muzıka-i Hümayun, 32
Muzikotek, 74
MÜZKO, 40
mythologization, 4, 17–18, 74, 93–94, 164–65, 213n3

nationalism, 5–7, 16, 19, 25–26, 82, 195, 216n6, 227n23, 230n1; and creativity, 84, 91, 97, 99, 101, 222n11; and everyday legality, 144, 160, 174; and folk music, 133–34, 142–48, 151, 160, 162, 198; and modernization, 32–33, 46; and traditionalism, 110, 122, 126. *See also* nation-building
Nationalist Movement Party (MHP), 230n1
nation-building, 6, 10, 82, 113, 117–18, 126, 197, 216n10. *See also* nationalism
NATO, 37
nazire tradition, 93, 104
negotiations, licensing, 7–10, 24, 28–29, 133, 147, 162, 221n21; and copyright statute, 172, 192; and legality, 33, 44–45, 69, 72, 76, 199
neoliberalism, 7, 11, 43, 125–26, 130, 144, 200
Neubauer, Eckhard, 94
New Jersey, USA, 55
new literature movement, 94–95
nightclubs, 42, 115, 143–44
Nilsson, Gül Okutan, 220n16
Nilüfer, 219n8
Nooshin, Laudan, 88
normative legal consciousness, 5, 14, 23, 30, 50–60, 67, 80–82, 167, 191–93, 213, 214n8, 218n1
nostalgia, 110, 113, 123–24, 218n2
notation, musical, 32, 92–93, 102–4, 111, 123, 222n5, 222n11; and copyright, 138, 160, 169, 179–85, 225n8, 231n8; and traditionalism, 116, 126, 128–29. *See also* lead sheets

Odeon, 41
Ong, Aihwa, 8
Only, Johnny, 190
ontology, 16, 120

orality, 26, 88, 164, 197, 200, 224n21, 227n27; and creativity, 91–93, 97, 100, 104; and traditionalism, 109–11, 120, 123–24, 130
orchestral arrangements, 151, 153, 230n15
Organization for European Economic Cooperation, 37
Orhon, Cüneyd, 224n1
Orientalism, 15, 73, 75, 87–88, 90
originality, 6, 59, 65, 94–95, 104–5, 123, 203–4, 222n7, 230n19; and everyday legality, 170–71, 175, 185, 189; and folk music, 139, 145, 148, 156–59, 164
Ottoman empire, 9, 70–71, 86–88, 91, 123, 152, 222n7, 222n11; and modernization, 31–35, 215n4, 216n6, 216nn8–9; post-, 85, 89–96, 99, 104, 106, 196, 222n6, 226n19, 227n26
Ottoman Public Debt Administration, 216n9
ownership, 6–9, 16–19, 49, 167, 191, 195–96, 199–200, 206, 214n8; and folk music, 102–5, 132, 139–42, 145, 162, 229n9
Özal, Turgut, 43
Özbek, Mehmet, 117, 177, 225n5, 225n7, 226n17
Özdemiroğlu, Atilla, 39, 43, 218n27
Özkan, Ali İzzet, 104, 227n28
Öztürk, İhsan, 124–26, 129
Öztürk, Veysel, 94–95

Pachtikos, Georgios, 222n11
Paris, France, 97–98, 203
Parlak, Erol, 105, 149
Parry, Millman, 109
Paşmakçı, Yücel, 22, 114, 119, 177, 225n5, 225n10
patronage, 10, 32, 91
Pehlivan, Osman, 143
penalties, 24, 45, 48
performers, 4, 20, 22, 25–26, 203–5, 214n7, 218n29, 219n8, 223n11, 227n24; and creativity, 92–96, 103, 105; and everyday legality, 171, 174–75, 178, 187, 189, 193; and folk music, 135–40, 143, 149–54, 159–63; and legality, 67, 77–80; and modernization, 42, 44; and traditionalism, 108, 115, 119. *See also* âşıklar (traditional singer-poets); radio

272 *Index*

musicians; recording artists; *individual performers*

performing rights, 3, 10, 63, 69, 77, 158, 160, 172, 218n30, 220n15; and modernization, 37, 39, 42, 44, 47

Perlman, Marc, 5, 221n3

personality theory, 17, 59, 88–89, 103, 156–57, 169–70, 213n5

personhood, 8, 196–97

Pinkfong, 190

piracy, 7, 9–12, 41, 44–45, 53, 77, 204, 214n6, 214n8, 217n24. *See also* unauthorized materials

plagiarism, 13, 103–4, 222n7

poetry, 94–96, 101–4, 109, 122. *See also* âşıklar (traditional singer-poets); deyiş (traditional poems)

Poland, 46, 56

policing, 45, 77, 81, 100, 140, 144

policymakers, 35–36, 49, 148. *See also* bureaucracies

political economies, 8, 12, 56, 94, 195

politics, 7–8, 11, 16, 195, 198; and creativity, 87, 95, 100–101; and everyday legality, 165–66, 190; and legality, 55–56, 68–69, 71, 73, 218n2; and modernization, 30, 32, 43, 45, 50

popularization, 17, 27, 134, 178, 189

popular music, 3, 34, 44, 122, 143, 151–52, 168, 226n16. *See also* Anadolu Pop

postcolonialism, 31, 49, 58, 200

Post-Ottoman art music, 26, 68, 111, 138, 174, 196, 221n4, 228n4; and copyright, 151, 156, 174; and creativity, 80, 88, 91–96, 99, 104, 106; and modernization, 33–34, 38–39; and traditionalism, 111, 118–20, 226n19

pragmatic legal consciousness, 218n1, 50–56, 60–65, 80–82, 199

Prague, Czech Republic, 98

preservation, 18, 24, 92, 108, 110–13, 121–22, 128, 158, 160

print culture, 34–36, 86–87, 201, 215n6, 216n8

private recording industry, 9, 112–13, 129, 143–44, 177–78

privatization, 9–10, 39, 42–44

production, 6–11, 102, 144, 151, 167, 196–97, 214n8; and creativity, 88–90; and legality, 58, 67, 79; and modernization, 34, 37, 40–41; and traditionalism, 110, 127. *See also* record producers; reproduction

professionalism, 30, 47, 74–75

profit, 9, 37, 41, 44, 50, 133, 166, 173–74, 229n11; and legality, 58, 61, 71, 73, 76, 78, 80; and traditionalism, 110, 122, 130

progress, 14, 30–32, 35, 50, 69, 72–74, 87–88, 108–10, 128, 219n3

property, 2, 10–11, 17–19, 116, 123–26, 165, 170, 191, 224n21; and creativity, 86, 89–90, 103; and legality, 53, 59, 92

protection, 17–18, 26, 50, 88, 203–5, 214n6, 222n9, 230n19; and everyday legality, 170–73, 187, 191; and folk music, 133, 142, 145, 155, 158, 229n8; and legality, 59, 75; and traditionalism, 90, 96, 106

protectionism, 35–36, 218n25

public domain, 18–19, 78, 196, 198, 223n12, 229n5, 229n9, 229n13–230n15, 232n15; and creativity, 85, 90–91, 96; and everyday legality, 166, 182, 187–93; and folk music, 130, 133–37, 142–53, 155–65

public good, 58, 157–58

public spaces (*umumi mahaller*), 10, 48, 55, 90, 217n30

publishing, music, 4, 19, 25, 47, 60, 73–74, 102; and copyright, 145–46, 152, 187, 189; and legality, 68, 74, 162, 176, 178, 219n5; and modernization, 37, 39. *See also names of specific publishers*

Qız, Sılemano, 100

racialization, 7, 16, 188, 215n11

radio, 33–34, 44, 76, 147, 218n30, 227n24. *See also* Turkish Radio and Television (TRT)

radio musicians, 22, 98–99, 111–12, 115, 117, 121–22, 176

Ranasinghe, Prashan, 55

Index **273**

reception, 6, 84, 90

recording artists, 10, 17, 23, 113, 130, 132, 219n8, 228n5, 228n33; and folk music, 134–40, 143, 173; and legality, 59, 61, 67, 71, 78; and modernization, 28, 39, 44, 47, 215n3, 217n21. *See also* performers

recordings, musical, 17, 79, 104, 124, 204, 214n7, 215n12, 227n21; and everyday legality, 167–68, 176–79, 218n24, 224n1, 232n12; and folk music, 135, 137–38, 140, 143, 147–50, 152–53, 158, 162–63; and legality, 52, 64, 75–82, 198, 217n17, 220n19; and modernization, 37, 44–45, 215n3, 218n24

recording technologies, 41, 104, 110, 123, 130

record labels, 10, 13, 24, 27, 109, 228nn33–34; and creativity, 88, 99, 221n4, 223n11; and everyday legality, 166, 178, 232n15; and folk music, 138, 140, 160, 162, 228n5, 229n11, 230n22; and legality, 52, 55, 61, 67–68, 70, 76–79, 220n19; and modernization, 32, 38–39, 41–42, 215n3, 217n17

record producers, 2, 4, 23, 25, 103, 129, 203–5, 221n20; and everyday legality, 138, 158, 160, 162, 168–69, 173–74; and legality, 61–64, 67, 77, 80; and modernization, 38, 41–44, 47, 50, 215n3, 218n24, 218n29. *See also* production

regionality, 97, 112, 114, 116–22, 174, 227n24, 227n30

registration, 10, 78–79, 196, 204, 220n19, 221n19, 225n7, 228n34, 229n5, 232n16; and creativity, 84, 86; and everyday legality, 125, 129, 135, 139–41, 147, 166, 172–74; and modernization, 38–39, 44

reproduction, 37, 45, 76–77, 80, 87–89, 197, 204–6, 217n24, 220n14, 221n20

republican era, 9, 31–32, 95–103, 151, 222n4

Republic of Turkey, 6, 25, 31, 33, 50–51, 70, 113, 216n8

resistance, 5, 12, 15–16, 84, 90, 125, 159–60, 193–94, 199, 216n6; and legality, 52–55, 66–72, 81; and modernization, 35, 47

Rey, Cemal Reşit, 151, 230n15

"Rêya'm dûr e" (song), 137

rightsholders, 10, 13, 187, 198, 207, 232n14; and folk music, 142, 148, 159, 163, 228n5, 229n10; and legality, 53, 55–56, 58, 62–64, 66, 69, 75–81, 219n4, 219n8, 221n20; and modernization, 28, 37, 39–40, 47–48, 50

rock music, 9, 28, 30, 54, 94, 113, 165, 168, 229n7; and folk music, 135–36, 143, 152

Roman (Romani) communities, 6, 91, 144, 228n34

Romania, 46

Romanticism, 6, 17–21, 91–96, 100–101, 106, 123, 148, 222n7. *See also* individualism

Rome Convention, 56–57, 218n28

royalties, 1–3, 10, 14, 26, 198–99, 201; and everyday legality, 168, 171–74, 178, 187–88, 232n15; and folk music, 134–35, 138, 145–49, 152–55, 157–63, 229n11, 230n16; and legality, 53, 55–56, 58, 60–63, 67–70, 75, 77; and modernization, 28, 37–42, 44, 47–48, 50–51, 218n30; and traditionalism, 109, 125, 127, 129–30, 228n32. *See also* 10 percent policy

rural practices, 25, 27, 33; and copyright, 135, 141, 149–50, 160, 173–74, 176–77; and creativity, 83–84, 86, 88, 90–91, 99, 105; and traditionalism, 115. *See also* 10 percent policy

Russian folk songs, 189

SACEM, 38–40, 43, 51, 70

sacrality, 60, 80, 99, 131, 133, 142

Sağ, Arif, 68, 130, 149, 178, 230n22

Said, Edward, 87

sales, music, 2, 37, 42, 44–45, 73, 77, 115, 205, 229n11, 232n15

Saltık, Hasan, 79, 140, 163. *See also* Kalan (music company)

SAMRO, 73

Samuels, David, 102

Şan, Tuğrul, 228n32

Sanlıkol, Mehmet Ali, 23

Sarat, Austin, 81, 166

274 *Index*

Sarısözen, Muzaffer, 33–34, 98–100, 111, 150, 223n15; and everyday legality, 168, 174, 176, 178–79; and traditionalism, 116–17, 121, 128, 225n4, 225n12–226n13

Sawkins, Lionel, 189

Sawkins v. Hyperion Records, Inc, 189

Saygun, Ahmet Adnan, 98, 151, 224n22

saz (instrument), 103, 141. *See also* bağlama (instrument)

Scherzinger, Martin, 18

secularism, 45, 72, 84, 95, 216n6

Seeger, Anthony, 17

Seeger, Pete, 188–89, 232n16

Şefizade, İzzet, 41

Şele, Kenan, 228n32

self, sense of, 7–8, 15, 56, 87, 195–97

Semercioğlu, Cengiz, 28–29

Şenel, Süleyman, 114, 119, 141, 223n15, 224n4, 225n5, 226nn14–15, 229n6

"Şenola düğün şenola" (song), 225n10

Şerif, Mahzuni, 178, 192

Sharia law, 34

Sharp, Cecil, 98

Sibley, Jessica, 11

Silbey, Susan, 15–16, 55–56, 60, 66, 82, 191, 200, 214n8

Şimşek, Ümit, 21, 149

Sinan, Mürsel, 184, 191–92

Şinasi, 87

"Sinsin Halayı / Elmaların Yongası / Kıyılı Halayı" (song), 150, 153

Sivas, Turkey, 120, 124, 227n24

social imaginaries, 8, 16, 148

sociality, 7, 71–72, 82, 92, 195, 199

songwriters, 4, 13, 25, 38, 49, 138, 160, 198, 219n8, 232n16; and legality, 55, 59–60, 76–77. *See also* composers; *individual songwriters*

Sorbonne, the, 98

soundtracks, 46, 50, 75, 151

source musicians, 100, 114, 129, 135–36, 200, 223n15, 225n7, 226n16, 228n32; and everyday legality, 171, 174–79, 182, 192

South Africa, 73, 188, 214n8

sovereignty, Turkish, 25, 30, 35–36, 50, 56 218n2

Soviet Union, 36

Spotify, 29, 45, 163

standardization, 34, 79

state, Turkish, 23, 38, 54, 57, 66, 70, 74, 82, 100, 137; and creativity, 84; and folk music, 142–44; institutions, 6, 9, 21–25, 33, 72, 84, 89, 94, 176, 192, 196, 200. *See also* conservatories; nationalism; nation-building; *individual institutions*

state broadcasting, 9–10, 20, 22, 34, 41, 68, 85, 99, 108–11, 130, 176. *See also* Turkish Radio and Television (TRT)

stereotypes, 15, 54, 82, 121, 188, 197. *See also* essentializing; Orientalism

St-Pierre, Pascale, Cornut, 13, 55, 214n9

streaming services, 28, 45–46, 48, 61, 70, 133, 163, 201. *See also* digital service providers

Su, Ruhi, 152, 168, 231n6

Sufism, 9, 31, 83, 91, 141

Sultan Mahmud II, 32

Sümer, Nevzat, 38–39, 44, 138, 142, 178, 217n16

Sunder, Madhavi, 18–19

Sunni orthodoxy, 22, 219n10

Sürmen, Erkan, 128

Suya people, 17

Swiss Civil Code, 34

Switzerland, 220n14

syntheses, musical, 33–34, 99, 122

Tan, Nail, 144

tango, 9

Tanzimat reforms, 32, 94

Taşan, Hacı, 105, 121

Taşlıova, Şeref, 186–87, 192

"Tatlı Dile Güler Yüze" (song), 137

Tatlıses, İbrahim, 126

Tayfur, Ferdi, 126

teachers, 4, 21–23, 33, 71, 78, 83, 92–93, 97, 113, 127, 149. *See also* conservatories; master musicians; music schools

Tecer, Ahmet Kutsi, 98

Index **275**

Technical Expertise Committees, 138–39, 141, 153–54, 158, 161, 186–87, 232n14

techniques, performance, 22, 149–50

Tekin, Gürsel, 230n2

television, 59, 67, 76, 143, 151, 205, 218n30, 225n8; and creativity, 84, 90, 99, 108; and everyday legality, 168, 177, 184, 186; and modernization, 34, 39–40, 44, 46, 48; and traditionalism, 111–12, 122

"Ten Anatolian Türkü" (composition), 151

Tez, Mehmet, 28, 51, 215n1

Top, Yavuz, 125

tourism, 52–54, 60, 71

trade policies, 35, 43–44

Trade Related Aspects of Intellectual Property (TRIPs), 44, 203

traditionalism, 26, 136, 142–44, 161, 226n19; and creativity, 88, 96; and state broadcasting, 108–10, 115, 117, 121–22, 127, 130–31

transcendental ideals, 4, 55, 60, 63–64, 197

transcription, 34, 102, 114, 126, 129, 150, 177, 181–83, 186

TRT Art Music Division, 111, 118

TRT Art Music Repertoire, 174, 225n7

TRT Folk Music Division, 22, 40, 109–13, 117–18, 121, 128, 225n8; and copyright, 135, 168–69, 177

TRT Folk Music Repertoire, 20–21, 34, 98, 140, 159, 174, 222n11, 223n18, 225nn6–8; and copyright, 150, 174, 178–86, 213n8, 228n32; and traditionalism, 112–14, 119–21, 128–29

TRT Turkish Art and Folk Music Special Advisory Committee, 111, 118–27, 140, 174

TTNet, 29

Tüfekçi, Gamzeçi Yazıcı, 120

Tüfekçi, Neriman Altındağ, 127

Tüfekçi, Nida, 142, 221n1, 226n15, 226nn18–19; and creativity, 89, 91, 96, 99, 104; and traditionalism, 108–22, 126–29, 224nn1–3, 225n7, 225n9, 225n12

Tura, Yalçın, 151, 223n12, 228n4

Turkcell, 29

Turkish art music. *See* Post-Ottoman art music

Turkish Civil Code, 221n21

Turkish classical music. *See* Post-Ottoman art music

Turkish Court of Cassation (Yargıtay), 10, 139, 170, 193, 217n21, 232n20

Turkish Cultural Ministry, 10, 44, 70, 77–79, 81, 144, 163, 172, 174, 201, 228n5

Turkish culture, 2–3, 7, 70–71, 87, 90. *See also* cultural policy

Turkish Finance Ministry, 84

Turkish Intellectual Property Civil Court, 171

Turkish music. *See* folk music

Turkish Music State Conservatory, 22, 112

Turkish Patent Institute, 44

Turkish Radio and Television (TRT), 10, 20–24, 26, 85, 221n4; and everyday legality, 168–69, 174–80, 182–86, 192, 231n8; and folk music, 135, 140–50, 229n6; and modernization, 39–40, 44, 217n18; and traditionalism, 108–9, 111–30, 224n1, 225nn5–7, 226n20, 228n32. *See also* state broadcasting; TRT Folk Music Division; TRT Folk Music Repertoire

"Turkish scenes" (composition), 151

Turkmenistan, 20

Türköz, Adnan, 150

türkü (folk songs), 196, 198, 225n4, 225nn7–8, 226n19, 227n30, 230n15; and collection, 27, 99, 127–30, 166–79, 187–94, 222n11; and copyright, 132–45, 149–51, 153–54, 156–58, 161–64; and creativity, 83–86, 90, 97–98, 103–6; and everyday legality, 169, 173, 175–78, 193; and traditionalism, 109, 111–30. *See also* ağıt (songs of mourning); deyiş (traditional poems); folk music (*halk müziği*)

türküleşme (türküfication), 103–4

Twitter, 29

ud (instrument), 23

Ufki, Ali, 92, 222n11

unauthorized materials, 41, 45, 207, 217n21, 217n24. *See also* piracy

United Kingdom, 46, 56, 113, 158, 213n5, 220nn14–15. *See also* London, England

United States, 206, 213n3, 213n5, 214n6, 214n8, 215n12, 217n25; and everyday legality, 156, 158, 191, 193; and legality, 46, 70–71, 75, 219n3, 219n7, 220n13, 220n15, 230n19, 232n20

universality, 52–53, 60, 87

Universal Music Publishing Group (UMPG), 162

Unkapanı, Istanbul, Turkey, 23, 41, 70. *See also* music companies; record labels

urbanization, 86, 110, 113, 130

urban practices, 9, 23, 26, 33, 119, 149, 156, 178; and creativity, 85–86, 88, 90–91, 106

Urfa, Turkey, 116–17, 177, 225n7, 226n18

"Urfalıyam dağlıyam, derde kerem" (song), 116

US Copyright Royalty Board, 75

Uzelli, Metin, 39

Uzelli Records, 39

value, 3, 5, 8, 20, 22, 26. *See also* 10 percent policy; financial concerns

van Gennep, Arnold, 98

variants and variations, 9, 20, 92–94, 102, 104, 150, 176, 224n21

"Varıp neğlemeli sılağı gayrı" (song), 228n32

Vartabed, Gomidas, 223n11

Veysel, Âşık, 38–39, 120, 123, 126, 223n20, 227n28, 228n3

violence, 73, 100

Voices from the Homeland ensemble, 22, 111–12

von Püttlingen, Johann Vesque, 88, 187

Vural, Oktay, 230n1

Washington, DC, 20

Weavers, The, 188

weddings, 99–100, 105, 117

"We Shall Overcome" (song), 189

Western art music, 9, 20, 32–34, 93, 96, 99, 106, 150–51

western European standards, 2–3, 10, 51; and copyright, 169, 193, 213n5; and creativity, 87–89, 93, 95; and legality, 57–59, 62, 65, 70–74, 82. *See also* Eurocentrism; international copyright standards

westernization, 3, 31–33, 36, 49. *See also* Eurocentrism; modernization

Western popular music, 113

Wihtol v. Wells, 189, 192

"Wimoweh" (song), 188

Wirtén, Eva Hemmungs, 87

women, 100–103, 124, 129

worldbeat, 17

World Cup, 75

World Intellectual Property Organization (WIPO), 17, 106, 132–33, 164

World War I, 31, 100

World War II, 36

"Yarım Senden Ayrılalı" (song), 126

"Yarınlar Bizim" (song), 38

Yekta, Rauf, 33

"Yeşil yaprak arasında kırmızı gül goncesi" (song), 225n7

"Yok Yok" (record), 42

Yönetken, Halil Bedi, 98

YouTube, 29, 45, 59, 137, 162–63, 168, 179, 184, 190, 232n19

Yurtseven, Taşköprülü Fikriye, 141

Zaw, U Khin, 19

zeybek, 99

Zhang, Taisu, 193–94

zurna (instrument), 99

Index 277

MUSIC / CULTURE

A series from Wesleyan University Press
Edited by Deborah Wong, Sherrie Tucker, and Jeremy Wallach

The Music/Culture series has consistently reshaped and redirected music scholarship. Founded in 1993 by George Lipsitz, Susan McClary, and Robert Walser, the series features outstanding critical work on music. Unconstrained by disciplinary divides, the series addresses music and power through a range of times, places, and approaches. Music/Culture strives to integrate a variety of approaches to the study of music, linking analysis of musical significance to larger issues of power—what is permitted and forbidden, who is included and excluded, who speaks and who gets silenced. From ethnographic classics to cutting-edge studies, Music/Culture zeroes in on how musicians articulate social needs, conflicts, coalitions, and hope. Books in the series investigate the cultural work of music in urgent and sometimes experimental ways, from the radical fringe to the quotidian. Music/Culture asks deep and broad questions about music through the framework of the most restless and rigorous critical theory.

FALL 2024

Benjamin Barson
Brassroots Democracy: Maroon Ecologies and the Jazz Commons

Donna Lee Kwon
Stepping in the Madang: Sustaining Expressive Ecologies
of Korean Drumming and Dance

Sumarsam
The In-Between in Javanese Performing Arts: History and Myth,
Interculturalism and Interreligiosity

SPRING 2025

Dave Fossum
Copyright Consciousness: Musical Creativity
and Intellectual Property in Turkey

A COMPLETE LIST OF SERIES TITLES CAN BE FOUND AT
https://www.weslpress.org/search-results/?series=music-culture

ABOUT THE AUTHOR

Dave Fossum is an assistant professor in the School of Music, Dance and Theatre at Arizona State University. He has received fellowships and grants from Brown University, the University of Pittsburgh, the American Research Institute in Turkey, and the Reed Foundation. His publications include "Westernizing Reform and Indigenous Precedent in Traditional Music: Insights from Turkmenistan" (*Ethnomusicology*, 2015), "Neset Ertas and the Ontologies of Turkey's Folk Music" (*Asian Music*, 2023), and "Authors and Burners: Imagining Creative Agency in Turkey's Musical Folklore" (*Ethnomusicology Forum*, 2023).